The Anarc Society at 40

Contemporary Challenges and Prospects

Edited by
HIDEMI SUGANAMI,
MADELINE CARR, AND
ADAM HUMPHREYS

OXFORD
UNIVERSITY PRESS

OXFORD
UNIVERSITY PRESS

Great Clarendon Street, Oxford, OX2 6DP,
United Kingdom

Oxford University Press is a department of the University of Oxford.
It furthers the University's objective of excellence in research, scholarship,
and education by publishing worldwide. Oxford is a registered trade mark of
Oxford University Press in the UK and in certain other countries

© Oxford University Press 2017

The moral rights of the authors have been asserted

First Edition published in 2017

Impression: 1

All rights reserved. No part of this publication may be reproduced, stored in
a retrieval system, or transmitted, in any form or by any means, without the
prior permission in writing of Oxford University Press, or as expressly permitted
by law, by licence or under terms agreed with the appropriate reprographics
rights organization. Enquiries concerning reproduction outside the scope of the
above should be sent to the Rights Department, Oxford University Press, at the
address above

You must not circulate this work in any other form
and you must impose this same condition on any acquirer

Published in the United States of America by Oxford University Press
198 Madison Avenue, New York, NY 10016, United States of America

British Library Cataloguing in Publication Data

Data available

Library of Congress Control Number: 2017931298

ISBN 978–0–19–877960–5 (hbk)
978–0–19–880514–4 (pbk)

Printed and bound by
CPI Group (UK) Ltd, Croydon, CR0 4YY

Links to third party websites are provided by Oxford in good faith and
for information only. Oxford disclaims any responsibility for the materials
contained in any third party website referenced in this work.

THE ANARCHICAL SOCIETY AT 40

Contents

Notes on Contributors vii

Introduction

1. Hedley Bull and *The Anarchical Society* Now at 40   3
   Hidemi Suganami

Part I. Reading *The Anarchical Society* Forty Years on

2. The Argument of *The Anarchical Society*   23
   Hidemi Suganami

3. Ordering the World: Hedley Bull after Forty Years   41
   Richard Falk

Part II. Three Foundational Critiques

4. *The Anarchical Society* as Christian Political Theology   59
   William Bain

5. *The Anarchical Society* and Human Rights   75
   Christian Reus-Smit

6. Decolonizing *The Anarchical Society*   92
   Mustapha Kamal Pasha

Part III. *The Anarchical Society* and World Politics Forty Years on

7. *The Anarchical Society* and the Control of Global Violence   111
   Robert Ayson

8. A Plea for Restraint: *The Anarchical Society* and Nuclear Proliferation   129
   Jan Ruzicka

9. International Society and Islamist Non-State Actors: The Case of the Islamic State Organization   145
   Harmonie Toros and Filippo Dionigi

10. Cyberspace and International Order   162
    Madeline Carr

11. *The Anarchical Society* and a Global Political Economy 179
    Louis W. Pauly

12. *The Anarchical Society* and Climate Change 198
    Robert Falkner

13. *The Anarchical Society* and Indigenous Peoples 216
    Paul Keal

14. Anarchy and Patriarchy in World Politics 234
    Jacqui True

Part IV. Augmenting *The Anarchical Society*

15. *The Anarchical Society* as Futurology 253
    Heikki Patomäki

16. International Society Encounters the Russian World: The Role of Representations in International Relations 270
    Katarzyna Kaczmarska

17. The International Society of 'Civilized States' 286
    Andrew Linklater

Conclusion

18. Bull's Political Vision 305
    Adam Humphreys

Consolidated Bibliography 323
Index 351

Notes on Contributors

Robert Ayson completed his MA as a Freyberg Scholar at the Australian National University and his PhD as a Commonwealth Scholar at King's College, London. Since 2010, he has been Professor of Strategic Studies at Victoria University of Wellington, New Zealand where he works closely with the Centre for Strategic Studies. He is also Adjunct Professor with the Australian National University's Strategic and Defence Studies Centre and Honorary Professor with the New Zealand Defence Force Command and Staff College. Ayson has a particular interest in strategic competition and cooperation, including the management of armed conflict. This work ranges from exploring the ideas of Hedley Bull (undertaken in part as a Senior Research Associate with the University of Oxford's Centre for International Studies) to studies of Asia-Pacific security and Australian and New Zealand responses to the changing balance between China and the United States. His key publications include: *Asia's Security* (Palgrave Macmillan, 2012), *Hedley Bull and the Accommodation of Power* (Palgrave Macmillan, 2012), *Strategy and Security in the Asia-Pacific*, co-edited with Desmond Ball (Allen and Unwin, 2006); *Thomas Schelling and the Nuclear Age: Strategy as Social Science* (Frank Cass, 2004).

William Bain holds degrees from the University of South Carolina (BA) and the University of British Columbia (MA and PhD). He is currently Associate Professor in the Department of Political Science, National University of Singapore. Before joining NUS he held appointments at Glasgow and Aberystwyth Universities. He has also been a Visiting Professor at Université Libre de Bruxelles. Questions of international relations, international political theory, and the history of ideas form the core of his research and teaching interests. He is the author of *Between Anarchy and Society: Trusteeship and the Obligations of Power* (Oxford University Press, 2003) and editor of, and contributor to, *The Empire of Security and the Safety of the People* (Routledge, 2006) and *Medieval Foundations of International Relations* (Routledge, 2017). He is also the author of several articles that explore aspects of the theory of international society, as well as medieval and early-modern international political theory. His current research activity is focused on a project that explores the theological foundations of international society, *Political Theology of International Order*.

Madeline Carr holds degrees from the University of Tasmania (BAHons) and the Australian National University (PhD). She worked for three years at Aberystwyth University and is now a Senior Lecturer in International

Relations at Cardiff University. Her research looks at the ways in which new technology both reinforces and disrupts conventional frameworks for understanding international relations and the implications of this for state and global security, order, and governance. Madeline has published on cyber norms, Internet Freedom, multi-stakeholder Internet governance, and the public/private partnership in national cyber security strategies (research funded by the British Council). Her book *US Power and the Internet in International Relations* is published with Palgrave Macmillan. Madeline is a co-lead on the Standards, Governance, and Policy stream of the UK's £10M PETRAS research hub on the cyber security of the Internet of Things. She was selected in 2014 for the Welsh Crucible as a future research leader and is a multi-award winning teacher.

Filippo Dionigi is Leverhulme Early Career Fellow at the LSE Middle East Centre, currently researching the impact of the Syrian refugee crisis on Arab statehood. He has published a book titled *Hezbollah, Islamist Politics and International Society*, and articles in *International Peacekeeping*, *The Journal of International Political Theory*, and *The European Journal of International Relations*. His main research interests lie at the intersection of constructivist International Relations theory and Middle Eastern politics.

Richard Falk obtained a Bachelor of Science in Economics from the University of Pennsylvania in 1952 before completing a Bachelor of Laws at Yale University. He obtained his Doctorate in Law from Harvard University in 1962. He began his teaching career at Ohio State University in the mid-1950s. He moved to Princeton University in 1961, where he was appointed Albert G. Milbank Professor of International Law and Practice in 1965, the position he now holds as Emeritus Professor. In 1999–2000, he worked on the Independent International Commission on Kosovo and has been associated with the Orfalea Center of Global and International Studies at the University of California, Santa Barbara since 2002. In 2008, the United Nations Human Rights Council (UNHRC) appointed him to a six-year term as a United Nations Special Rapporteur on the 'situation of human rights in the Palestinian territories occupied since 1967'. He is the author or co-author of twenty-five books and the editor or co-editor of another twenty-five volumes. His most recent book is *Humanitarian Intervention and Legitimacy Wars*.

Robert Falkner holds degrees in politics and in economics from Munich University and a doctorate in international relations from Oxford University. He is Associate Professor of International Relations at the London School of Economics and Political Science (LSE), where also he serves as Co-Director of the Dahrendorf Forum and Academic Director of the TRIUM Global Executive MBA, an alliance between LSE, NYU Stern School of Business, and HEC School of Management. He is also an associate of the LSE's Grantham

Research Institute on Climate Change and the Environment and an associate fellow of Chatham House. In 2006–7 he was a visiting scholar at Harvard University. He has published widely on global environmental politics and international political economy, including *The Handbook of Global Climate and Environment Policy* (Wiley-Blackwell, 2013) and *Business Power and Conflict in International Environmental Politics* (Palgrave Macmillan, 2008). One of his current projects engages English School theory in a study of the rise of global environmental responsibility in international society.

Adam Humphreys holds a BA in Philosophy, Politics, and Economics, an MPhil in International Relations, and a DPhil in International Relations from Oxford University, where he was a British Academy Post-Doctoral Fellow (2007–10) and Fellow in Politics at Brasenose College (2010–13). He joined the University of Reading in 2013 as Lecturer in International Relations. He is interested in all areas of International Relations theory, especially: realism and the work of Kenneth Waltz; the nature of theory, how it is applied, and how it explains; the philosophy of science and meta-theory; and the relationship between theory and history. He also has research interests in British foreign policy and the ethics of war. Recent publications include: 'Causation, Complexity, and the Concert: The Pragmatics of Causal Explanation in International Relations', *Journal of International Relations and Development* (forthcoming); 'From National Interest to Global Reform: Patterns of Reasoning in British Foreign Policy Discourse', *British Journal of Politics and International Relations*, 17:4 (Nov 2015), 568–84; 'Realpolitik', in Michael T. Gibbons (ed.), *The Encyclopedia of Political Thought* (Wiley-Blackwell, 2014); 'Waltz and the World: Neorealism as International Political Theory?', *International Politics* 50:6 (Nov 2013), 863–79. He is co-editor, with Hidemi Suganami, of a forthcoming special issue of *Journal of International Relations and Development* on 'Problems of Causation in World Politics'.

Katarzyna Kaczmarska is Marie Skłodowska-Curie Fellow at Aberystwyth and St Petersburg State Universities. She holds a degree in Development Studies from the University of London and in International Relations from the University of Lodz. She was awarded a doctoral training scholarship and completed her PhD in International Politics at Aberystwyth University. Her research interests centre on sociology of knowledge with respect to international relations. Her current research project looks at knowledge on international politics produced in Russia. Prior to coming to Aberystwyth University, she worked as a Research and Teaching Fellow at the OSCE Academy in Bishkek and as analyst and policy practitioner in development cooperation, a field she has since returned to several times as a consultant. She has published on post-Soviet politics, the concept of international society, and the role of political myths in the discourse of development cooperation.

Paul Keal holds a BA from Flinders University and a PhD from the Australian National University. He has held appointments in the University of New South Wales at the Australian Defense Force Academy, the Australian National University, and La Trobe University, and had visiting appointments at Princeton University, Stanford University, the Russian Diplomatic Academy, Keele University, and the University of British Columbia. Between 2004 and 2010, he was Senior Fellow in the Department of International Relations, School of International, Political, and Strategic Studies, College of Asia and the Pacific, Australian National University. Keal's main interests are indigenous rights in world politics, indigenous sovereignty, and self-determination in world politics, and ethical and cultural factors in the political rebuilding of societies emerging from conflict. He is the author of *European Conquest and the Rights of Indigenous Peoples: The Moral Backwardness of International Society* (Cambridge University Press, 2003); *Unspoken Rules and Superpower Dominance* (Macmillan, 1983), co-editor with Andrew Mack of *Security and Arms Control in the North Pacific* (Allen & Unwin, 1988), and editor of *Ethics and Foreign Policy* (Allen & Unwin and the Australian National University, 1992).

Andrew Linklater was educated at Aberdeen, Oxford, and London Universities. He joined Aberystwyth University as Woodrow Wilson Professor in 2000, having previously been Professor and Dean of Postgraduate Studies at Keele University. He had earlier taught at Monash University and the University of Tasmania. He is a Fellow of the British Academy, the Academy of the Social Sciences, and the Learned Society of Wales. Linklater was involved in developing new linkages between political theory and international relations in the 1970s and 1980s, and then in forging connections between critical social theory and world politics. His most recent research investigates the problem of harm in world politics—specifically the problems that arise as societies acquire the capacity to harm and face the challenge of controlling that destructive capability. This has led to a major engagement with process sociology, as developed by Norbert Elias. Current research is geared towards producing a major three-volume study of the problem of harm in world politics which develops new connections between international relations, process sociology, and world history. Linklater's major publications include: *Men and Citizens in the Theory of International Relations* (Macmillan, 1982/1990); *Beyond Realism and Marxism: Critical Theory and International Relations* (Macmillan, 1990); *The Transformation of Political Community: Ethical Foundations of the Post-Westphalian Era* (Polity, 1998); (with Hidemi Suganami) *The English School of International Relations: A Contemporary Reassessment* (Cambridge University Press, 2006); *Critical Theory and World Politics: Sovereignty, Citizenship and Humanity* (Routledge, 2007); and *The Problem of Harm in World Politics: Theoretical Investigations*

(Cambridge University Press, 2011). Works in progress include: *Violence and Civilization: States-Systems in the West* (Cambridge University Press, 2016); and *Political Symbols and Global Civilizing Processes* (in preparation).

Mustapha Kamal Pasha holds a BA (Forman Christian College), an LLB (Punjab University Law College), a Diploma in International Affairs (Punjab University), an MA (Graduate School of International Studies, University of Denver), and a PhD (Graduate School of International Studies, University of Denver). In 2013, he took up a chair in International Politics at Aberystwyth University, having been Sixth Century Chair and Head of International Relations at the University of Aberdeen since January 2006 and taught previously at the School of International Service, American University in Washington, DC. He was Vice-President of the International Studies Association in 2012–13. His work is broadly located within Post-Western International Relations and draws from varied genealogies, notably decolonial thought, postcolonialism, poststructuralism, critical theory, and classical political economy (influenced by Hegel, Marx, Gramsci, and Subaltern Studies). He is currently completing an original monograph on Islamic Nihilism. His second major project extends his abiding interest in old and emergent forms of global inequalities and stratifications. His recent publications include: (Editor), *Globalization, Difference and Human Security* (Routledge, 2013); 'Nihilism and the Otherness of Islam', *Millennium* 42 (2013): 177–97; 'The Bandung Impulse and International Relations', in Sanjay Seth (ed.) *Postcolonialism and International Relations* (Routledge, 2013); 'Islam and the Postsecular', *Review of International Studies* 38 (2012): 1041–56; 'The Secular Subject of Critical International Relations Theory', in S. Brincat, L. Lima, and J. Nunes (eds.), *Critical Theory in International Relations and Security Studies* (Routledge, 2012), 105–14; 'Islam, Nihilism and Liberal Secularity', *Journal of International Relations and Development* 15 (2012); 'Western Nihilism and Dialogue: Prelude to an Uncanny Encounter in International Relations', *Millennium* 39 (2011), 683–99; 'Global Leadership and the Islamic World: Crisis, Contention and Challenge', in Stephen Gill (ed.), *Global Crises and the Crisis of Global Leadership* (Cambridge University Press, 2011), 144–60; 'Untimely Reflections', in Robbie Shilliam (ed.), *International Relations and Non-Western Thought* (Routledge, 2011), 217–26; 'Symbiosis and Fracture: Civil Society and Weak States in South Asia', in T.V. Paul (ed.), *South Asia's Weak States: Understanding the Regional Insecurity Predicament* (Stanford University Press, 2010), 122–44.

Heikki Patomäki is Professor of World Politics at the University of Helsinki since 2003. Previously, he was Professor of World Politics and Economy at the Nottingham Trent University (1998–2003) and RMIT University, Melbourne (2007–10), and, in 2012, he was a Visiting Professor at the Ritsumeikan University in Kyoto. Patomäki's research interests include philosophy and methodology of social sciences, peace research, futures studies, economic theory, global political economy, and global political theory. His most recent book on the future of economic theory and policy was published in January 2015 in Finnish (*Suomen talouspolitiikan tulevaisuus: teoriasta käytäntöön*); other editions will follow. Patomäki's books in English include *The Great Eurozone Disaster: From Crisis to Global New Deal* (Zed Books, 2013); *The Political Economy of Global Security* (Routledge, 2008); *A Possible World: Democratic Transformation of Global Institutions*, with T. Teivainen (Zed Books, 2004); and *After International Relations* (Routledge, 2002). He is currently working on two new books in English, *Unprincipled Economics* (Routledge), with Jamie Morgan; and *Global Futures*.

Louis W. Pauly, now Chair of the Department of Political Science at the University of Toronto, has held the Canada Research Chair in Globalization and Governance since 2002. As Director of the Centre for International Studies from 1997 to 2011, he helped build the foundations for the Munk School of Global Affairs, where he remains a member of the faculty. A graduate of Cornell University, the London School of Economics, New York University, and Fordham University, he is a Fellow of the Royal Society of Canada. He recently held the Karl W. Deutsch Guest Professorship at the WZB Berlin Social Science Center. With Emanuel Adler, from 2007 to 2012 he edited the journal *International Organization*. In 2015, he was the recipient of the Distinguished Scholar Award from the International Political Economy Section of the International Studies Association. His personal and collaborative publications include *Power in a Complex Global System* (Routledge, 2014); *Global Ordering: Institutions and Autonomy in a Changing World* (UBC Press, 2008); *Global Liberalism and Political Order* (SUNY Press, 2007); *Complex Sovereignty: Reconstituting Political Authority in the Twenty-First Century* (University of Toronto Press, 2005); *Governing the World's Money* (Cornell, 2002); *The Myth of the Global Corporation* (Princeton, 1998); *Who Elected the Bankers? Surveillance and Control in the World Economy* (Cornell, 1997); and *Opening Financial Markets: Banking Politics on the Pacific Rim* (Cornell, 1988).

Christian Reus-Smit is Professor of International Relations at the University of Queensland and a Fellow of the Academy of the Social Sciences in Australia. Before joining UQ, Reus-Smit held Chairs at the European University Institute and the Australian National University (where he was Head of the Department of International Relations from 2001 to 2010). He is co-editor of the Cambridge Studies in International Relations book series, the journal *International Theory*, and a new multi-volume series of *Oxford Handbooks of International Relations*. In 2013–14, Reus-Smit served as a Vice-President of the International Studies Association. His major publications include: *The Globalization of International Society* (Oxford University Press, 2017);

Individual Rights and the Making of the International System (Cambridge University Press, 2013); *Special Responsibilities: Global Problems and American Power* (Cambridge University Press, 2012); *The Oxford Handbook of International Relations* (Oxford University Press, 2008); *American Power and World Order* (Polity, 2004); and *The Moral Purpose of the State* (Princeton University Press, 1999).

Jan Ruzicka is Lecturer in Security Studies in the Department of International Politics, Aberystwyth University. He also serves as Director of the David Davies Memorial Institute. He was educated at Charles University Prague, Central European University, and Brandeis University. He received his PhD in International Politics from the University of Wales, Aberystwyth. He was Research Assistant on the RCUK-funded project 'Challenges to Trust-Building in Nuclear Worlds' in 2009–11. Prior to his academic career, he worked as the chief aide to a ranking member of the Committee on Foreign Affairs, Defence, and Security of the Senate of the Czech Republic in the years 2004–6. His research explores implications of nuclear weapons, trusting relationships, and revolutions for international security. His articles on these topics have been published in *Ethics & International Affairs, International Affairs, International Relations, Medicine, Conflict and Survival, Journal of Trust Research, RUSI Journal, Review of International Studies*. He was the guest editor of a special issue of the journal *International Relations* (September 2014) dedicated to Karl Deutsch and his impact on the discipline of IR. He is primary investigator on the project 'Alliances and Trust-building in International Politics' supported by the British Academy.

Hidemi Suganami studied at Tokyo, Aberystwyth, and London Universities. He took up his first academic post at Keele University in 1975, where he later became Professor of the Philosophy of International Relations. In 2004, he moved to Aberystwyth University, where currently he is Emeritus Professor of International Politics. His major publications include: *The Domestic Analogy and World Order Proposals* (Cambridge University Press, 1989; Japanese edition, 1994); *On the Causes of War* (Clarendon Press, 1996); and, with Andrew Linklater, *The English School of International Relations* (Cambridge University Press, 2006). Suganami has written extensively on the English School of International Relations and some of its central figures, C.A.W. Manning and Hedley Bull, in particular; he was also a contributor to one of the key texts of the English School, Hedley Bull and Adam Watson (eds), *The Expansion of International Society* (Clarendon Press, 1989; Italian edition, 1994), based on the work of the British Committee on the Theory of International Politics. His long-standing interest in the philosophy of law has led to the publication of 'Understanding Sovereignty through Kelsen/Schmitt', which won the British International Studies Association's best-article-of-the-year award in 2007. Suganami is also a co-editor, with Richard Ned Lebow and

Peer Schouten, of *The Return of the Theorists: Dialogues with Great Thinkers in International Relations* (Palgrave, 2016). Over a number of years, he has been writing on philosophical issues surrounding causation and explanation in social science and history with a view to clearing the ground where International Relations meets philosophical analysis. This will form the basis of a monograph on *Causation and Explanation in International Relations: A Philosophical Investigation,* co-authored with Adam Humphreys.

Harmonie Toros holds a BA in Contemporary History (Sussex), a Maîtrise in History (Paris IV- Sorbonne), an MA in Conflict Resolution (Bradford), and a PhD from Aberystwyth University. She worked as reporter and editor for major international news agencies (The Associated Press and Agence France-Presse) before returning to academia in 2003 to research the potential of negotiations and dialogue in the transformation of conflicts marked by terrorist violence. She is author of *Terrorism, Talking and Transformation: A Critical Approach* (Routledge, 2012) and editor of two volumes investigating the crossroads between terrorism and peace and conflict studies (Routledge, 2014 and 2015). A senior lecturer in international conflict analysis at the University of Kent, she is currently investigating the role of the human experience of war and political violence in international relations.

Jacqui True is Professor of Politics & International Relations and an Australian Research Council Future Fellow (2015–19) in the School of Social Sciences at Monash University, Australia. She received her PhD from York University, Toronto, Canada and has held academic positions at Michigan State University, the University of Southern California, and the University of Auckland. She is specialist in Gender and International Relations and has made contributions to theorizing gender mainstreaming in global governance and feminist research methodologies in international relations. Her current research is focused on understanding the political economy of post-conflict violence against women and the patterns of systemic sexual and gender-based violence in Asia Pacific conflict-affected countries. Her book, *The Political Economy of Violence Against Women* (Oxford, 2012) won the American Political Science Association's 2012 biennial prize for the best book in human rights and the British International Studies Association International Political Economy book prize in 2013. Recent publications include 'Reframing Conflict-Related Sexual Violence', in *Security Dialogue* with Sara E. Davies and *Scandalous Economics: The Politics of Gender and Financial Crises* (New York: Oxford University Press, 2016) edited with Aida Hozić.

Introduction

1

Hedley Bull and *The Anarchical Society* Now at 40

Hidemi Suganami

ORIGINS OF OUR BOOK

'I am calling it "The Anarchical Society"', said Bull of his book with a twinkle in his eye as we sat for tea. This was at Keele, in the academic year of 1975–6, my first year of teaching.[1] That was a memorable afternoon; Bull, our distinguished guest speaker that day, had just given an impressive lecture to our students. He titled it 'The Obsolescence of the States System?', though as we walked across to the packed lecture theatre, he told me with a smile, 'I had thought of calling it "The Decline of the West?".' That afternoon's lecture became a basis of the third part of his book, *The Anarchical Society* (1977). Meanwhile, the abandoned title of the lecture, 'The Decline of the West?' appears not to have been forgotten entirely. It changed to 'The Revolt against Western Dominance', the title of the second part of the Hagey Lectures Bull delivered several years later (Bull 2000c [1984]; see also Bull 1984b).

When, in the first quarter of 1977, I learnt that the book was finally out, I bought a copy straightway and read it with great excitement. Though it left me with several puzzles—some of which I seek to resolve in my other essay in this volume—I had little doubt that it raised the standard of textbook-writing in International Relations (IR) to a level in some ways unrivalled in the previous two decades. Geoffrey Goodwin, the then Montague Burton Professor of International Relations at the LSE, visited Keele that June as our external examiner and he too was deeply impressed by what 'Hedley' had done. *The Anarchical Society* became one of the books then most strongly recommended to IR students in the UK, on a par with Carr's *Twenty Years' Crisis* (1939) and

---

[1] I am grateful to my two co-editors for their support, encouragement, and advice without which I could not have written this essay in the way it has materialized.

Waltz's *Man, the State and War* (1959), the latter soon to be superseded by the same author's *Theory of International Politics* (1979). The rest is history—in which, as has been told many a time, several 'isms' and 'schools' began to be seen to inhabit the terrain of IR.

My forty years in the university teaching of International Relations have roughly coincided with the life of *The Anarchical Society*, which is currently in its fourth edition (2012). When, in my final year of teaching at Aberystwyth, I was asked to deliver six consecutive lectures to our first-year students, with two other colleagues each doing the same, I chose *The Anarchical Society* as one of the key texts. This was not an unexpected choice for a module titled 'Exploring the International, Part One'. And the choice was natural particularly for my section of the module: our remit had been to give one coherent account of 'the international' from a perspective we were each most familiar with and, for me, that was the 'English School of International Relations'; Bull's book came with that choice.

While a majority in the Department at large seemed to consider that 'exploring the international' expressed the most obvious focus of our pedagogy, there were also some dissenting voices, which I respected, suggesting that this was *not* the best way to study or teach contemporary world politics. However, I felt that nothing is lost, and much will be gained, by acquainting our beginners, in my part of the module, with one clearly articulated line of argument that Bull, and others in the English School, have developed.[2]

However, I was uneasy. Bull's way of representing the world is a significant one and his argument is definitely worth getting to know in the study of international politics. But his approach faced many serious challenges from within IR, where other stances compete with that of the English School, and from within the contemporary phase of human history itself, in which a number of acute problems confront us: uncertainties in the future of great power relations after the end of the Cold War; ubiquitous violence that appears increasingly to affect our everyday lives even in relatively well-governed societies; and, above all, climate change with a wide range of serious repercussions for our ways of living everywhere on this planet. None of these problems seem to sit comfortably with that strangely sanguine title, *The Anarchical Society*, which, over forty years ago, Bull spoke of with a twinkle in his eye—a title which neatly captures his central puzzle: what combination

---

[2] For a fuller account of the English School and its thinking, see Linklater and Suganami (2006). On how to treat 'the international' in the teaching of world politics, the approaches taken by Edkins and Zehfuss (2005) and Rosenberg (2016) are, in their different ways, worthy of close attention in contrast to the distinctly juridical line adopted by Bull and, incidentally, also by Waltz (1979). Almost entirely neglected, Hans Kelsen has articulated the juridical idea of 'the international' (and thereby also 'anarchy' and 'sovereignty') with unrivalled clarity in his discussion of 'centralization and decentralization as legal concepts' (1945, 303–27). On Kelsen's treatment of sovereignty, see Suganami 2007.

of historically contingent features of the modern states system has contributed to the degree of cooperation, or 'society', that exists among states coexisting under 'anarchy'.

That uneasiness was at the back of my mind when I suggested to Madeline Carr, then one of my colleagues at Aberystwyth, to co-edit a collection of essays under the title, *The Anarchical Society at 40: Contemporary Challenges and Prospects*. 'I will write the first chapter, summarizing Bull's argument', I reassured her, thinking to myself that that would be an easy part. 'But', I added, 'I want to know more—and the students, too. I will invite people to write about aspects of contemporary world politics covered, and not covered, by Bull. You can write on the significance of the Internet to world politics. He certainly didn't know about that!' Without any hesitation, and with much enthusiasm, we decided to work together. Later, in June 2016, when Madeline ably organized a two-day international workshop at Cardiff, with generous funding from the University, to facilitate discussions on our papers, Adam Humphreys, who had earlier agreed to write a conclusion to this volume, joined the editorial team, adding a valuable third eye. On behalf of the editorial team and contributors, I wish to express here our gratitude to Cardiff University, School of Law and Politics, for their part in enabling us to bring our project to fruition.

Before we present the outcomes of our collective endeavours over the past two years, I wish to touch on a few questions by way of introducing the essays that follow: 'what sort of scholar was Bull?'; 'what kind of book is *The Anarchical Society*?'; and 'what, in outline, does *The Anarchical Society at 40* deliver?'.

HEDLEY BULL: AN ANALYTICAL SYNTHESIZER

Back in the 1970s again, one of my former teachers at Tokyo University asked me the first of these questions when he suggested that I write an article for a Japanese journal, outlining the study of international relations in the UK. 'I only know him through his style of intellectual engagement', I replied, 'but he strikes me as the kind of person who is driven to qualify almost everything he says; he is very careful, he doesn't suffer fools easily, and we have to qualify almost anything we say to him.' John Vincent, then a colleague of mine at Keele and one of Bull's former PhD students at Canberra, confirmed my assessment. He would see Bull regularly for supervision, each time he would explain what his research project was about, and each time he would come out feeling utterly demolished. This apparently went on for quite some time, for the whole first year or more (see Vincent 1974).

I had a comparable experience with Bull though I only saw him several times in all. Once he invited me to Oxford, in 1976, during his visiting fellowship at All Souls.[3] Over lunch he asked me how I was getting on with my PhD thesis 'in progress' on the theme of the domestic analogy, a subject on which he had written a pioneering work (1966b). He listened to me mumble a bit and told me straightway with much bluntness, a quality for which he was well known: 'The domestic analogy isn't the issue'! I worked hard to prove him wrong, or at least *qualify* his main thrust, but it took me a very long time to get there (see Suganami 1989).

It is interesting to note how Bull combined the outspoken way in which he rejected what he saw as intellectually not worth pursuing with the extremely careful way in which he qualified everything he argued for. For him, it seemed, certain things were intellectually beyond the pale, quantitative international politics amongst them (Bull 1969); and within the realm of what he took to be intellectually worthy, he was clear that lucid argumentation and judicious judgement must guide one's exploration.

Bull may have been operating under the influence of once pervasive Logical Positivism, according to which all statements are either meaningful or not, and only those which are can be either true or false, requiring, and therefore warranting, careful empirical or logical examination (Ayer 1971 [1936]). But, of course, where the boundary of meaningfulness or intellectual worthiness lies in turn becomes a contentious issue. It is pertinent to note in this regard Bull's claim that, unlike his mentor Martin Wight, he studied closely what was being done at that time under the rubric of 'scientific studies of international relations' before rejecting it (Bull 1991 [1976], xi). Bull's verdict on Richard Falk's vision took a comparable path—though he did not fail to acknowledge that '[Falk's] is one of the most significant points of departure in the study of world politics today' (Bull 1977, ix; Falk 1971 and Ch. 3 in this volume). Even with respect to Brian Midgley's theological work on natural law, mostly neglected or treated with disdain in IR circles, Bull took it seriously enough, on the face of it, to write a lengthy review article on it (Bull 1979c; Midgley 1979; and Bain, Ch. 4 in this volume).

Bull clearly was a careful, painstaking, analytic thinker. But such an intellectual disposition at times conflicts with the need to learn from a wide range of literature pertinent to one's study. This appears true of Bull; in his thinking he relies heavily on a relatively narrow range of intellectual resources which he had under his firm command. These included, and did not appear to have gone much beyond, certain key ideas of C.A.W. Manning and Martin Wight in International Relations, those of his 'Oxford teacher', H.L.A. Hart in the theory of law and society, the teaching of the philosopher John Anderson,

---

[3] In the following year Bull became the Montague Burton Professor of International Relations at Oxford, a position he held until his tragically early death in 1985.

to whom Bull acknowledges his 'greatest intellectual debt' (Bull 1977, ix–x), and, from among the classics of international law that interested him, Vattel's *The Law of Nations* in particular (see Bull 1966c, 1977, 322 n. 3; Vattel 1916 [1758]). Intellectually, Bull was a synthesizer but with a relatively narrow cluster of ideas shaping his basic outlook.[4] Still, he thought deeply about a variety of arguments then dominant in IR regarding the political organization of the world. He wrote:

> When still an undergraduate I was very impressed (I now think too impressed) by the dictum of Samuel Alexander, the author of *Space, Time and Deity* (London: Macmillan, 1920) that 'thinking is also research'. My book reflects the limitations of an attempt to deal with a large and complex subject simply by thinking it through. (1977, x)

There are, of course, limitations; there are no books without. Still, Bull's analytical mind has produced a well-synthesized book, which has come to be widely acknowledged as one of the contemporary classics of international political theory.

THE ANARCHICAL SOCIETY: A 'RATIONALIST' TEXT

What kind of book, then, is *The Anarchical Society*? To those relatively limited circles of IR scholars, mainly in the UK, who were already familiar with Wight's study of the historically recurring patterns of international thought (Wight 1966a, 1966b; Bull 1991 [1976]), it was immediately clear that Bull's book focused on systematic exposition of what Wight called 'Rationalism', in contrast to 'Realism' and 'Revolutionism' (Wight 1991), and application of that particular tradition of thought to discussing contemporary world politics and its future.

According to Rationalism, despite the overall anarchical, or legally decentralized, structure of the international system, (i) sovereign states, through the workings of historically evolving rules and practices—or 'institutions of international society' (Bull 1977, xiv)—have managed to maintain a semblance of order in their inter-relations; (ii) this, in turn, has contributed to the maintenance of order in human social relations as a whole; and (iii) strengthening the element of international society in world politics remains the key to enhancing the prospect for order in global human social relations.[5]

---

[4] Although I have no space to develop my argument here, I would suggest that this cluster comprises utilitarian liberal individualism and empiricism.

[5] According to Wight, the term 'Rationalism' derives from John Locke's idea that 'men are reasonable, and that they live together according to reason even when they have no common government, as in the condition of international relations' (1991, 14). Wight's 'Rationalism'

'Realism', by contrast, sees in the anarchical structure of the states system that emerged from Western Christendom a condition under which war is a perpetual possibility between any states, where 'political action is most regularly necessitous' (Wight 1966a, 26). 'Revolutionism', on the other hand, advances an interpretation of world history as a struggle towards an ultimate goal of world peace and justice brought about by progressive forces transcending humanity's division into sovereign states (Bull 1991, xii).

However, Wight's '3Rs' remained relatively unknown to IR scholars even within the UK while leading figures of the increasingly global IR community showed a clear tendency to identify their positions in relation, and often in opposition, not to Bull's book, but to Kenneth Waltz's 'neorealist' classic, *Theory of International Politics* (1979) published two years later (see Keohane 1986). This has meant that the IR community remained somewhat unclear about the precise identity of Bull's book in IR 'isms' terms (Finnemore 2001)— although some commentators later came to discuss Bull's position in terms of its proximity to, or distance from, constructivism, liberal institutionalism, and neorealism (Dunne 1995; Hurrell 2002, 2012).

When, at the end of the 1970s, those two now-classic works in IR were in full circulation, it might have been noted, in social science methodology terms, that Bull's book embodied 'interpretivism' (or 'hermeneutics') in contrast to Waltz's which embraced 'positivism'. However, even though it was very common in the 1970s for works in the philosophy of social science to juxtapose these two approaches, usually with a view to exploring a possible third (Lessnoff 1974; Bernstein 1976; Benton 1977), there was little awareness within the IR community then that *The Anarchical Society* and *Theory of International Politics* might constitute a contrasting pair. The juxtaposition between 'interpretivism' and 'positivism' was brought to the attention of the IR community at large only later, mainly through the publication of Hollis and Smith's *Explaining and Understanding International Relations* (1990).[6] And in the same year, Linklater's pioneering work, *Beyond Realism and Marxism: Critical Theory and International Relations* appeared, in which he drew attention to the contrast between Wightian Realism and

---

therefore points to the ability of states to find ways to coexist and cooperate under anarchy and should be distinguished from 'rationalism' in the North American political science of international relations which sees states as rational utility-maximizers (see Wendt 1999).

[6] Hollis and Smith's (1990) well-known 'explaining'/'understanding' dichotomy, corresponding to the positivism/interpretivism contrast, points to two supposedly distinct modes of account-giving; the former in terms of 'causes of events' and the latter 'reasons for actions'. This dichotomy assumes that causes and effects are connected (solely) by externally observable regular conjunctions while the linkages between reasons and actions are inter-subjectively intelligible to observers who put themselves in the situations of the relevant actors in their social contexts (see Winch 1958).

Rationalism, embodied in the writings of Waltz and Bull, as exemplifying positivism and hermeneutics.[7]

For the ten years or so following its publication, therefore, *The Anarchical Society* stood in some splendid isolation in IR. This period ended when the book came to be acknowledged, in the global market of ideas and brands, as the representative text of British IR (Hoffmann 1995, vii) and, more specifically, of the English School of International Relations—particularly through the publication of Tim Dunne's *Inventing International Society: A History of the English School* (1998b), followed by Barry Buzan's call in 1999 to 'reconvene the English School' (2001). These two scholars' works have enabled the label 'The English School' to be added to a standard menu for choice in the expanding list of 'theoretical perspectives' in IR.[8]

This much-used term, 'theoretical perspective' is in fact quite useful in clarifying the kind of book that *The Anarchical Society* is. What it offers is a 'theory' in the sense of a 'conceptual scheme' *through* which we can *see* (as implied by the etymology of the word 'per-spective')—by means of which we can make sense of—what goes on in the world political system.

It is pertinent to recall here that Manning had a formative influence on Bull's approach to the study of international relations; and he, too, had presented a conceptual scheme to help make sense of the relations of states. But Manning's claim had been that he was merely replicating the ideas in the light of which day-to-day international intercourse was being carried out by states' official agents themselves; the conceptual scheme he articulated was, emphatically, that very set of ideas in terms of which, he claimed, those who talked and acted in the name of their states understood and conducted their inter-state relations (Manning 1975). Bull has at least partially inherited this 'anthropological' stance. But Bull is somewhat more ambiguous on this point; he can also be interpreted as offering a conceptual scheme, or set of ideas, which *he* formulated to covey the images *he* has of the world; hence his deployment of a set of conceptual idioms—'international system', 'international society', and 'world political system', chief amongst them—whose meanings must be understood as Bull defined them in order to make sense of

---

[7] Following Habermas, Linklater held that these two orientations represented distinct knowledge-constitutive interests—a technical interest in enabling survival through manipulation and control in the anarchic international environment and a practical interest in strengthening the bases of international order—and he argued that an interest in the emancipation of the human species, which he associated with Revolutionism, dialectically transcends them both (Linklater 1990, 8–33).

[8] The name 'English School' was used initially by Roy Jones in his 'The English School of International Relations: A Case for Closure' (1981). This polemical piece effectively demonstrated by its own example how little understood the School's central views were then, even within the UK IR community.

his interpretation of the world and argument about it (on which see Suganami, Ch. 2 in this volume).[9]

There is another ambiguity in Bull's methodological stance. His argument has a clear *causal* dimension to it, bringing him closer to the 'explanation' side of Hollis and Smith's dichotomy, away from the 'understanding' side. His key contention is that what he has identified as the rules and institutions of international society have contributed to the achievement of international order. He wrote:

> A central theme in this study is that the rules and institutions to which reference has been made carry out positive functions or roles in relation to international order. In this study what is meant by statements of this kind is simply that these rules and institutions are part of the efficient causation of international order, that they are among the necessary and sufficient conditions of its occurrence.
>
> (1977, 74–5)

But to say that Bull's study contains statements of a causal kind as its key component is not the same as saying that his book investigates the causes of a range of phenomena or events relating to the subject of 'international order'; there is nothing in the book about the causes of war or imperialism, for instance. And, although he acknowledges the existence of causes of the world's ills deeper than its institutional structure, he does not investigate such causes nor even examine works that do (see Patomäki, Ch. 15 in this volume). Bull's attention is narrowly focused on explaining the extent to which, despite international anarchy, states manage to coexist and cooperate in orderly ways and, more specifically, on identifying the institutional bases of international order.

The best answer to what kind of book *The Anarchical Society* is will therefore be that its author focused on articulating and developing the 'Rationalist' tradition of international political thought in Wight's sense and applied its intellectual resources to discussing contemporary world politics,

---

[9] Bull's use of conceptual schemes for the purpose of interpreting world politics is found, for example, in his discussion of 'war'. He wrote: 'From the vantage-point of the individual state, war remains an instrument of policy... From the point of view of the international system, war remains a basic determinant of the shape of the system... From the perspective of international society, war retains its dual aspect: on the one hand, a threat to be limited and contained; on the other hand, an instrumentality to be harnessed to international society's purposes' (1977, 194–8). It is interesting to ask here what Bull could have meant by the three innocuous-sounding phrases, 'from the vantage-point of', 'from the point of view of', and 'from the perspective of'. He may have used the first of these almost literally to suggest that if we put ourselves in the position of the leader of a state, observing what is going on outside its borders, we will consider war as an instrument of our national policy. But it is clear that he is using the latter two phrases non-literally—to suggest 'if we *interpret* the world to constitute an international system *or* international society', then war can be understood in this way or that. Of course, it is also possible that, in the first case, Bull was thinking that if we *interpret* the world as consisting of states in competition with one another, as Realists do, then war will be understood as an instrument of national policy.

and its future directions, at the time of his writing. This points to one of the book's important features: the key aim of *The Anarchical Society* is neither simply 'understanding' (in Hollis and Smith's sense), nor 'causal explanation' (as Bull explained it above), of world politics, but encompasses a normative or practical dimension. This consists in a fundamental endorsement of the institutional structure of world politics as the anarchical society of sovereign states and an exploration of how its contributions to order and other related goals may be strengthened in the face of various challenges which Bull sensed at his particular historical juncture.

It is well to note, however, that just as there are no books without limitations, there are no texts without potentials. It is of course important to read a text critically and uncover assumptions and judgements that shaped its author's argument and even perhaps set a broad limit to what she could coherently present as its main thesis. But it is also important to look into various corners of her textual architecture to find some hidden elbow room, some space to manoeuvre the text out of its apparent encasement.

In reading *The Anarchical Society* forty years after its publication, it is instructive to work with both these reading strategies. The book requires, and enables, both these kinds of engagement because of its relatively narrow basis and focus as well as its aging effects combined with its author's well-known tendency to carefully qualify everything he advances as his main thesis. There may be more we can read into or out of *The Anarchical Society* than Rationalism or the international society perspective pure and simple. However, as Adam Humphreys points out in his essay 'Bull's Political Vision', with which we conclude this volume, it is not in Bull's use of the Wightian trichotomy—transposed to the concepts of 'international system', 'international society', and 'world society'—that we can find an opportune space to develop Bull's argument further beyond its Rationalist framework and focus. Rather, the 'elbow room' is in Bull's own idea of the 'world political system' *as already a contemporary reality*, comprising state and non-state actors and subsuming the international system with a varying element of international society in it.

THE ANARCHICAL SOCIETY AT 40: AN OUTLINE OF OUR BOOK

Before we get to all that quite complex line of thinking, we invite the readers to go through sixteen substantive essays in all. The contributors come from a variety of backgrounds in terms of their intellectual orientations, academic specializations, and educational, professional, and other life experiences and they collectively exhibit wide-ranging manners in which Bull's text can be approached. Still, their essays are interlinked in many criss-crossing ways as Humphreys notes in his concluding essay (Ch. 18); and there are several clusters each of which exhibits closer similarities in terms of the subjects covered and/or the attitudes of the authors to Bull's approach or contentions. I outline below the arguments of the sixteen essays in the light of the clusters I find among them. These essays, followed by Humphreys', which I also outline at the end of this introduction, articulate our individual and collective judgements about *The Anarchical Society*, its limits, and resilience forty years after its publication.

It is an intriguing feature of Bull's book that, despite his careful, systematic style of writing, it does the very thing that he is at pains to stress that it does not while it does *not* do what he acknowledges *needs* to be done. First, Bull claims he does not canvass any solution to the problems that humankind faces, yet this is precisely what he does. Second, contrary to what the book's subtitle, *A Study of Order in World Politics* signifies in his own terminology, and to how he thinks the '*world* political system' should be studied, the book remains a more narrowly focused study of *international* order in the contemporary global '*international*' system'. In Chapter 2, 'The Argument of *The Anarchical Society*', I first outline the complex moves the book makes and then investigate the underlying sources of these two discrepancies to obtain a deeper understanding of Bull's thought structures. The chapter ends by outlining what, in the light of what Bull has said but not done, other scholars could fruitfully pursue to make further contributions to a study of order, and other related goals, in contemporary world politics.

This is followed by Richard Falk's 'Ordering the World: Hedley Bull after Forty Years', in which he reviews some of the main contentions of *The Anarchical Society* with the benefit of forty years' hindsight. This exercise is of special interest not least because of Bull's critical engagement with Falk's work in *The Anarchical Society* itself. Against certain well-known realists, such as Henry Kissinger and Hans Morgenthau, Falk finds himself on the side of Bull in stressing the *social* character of international relations but situates himself closer to Robert Cox, who emphasizes the constitutive roles of the world economy and civil society actors to a far greater degree than did Bull. Falk was prescient to warn us of the dangers facing our planet yet, he acknowledges, Bull was right to think that radical changes of the sort Falk urged were unrealistic. Whether, in retrospect, Bull was right also to suggest that these threats to human existence could be dealt with adequately through international cooperation is one of the important questions discussed by Falk and later revisited by Robert Falkner in Chapter 12, '*The Anarchical Society* and Climate Change'.

These two preliminary essays, forming 'Part I: Reading *The Anarchical Society* Forty Years on', are followed by a cluster of three essays in 'Part II:

Three Foundational Critiques', in which William Bain, Christian Reus-Smit, and Mustapha Kamal Pasha take turns to engage in a deep-level critique of Bull's thought as expressed in his text.

In Chapter 4, '*The Anarchical Society* as Christian Political Theology', Bain points out that Bull, who found no place for theology as a basis of acceptable scholarship in the study of international relations, was unaware of a Christian theological foundation of his own international political theory. Bull's thought, Bain argues, descends from that line of Christian theological doctrine according to which the basis of order resides in 'will and artifice' not in 'reason'—a doctrine upon which, significantly, Hobbes had built his political philosophy. This makes it a serious history-of-ideas error to call Bull's version of Rationalism 'Grotian' (rather than 'Hobbesian') as is conventionally done by the English School writers, including Bull himself. According to Bain, the Christian theological origins of Bull's understandings of order in world politics alerts us to the extent to which Western culture still permeates a dominant understanding of the contemporary states system. Bain also argues that since, for Bull, there is no ultimate reason why anything ought to be done, he will be unable to defend the values of international society, 'life, truth, and property', or, more fundamentally, individual human rights without invoking 'a kind of faith'—despite his outright rejection of it as a foundation of knowledge.

In Chapter 5, '*The Anarchical Society* and Human Rights', Christian Reus-Smit observes that Bull is an arch-taxonomist who thrived on fine conceptual distinctions. Especially significant amongst them, in terms of the ways they shape Bull's account of order in world politics, are those between 'international order' and 'world order', 'international society' and 'world society', and 'international justice' and 'human justice'; and underlying all these, Reus-Smit claims, is the most fundamental, and problematic, distinction between 'order' and 'justice'—a point which I also pick up in Chapter 2 in this volume. Razor-sharp though Bull's analysis often was, he lacked a historical understanding of the interplay and contestation between individual human rights and state rights, which, Reus-Smit argues, has shaped the nature of states, international society, and world society. Reus-Smit suggests that greater attention to the nature and politics of human rights can aid significantly in generating a theory of social change which Bull was unable to develop within the parameters of his decidedly taxonomic intellectual disposition.

In Chapter 6, 'Decolonizing *The Anarchical Society*', Mustapha Kamal Pasha critiques Bull's treatment of the Third World's demands for justice. While expressing his concerns for redistributive justice, and thereby acknowledging the presence of 'coloniality', Bull never incorporates into his discussion the injustices of colonialism on which post-colonial international society/ order has been built—a theme that also concerns Keal (Ch. 13 in this volume). The goal of 'order' that Bull values when discussing its relation to 'justice' has been abstracted from the history of colonialism which haunts Bull's text inerasably. Consideration of the problem of justice, Pasha points out (Ch. 6 in this volume, pp. 92–3), needs to include three components: '(i) an acknowledgement of particular (exclusionary) historical settlements that have shaped the contemporary international order; (ii) recognition of racially differentiated space (or "coloniality") as a durable feature of past and present international order; and (iii) exposure of some of the more potent effects of this differentiation on the capacity or power of (unequal) actors (sovereign states in Bull's formulation) in the international system.'

These three essays, comprising Part II, point to what their respective authors each present as quite fundamental limitations intrinsic to Bull's intellectual orientation underpinning his work, in particular, the a-historicity of his conceptual theorizing. By comparison, the next eight essays, forming 'Part III: *The Anarchical Society* and World Politics Forty Years on', are not quite so fundamentally critical of Bull's framework. Indeed, the contributors to this part apply, to the extent they find it possible and helpful to do so, Bull's ideas and insights to certain specific issues of contemporary world politics. And their essays cluster around certain identifiable common themes. Chapters 7–9 deal with contemporary world political issues relating to violence and security. Chapters 10–12 examine the contemporary relevance of *The Anarchical Society* against the background of much increased global interconnectedness. Chapters 13 and 14 discuss 'indigenous peoples' and 'women', respectively, as global classes neglected in Bull's treatment of world politics.

There are of course a number of readily usable elements in *The Anarchical Society* in discussing world political issues even forty years on and these are most pronounced in relation to the subject of violence and security. In Chapter 7, '*The Anarchical Society* and the Control of Global Violence', Robert Ayson draws attention to Bull's neglected scholarly identity as a military-strategic thinker and to his emphasis on the importance of informal rules concerning the control of violence which emerged in the nuclear era. They were underpinned by a degree of common interest in mutual restraint acknowledged by the great powers. The end of the Cold War, the rise of China as a great power in Asia, and the intensification of terrorism and counter-measures since 9/11 provide a volatile background, against which Ayson conducts his analysis of the threats to international order and the extent of common interest in containing them. He warns that without restraint by all the major powers, any confidence that there is a system of informal rules for the control of global violence may be dented even where major inter-state war has been avoided as in Crimea or Ukraine; and further that the very idea of the anarchical society of sovereign states, where order is sustained by informal rules controlling global violence, is challenged by violent non-state actors and divisive international responses to them so far in Libya, Syria, and Yemen, for example.

In Chapter 8, 'A Plea for Restraint: *The Anarchical Society* and Nuclear Proliferation', Jan Ruzicka focuses on Bull's nuanced position on the implications of nuclear proliferation for international order. Characteristically, Bull was neither a proliferation optimist (like Kenneth Waltz) nor a proliferation pessimist (like Graham Allison) but an agnostic, which Ruzicka argues may have contributed to the relative neglect of Bull's noteworthy contribution in the subsequent debates about nuclear proliferation. Ruzicka outlines the complex interplay of forces for and against nuclear proliferation, both 'horizontal' and 'vertical'. And against that background, he draws attention to the continued importance of Bull's stress on restraint. Bull's idea of restraint involved a degree of superpower cooperation to prevent some, though not all, states from going nuclear; however, he held, the exercise of *self*-restraint on the part of superpowers was equally important to the maintenance of international order because their failure to show restraint would increase the feelings of injustice and spur further proliferation. Despite his agnosticism, Bull did worry that the world of many more nuclear powers represented a particular threat to it; nuclear weapons exposed states to the prospect of sudden and complete destruction as in the Hobbesian state of nature. Faced with such a possibility, the logical step might be to form a world government, an idea to which Bull was strongly opposed on normative grounds, Ruzicka reminds us.

In their co-authored Chapter 9, 'International Society and Islamist Non-State Actors', Harmonie Toros and Filippo Dionigi examine the case of the so-called Islamic State (IS). They draw attention to IS's apparent eagerness to conform to the conventional idea of statehood accepted by international society. This seems consonant with Bull's judgement that non-state violent actors of his time were all aiming to become sovereign states in the conventional sense and seems also to support the idea propounded by English School writers and others that international society exerts socializing pressures on revolutionary actors. However, IS has also spectacularly flouted international society's norms regarding human rights and the control of violence. Toros and Dionigi show that the use of international society's vocabulary, practices, and institutions constitutes for the IS a way to attempt to elevate its status from informal organization to state—an attempt which its opponents try to delegitimize by their concerted use of the prefix 'so-called' when referring to IS. However, they argue, once established as a 'para-state' entity, IS has engaged in norm contestation whereby it has confronted the Western-centric conception of international order and countered it with the ideal of a 'caliphate' as a religious supranational order.

The essays by Madeline Carr, Louis Pauly, and Robert Falkner come next. They each look at an important aspect of increased global interconnectedness—the impact of the Internet on international order, management of the global systemic financial crises, and responses to climate change, respectively, exploring how far, in a changed global environment forty years on, some of Bull's ideas and insights may still be applied or need to be recalibrated.

In Chapter 10, 'Cyberspace and International Order', Carr notes that Internet technology may undermine much of what Bull says about order and its maintenance because his unspoken assumption about the ready identifiability of a disturber of order does not hold well in cyberspace. She explores contending views about whether cyberspace has created a potentially more violent and disorderly environment for international relations and outlines the gradual evolution of norms contributing to the formation of a cyber regime. While acknowledging the extent to which the problem of attribution would make it easier for potential perpetrators to resort to cyberattacks, thereby flouting any relevant emerging norms, Carr finds in Bull's discussion of why states obey international law an insight into how a semblance of order may still be maintained even in this area.

In Chapter 11, '*The Anarchical Society* and Global Political Economy', Pauly speculates that, if Bull came back today, he would likely add a chapter to his book, discussing the economic forces that transformed our world during the past four decades. Among other systemic changes, Pauly points out, the radical unleashing of finance and the partial return of a pre-1914 economic ideology, justifying open and integrating capital markets, might have surprised an advocate of the virtues of the states system, which Bull clearly was. Still, by following Bull's reasoning, his basically empiricist orientation, and his underlying moral sensibilities—as well as suggestions from his constructive critics—Pauly traces the emergence since the late 1970s of a 'variegated global capacity' to assess systemic financial risks, to design collaborative policies to prevent systemic crises, and to manage them when they nevertheless occur. That its embryonic instruments would be fragile and more attuned to efficiency and effectiveness than to justice should be no surprise to Bull's intellectual descendants. However, as in other contemporary policy arenas where the challenges can only be addressed globally, they do clearly suggest, Pauly believes, the emergence of the global society glimpsed in a book that was more nuanced than its main title implied. The challenge of legitimating that complex capacity remains, which means that considerations of justice must soon be addressed, he concludes.

In Chapter 12, '*The Anarchical Society* and Climate Change', Falkner notes that Bull was the first in the English School to address international environmental issues—though, writing four decades ago, he did not mention global warming specifically. But now, Falkner points out, managing climate change ought to be treated as an integral part of any study of the foundations of order in world politics. Still, he finds in Bull's 'pluralist' interpretation of international society some basic insights that continue to be relevant today: (i) it highlights the persistent differences in values and interests that stand in the way of deeper international cooperation; (ii) it suggests that inter-state bargaining remains a central method for resolving international differences on how to reduce global carbon emissions; and (iii) it stresses the importance of crafting cooperative solutions which are reflective of the realities of international power asymmetry. However, as Falkner notes, Bull also wrote that '[i]n the long run it [is] unlikely that action at the purely state level will be sufficient to cope with environmental dangers' (1977, 294–5), suggesting also that in order for humanity to tackle environmental threats, there would need to be 'a greater sense of human cohesion than now exists' (1977, 295). These clearly are important qualifications—although, as Falkner points out, Bull did not himself address how a shift towards a more 'solidarist' response might occur and did not recognize the role of non-state actors in developing new forms of transnational governance beyond the state-centric climate regime.

There then follow contributions by Paul Keal and Jacqui True, each discussing a global class neglected in Bull's book. Keal points out in Chapter 13, '*The Anarchical Society* and Indigenous Peoples', that Bull's neglect of this group even when discussing human rights is partly due to his individualistic bias which prevented him from taking seriously the need to recognize the human rights of collectivities. Keal also suspects that Bull could not have accommodated in his neat conceptual vocabulary the inchoate notion of indigenous sovereignty, which Keal himself has come to appreciate as a politically significant concept for the reconciliation of the historical injustices suffered. Still, Keal finds in Bull's idea of world order and justice among all human persons a promising starting point for considering this neglected subject.

One of Bull's concluding assertions is that contemporary global international society may need to find a cosmopolitan cultural underpinning; that, to the extent that such a culture has come into existence, it is to a large extent based on the Western culture of modernity; and that if a cosmopolitan culture is to support and strengthen international society at the global level, it will need to incorporate non-Western elements to a much greater degree. Keal is firm in his judgement, however, that it is not enough to talk of incorporating 'non-Western' elements into the cosmopolitan culture if the cultures of the indigenous peoples, and their claim to indigenous sovereignty, continue to be neglected.

In Chapter 14, 'Anarchy and Patriarchy in World Politics', True finds merit in Bull's basic appreciation of the complex societal nature of his subject matter; this opens up the possibility to bring patriarchy to our attention—a hierarchical social principle underpinning states and their interactions. True notes that the increasing breakdown of patriarchy in the West and other parts of the world, in part due to the forces of economic globalization, has weakened the traditional patriarchal cultural foundation of international society, thereby possibly encouraging transition towards less hierarchical inter-state practices. However, it has also caused backlashes, fuelling gendered violence at all levels. In the circumstances, True believes, paralleling Keal, that it will be inadequate, indeed misguided, to talk of incorporating 'non-Western' elements into the cultural foundation of global international society. Instead, she argues that it is the responsibility of states, working with transnational feminist networks, to counter misogynistic backlashes as well as non-Western forms of patriarchy and encourage transition towards a more just society as, she believes, a stable world order will not be constructed without gender justice together with social and economic justice for all subordinated groups.

Our final cluster comprises three essays written by Heikki Patomäki, Katarzyna Kaczmarska, and Andrew Linklater, respectively. What these contributors to 'Part IV: Augmenting *The Anarchical Society*' have in common is their interest in the particular path they pursue in order to strengthen *The Anarchical Society* and generate what they take to be a more fruitful research programme.

This part opens with Chapter 15, a multidisciplinary essay, '*The Anarchical Society* as Futurology', by Patomäki. He notes the book's serious methodological inadequacies and stresses the need, for the study of world order processes, to engage in fuller causal investigations. Patomäki sees causation in world politics as a process through which a number of causal propensities operate in an open system to generate an outcome. He points out that a particularly pertinent question for Bull in 2017—*The Anarchical Society*'s 40th anniversary year—will be why the post-Cold War moment of cooperation, shared values, and solidarity was so short-lived and the world is again sliding back to nationalist statism, militarized conflicts, and arms races, notwithstanding the sway of globalizing forces and emergence of elements of world statehood. Patomäki offers, by way of illustration, a causal analysis of the major mid-2010s conflict centring on Ukraine, paying attention to the much neglected connections between military/security and political economy spheres. In so doing, Patomäki demonstrates one significant way in which the approach of Bull's book needs to be expanded and deepened.

In Chapter 16, 'International Society Encounters the Russian World: The role of Representations in International Relations', Kaczmarska outlines how Russia's status has been characterized in various ways by Bull and other English School writers within their conception of international society. However, they have paid no attention to Russia's own discourse on international relations. Interestingly, Russia appeared at one time to internalize the Western perspective, epitomized in the English School narrative, Kaczmarska points out; however, it also began to assert a more independent line, crystalized around the idea of the 'Russian world'. Importantly, Kaczmarska's key message is not an endorsement of the 'clash of civilizations' thesis but rather a reminder to those who readily take from Bull and other English School writers an idea of '*world* international society', i.e. a society of states encompassing the whole world, that they should reflect on the 'situatedness' of their own knowledge claims given their readiness to criticize the Russian claims as merely rhetorical and ideological.

In Chapter 17, 'The International Society of "Civilized States"', Linklater draws attention to Bull's distinction between 'the common stock of ideas and values possessed by the official representatives of states' (or 'diplomatic culture') and 'the intellectual and moral culture that determines the attitudes towards the states-system of the societies that compose it' (or 'international political culture') (Bull 1977, 316–17). Linklater's aim is to shed light on long-term developments in the states-system by transferring Bull's somewhat fragmentary sketches of these two cultures and their relationships onto a larger canvas on which the sociologist Nobert Elias has given a detailed account of the European 'civilizing process'—a process through which the Europeans came to regard themselves as more advanced than other peoples. This generates an understanding of the close connection between the diplomatic and international political cultures in eighteenth-century Europe, comprising absolutist court societies, and the subsequent emergence of the idea of the 'standard of civilization' in the nineteenth century, which was challenged by 'the revolt against the West' in the twentieth century. Linklater concludes his discussion by extending this line of thinking to analyse recent perspectives on world politics that have explored the relationship between cultural convergence and divergence in what he, following Bull, considers as the first universal society of states.

Although these three contributors each have a specific subject they deal with (political economy and military security; Russia/Russian world; the civilizing process), their more general message concerns the ways of studying world politics more adequately than Bull had done. Patomäki stresses the need to engage in proper causal enquiry, Kaczmarska the importance of reflexivity in knowledge production, and Linklater the relevance of Elias's historical sociological work to developing further what Bull only touches on when discussing the cultural dimension of international relations.

It is noteworthy that the contributors to this volume, including those who are highly critical of Bull's intellectual orientation, such as Bain, Reus-Smit, and Pasha, agree that *The Anarchical Society* provides us with a significant point of departure. Interestingly, that was in effect what Bull said of a 'British orthodoxy' status which I once attributed to him and his English School colleagues.[10] I do not think such a label gave an inaccurate description of where Bull and a few others stood in the latter part of the 1970s in the then much smaller IR community in the UK, although, of course, the study of International Relations has much diversified since that time, with various approaches filling and dividing the field. Interestingly, Bull was not entirely

---

[10] This was at the 1980 British International Studies Association Conference where I convened a panel on 'British Orthodoxy in International Relations' and gave a paper, later published as 'The Structure of Institutionalism: An Anatomy of British Mainstream International Relations' (1983). Bull joined the audience at the back of the packed room.

persuaded that his approach represented the 'British orthodoxy' at that time. However, he remarked that it would not necessarily be a bad idea if there were to be such a thing because others would then have a body of thought against which they could formulate theirs as alternatives. His implicit allusion here to Wight's idea of conversations between traditions as a key to understanding international relations (Bull 1991 [1976]) may have escaped many; but the confidence in Bull's voice was for everyone to hear. As a point of departure, the contributors to this volume find, even forty years on, that this confidence was broadly justified. 'Whereto, from here?' therefore becomes a key question. In his concluding essay, 'Bull's Political Vision' (Ch. 18 in this volume), Humphreys weaves his own thoughts on this issue into the tapestry of ideas that he sees as emerging from the preceding contributions to this volume.

It has often been pointed out that the strength of the English School methodology, as represented by Bull, lies in its pluralism, combining 'Hobbesian' Realism, 'Grotian' Rationalism, and 'Kantian' Revolutionism (Hoffmann 1995; Little 2000; Buzan 2001). However, in Humphreys's judgement, it is not this triad, derived from Wight's 3Rs, but rather Bull's own concept of 'the world political system' that gives us an important starting point. Taking *The Anarchical Society* as a significant point of departure forty years on means, first and foremost, broadening our focus from the system/society of states to the world political system of which it is just a part—a move Bull had endorsed in principle (1977, 277).

To give the world political system a more prominent place than did Bull is not to suggest that non-state actors are now more important than states in the world political arena; nor is it to suggest that what Bull sees as a world society—underpinned by a cosmopolitan culture embodying common values and interests—has emerged. But we must acknowledge the fact that the transnational dimension of world politics is much more significant than it was in Bull's day. There are complex political interactions among states and non-state actors in many directions, underpinned by cultural divergence as well as convergence, which can no longer be excluded from our study of world order.

It does not follow, of course, that once this shift of focus is implemented within the Bullian paradigm, we can hope for a comprehensive theory of world order. There are limits to what can be achieved within this paradigm, Humphreys points out, reminding the reader of the key critical observations that criss-cross many contributions to this volume. To go beyond such limits, Humphreys suggests three possible paths: to develop a more adequate study of the process of change, to deepen our awareness of the situatedness of our knowledge, and to explore what a just world order might now consist in.

As William Bain remarks in Chapter 4, quoting Michael Mandelbaum, 'Bull has written that rarest of books: It is not the last, but the first word on its subject' (Mandelbaum 1977, 575).

Part I

Reading *The Anarchical Society* Forty Years on

2

The Argument of *The Anarchical Society*

Hidemi Suganami

INTRODUCTION

Hedley Bull is well known for his careful, systematic style of writing. Almost every page of *The Anarchical Society* reveals the very tight control he imposes on his text. Given this, it is remarkable the extent to which the book does the very thing that he is at pains to stress that it does not—while it does *not* do what he acknowledges *needs* to be done. First, Bull claims he does not canvass any solution to the problems that humankind faces—peace and security, economic and social justice, and the management of the environment; yet this is precisely what he does. Second, contrary to what the book's subtitle, *A Study of Order in World Politics*, signifies in his own terminology, and to how he thinks 'the *world* political system' should be studied, the book remains a more narrowly focused study of *international* order in the contemporary global '*international* system'. As I look back at it again after forty years, these features of the book appear particularly noteworthy in an intellectual and world political environment which has altered in some ways quite significantly since Bull was writing it.

It by no means follows, however, that Bull's answers to the questions he does address are unsound; they are for the most part judicious and persuasive. In this chapter I first outline the complex moves Bull makes in propounding his main argument. I then investigate the two discrepancies noted above and identify their underlying sources. In relation to a set of avenues Bull felt should be explored but did not himself pursue, I conclude by noting what could fruitfully be done by others to make further contributions to a study of order, and other related goals, in contemporary world politics.[1]

---

[1] I am grateful to Andrew Linklater, Richard Beardsworth, and Adam Humphreys for their detailed comments on earlier drafts of this essay and thank Hedley Bull's literary executor, Mary Bull, for her permission to quote any passages from *The Anarchical Society*. Bull, Hedley, *The*

THE ARGUMENT

Given the centrality of Bull to the 'English School of International Relations' and its association with the idea of 'the society of states', it is noteworthy that what he presents as the most basic, enduring structural feature of modern world politics is not 'international society' but 'the states system'.

Bull identifies the latter's defining attributes to be 'a plurality of sovereign states' and 'a degree of interaction among them', suggesting that, where in addition there is 'a degree of acceptance of common rules and institutions', the states system can be said to form a society (1977, 233). Interactions among states in the modern international system, he acknowledges, have always exhibited this 'element of a society', of 'co-operation and regulated intercourse among states', but, he stresses, 'only as one of the elements in it, whose survival is sometimes precarious' (1977, 41). Following Wight (1991), he argues that the ('Grotian') element of society is challenged by two other elements which also characterize the conditions of the states system: 'the ["Hobbesian"] element of war and struggle for power among states' and 'the ["Kantian"] element of transnational solidarity, cutting across the divisions among states' (1977, 41).[2] In Bull's judgement it is erroneous therefore 'to interpret international events as if international society were the sole or the dominant element' (1977, 51). 'In different historical phases of the states system, in different geographical theatres of its operation, and in the policies of different states and statesmen, one of these three elements may predominate over the others', he speculates (1977, 41).[3]

According to Bull, this basic structure of the world is unlikely to change for the foreseeable future (1971, 257–81), by which he means within a few decades from the time of his writing. His view on this important subject betrays the influence of Manning (1975) and Wight (1991), in particular the former's stress on the need to draw fine conceptual, and often legal, distinctions and the latter's emphasis on the importance of studying the present in the light of the knowledge of the past.

Bull's argument here comprises three key moves. First, he points out, '[t]here is not the slightest evidence that sovereign states in this century will agree to subordinate themselves to a world government founded upon consent'

Anarchical Society 1, published 1977 [The Macmillan Press], reproduced with permission of Palgrave Macmillan.

[2] See, however, Bain, Ch. 4 in this volume and Linklater and Suganami (2006) for the misuse of the three labels, 'Grotian', 'Hobbesian', and 'Kantian'.

[3] However, this does not alter the fact that the focus of *The Anarchical Society* is on the element of international society. See Little (2000) and Buzan (2001); compare Linklater and Suganami (2006, 31–2) and also Ch. 1 in this volume.

(1977, 261-2); and '[i]n the late twentieth century... the prospects that world government will be established by conquest appear slight' (1977, 263).

Second, despite some 'features of contemporary world politics which provide *prima facie* evidence' for the emergence of a 'New Mediaevalism'—'a secular reincarnation of the system of overlapping or segmented authority that characterised mediaeval Christendom' (1977, 264)—there is, he contends (1977, 275), 'no clear evidence that in the next few decades the states system is likely to give place' to such an alternative on the global scale.

Third, Bull acknowledges, '[t]he contraction and disappearance of the element of international society... [is] entirely possible' (1977, 260); even '[t]he disappearance of the element of a system from the present pattern of universal politics could come about' (1977, 260)—but, he speculates, in a passage suggestive of his close engagement with Falk's insightful analysis (see Bull 1977, ix; Falk 1971), 'only as the consequence of the collapse of our present scientific, industrial and technological civilisation' (Bull 1977, 260), 'induced by global nuclear war', 'the exhaustion of sources of energy and a consequent breakdown in global transport and communication, or a revolution in human values that brought about a universal turn to a simpler and more localised style of life' (Bull 1977, 261).

Importantly, however, this fundamental and enduring structure of world politics as a global system of states, Bull qualifies, is only part of 'a wider world political system' or 'the world-wide network of interaction that embraces not only states but also other political actors, both "above" the state and "below" it' (1977, 276); and therefore the 'study of world politics should be concerned with the global political process as a whole, and this cannot be understood simply in terms of interstate politics in the strict sense' (1977, 277)—a point he had already conceded five years earlier (1972a, 255) in response to the work of Robert Keohane and Joseph Nye (1972, 255). Nevertheless, Bull points out, '[t]he states system has *always* operated within a wider system of political interaction' (1977, 281; emphasis added), i.e. this is not a new phenomenon, and he claims with some confidence that 'within the world-wide political system of today the primacy of states system is *for the time being* assured' (1977, 281; emphasis added).

A summary of Bull's conceptual vocabulary will be useful at this point. As may have been noted already, 'system of states', 'states system', and 'international system' are interchangeable as are 'society of states' and 'international society'. Bull considers that the system of states has come to cover the whole world and therefore we now have a global 'international system', in which, he believes, a spatio-temporally varying 'element of international society' is also present. This international, or inter-state, structure forms part of what Bull calls 'the world political system', comprising state and non-state actors.

'The world political system', which Bull presents as an undeniable political reality (1977, 276-81), is not the same sort of thing as what he calls 'a single world society or the great society of all mankind' (1977, 23). This last term was used in earlier times to refer to 'a notional society' (1977, 20) to express the idea of the universal moral order governing the entire human race, whose ultimate units, Bull argues, are individual human beings (1977, 22). He also makes it clear that 'the factors consolidating the world political system do not in themselves assure the emergence of an integrated world society' grounded in 'a sense of common interest and common values, on the basis of which common rules and institutions may be built' (1977, 279).[4]

Though marginalized in his discussions, 'the world political system' is in fact central to Bull's entire conceptual edifice. This becomes clear once we ask what the entity is concerning which it makes any sense at all to think, as does Bull, in terms of the three competing elements—'Hobbesian' international system, 'Grotian' international society, and 'Kantian' world society. *It clearly cannot be any of the three elements*; and within Bull's conceptual scheme, this hidden-but-fundamental entity will have to be none other than 'the world political system'—comprising non-state actors and states, the latter forming a system with a varying element of society within it and interacting with the former in complex ways.[5]

How, then, is order maintained in this complex setting? To address this central question, Bull begins by defining what he calls 'order in social life' as a state of affairs in which 'a pattern of human activity [exists] that sustains elementary, primary or universal goals of social life' (1977, 5). These goals are: 'ensuring that life will be in some measure secure against violence resulting in death or bodily harm', 'that promises, once made, will be kept, or that agreements, once undertaken, will be carried out', and 'that the possession of

---

[4] In '*world* society' or 'the *world* political system', the modifier 'world' is being used in contradistinction to 'international'/'inter-state'; 'world society' comprises individuals and 'the world political system' contains non-state actors and therefore neither is 'inter-state' (either purely or at all). However, when Bull rather confusingly talks also of '*world international* society' (1977, 317; emphasis added), he is simply expressing the idea that the element of the society of states, with its historical origins in Europe, is now 'global in extent'.

[5] In his systematic attempt to go beyond the English School's conceptual scheme, Buzan presents the 'human social world' (2004, 126) as a combination of inter-state societies, inter-human societies, and transnational societies, consisting of states, individual human persons, and transnational actors, respectively, and each capable of being global or regional in extent (2004, 90–138). Inter-state social relations are part of the human social world as Buzan presents it just as the system/society of states is part of 'the world political system' as Bull conceptualizes it; neither Buzan's 'human social world' nor Bull's 'world political system' (necessarily) signals the end or transcendence of inter-state relations, therefore. In his second major study on 'international legitimacy', Ian Clark reserves the term 'world society' to refer to 'the realm of the individual, of the non-official group or movement, and of the transnational network of nongovernmental agents' (2007, 6), which basically corresponds to Buzan's inter-human and transnational societies combined. All these authors demarcate the realm of the states or 'the realm of the governmental' (Clark 2007, 6) from the rest on the basis of the distinction between 'official' (or public) and 'non-official' (or private)—a distinction feminist writers see as gendered. See Ch. 14 in this volume.

things will remain stable to some degree, and will not be subject to changes that are constant and without limit' (1977, 4–5); or 'life, truth and property' (1975, 5), for short. The idea that these goals are fundamental to the social life of human individuals stems from Hart's argument, concerning what he calls 'the minimum content of Natural Law' (1961, 189–95), which, in turn, derives from Hume's theory of 'the origins of justice and property' (1985[1739/40], 536–52).

According to Bull, this idea of 'order in social life' applies to *any* society comprising human persons and therefore not only to domestic societies but importantly also to social life hypothetically envisaged as taking place in 'the great society of all mankind' or 'world society' (1977, 20). But here comes a twist. Bull acknowledges that '[o]rder in world politics may *one day* take the form of the maintenance of elementary goals of social life in a single world society or great society of all mankind' (1977, 23; emphasis added). But, as we know, he believes that the political organization of mankind in the present phase is primarily a system of states and that this is unlikely to alter for the foreseeable future. Therefore, Bull suggests, 'we are still accustomed to thinking of order in world politics as consisting of domestic order, or order within states, and international order, or order among them' (1977, 23). Thus, *world order = domestic order + international order*. Without further ado, Bull decides to go along with this formula, which, as I show in the section on 'The Discrepancies', brings some serious problems.

At this point it is important not to lose sight of what Bull means specifically by '*international* order' in contradistinction to order in the social life of *human persons*. By '*international* order', he means 'a pattern of activity that sustains the elementary or primary goals of the society of states' (1977, 8) or of social life *among states*. Given Bull's well-known stress on the insight that social life among states is qualitatively different from that among individual human persons (1966b; 1977, 46–51), we would expect him to deal with 'international order' somewhat differently from his treatment of order in the social life of individual human persons. And we do see this in the *six* basic goals of the social life of states which he postulates and briefly supports with some selected historical illustrations (1977, 16–9).

They are: (i) the preservation of the system and society of states itself against challenges to create a universal empire or challenges by supra-state, sub-state, and trans-state actors to undermine the privileged position of sovereign states as the principal actors in world politics; (ii) the maintenance of the independence or external sovereignty of individual states; (iii) peace, or the absence of war, among states as the normal condition of their relationship, to be breached only in special circumstances and according to generally accepted principles; (iv) limitation of violence; (v) observance of international agreements; and (vi) respect for one another's spheres of jurisdiction.

Bull acknowledges that (iv)–(vi) are international analogues of the 'common goals of all social life' (1977, 18–19); and there are some untidy conceptual overlaps among (i)–(vi), so that the total number of goals could be fewer than six. Nevertheless, it is significant that the goals Bull has identified in articulating the concept of *'international* order' are not reducible or identical to his three basic goals of all social life among human persons.

Importantly, Bull acknowledges that '[i]f international order [articulated in this way] does have value, this can only be because it is instrumental to the goal of order in human society as a whole' (1977, 22). He even declares that 'there is nothing historically inevitable or morally sacrosanct about the idea of a society of states' (1977, 68) and that therefore there is no *intrinsic* moral value to *international* order as such. This can be contrasted to Bull's characterization of 'life, truth, and property' as 'elementary, primary, or universal' goals of all social life, which, contest though he may, suggests their significant moral import.

Interestingly, Bull concedes that *international* order could be maintained even if states 'formed an international system only, and not also an international society' (1977, 65). However, he contends that 'the modern international system is *also* an international society, at least in the sense that international society has been one of the elements permanently at work in it' (1977, 51; emphasis added). And this judgement leads him to his central contention: what has contributed mostly to the maintenance of international order in the modern states system is this *additional* element of international society, with its rules and institutions.

Bull defines an 'institution' as 'a set of habits and practices shaped towards the realisation of common goals', distinguishes it from 'an organisation or administrative machinery' (1977, 74), and sees the 'institutions of international society' to comprise 'the balance of power, international law, the diplomatic mechanism, the managerial system of the great powers, and war' (1977, 74) as well as sovereign states themselves, acting as organs of the anarchical society of states in operating its 'rules' (1977, 71). These rules, which he distinguishes from 'institutions', are of three kinds: 'the complex of rules that states what may be called the fundamental or constitutional normative principle of world politics' (1977, 67), 'the rules of coexistence' (1977, 70), and 'the complex of rules concerned to regulate co-operation among states' (1977, 70). Partly to explain the significance of separating 'rules' from 'institutions', Bull points out that these rules do not necessarily have to be 'legal' in character (1977, 67). 'That modern international society includes international law as one of its institutions', he contends, 'is a consequence of the historical accident that it evolved out of a previous unitary system, Western Christendom, and that in this system notions of law—embodied in Roman law, divine law, canon law and natural law—were pre-eminent' (1977, 142).[6]

---

[6] Bull's idea of the double-layer (rules-and-institutions) underpinnings of international order can be compared to Hart's (1961) concept of law as a union of primary and secondary rules, or

The Argument of The Anarchical Society

Now comes a further twist; Bull is not optimistic about the contribution the element of international society will continue to make to the maintenance of international order. He explains:

> The ideological divisions following upon the Bolshevik Revolution, the revolt of non-European peoples and states against Western dominance, and the expansion of the states system beyond its originally European or Western confines, have produced an international system in which the area of consensus has shrunk by comparison with what it was in 1914. It may readily be imagined that in the next few decades such stresses will be placed on this remaining area of consensus that it will decline drastically or even disappear altogether. (1977, 257–8)

Notwithstanding his pessimism, arguably quite apt in today's context, Bull does not think that the contraction and disappearance of the element of international society 'is *bound to* occur' (1977, 260, emphasis added). And he argues that the states system with an additional element of international society, with its rules and institutions operating effectively, is still, in the foreseeable future, humanity's best bet—known to be tolerably good while other options are not guaranteed to be as good or better—to address the problems facing mankind: peace and security, economic and social justice, and the management of the environment (1977, 282–96).

Bull's argument is threefold regarding each of these issue areas: there is no guarantee that other conceivable ways of organizing the world as a whole will be better at dealing with them because the causes of the problems are deeper than the world's institutional structure; we must not overlook the positive role the states system actually plays towards the achievement of a variety of goals; and there is at least a possibility in the current organization of the world to expand its management of the problems we face (1977, 284–95).

It will have been noted that Bull is no longer confining his attention to how to maintain 'world order', defined earlier in the book in terms of 'life, truth, and property'; he is now, in the final part of the book, discussing how adequately to address a cluster of urgent contemporary world political issues. Regardless, if the states system, with an additional element of international society, with its rules and institutions operating effectively, is likely to be humanity's best means in the foreseeable future to address these difficult problems, this will require that 'the element of international society... [be] preserved and strengthened' (1977, 315). This leads Bull to stress the need to maintain and extend 'the consensus about common interests and values that provides the foundation of [international society's] common rules and institutions, at a time when consensus has shrunk' (1977, 315).

---

rules of conduct and rules about rules. At the 1980 Annual Conference of the British International Studies Association, Bull remarked that he did not consciously apply Hart's theory but that, having heard me point out the similarity, he could now agree that there was a parallel.

As we saw, this shrinking of consensus has happened, Bull believes, along three axes since the outbreak of the First World War: the ideological divide between 'the East' and 'the West', the have-and-have-not divide between 'the North' and 'the South', and the cultural divide between 'the West' and 'the Other'. Accordingly, his considerations of the future viability of the system/society of states are three-pronged. *Firstly*, in relation to the East–West divide, he argues:

> [The] consensus [maintaining and extending the element of international society] must include a sense of common interests among the great powers, sufficient to enable them to collaborate in relation to goals of minimum world order, and especially the avoidance of nuclear war. (1977, 315)

Secondly, however, a consensus founded upon the great powers alone cannot be expected to endure, argues Bull:

> No consensus is possible today that does not take account of the demands of Asian, African and Latin American countries and peoples for just change in respect of the elimination of colonialism and white supremacist governments, the relationship of dependence or subordination in which most of them stand to rich countries. (1977, 300)

Thirdly, in relation to the global cultural divide, Bull writes:

> The future of international society is likely to be determined, among other things, by the preservation and extension of a cosmopolitan culture, embracing both common ideas and common values, rooted in societies in general as well as in their elites, that can provide the world international society of today with the kind of underpinning enjoyed by the geographically smaller and culturally more homogenous international societies of the past. To say this is not to imply that any cosmopolitan culture is likely to become dominant throughout the world, engulfing cultural particularisms, or that it is desirable that such a development should take place. We have also to recognise that the nascent cosmopolitan culture of today, like the international society which it helps to sustain, is weighted in favour of the dominant cultures of the West. Like the world international society, the cosmopolitan culture on which it depends may need to absorb non-Western elements to a much greater degree if it is to be genuinely universal and provide a foundation for a universal international society. (1977, 317)

This, as I see it, is the argument of *The Anarchical Society*. I continue to be struck by Bull's clear, careful, and systematic deliberation. Although I have no space for a detailed exposition here, I am also impressed by his ability to combine an analytical mode of enquiry with historical understanding and apply them to discussing important world political issues of his time. I have much sympathy with his aversion to a host of clichés about our often too-readily-oversimplified subject matter and endorse his sceptical stance which I find intellectually vital. But there are problems. Next, I offer some critical observations on this landmark contribution from the 'English School', focusing on the two discrepancies noted at the beginning of this chapter.

THE DISCREPANCIES

A first discrepancy is Bull's insistence that he is not engaged in normative advocacy although this is precisely what he does in the book. Following Hume and Hart, Bull characterizes the basic values of 'life, truth, and property' as goals which will be *instrumentally rational* for human beings, *wishing to engage in social life*, to pursue, given what they and their environment *contingently* are. Such a formulation, with its emphasis on instrumental rationality and contingency, may have a rhetorical effect of making it seem as though Bull were not engaging in any normative argumentation. But he makes his prescriptions seem like optional guidelines, rather than normative principles, only because he makes it sound as if joining a society, like baking an apple pie, is a matter of individual choice. But the idea of individual human beings existing outside society, wondering what best to do if they choose to form a society, is absurd. Once this point is appreciated, Bull's talk of strictly instrumental rationality loses what appeal it may have seemed to possess at first sight.

In line with his self-imposed stricture, Bull abstains from saying that human beings have a moral duty, *in any absolute sense*, to pursue the basic goals of social life (1977, 6). He is of course right to refrain from saying this for circumstances are conceivable where it is morally reasonable to argue that 'life, truth, or property' has to be sacrificed for certain other ends. However, refraining from saying that these values are morally sacrosanct is not the same as abstaining from a normative international political discourse, which is about arriving at a reasoned judgement on how the world should be organized and what actions should be taken in the existing setting. In fact, this is exactly what Bull does. It therefore comes across as an understatement when he remarks towards the end of the book that his 'argument is an *implicit* defence of the states system' (1977, 318, emphasis added). As shown in the previous section, *The Anarchical Society* contains an *explicit* defence of—and *advocacy* for—the states system with an additional element of international society in it.

Still, being shy of openly crossing the empirical/normative boundary, which he equates with the objective/subjective distinction, Bull remarks that his book is a study of order and not of justice, adding his unexamined belief that '[u]nlike order, justice is a term which can ultimately be given only some kind of private or subjective definition' (1977, 78). In other words, his declared intention is to stay away from what he regards as the ultimately subjective realm of the justice talk and to focus squarely on the study of what 'order' is and how it is maintained, both of which, Bull believes, can be (more) objective. But he does not, in fact, stay clear of the issues of justice.

As we saw, his main argument is that the states system is the best means, among those likely to be available in the following few decades, for securing, among other things, the goal of economic and social *justice* (1977, 288–92). Moreover, in the earlier part of the book, he discusses the relationship between order *and* justice and makes a number of pertinent observations. He states that 'justice, in any of its forms, is realisable only in a context of order' (1977, 86); but, significantly, he also acknowledges that '[i]t does not follow from this... that order is to be preferred to justice in any given case' (1977, 97; see also 315). He elaborates:

> It is sometimes possible... to bring about a change agreed to be just with the consent of the parties affected, and... there may be no injury to the foundations of international order... It is clear also that even where there is not consent by all the parties affected, but there is overwhelming evidence of a consensus in international society as a whole in favour of a change held to be just, especially if the consensus embraces all the great powers, the change may take place without causing other than a local and temporary disorder, after which the international order as a whole may emerge unscathed or even appear in a stronger position than before. It can scarcely be doubted that an international society that has reached a consensus not merely about order, but about... justice, is likely to be in a stronger position to maintain the framework of minimum order or coexistence than one that has not...
>
> When... demands for justice are put forward in the absence of a consensus within international society as to what justice involves, the prospect is opened up that the consensus which does exist about order or minimum coexistence will be undone. The question then has to be faced whether order or justice should have priority. (1977, 95–6)

All this suggests that, in *The Anarchical Society* itself, Bull has written as much as he could say about 'justice' *at the very general level at which he was operating in the book*. He is well known for suggesting that a 'study of justice in world politics, which may be envisaged as a companion volume to the present one, might yield some very different perspectives' (1977, xiii). But he could not have been thinking that, in the companion volume, he would raise *the same* set of questions concerning justice as he touched on in *The Anarchical Society* and that they might yield different answers because of the shift of perspectives. It is more plausible that the new perspectives would have led him to address a different, though related, set of questions. An example might be one demanding more detailed, case-based, investigation into the range of circumstances under which the pursuit of justice should be given priority over the demands for order—as done by Wheeler (2000), for instance. It cannot, in any case, be said that *The Anarchical Society* is a study of order, and not *also* of justice, in the categorical way in which Bull puts it; one of the key questions he raises there concerns the *relationship* between them, though examined at a very general level.

Given this degree of discrepancy between the argument of *The Anarchical Society* and Bull's own characterization of it, we may wonder what was really troubling him; why did he not present his book straightforwardly as a contribution to *normative* international political theory? Bull's clear desire not to be seen to make prescriptions—other than 'hypothetical' ones of the form 'if you want to achieve X, then Y is the way to do it'—stems from his strong conviction, which runs through his book, that advocacy is inimical to scholarship (1977, xv, 319–20). This is in fact unsurprising. In the period between mid-1960s and mid-1970s, when Bull formed his ideas articulated in the book, the intellectual atmosphere that prevailed in IR in the UK and elsewhere was predominantly 'positivist', according little or no legitimacy to the activity of generating substantive normative judgements.

We may recall here that two path-breaking contributions to explicitly normative international political theory—Beitz's *Political Theory and International Relations* (1979), based on Rawls's *A Theory of Justice* (1971) which was much discussed then mostly outside of IR, and Linklater's inspirational *Men and Citizens in the Theory of International Relations* (1982), which introduced Hegelian dialectical thinking to IR—only appeared, respectively, two years, and five years, after the publication of *The Anarchical Society*. Bull's book, which was in gestation for over a decade, predates the beginning of a new epoch in which openly engaging in normative enquiry began to recover some intellectual legitimacy in International Relations as an academic discourse.

Bull was himself a 'positivist' in the sense in which 'legal positivists', such as Kelsen (1967) and Hart (1961), were 'positivist', drawing a sharp distinction between 'is' and 'ought' and considering it their aim to identify and state the content of the law as it exists in a given society. Similarly, Bull saw it as his primary aim to identify the institutional principles of the world. But he went on to examine their workings and in so doing *commended* in broad terms what he identified as 'the institutions of international society' (1977, 74) as providing the best means, in the current circumstances, with which to address the problems of peace and security, economic and social justice, and the management of the environment. And because these goals cannot possibly be regarded as *optional* for 'the great society of all mankind', divided into interacting sovereign states, Bull's persistent refrain that he only deals in 'hypothetical', not 'categorical', prescriptions sounds hollow.[7]

---

[7] While broadly endorsing 'the institutions of international society', including that of international law, Bull was critical of the twentieth-century trend in international law to curtail the state's freedom to use force as possibly interfering with the workings of the institution of the balance of power (1966c; 1977, 143–4, 238–40). He was also concerned that the recent

There is a second discrepancy found in *The Anarchical Society*. The book remains almost exclusively a study of '*international* order' in the contemporary 'global *international* system' even though, if its subtitle is to be taken at its face value, it promises to be a study of order in *world* politics, taking place in the '*world* political system', of which the 'global *international* system', in Bull's own conceptual vocabulary, is only part. Most probably unnoticed hitherto, this is facilitated partly by his sharp division between order and justice. To explain how this is so, I present below a close analysis of the moves that Bull makes in this connection. This demonstrates, among other things, that we may make a mistake in our thinking, not only when we conflate concepts that, for our purposes, should really be kept apart, but also when we take a given conceptual distinction for granted, without paying sufficient attention to the consequences of so doing.

Now, Bull is keenly aware that what he calls the institutions of international society, 'especially when they are working properly' (1977, 91), are often inimical to the achievement of what justice demands according to our 'everyday notions of justice' (1977, 91). In an uncharacteristic *over*statement, he remarks that 'the institutions and mechanisms which sustain international order... *necessarily* violate ordinary notions of justice' (1977, 91, emphasis added). He writes on this subject with great eloquence:

> Consider... international law... [W]hen the law is violated, and a new situation is brought about by the triumph not necessarily of justice but of force, international law accepts this new situation as legitimate... [I]nternational law condemns aggression, but once aggression has been successful it ceases to be condemned. The conflict between international law and international justice is endemic because the situations from which the law takes its point of departure are a series of *faits accomplis* brought about by force and the threat of force, legitimated by the principle that treaties under duress are valid...
>
> Or consider the role that is played in the maintenance of international order by the special position of the great powers... [T]he great powers, when they perform these services to international order, do so at the price of systematic injustice to the rights of smaller states and nations, the injustice which has been felt by states which fall within the Soviet hegemony in Eastern Europe or the American hegemony in the Caribbean. (1977, 92–3)

---

developments in international criminal law and human rights law were potentially subversive of the very idea of the society in which sovereign states coexist (1977, 152–3). On the latter point, see Reus-Smit, Ch. 5 in this volume. Bull's underlying prioritization of coexistence over cooperation is criticized by Falkner (Ch. 12 in this volume) in relation to climate change. However, it is also Bull's view that 'it is surely the duty of all intelligent and sensitive persons... to recognise' the desirability of a 'world society or community, characterized by a sense of the common interests and values of all mankind' and 'dedicate themselves to work for it' (1977, 289).

It is vital to notice here that Bull is making these claims *exclusively* with respect to 'justice', which, as we know, he distinguishes sharply from 'order'. And, importantly, he does not discuss how far, or in what ways, the maintenance of 'international order' may hinder, and has hindered, the fulfilment, in separate domestic societies, of certain basic values, which he classifies under the rubric of '*order*', such as freedom from violence or relative stability of possession. This silence is problematic. Why is this so?

Clearly, if a people were to be subjected to conquest or forceful control by an imperial or hegemonic power, legitimated by international law or the special position of the great powers in the name of international order, not only could they, or their community, be said to suffer 'injustices' but many of them would be forced to endure 'disorder' in terms of the harms done to their lives, possessions, and wellbeing derived from the sanctity of contractual obligations. Bull may conceivably respond that, even under such conditions, the target people can still be said to enjoy 'orderly' social life in so far as they are not *totally* deprived of 'life, truth, and property' and that what we can reasonably say in such circumstances is that they are treated *unjustly* according to our everyday notions of justice. But it would seem far more reasonable not to insist here on the supposed sharp divide between 'justice' and 'order', but to simply accept that what the target people would suffer could come under the rubric not only of 'injustice' but also of 'disorder' in our everyday notions. Indeed, we think of such a predicament as 'unjust' precisely because of the 'disorder' unfairly forced upon them.[8]

But that is not how Bull proceeds. Whereas he is fully cognizant of the extent to which the maintenance of international order could be detrimental to the pursuit of *justice*, he has nothing to say about the possibly negative impact of the maintenance of international order on the pursuit of *order* in separate domestic communities.

To see the significance of these comments, we need to recall Bull's basic formula: *world order = domestic order + international order*. Within this formula, he is failing to pay attention to the extent to which 'international order' may not be added purely *as a positive value* to 'domestic order'. The pursuit of international order may curtail the enjoyment of *order* in certain domestic societies as much as it may cause *injustices* to them, though Bull only explicitly acknowledges the latter. His silence on the international order/domestic order nexus, facilitated by his sharp demarcation between order and justice, contributes to making it appear as though—on the order side of things—international order were a benign force, likely to support, not hinder, the pursuit of order in separate domestic realms, such that it will contribute only positively to what is achievable cumulatively as world order.

---

[8] On international society's historical connivance with colonial conquests, see Keal (2003) and his Ch. 13 and Pasha's Ch. 6 in this volume. See also Linklater (2011) and Clark (2013).

Now, the negative impact of the pursuit of international order specifically on justice, to which Bull pays much attention in the above-quoted paragraphs, is not the book's main concern inasmuch as it is said to be not about justice. The (supposedly relatively benign) contribution that international order makes towards the maintenance of order in world politics therefore comes to the fore; and the pursuit of *international* order through the element of international society within the *global states system* comes to occupy a central place in Bull's study, even though the book is supposed to be a study of *order* in *world politics*.

There is one related factor which I should mention here as further reinforcing Bull's concentration on international order as his central focus. This is his almost total neglect of domestic order itself. This is, of course, understandable given that Bull specializes in International Relations. But if, as he believes, *world order = domestic order + international order*, the pursuit of order in separate domestic societies must be crucial to achieving world order. It is natural to think so given Bull's definition of world order, understood as order in the human social life as a whole, and that of order in separate domestic societies; they are both given in terms of the same basic goals of 'life, truth, and property'. In other words, in Bull's thinking, 'world order' and 'domestic order' are qualitatively the same, differing only in scale, whereas, as we noted earlier, 'international order' or 'order among states' is qualitatively different from both. But Bull does not enquire how far, in their separate domains, diverse domestic societies, inhabiting the contemporary world, succeed in maintaining the three basic goals and thereby contribute substantively to the maintenance of these very same goals for mankind as a whole. He leaves that question aside and focuses on how *international* order is maintained in the contemporary global system of states (see 1977, 22, 99–229).

But this focus is problematic in Bull's own scheme. He has acknowledged that the states system, with an element of international society added to it, is only part of 'a wider world political system' (1977, 276). He even claims openly that the 'study of world politics should be concerned with the global political process as a whole, and *this cannot be understood simply in terms of interstate politics in the strict sense*' (1977, 277; emphasis added). However, he does not in fact investigate how 'the world political system', or 'the world-wide network of interaction that embraces not only states but also other political actors, both "above" the state and "below" it' (1977, 276) contributes, positively or negatively, to order and other items on the agenda of world politics. His focus is on the contribution of the global states system, with an element of international society within it, to international order and other related goals.

There is a perplexing issue, concerning which there has been much debate in IR, that underlies this discrepancy between what Bull acknowledges should be done and what his book actually does. This centres on the relative

The Argument of The Anarchical Society

significance of the state and non-state actors on the world political scene.[9] On this question, Bull appreciates, *on the one hand*, that subnational actors do directly engage in world political processes. He states:

> Political groups within a state do not simply affect world politics through the influence they may have on their own state's foreign policy. First, they may enter into relations...with political groups in other states...Second, they may enter into relations with foreign states...Third, they may enter into direct relations with an international organisation. (1971, 277)

On the other hand, we also see Bull propound a decidedly more state-centric view:

> The great mass of political mankind does not have the means of interest articulation and aggregation which...are the hallmarks of a political system. In so far as the interests of mankind are articulated and aggregated, and a process of political socialisation and recruitment moulds a universal political system, this is through the mechanism of the society of sovereign states. For guidance as to what the interests of the world as a whole might be, for example with regard to the control of arms, or the distribution of population and resources, or the conservation of the environment, we are forced to look to the views of sovereign states and of the international organisations they dominate. (1977, 85)

Accordingly, while acknowledging the presence of individuals and non-governmental groups, concerned to promote their visions of the common good of the world, Bull insists that their views are not authenticated by 'any political process of assertion and reconciliation of interests' (1977, 85); they may at best 'speak with authority on their particular subject' (1977, 86). Bull's pronouncements are quite extreme here:

> [T]he views of these individuals provide even less of an authoritative guide to the common good of mankind than do the views of the spokesman of sovereign states, even unrepresentative or tyrannical ones, which at least have claims to speak for some part of mankind larger than themselves. (1977, 86)

To balance such a claim, Bull acknowledges that states (even in the universal ideologies they espouse) are 'notoriously subservient to their special interests, and agreements reached among states notoriously the product of bargaining and compromise rather than of any consideration of the interests of mankind as a whole' (1977, 86).

What Bull fails to notice in his deliberation here is the simple fact that the assertions of the views of these individuals (or 'activists') and non-governmental groups are clearly not an integral part of the global states system (with an element of international society), but they *are* of the world political system and its processes. His idea that these entities lack *authority* points to

---

[9] See, among many others, Hall and Biersteker (2002) and Suganami (2004).

their lack of full formal international legal standing in the global system/society of states. By no means does this show, however, that they have no *power* to take part in the processes of the world political system or that they may not exercise that power with considerable *moral authority*, effectuating changes in inter-state relations (see Clark 2007). And hence such actors need to be granted a more central place in any full account of *world* (as distinct from *international*) order. This observation is particularly relevant to contemporary world political processes in which non-state actors (including some violent ones) can be said to have strengthened their presence since Bull's time (see Chs. 9, 11, and 12 in this volume).

It appears then that Bull spoke of the need to see the global system of states as part of the world political system when he was alerted to the seeming competition for primacy between states and certain non-state actors; when, however, he was acting on his judgement that the states are the more dominant 'for the time being' (1977, 281), his focus was on the global states system's contribution to (world order *via*) the maintenance of international order and other related goals. This explains the discrepancy or apparent tension between, on the one hand, his acknowledgement that 'study of world politics should be concerned with the global political process as a whole, and this cannot be understood simply in terms of interstate politics in the strict sense' (1977, 277) and, on the other, his almost exclusive focus on the contribution of the global states system, with an element of international society, to international order and other related goals.

CONCLUSION

To say that Bull's book is not what he claims it to be or does not do what he acknowledges should be done is not to say that what he does do is seriously flawed. On the contrary, Bull's defence of the global system of states, with an admixture of a spatio-temporally varying element of international society, as more realistic than other alternatives *at the global level in the near future* is well argued—although we must enter a reservation here that describing the world as a 'global' system of 'states' may be problematic to the extent that there are different kinds of states in this system and some of them do not function well as 'states'.[10] Still, Bull's cautiously optimistic assessment that the then existing formal international structure could be a reasonably effective way to secure the goals of peace and security, economic and social justice, and the management of the environment was not implausible at the time of his

---

[10] See Jackson (1990).

writing. His stress then on the need for reconciliation along the three axes of world conflict was rational and even prescient.

Bull's book is also suggestive of what could be done by others in the study of contemporary world politics.[11] First, if, as Bull notes, the pursuit of world order can be thought of as comprising the pursuit of order *among states and within them*, then a study of how order is pursued with varying degrees of success in a diverse range of polities is vital as he in fact acknowledges (1977, 22). This is made very complex, however, by the fact that the pursuit of order (and other values) within a given polity, or class of polities, is likely to be affected in various ways by the workings of the global states system (with an element of international society); and this system, according to Bull, forms part of the world political system and is therefore in turn affected by the workings of that system. But if, as he acknowledges, a study of order (and, by extension, other goals) in world politics must take into account the political processes of the world political system as a whole, then we should aim to fulfil that need in some manageable ways. Such a study is likely to reveal that some world political processes work in such a way as to *hinder* the pursuit of order and other values across diverse polities.[12]

Second, Bull was right to acknowledge the operation of 'deeper causes' (1977, 285, 291) than the institutional structure of world politics as significantly contributing to the world's ills. But he seems in retrospect to have underestimated the extent to which the states, contrary to the optimism he had expressed in defence of the states system, would continue to fail to counter these causes 'deeper than any particular form of universal political order' (1977, 294) with requisite force in relation to crucial issues, such as, most notably, climate change (see Falk, Ch. 3 and Falkner, Ch. 12 in this volume). Why they have failed could not be understood, of course, without first enquiring what such 'deeper causes' are (see Patomäki, Ch. 15 in this volume). That Bull did not deal with this in his book is quite understandable; no single book-length project could cover so much. But this was not what he suggested *he* might study in a companion volume. Clearly, others can step in here.

Third, it may seem reasonable at first glance for Bull to suggest that '[l]ike the world international society, the cosmopolitan culture on which it depends may need to absorb non-Western elements to a much greater degree if it is to be genuinely universal and provide a foundation for a universal international society' (1977, 317). But he is silent on who should or could do what to meet such a need.[13] Meantime, the conflict, which Bull later characterized as the

---

[11] Here I focus on what Bull has *said quite emphatically but not done* and do not deal with many other things that he *could or should have said and done* in relation to his subject-matter.

[12] See Tosa's (2009) insightful work in this regard.

[13] Onuma's *Treatise* (2017) is based on his lifelong commitment to the responsibility of international lawyers in this regard.

cultural 'revolt against the West' (1984b), appears to have intensified since the time of his writing, pointing to the urgent need to consider how his recommendation of conciliatory moves in this area, if they are to be pursued, may be implemented in the current world political settings (see Chs. 13, 14, and 17 in this volume).

In these endeavours, and in drawing implications from what they may produce, there is one thing we might learn from Bull's example: his epistemic cautiousness, which runs through his whole text. This is how he ends it:

> The fact is that while there is a great desire to know what the future of world politics will bring, and also to know how we should behave in it, we have to grope about in the dark with respect to the one as much as with respect to the other. It is better to recognise that we are in darkness than to pretend that we can see the light. (1977, 320)

With this, I concur wholeheartedly.

3

Ordering the World: Hedley Bull after Forty Years

Richard Falk

DURABILITY AND ANACHRONISM OF THE ANARCHIC SOCIETY HYPOTHESIS

With the awareness that forty years is the canonical biblical interval, it is rather remarkable that forty years after the publication of *The Anarchical Society* its central argument is still conceptually distinctive enough and sufficiently historically relevant to engage students of world politics. Many scholarly authors of the twentieth century with great intellectual and political influence at their time of writing have mainly fallen by the wayside when it comes to serious current reflections about world order. Bull has not.

By way of invidious comparison, I would mention Hans Morgenthau and George Kennan as prominent in their day but who now are barely discernible presences on the intellectual landscape, of interest, if at all, only for those concerned with the history of Western statecraft. A similar assignment to the dingy dustbin of the history of ideas and practice of statecraft awaits Henry Kissinger, who despite his several hefty books published over the course of the last decade, is likely to be remembered mainly as an opportunistic, if effective, diplomatic practitioner and an alleged war criminal (Falk 2015; Hitchens 2001).

What makes Bull's work stay alive and relevant is a combination of ahistorical theorizing and an illuminating conceptual emphasis on the realities of international life as constituted over the centuries by a distinctive form of society that has become operative in relations among sovereign states. These contributions paradoxically flow from Bull's deep knowledge of the history of international relations and relevant philosophizing and his informed disdain for an unduly abstract social scientific approach whether by way of systems theory or empirical methodologies.

It seems more clarifying to compare Bull's worldview with that of Robert Cox who also relies on a mixture of history and philosophy to construct his understanding of world order, and is suspicious of 'scientific' claims for what is inherently an interpretative undertaking. Both Bull and Cox seem best understood as 'classical realists' in Cox's taxonomy (1996, 503–5). At the same time they are very different in their diagnoses of world order, and what might be done to humanize its operations. Cox emphasizes the constitutive roles of the world economy and civil society actors to a far greater degree than Bull, which to some extent may reflect the fact that Bull did his formative work a decade earlier than Cox. Bull is rather reluctant to prescribe any institutional or ideological departures from statist logic as he is deeply sceptical of the value of normative innovations, although exhibiting a sympathetic reading of the argument put forward by Rajni Kothari as to development imperatives shaping the behaviour of the (then recently) independent sovereign states that had emerged from many decades of colonial rule (1977, 307–11). In my view, Bull seems ontologically sceptical, if not completely opposed, to attempting structural reforms in world order, which he believes create false expectations of societal potential that ends up shifting attention away from opportunities to make international society function more smoothly within its fixed parameters.

Cox, in contrast, premised on a different interpretation of historical context, is very much convinced that structural approaches to the study of world order are oblivious to opportunities for change and reform. At the same time Cox is influenced by Marx, and Marxist thinkers, particularly by Gramsci, who supposed that desirable change of transformative scope will emerge by way of a bottom-up pattern resulting from the mobilization of global civil society (1996, 535). Cox is not optimistic about the prospects, and describes himself as a 'pessimist' in contrast with mainstream realist 'problem-solvers' who regard world order as generating technocratic problems within fixed limits that are invariably capable of solution (1996, 88–9).

Bull (1977, ix) mentions me as a friendly antagonist, taking particular issue with my book *This Endangered Planet: Prospects and Proposals for Human Survival* (Falk 1971) which preceded the publication of *The Anarchical Society* by a few years. Both with a more Grotian orientation and a greater appreciation of the ecological dimensions of the challenges to existing world order, it is evident why Bull would regard my views as unrealistic, even to the extent of labelling them 'salvationist' (1977, 302–5).[1] From the perspective of the early

---

[1] Bull used 'Grotian' in two senses: (1) 'to describe the broad doctrine that there is a society of states' and (2) 'to describe the solidarist form of this doctrine, which united Grotius himself and the twentieth-century neo-Grotians, in opposition to the pluralist conception of international society entertained by Vattel and later positivist writers' (1977, 322 n. 3). Here I am using the term in the second sense. 'Solidarism' and 'pluralism' differ basically in their respective judgements about the degree of solidarity and consensus present in inter-state relations, the former placing the estimated level of solidarity markedly higher than the latter (Bull 1966c). For a

twenty-first century, Bull's anti-Grotian assessments of forty years ago might have softened over the years, and yet even now seem to be on balance more descriptively persuasive than my analysis that rested on a discredited postulate of the urgency of change and a belief in the long arc of positive moral evolution in human affairs. Those who could be truly presented as world order optimists can point to the proliferation of international tribunals, and especially to the establishment of the International Criminal Court and the avoidance of ecological collapse, as steps in the problem-solving direction.

Despite this acknowledgement of Bull's perspicacity with respect to the normative dimension of international society, I would nevertheless argue that my insistence in 1971 on taking seriously the ecological challenges to a politically fragmented world seem to have greater traction in the contemporary world than Bull's 'enlightened statism'. Such a claim seems reasonable given the scientific and intergovernmental consensus that has formed around the collective need to reduce worldwide greenhouse gas emissions in the next several decades or else face severe adverse consequences (Falk 2012a; Falk 2012b; 2016). The *Paris Agreement on Climate Change of 2015* is widely regarded as a triumphal achievement from the perspective of international cooperation and celebrated as a protection of the global public good, but it is also understood as falling disastrously short of what is needed and desirable if evaluated on the basis of protecting the human and species interest. In other words, Paris achieved the most that can be expected by states acting together, promoting shared collective goals while upholding distinct national interests premised on differing national circumstances and perceptions of responsibility and capability. What is demonstrated is that the prudent protection of the global public good requires something more than states, acting on their own, can be expected to achieve. It requires stronger *global* mechanisms of problem-solving that are not tied to statism, that is, the aggregation of the separate state interests. In this respect, the parts are greater than the whole in the anarchical society when faced with a serious policy challenge of the sort presented by the threats associated with global warming. If the whole is to be adequately protected it will need stronger central institutions (see Falkner, Ch. 12 this volume).

I interpret this line of analysis as validating the Cox emphasis, which I share, on the need for structural transformation given the historical and material conditions presently tending to create challenges that state-centric multilateral cooperation could not hope to meet even if pushed toward maximal levels of agreement by dominant state actors (Falk 1971, 1975). In fairness, Bull was increasingly disposed to incorporate newly independent, post-colonial,

---

detailed analysis of the meanings of the two terms used by Bull and subsequent English School writers, see Linklater and Suganami 2006, 59–74. Bull's use of 'Grotian' in the first sense is critiqued by Bain, Ch. 4 in this volume.

non-Western states into his conception of international society, urging sensitivity to claims being put forward for a reframing of world order along globally inclusive lines as indispensable if the anarchic society was to adapt to the changed global circumstance brought about by the collapse of European colonialism (1977, 305–11; also Bull and Watson 1984; see, however, Pasha, Ch. 6 in this volume). In effect, Bull was arguing that the normative order of the anarchic society based on greater equity and equality was essential if statism was to continue to provide an effective world order.

Perhaps, Bull's realist embrace of statist thinking is more compatible with the ecological preoccupations of the late twentieth century when adequate environmental agreements were feasible via statist mechanisms, as with the Montreal Protocol regulating effectively the depletion of the ozone layer. It is also true that Bull entertained the possibilities that non-state structures were emergent in international political life, and responsive to new policy imperatives, including the 'neo-mediaevalist' rise of non-state actors of various categories (1977, 264–76). After all, climate change was addressed, at least temporarily, by the *Paris Agreement via* the medium of multilateralism, and, at least formally, avoided either a hegemonic solution imposed by the most powerful states (e.g. via a US/China duopoly) or abandoning statism by conferring on the United Nations authority to identify and implement the global interest, and then allocating responsibilities among states to promote the general welfare.

Since Bull there have been other developments complicating an understanding of the anarchical society. In reaction to deindustrialization and outsourcing in the West, migratory flows, and the perception of Islam as the source of anti-Western terrorism, there has been a resurgence of support for identity politics drawing on ultra-nationalist sentiments and foreign policies that adhere to national interests rather than sacrificing territorial interest so as to benefit global capital (see Patomäki, Ch. 15 in this volume). In a sense, there is, despite the need for global solutions of climate change, a resurgent and regressive statism that is testing the limits of the anarchical society in ways that could not have been anticipated in Bull's lifetime. In effect, the major premise of the anarchical society, as set forth by Bull, is being rearticulated in the current international context. This involves both a retreat from globalism and a renewed reliance on great power management of common problems, although considerably globalized if compared to the Euro-centric operations of Westphalian statism up through the middle of the prior century.

BULL'S ANARCHICAL SOCIETY

Bull's approach to international relations has become unfashionable in American academic and think-tank circles despite its continuing relevance to an evolving international set of conditions. He is what I would call 'a qualitative thinker', who has proved attractive over several decades to a rather wide range of talented (once) younger scholars declaring their affinities by proclaiming an adherence to a rather vibrant 'English School' (Dunne 1998b). In the main, the English School over the course of its existence has adopted variants of the outlook developed in *The Anarchical Society* as its iconic starting point for an understanding of both global politics and world order.

The originality of Bull involves developing the linkages between power and order in a context of shared norms and understandings that lend plausibility to an inference of 'society'. In this regard, Bull is affirming the reality of an international normative order, including the limited efficacy of international law, in the international political domain that lacks governmental institutions, and is hence most accurately depicted as 'anarchic'. Such an intellectual understanding of the distinctiveness of an operative international order built around the interaction of states, with weak central institutions devoted to cooperative undertakings, is what makes it accurate to distinguish Bull's understanding of the world from 'classical realists' in Hobbes' tradition of thought (see, however, Bain, Ch. 4 in this volume). Bull is convinced, and convincing, to the effect that the overriding goal of international order has been to establish security for a system of sovereign states. It is this pluralist international order originating in a shared European cultural experience that facilitates and structures cooperation for the multiple dimensions of mutual coexistence, which has three principal goals: ordering international relations, facilitating the pursuit of enlightened national interests on the part of governments of sovereign states, and, in most instances, upholding the autonomy of domestic political systems as providing the most hospitable setting for pluralist arrangements of power and authority within the enclosures of sovereign, international borders.

This postulation of 'anarchic society' retains its significance for two main reasons: first, it rejects the dichotomy between a normless anarchy and an extension of government to encompass all political relations in the world (that is, world government) or even an arrangement or entity with sufficient authority to define and implement global interests in those policy settings where aggregations of national interests cannot generate satisfactory solutions given current global conditions. It is this middle ground of anarchic society that possesses structural originality: it should not be confused with the domestic governance structures and civilizational traditions of established sovereign states, nor should it to be regarded as normless zone where there are no rules. Bull also makes clear that international norms are not to be exclusively identified with law and its enforcement, but more significantly pertain to political expectations of how best to maintain orderly relations, as by way of great power management arrangements, maritime and aviation rules of the road, the balance of power, and a variety of political norms of abiding relevance and guidance (1977, xiii, 65–74, 101–229). Bull was of course aware that genocide and mass atrocities are transgressive of moral norms, but he did not think this provided a foundation for imposing *individual* accountability on those who act on behalf of sovereign states (1977, 152).

Bull rejects any form of meta-state normative authority, whether associated with the UN or the claims of victors in a major war as embodied in the Nuremberg tradition that held the surviving political and military leaders of the defeated German and Japanese governments accountable in their individual capacities (Bull, 1966c).[2] In this respect, Bull is a statist who sees criminal law as appropriate only in the sort of strong political communities established within sovereign states, and thus the imposition of international criminal law is seen as nothing other than an expression of power by the victor rather than the application of law premised on sovereign equality. It is true that the celebrants of international criminal law, whether explicitly or not, are Grotians, or more conventionally identified in America as 'liberals', those who, while admitting the shortcomings of such one-sided law, view it, nevertheless, as an important incremental step towards a global rule of law, and as confirmation of the Kantian belief in moral evolution.

Secondly, Bull posits this pluralist state-centric form of world order as itself a global public good that would likely be weakened by creating a more centralized set of global regulatory mechanisms (see Bull 1966c). In this sense, Bull is implicitly rejecting both Kantian and Grotian evolutionary expectations of a more morally attuned and legally ambitious world order emerging over time that could eventually sustain a structure of 'perpetual peace' among sovereign states governed on the basis of republican principles. Such a globalized world order rejects diversity, and as such is inconsistent with Bull's preference for pluralism with respect to domestic public order as well as internationally with regard to the juridical equality of states (see Bull 1966c; 1977, 252–4). If my reading is correct, then Bull regarded the existing state system to be *structurally* as good as world order is likely to become, although it is admittedly contingent, even precarious, and thus deserves to be strengthened in accord with *this distinctive* logic (Suganami 1989, 160–2).

Whether Bull would continue to adhere to this assessment given the current unmet and menacing challenges of economic globalization, nuclear weaponry, transnational terrorism, and climate change is uncertain. One clue as to how he would view the world of the present is his failure to favour institutional

---

[2] Bull is not clear whether he would support collective forms of accountability as is associated with preventing and responding to the crime of genocide, which might have been treated as an exception to his overall opposition to intervention claims, including so-called humanitarian intervention. As well as adhering to strong anti-intervention views on pluralist grounds, Bull supported the complementary idea of territorial sovereign autonomy.

centralization in the face of the advent of nuclear weapons of which he was deeply cognizant and appropriately concerned (compare Deudney 2007; see Bull 1961; see also Ruzicka, Ch. 8 in this volume). Yet unlike climate change and the other challenges of global scope, it could be maintained that the doctrine of deterrence combined with the non-proliferation regime was the safest approach to the avoidance of nuclear war, and thus preferable to a nuclear disarmament process administered by the United Nations or some international institutional arrangement established for this purpose.

For the optimal attainment of global security in the nuclear age, Bull stresses the role of norms and historically validated understandings. His conception of norms is inclusive, encompassing both legal norms based on agreement and custom as well as political norms derived from such conceptions as balance of power, deterrence, principles of coexistence, a taboo on the use of nuclear weapons, and the logic of reciprocity (Bull 1977, 211; and Ayson, Ch. 7 in this volume). The current absence of sharp ideological cleavages that challenge the legitimacy of existing sovereign states and the presence of a shared civilizational experience are features of a successful anarchical society that Bull recognized as being stretched and severely tested by what he identified as 'the expansion of international society' to include the active and equitable participation of non-Western fully independent sovereign states (Bull and Watson 1984).[3] Despite Bull's celebration of the anarchical society, through his study of history, he was acutely aware of the contingency of all political arrangements.

THE CONTINGENCY OF A GLOBAL ANARCHICAL SOCIETY

Bull was among the early commentators to acknowledge fundamental challenges to the stability and even durability of the anarchical society since the end of the First World War (1977, 257–8). He believed that both the Russian Revolution and the dynamics of decolonization placed strains on the underlying dependence of the societal aspects of world order on what might be described as a dynamic European 'civilizational consensus'. Bull also recognized that there were common human interests that could not be adequately protected by the kind of state-centric procedures of problem-solving available to the anarchical society (1977, 20–2). Despite the Cold War denial of the legitimacy of diverse public order systems within states,

---

[3] Bull affirmed the importance of promoting global justice in the post-colonial world, especially in the context of world economic arrangements governing trade and investment.

there developed a profound shared societal interest transcending ideological differences in avoiding nuclear war or any major violent encounter that could produce a third world war (1977, 189–99, 226). Geopolitical prudence in the Cold War era gave rise to an informal, yet operative, nuclear taboo that reflected a commitment to the preservation of the pluralist world order to which Bull subscribed. Bull also regarded the emergence of a deterrent balance between nuclear adversaries in the Cold War as evidence that sufficient societal commonalities existed between these intense ideological rivals to undergird their cooperation to avoid mutual disaster. Yet Bull's attentiveness to history made him aware that there was no guarantee that such rationality would prevail over time (1977, 191).

In more recent times, Bernard Lewis and Samuel Huntington expressed extreme versions of this precariousness of world order, both scholars stressing the disruptive impact of an Islamic resurgence as giving rise to 'a clash of civilizations' posited as fundamentally incompatible with sustaining minimum order in international relations based on Western models, interests, and values—that is, positing limits on acceptable degrees of diversity (Lewis 2002; Huntington 1996). The 9/11 attacks in 2001 re-securitized international relations, displacing the post-Cold War economism of the 1990s, in ways that did threaten the most basic organizing principle of the state-centric pluralism, namely, national sovereignty. Both the non-state identity of the principal antagonists in 'the war on terror' and the disregard of normally applicable non-intervention rules due to the de-territorialization of conflict and the incentives to shift war planning from *reactive* postures of self-defence to *pre-emptive* approaches undermine the normal ordering dynamics of an international anarchic society (Falk 2002).[4]

More recently Henry Kissinger in *World Order* has voiced similar concerns in a more generalized manner, and without any attention even to the societal elements of world order. In his words, '[O]ur age is insistently, at times almost desperately, in pursuit of a concept of world order . . . Are we facing a period in which forces beyond the restraints of any order determine the future?' (Kissinger 2014, 2). Less deterministic than Huntington and more geopolitical than Bull, Kissinger believes that the challenge can only be met by bringing China into a reconstituted anarchical system (not society) that is global in scope, and this will only be achieved if the reframing of relations among states appears to be 'legitimate' by its major political actors, which are the dominant states. I would suppose that Bull would regard Kissinger's framing of world

---

[4] The United States is 'a global state' and Al Qaeda and to some extent ISIS are non-states. Of course, the United States is also a state in the conventional sense, and ISIS currently holds and governs territory and claims to satisfy the features of state. Both actors claim and treat the entire world as a potential battlefield, an extraordinary departure from the conceptualization and experience of war as a characteristic of Westphalian statecraft (See Toros and Dionigi, Ch. 9 in this volume).

order as unsatisfactory because Kissinger is seeking legitimacy for a system of states bound together by interests alone rather than to an anarchic society that achieves order on the basis of shared *traditions* and *values* as well as interests. Kissinger seems to rely on statecraft as the sole durable basis of stability, and has always viewed with cynical dismay any stress on shared values and cultural traditions, however intense and mutual, as giving rise to international law and norms of political prudence and moral conviction (Kissinger 2014, 249–52). As well, despite the impacts of neoliberal globalization and the rise of transnational civic activism, Kissinger ignores the relevance of both market and social forces, and conceives of change as a top down process essentially driven by technological innovation, especially in war-making (see Chs. 11 and 15 by Pauly and Patomäki in this volume). The contrast of both Kissinger and Bull with Robert Cox here is striking. Cox treats structural change as an urgent priority, but assumes that it must come about, if at all, by a bottom-up dynamic, hopefully taking the form of a global populist movement that drastically alters the political climate in ways that make adaptive change feasible.

ALTERNATIVES TO THE GLOBAL ANARCHICAL SOCIETY

Far more than Bull, Kissinger is of the opinion that it is not constructive to speculate on alternatives to the state system, although he does recognize that his call for a reframing of European Westphalia must be perceived as 'legitimate', at least by China, and that to do so it must dispense with its historical regional trappings: 'Westphalian principles are, at this writing, the sole generally recognized basis of what exists of a world order' (Kissinger 2014, 6). What is unclear in Kissinger's presentation is whether he seeks to christen a new 'Global Westphalia' or is merely proposing a widening of Westphalia's hegemonic dimension to achieve a Sino-American Westphalia, which amounts to a geopolitical duopoly. This type of political reasoning ignores the *societal* aspects of Westphalia, which as Bull clearly recognized (1977, 27–41) depended for effectiveness on Europe being a civilizational grouping and not merely a 'system' whose preoccupation was to consolidate and stabilize power relations among states in Europe at a given time, and govern the rest of the world hierarchically. This is a crucial difference. On other dimensions of world order these two influential thinkers are closer together. Both Bull and Kissinger seriously understate the degree to which market forces operating in a neoliberal ideological climate erode stability and subvert legitimacy by accentuating inequalities within states, which in turn, generate tensions and nativist backlashes that imperil the cooperative dimensions of the anarchical society and threaten protectionist policies (see Patomäki, Ch. 15 in this volume).

Bull devotes serious attention to three candidates to replace his conceptions of a state-centric and pluralist international society: a great power concert, global centralism, and regionalism (1977, 249–52). He does not find the re-establishment of a great power concert of the sort that existed in Europe after the Napoleonic Wars as feasible, nor does he regard a centralized world order as desirable because of its challenge to pluralism at the state level. Bull is more positive about regionalism, regarding it as having the potential to achieve more ambitious forms of cooperation than statecraft can manage, while not being compelled to face directly the complexities of global arrangements.

What most differentiates Bull from many mainstream Western thinkers is his acknowledgement that non-Western demands must be addressed if a new legitimating consensus of the expanding anarchic society is to be achieved. 'No consensus is possible today that does not take account of the demands of Asian, African and Latin American countries and peoples for just change in respect of the elimination of colonialism and white supremacist governments, the redistribution of wealth and resources, and the ending of the relationship of dependence or subordination in which most of them stand to the rich countries' (1977, 300). Bull makes it clear that the global weight of these countries cannot be calculated by reference to their meagre military capacity to challenge the West, but arises from the fact that they 'represent a majority of the states in international society. Moreover, they represent a majority of the world's population, and are the predominant element in that world society' (1977, 301). Such a passage beckons toward a latent democratic foundation for upholding the societal claims for the reform of international anarchy based on notions of fairness and populist sentiments rather than, as with Kissinger, on the basis of an adjustment to shifting geopolitical realities. Bull's position supporting the normative accommodation of the post-colonial non-West is strikingly at odds with the perception that Bull is properly classified as falling within the realist tradition of hard power determinism. By comparison, it would be hard to find such concern for ethics and justice anywhere in the large corpus of writing of such leading realists as Kissinger, Kennan, Krasner, or even Morgenthau.

The importance of non-Western legitimation becomes even clearer in Bull's related assertion: 'an international regime that cannot respond to their demands will be lacking in moral authority even within the "have" countries and will be incapable of achieving the kind of consensus that world order will require' (1977, 301). I regard this kind of diagnosis of what is needed to reconstitute the West-centric embodiment of the anarchical society as basically resting on a soft power approach to reconstituting a viable post-Westphalian world order. This does not imply an indifference to the continuing major relevance of hard power dimensions of order, but it avoids reducing the march of history to battlefield victories and defeats. In other writings, Bull assuredly exhibits his sensitivity to the relevance of hard power with respect to geopolitical sustainability in the nuclear age, placing an unprecedented premium on cooperation among even the bitterest of rivals to avoid a mutually catastrophic breakdown of minimum order (1961).

To summarize this central point, Kissinger believes that the rise of non-Western states requires a new enlargement of shared understandings and mutual appreciations (the foundations of legitimacy in international relations) among diverse states representing the leadership of diverse civilizations. Such a globalization of Westphalia will be needed to restore the quality of world order if it is to equal or surpass its eighteenth- and nineteenth-century operational achievements in Europe. In marked contrast, Bull writing almost forty years earlier than Kissinger, is insisting on the central relevance of 'moral authority' to the formation of the kind of consensus needed for an anarchic society of global scope to function effectively under contemporary conditions (1977, 95–6, 300). Kissinger seems to believe that inter-civilizational sensitivity to a changing power ratio among major states is sufficient, and treats the reformist demands of the global South as irrelevant (or worse) in fixing what he contends to be the broken system of world order.

A SYMPATHETIC CRITIQUE OF BULL'S APPROACH TO POLITICAL GLOBALIZATION

Having the benefit of a retrospective assessment, it becomes clear that Bull was at once prescient and insensitive to certain realities that would challenge his diagnosis of how to adapt to the changes associated with the emancipation of non-Western countries and peoples from colonial rule and from the associated structures of hegemony. In particular, Bull does not accord sufficient attention to contradictory impacts of a globalizing world economy being shaped by a neoliberal ideology (Ikenberry 2011). On the one side, the ideological convergence and selective material success of this neoliberal global system has created a kind of socializing consensus, epitomized by Margaret Thatcher's TINA ('there is no alternative') and by the IMF/World Bank 'Washington consensus'. This liberal world order has been challenged by various contentions that these economic arrangements are predatory and at odds with perspectives of ecological sustainability (climate change) and equity (persisting poverty—3 billion earning below $2.50 per day; gross inequalities). The central critical contention being made is that the world economy has become unacceptably responsive to the priorities of *capital* rather than dedicated to the wellbeing of *people* (Falk 1999; Gill 2008). From these perspectives, the current realities lack moral authority, and thus cannot meet the precepts of minimum world order, but the deficiency cannot be overcome on a simple West/non-West basis. Also important is the uneven experience of success and failure with respect to economic globalization that has fractured, or at least decisively weakened, such categorizations as 'the Third World', 'the global South', and 'the non-aligned movement'. These developments have produced several effects, including the incorporation of non-Western countries in the structures of economic governance (G20), the weakening of leverage by the non-West, and the emergence of an increasing number of 'failed states' that are unable to provide minimum internal order or tolerable levels of human security for their populations. These geopolitical black holes have become highly significant sites of tension and intervention in an era of high intensity, transnational, non-state violence and crime. Bull does not anticipate these forms of incoherence among formally independent sovereign states.

At the same time, with an opposite impact, it can be argued that Bull failed to appreciate the hegemonic potentials of the American role as provider of global security beyond the confines of Europe, especially as geopolitics has been reconfigured since the end of the Cold War (Brooks and Wohlforth 2016). The United States operates as a meta-territorial global state that has a domineering military presence in more than 100 countries, every ocean, and in space, coercing compliance with its geopolitical priorities: non-proliferation, neoliberalism, 'special relationships' (Israel and Saudi Arabia), and alliances. In this respect, international law is compromised as a source of order if conflicting with these other goals, and as well, the maintenance of autonomous sovereign states, a prime normative goal of the sort of pluralist world ordering system favoured by Bull.[5] There are alternative legal/political norms that are more congenial with the regulatory precepts of neoliberal globalization seeking connectivity with the world economy and the world community responsibility to avoid mass atrocity: interventions to achieve regime change or fulfilling the mandate of a responsibility to protect. Such solidarist elements posit a form of minimal order that acts as an alternative to the idea of consensus, that is, the agreement of governments acting within such institutional settings as the UN Security Council as an ingredient of a hybrid world order, combining 'leadership' with 'coercion' while continuing to conceive of most political relations through a state-centric lens.

In one respect, the soft power emphasis in Bull that was anti-interventionist and supportive of genuine pluralism, has been vindicated in ways that he did not anticipate. Especially, the declining capacity of military intervention under

---

[5] I would expect Bull to be critical of the overly militarized geopolitics that has become associated with the American role as global leader, especially its continuing reliance on regime changing intervention. At the same time he would be sensitive to the security imperatives in a post-9/11 global setting.

Western auspices to reconfigure the political orientation of militarily weaker states has imposed limits on hegemonic effectiveness, although the failure to accept these limits has added to the turbulence of international relations, especially in the Middle East. American interventionary disappointments in Vietnam, Afghanistan, Iraq, and Libya, despite hard power domination in each of these combat zones, confirms this observation, as did the earlier Soviet experience in Afghanistan and ongoing Saudi frustrations in Yemen. In the present global settings, political actors other than the United States have better understood this diminished historical agency of military superiority, and acted accordingly with greater restraint. Unfortunately, the US continues to be in the grips of what can be described as 'geopolitical hubris,' which has been translated by political leaders into a series of costly military misadventures (compare Lebow 2003).

In the aftermath of the Second World War, when international institution-building was focused on war prevention and the avoidance of a recurrence of the Great Depression, the US leadership was widely appreciated except by the Soviet bloc of countries. Later tensions between the core members of the Westphalian community emerged as a result of colonial wars and controversial efforts by the West to contain the spread of Soviet and Marxist influences in the Third World *via* interventions in a series of countries, including in Iran (1953), Guatemala (1954), and most of all Vietnam (1963–75).

Overall the expansion of the Westphalian reach to encompass the entire world may have been effective in this period because several important non-Western powers were able to enjoy the benefits of rapid economic growth, most notably China, which substituted for meeting the demands of the non-West that Bull had identified. Note that the effort of the South to achieve a more balanced international economic order in the 1970s was frustrated by Western resistance, and a determined pushback against the Nonaligned Movement and other initiatives that were led by such capitalist formations as the Trilateral Commission and the World Economic Forum. In other words, Bull's outlook was insufficiently attentive to the role of market ideological factors and American militarism in sustaining by force the Westcentric shape of world order that managed the transition from the colonial projection of Western hegemony to a post-colonial variant sustained by the control of world economic policy and through the shaping of global security structures in the nuclear age.

The end of the Cold War, followed by the collapse of the Soviet Union, altered the role of security norms in the anarchic setting, especially diminishing the centrality of political doctrines associated with deterrence and containment. American military hegemony filled the geopolitical vacuum, but weakened the normative and institutional features of international society, especially in relation to upholding security considerations (Mandelbaum 2002, 2005). International law and the United Nations were both weakened. Perhaps the geopolitical enforcement of some hegemonic security policies, most notably coercion to inhibit or prevent the proliferation of nuclear weapons to certain states deemed hostile or dangerous, would be treated as establishing new political norms that contribute to the maintenance of minimum order. It could be argued, in opposition to this interpretation, that nuclear disarmament is indispensable for the long-term security of international society, and such a major instance of cooperation to sustain a pluralist world order based on mutual interests (Falk and Krieger 2012). This raises a defining question: given the challenges of the twenty-first century, is the anarchic society the best of attainable world order frameworks?

ARE THERE ATTAINABLE PREFERRED ALTERNATIVES TO THE ANARCHICAL SOCIETY?

In my view, the anarchical society as projected so brilliantly by Hedley Bull, even if strengthened as he proposed, seems structurally incapable of overcoming the gap between what is feasible (politics as the art of the possible) and what is necessary (protecting the peoples of the world against various forms of catastrophic harm) (Falk 2012a). The basic structural deficiency is associated with the absence of effective means to uphold the global interest in situations where multilateralism as the aggregation of national interests is unable to produce sufficiently effective cooperative arrangements. Climate change, upholding biodiversity, eliminating nuclear weapons, and moderating inequality are prominent examples (see Ruzicka, Ch. 8 and Falkner, Ch. 12 in this volume). It is not that the anarchical society cannot ever reach agreements that adequately uphold global interests, but that where sharp differences in national circumstances exist and high stakes are involved, such agreements have not been forthcoming despite major efforts.

Nevertheless, as suggested at the outset, the basic framework set forth by Bull in *The Anarchical Society* remains conceptually illuminating as descriptive of the way in which international political life continues to be structured in the twenty-first century. Unlike more policy-oriented forms of realist thought, the approach followed by Bull takes account of the cooperative potential of international relations and it also accords a positive, although limited, role to international law and morality.

From an empirical standpoint, Bull's opposition to Grotian optimism about the evolution of international society seems validated. In view of intervening developments, however, especially the profound dangers associated with the failure to address global warming in a timely and effective fashion, whether Bull would alter his reluctance to endorse structural modification is impossible to say. On the one side, Bull was not sympathetic with radical challenges to the prevailing order, while on the other side, Bull was impressively responsive to changes in the character of world order as, for instance, brought about by the collapse of European colonialism and the globalization of statism. What does seem evident is that Bull's worldview retains relevance for both critics and apologists in their respective attempts to solve the puzzles of contemporary world order.

Part II

Three Foundational Critiques

4

The Anarchical Society as Christian Political Theology

William Bain

Hedley Bull is the most influential theorist of order in International Relations; *The Anarchical Society* is the most important account of order in international relations.[1] Michael Mandelbaum, writing in the pages of *Political Science Quarterly* shortly after its publication in 1977, said 'Bull has written that rarest of books: It is not the last, but the first word on its subject' (1977, 575). Mandelbaum was certainly correct in his judgement: Bull's influence is such that no theorist of order can afford to ignore him. Engagements in theorizing order typically begin with the framework that Bull lays out in the opening pages of *The Anarchical Society*, and especially the ubiquitous three traditions he ascribes to Hobbes, Grotius, and Kant. And yet, conspicuous influence notwithstanding, even masterpieces suffer from blemishes of various kinds. Barry Buzan (2004, 28–44) describes the idea of world society as an 'analytical dustbin' that elicited little intellectual enthusiasm from Bull, and Martha Finnemore complains that Bull fails to make explicit important causal connections in his account of order (2001, 510. Also see Patomäki, Ch. 15 in this volume).[2] Others struggle with the moral ambiguity that pervades the relation of order and justice, and the extent to which Bull shifted his position away from the grim reality that 'terrible choices' must sometimes be made toward a more sympathetic accommodation of the demands of justice (Dunne 1998b, 145, 155; Rengger 2006, 44-2; Wheeler and Dunne 1996, 91–107).

---

[1] I am grateful for the comments on this chapter from Madeline Carr, Ian Hall, Adam Humphreys, Terry Nardin, Luke O'Sullivan, Haig Patapan, and Hidemi Suganami.
[2] Finnemore's allegation that Bull does not present his work in causal form is belied by his contention (1977, 74–5) that 'rules and institutions are part of the efficient causation of international order, that they are among the necessary and sufficient conditions of its occurrence'.

But, limitations notwithstanding, no other book gives the idea of order in international relations a more prominent hearing.

Bull understood himself as providing an implicit defence of the states system, and specifically the kind of order he associated with international society. But what exactly is the character of this element of society, as Bull calls it? He asserts that order, in general, presupposes a pattern in terms of which things are related, thus a shelf of books discloses order in a way that a heap of books on the floor does not. Order in social life consists in this, but crucially, in something more; it consists not in any pattern, 'but a pattern that leads to a certain result, an arrangement of social life such that it promotes certain goals or values' (1977, 4). An assortment of books exhibits order in this sense when they are arranged according to author, or title, or some other principle. Therefore, order in social life is purposive in character and the pattern it imparts is intelligible in the context of fundamental goals: limiting violence, keeping promises, and ensuring stability of possession, or what Bull calls life, truth, and property (1977, 4–5). These goals are elementary in the sense that no society is properly a society without them: 'a constellation of persons or groups among whom there existed no expectation of security against violence, of the honouring of agreements or of stability of possession we should hardly call a society at all' (1977, 5). Goals of this kind are formal in character; their existence and their authority, when formulated as rules of conduct, are related, not to the realization of a substantive human or international good, but to negative prohibitions that are given to a system of mutual forbearance and compromise (Hart 1961, 185–91).

It is this conception of international life—states associated in respect of rules pertaining to life, truth, and property—that Bull wished to defend against the appetite of power and the pride of emancipation. Such an association reposed most clearly in the idea of international society, to which he looked to Hugo Grotius, the Miracle of Holland, for inspiration (Hoffmann 1990, 24). It is widely accepted that *The Anarchical Society* lays out a Grotian conception of international society that is the English School's distinctive contribution to international theory. This conception is held out as the well-known alternative, or *via media* in English School parlance, between the forbidding world of realism and the aspirational world of various utopian programmes for change. But is this Grotian conception of international society what Bull says it is? In this essay, I argue that Bull's theorization of order is radically incomplete, enough so that it calls out for reconsideration. I argue, furthermore, in light of this incompleteness, that his identification of international society with Grotius is substantially incoherent. Both of these arguments are drawn out and elaborated with the help of an unlikely resource: medieval theology. Bull's thinking about order, though often confused in formulation and ultimately incoherent in what it claims, is symptomatic of a medieval debate about the nature of God and the extent of his power. When the idea of international order is considered in this context it is apparent that what Bull describes is consistent, not with Grotius, but with the thought of Thomas Hobbes.

ORDER AS A PROBLEM OF THEOLOGY

To suggest that Bull's theory of international society is in some way indebted to theology is likely to elicit marked expressions of scepticism, if not outright incredulity. Bull had no truck with religion, a position made abundantly clear in his exchange with E.B.F. Midgley on the relevance of natural law in the study of international relations. Bull readily acknowledged the historical significance of natural law in explaining the emergence and development of the modern states system (2000b, 157–8). But history is history and Bull was clear in saying that international society had outgrown its Christian and then its European origins. A cosmopolitan culture had supplanted, albeit tentatively, the *faux* universalism of a natural law that inhabited the minds of early-modern theologians and jurists. In reply, Midgley (1979, 265) describes, and disparages, Bull's evolutionary story about the progressive development of international society and the gradual falling away of natural law as 'semi-philosophical', and symptomatic of the (mistaken) belief that intellectual dialogue should and must be uncontaminated by talk of God. Here, the nature of their disagreement is laid bare. Midgley bemoans the decline of religion in public life, noting that it is impolite to state or conclude that God is the author of natural law, or worse, that the author of natural law is the same author of revelation contained in Scripture. There can be no doubt that Bull subscribes to this secularist sensibility. Unlike Midgley, he dismisses religion as a legitimate source of knowledge; rational argument, rather than theological belief or revealed truth, is the only appropriate method for studying international relations (Bull 2000b, 168–9).

Despite his disdain for scholarship rooted in religion, Bull calls on none other than Augustine of Hippo to explain what he means by 'social order'. Order consists in discrepant parts, arranged in a good pattern, which leads to a particular result, or as Augustine himself puts it: 'order is the disposition of equal and unequal things in such a way as to give to each its proper place' (Augustine 1998, 938). Of course, Bull is unconcerned with the theological compass within which Augustine derives the character of order. He does not subscribe to Augustine's belief (1998, 940) that God creates and ordains all natures, and that these natures are arranged in an order of concord that gathers in God for the enjoyment of God. Augustine provides nothing more than a heuristic starting point that simply ignores any and all theological baggage as an unwelcome distraction that impedes the quest for understanding. But Bull's opportunistic appropriation slides into confusion when, developing this Augustinian starting point, he says that the purposive character of order is necessarily relative in character. Social and political systems can conflict with one another and still disclose intelligible patterns of order because discrepant parts can be arranged in a number of different ways. There is, then, no truth to any given order as such. Purpose is judged from the standpoint of utility, so if a neo-medieval order is judged likely to be more violent than a world of sovereign states, it is to that extent correctly regarded as inferior to the order afforded by the states system (Bull 1977, 4, 255).

Clarifying what Augustine means by order opens a space in which to rethink Bull's conception of order. In doing so, we are drawn to yet another unlikely place, not further from the other-worldly domain of theology, but closer: the doctrine of creation. The story of creation related in the book of Genesis seems a distant illusion or fantasy when compared to the concrete reality of international relations. Yet the Genesis story, and the way in which it is interpreted, is bound up with historical understandings of the constitution of reality, prominent in Western thought over scores of centuries, and has profound implications for politics, law, and ethics, as well as modern natural science. Emil Brunner, a Protestant theologian, expresses the essence of this claim when he says the doctrine of creation structures our comprehension of reality and the way in which it is known as object of knowledge: '[a]ll coordinates of the picture of reality—the above and the below, the whole system of weights, and the whole hierarchy of values—and therefore the whole conception of culture and civilisation is determined by it' (1948, 18). Augustine makes the same point: 'From [God] comes every mode, every species, every order; from Him comes measure, number, weight; from Him comes everything which exists in nature, whatever its kind and whatever its value' (1998, 206).

One of the central claims of this essay is that Bull's thinking about order reflects a particular interpretation of the Genesis story. The idea of order in Western thought has been decisively shaped by the so-called encounter between Athens and Jerusalem, which yielded rival interpretations of the doctrine of creation. One of these interpretations can be traced to neo-Platonist readings of Plato's *Timaeus*, in which the order of the cosmos is attributed to a Demiurge who makes order out of disorder by arranging pre-existing matter with pre-existing form. The activity of arranging the order of the cosmos is guided by an eternal and unchangeable pattern that is intelligible to the intellect; '[a]nd having been created in this way, the world has been framed in the likeness of that which is apprehended by reason and mind and is unchangeable, and must therefore of necessity, if this is to be admitted, be a copy of something' (Plato 1961, 1162). Crucially, this world is not just a copy; it is the only possible copy. The order of the cosmos is a necessary arrangement, so when asked if the world is merely one of many possible worlds, Timaeus replies: 'There must be one only if the created copy is to accord with the original' (1961, 1163). Of course, no Christian can accept all that is said in *Timaeus*. Plato's Demiurge is not a creator properly so called; he is merely a craftsman who arranges what already exists, just as a carpenter brings together the idea of a chair with the material out of which a chair is made. In contrast, Genesis tells of an all-powerful God who truly created the world out of nothing (*ex nihilo*), and so created *this* particular world out of many hypothetically possible worlds.

But, defects notwithstanding, the Platonic account of the order of the cosmos was close enough to the biblical story of creation that it was assimilated into Christianity with the help of Hellenized Jews, foremost among them Philo of Alexandria (Augustine 1998, bk. vii, ch. 11; Oakley 1979, 145-60). Augustine followed in Philo's footsteps, helping to cement a rapprochement between Athens and Jerusalem in Christian thought. Augustine conflates the Platonic Demiurge with the Old Testament God of power and might, which leads to a distinct conception of order. In doing so, he denies the extra-mental independence of Plato's forms and instead locates them in the mind of God: 'the ideas are certain original and principal forms of things, i.e., reasons, fixed and unchangeable, which are not themselves formed and, being thus eternal and existing always in the same state, are contained in the Divine Intelligence' (1982, 80). These ideas are not imposed from without, as a sculptor moulds clay into a figurine; they are bestowed on things from within God's mind. Therefore, God is present in all things in proportion to their perfection: 'It is His hidden power, pervading all things and undefilably present in them all, which causes all that exists in any way to have whatever degree of being it has' (Augustine 1998, 536).

This notion of degree informs the relation between creator and what is created. God is immutable, says Augustine, because he supremely *is*; and he gave being to other things, through the act of creation, but being unlike his own. Created things have distinct modes of existence that are described in terms of fitness and determine place and purpose: 'To some He gave being more fully, and to others he gave it in a more restricted way; and so he arranged natural entities according to their degrees of being' (1998, 500). This relation of creator and what is created entails a hierarchical conception of order. Man, as a rational animal, is nearer to God in nature than irrational animals that lack the capacity for thought and reflection (Augustine 1998, bk. xi, ch. 26). Therefore, the natures of things 'give shape to the visible structure of the world' and the wisdom of this arrangement, emanating as it does from the divine intellect, is luminous to human reason. Indeed, for Augustine, the perfection of this order is no manifestation of chance, or fate, as the Stoics would have it: 'Neither heaven nor earth, neither angel nor man, not even the inward parts of the smallest and most inconsiderable animal, nor the feather of a bird, nor a tiny flower of a plant nor the leaf on the tree, has God left unprovided with harmony and, as it were, at peace among its parts' (1998, 206). Order in the Augustinian sense cannot be relative as Bull suggests. Order connotes a necessary pattern of place and purpose; all other configurations are disordered, as when the body is corrupted by a diseased limb that no longer performs its function.

The doctrine of creation so understood, and the corresponding conception of order, held the field in the Latin West for several centuries. But in the thirteenth and fourteenth centuries theologians associated with the so-called nominalist school saw the reason and consequent necessity of the Augustinian synthesis of Athens and Jerusalem as posing a threat to God's freedom and omnipotence. A world created in respect of ideas located in the divine intellect cultivated doubt as to whether God was subject to the reason of what he had created. The problem, as Oakley explains, turned on a deep-seated tension between a rational order of the world and God's unimpeded will: 'If the universe was truly rational and ultimately intelligible, could God ever be wilful? If God could really be wilful, could the universe fully be rational?' (1979, 160). The attempt to resolve this tension yielded an alternative interpretation of the doctrine of creation and a corresponding way of thinking about order. William of Ockham, one of the most influential nominalist theologians, set out to vindicate biblical testimony of God's omnipotence by rejecting Augustine's doctrine of divine ideas. In doing so, Ockham dissolved the rational pattern that defines the nature of things and holds them in place, in a state of relational harmony. There is no reason to what God creates, or why he creates: God creates simply by sheer force of will. (1990, 144). Consequently, order is nothing more than a pattern mandated by divine fiat.

The primacy that Ockham ascribes to the will results in a radically contingent conception of order. Created things are singular in character; they exist in themselves, in isolation from all other things, when severed from the ideas in God's mind that define place and purpose (Oakley 2005, 29). Knowledge of such things is acquired by observing empirical behaviour because there is no reason of things to intuit. Things impart order only so far as order is imposed on them. It is in this context that Bull's analogy between order and a shelf of books makes sense: order consists in an assemblage of things that are arranged according to some principle, such as author or subject. There is no intrinsic rationality to such an arrangement; the relation of parts and whole, whether of books or states, can be made and unmade. As things are contingent, so too is order conditional. Thus, Ockham precipitates a shift away from reason and rationality as the ground of a regular and reliable order, so that questions of regularity and reliability are resolved in the biblical language of promise and covenant, or in the vernacular of modern politics, consent and contract. God is bound by the order of the world he chose to create freely, not because of its reason, but because of his promise to 'remain faithful to the covenant that, of his kindness and mercy, he has instituted with man' (Oakley 1984, 62).

The Ockhamist conception of order presupposes a different and distinct mental universe in terms of which to know and to explain the world. The idea of order no longer calls to mind an interconnected whole, permeated by an indwelling reason, which explains the relations of the parts; the parts of Ockham's whole can be arranged in numerous indeterminate patterns. It calls to mind a mechanical system, like a clock, which operates according to laws or norms imposed upon it by its maker (Oakley 1979, 165). Such an order is explained as an object of knowledge with reference to the external relations of individual things; that is, it is explained by way of empirical observation and the investigation of efficient causes (Oakley 1979, 165–8; Oakley 2005, 30). In contrast, the Augustinian conception of order is explained with reference to internal relations, according to which the natures of things disclose an intrinsic pattern of mutually constituted connections. Knowledge of this pattern is acquired by investigating these connections, using a priori reasoning, which focuses on both efficient and final causes (Oakley 2005, 27–33). Here, the parts jointly constitute a whole that is determined by certain and true (as opposed to indifferent and contingent) purposes or goods.

TWO KINDS OF SOCIETY

The Grotian and Hobbesian traditions of thought described in *The Anarchical Society* correspond with the Augustinian and Ockhamist conceptions of order and their distinct theological frames of reference. Taking these theological frames of reference seriously forces a revision of Bull's understanding of order as well as the related idea of international society (1977, 33, 41). The distinction between Grotian and Hobbesian patterns of order marks the boundary between an international society and an international system, or rather between society and 'not society'. The emphasis on society is rooted in Martin Wight's (1987, 222, 224–6) dissatisfaction with the realism–utopianism dichotomy laid out most famously in E.H. Carr's *The Twenty Years' Crisis*. Wight uses Hobbes to frame the terms of debate when he says the 'initial question, "What is international society?" seems to resolve itself into the question, "What is the state of nature?", and the answers to both questions will be the same' (1991, 31). In the Hobbesian state of nature, which is a state of war, power and interest are impervious to the civilizing effects of law and morality. Society exists within states, rather than between them. So, when confronted with the question 'what is international society?' Wight's realist, for whom Hobbes is the iconic spokesman, replies: 'nothing' (1987, 222). Wight contrasts this grim conclusion with the rationalist position, which 'assumes that moral standards can be upheld without the heavens falling. And it assumes that the fabric of social and political life will be maintained, without accepting the doctrine that to preserve it any measures are permissible' (Wight 1968, 130; Wight 1987, 222–3).

Bull essentially reproduces Wight's distinction in *The Anarchical Society* where Hobbes stands for realism and Grotius for rationalism. He says the Hobbesian tradition sees the state as 'free to pursue its goals in relation to other states without moral or legal restrictions of any kind. Ideas of morality and law, on this view, are valid only in the context of a society, but international life is beyond the bounds of any society' (1977, 25). Of the Grotian tradition he says, again closely tracking Wight's scheme, that states are bound by the rules of the society they form, so '[a]s against the view of the Hobbesians, states in the Grotian view are bound not only by rules of prudence or expediency but also by imperatives of morality and law' (1977, 27). There is a theological genealogy to all of this that has an important—and for Bull unacknowledged—bearing on the way in which these claims are understood. It is a genealogy that begins with a particular conception of God, and from this conception follows the character of order. Order for Hobbes is a modern reflection of medieval Ockhamist theological discourse. Hobbes's God is the all-powerful voluntarist God of the Old Testament who creates without reason. Efficacious speech, and nothing else, explains the 'is' and the 'why' of all things: 'the *power* of God alone without other helps is sufficient *justification* of any action he doth' (Hobbes 1840, 248–50). The character of order follows in train: in a radically contingent world singular things impart order only so far as order is imposed on them.

Hobbes's political philosophy is plotted in respect of these theologically defined coordinates. The state of nature is composed of individuals that have no inherent connections; they are alone in the world, their fortune determined solely by self-defined desires and their own personal account of power. These individuals impose order on themselves through a concatenation of speech acts that signify acts of will, knowledge of which is secured in contracts that explain both the force and the agency by which the commonwealth is brought into existence. In other words, human beings institute the commonwealth in the same way that God created the world, or as Hobbes puts it: 'NATURE (The Art whereby God hath made and governes the World) is by the *Art* of man, as in many other things, so in this also imitated, that it can make an Artificial Animal' (2012, 16; Oakeshott 1975, 60). This theological frame of reference is especially significant for correctly ascertaining the character of Hobbes's laws of nature. When viewed from the standpoint of reason, these laws are merely prudential theorems that are conducive to self-preservation. In contrast, their legal character is 'delivered in the word of God, that by right commandeth all things; then are they properly called Lawes' (Hobbes 2012, 242). Therefore, order is something made rather than discovered; human beings impose order on themselves as God imposed order in matters pertaining to ethics and nature.

Turning to Grotius, we find that a different conception of God leads to a different conception of order. Grotius affirms God's omnipotence but the character of omnipotence is mediated by God's rational nature. So, when God speaks the world into existence, utterance is not without reason: 'The very Figure of the World, which is the most perfect, *viz.* round, inclosed in the Bosom of the Heavens, and placed in wonderful Order, sufficiently declares that these Things were not the Results of Chance, but the Appointment of the most excellent Understanding' (Grotius 2012, 38; Grotius 2006, 20–1). It is Grotius's emphasis on understanding that informs a very different conception of order than is the case with Hobbes. God is the efficient, as well as the final, cause of the world, as a whole and in its parts. Consequently, all things, moral and material, exist *because* of God and they continue to exist *for* the sake of God (Grotius 1988, 112). The result is a rationally intelligible hierarchy of mutually dependent causes that embraces all things, without exception, and explains their divinely ordained place and purpose. Indeed, the world for Grotius is an interconnected whole, for all things are arranged for their particular good and the good of the whole, so as to effect a unity; and the law of this unity is reason, which Grotius says 'we call *God*' (Grotius 2012, 37).

Grotius's international thought is inextricably a part of this divinely ordained, purposive order of the world. Take, for example, his defence of freedom of navigation on the seas, which is rooted in beliefs about the appropriate direction of God's creation. Free navigation, and by extension trade, is the way in which Grotius reconciles the right of proprietary possession with the duty of mutual assistance. As nations do not possess all that is required for life, use of the sea is required so that man can attend to his own needs and those of his neighbours. This, Grotius contends, is what underwrites the lawfulness of free navigation, for God established that 'one nation should supply the want of another by the appointment of divine justice' (2004, 10–12, 38, 51). The right of war, that aspect of Grotius's thought that is of greatest interest to international theorists and international lawyers, is similarly bound up in a divinely ordained order that is shot through with notions of place and purpose. War is a remedy of injustice, manifest as a violation of rights; it is an activity, the resort to which is justified in response to disorder that disrupts what God intended and established. Grotius says in this regard, citing Augustine, that war is justified for the sake of restoring 'a well ordered and disposed concord'—that is, the divinely ordained design and end of human society (2005, 184; 2004, 57).

Uncovering these theological foundations suggests that the contrast between Hobbesian and Grotian patterns of order is not, as Bull suggests, drawn out in the difference between a Hobbesian absence of society and a Grotian presence of society. Hobbes and Grotius stand for contrasting ideas of society. Order for Hobbes is something made, as when a heap of bricks are arranged so that they form a house. But there is nothing necessary about this particular arrangement. Individual bricks do not strive to come together in such a way that they form a house, and so assume their proper place and fulfil their necessary purpose. Freedom is the underlying condition, rather than the goal, of Hobbes's approach to order. Therefore, individual bricks are in themselves indifferent as to place and purpose; so instead of a house they could just as easily be arranged to form a retaining wall, a garden path, or a furnace. And so it is with states. Order between states arises in respect of contractual arrangements that facilitate trade as well as alliances and confederacies that address circumstantial purposes, such as the provision of mutual defence. But none of this, Hobbes insists, depends on the existence of an international sovereign: 'Leagues between Common-wealths, over whom there is no humane Power established, to keep them in awe, are not onely lawfull, but also profitable for the time they last' (2012, 370). The authority of such arrangements derives from eternal and immutable laws of nature; that is, genuine *lex* that binds in the sight of God. Consequently, Bull's elementary goal of truth is not absent in the international realm. As Hobbes makes clear, '[s]o that before the time of Civill Society, or in the interruption thereof by Warre, there is nothing can strengthen a Covenant of Peace agreed on, against the temptations of Avarice, Ambition, Lust, or other strong desire, but the feare of that Invisible Power, which they every one Worship as God' (Hobbes 2012, 216).

The distinguishing characteristic of Hobbes's conception of order is the presumption of freedom to make and unmake the world; order in this sense rules out a substantive common good that amounts to something greater than the sum of shared interests. States, and the people residing within them, are not meant to be anything in particular because there are no substantive ends or goods to achieve. Freedom is strictly formal in character; there is no coordination of efficient and final causes, as with Augustine's conception of order, which explains why there is order *and* why this particular order is good. Bull's elementary goals of order—life, truth, and property—are similarly indifferent as to the achievement of a substantive state of affairs; they are given to formal coexistence that regulates the exercise of freedom. Consequently, the condition of anarchy that is attributed to Hobbes does not loose the pursuit of interest from all restraint, as Bull claims. Cooperation is not as elusive as it is made out to be and violence is not as pervasive or uncontrolled. Moral rights and duties exist in the international state of nature, as do valid pacts and covenants founded on juridical rights and duties. In this sense, Hobbes is properly regarded as a theorist of international society, albeit a society of a particular kind (Malcolm 2002, 452). These rights are not harmonized by nature to form a general pattern that directs all things to their proper place and their respective good. Outside the state there is only a partial pattern established by convention, which is contingent evidence of a journey that has no definite or necessary destination (Malcolm 2002, 453–6). There is, then, no room in Hobbes's thought for an international order in which discrepant parts are arranged for the good of the whole.

In contrast, order for Grotius is discovered rather than made. This does not mean that relations established by contract and consent are ruled out. The pursuit of mutual advantages can be secured in contracts underwritten by consent, and such arrangements oblige 'by virtue of the natural law stating that agreements must be kept' (Grotius 2001, 249). However, the freedom to institute arrangements closer than the society that is common to all human beings is not as it is for Hobbes. God's reason, which directs all things to their appointed place and purpose, harmonizes discrepant parts in a natural unity as opposed to a constructed union. In other words, order for Grotius is grounded in the principle 'that every part as a part is arranged for the good of the whole' (2001, 249). And it is God's reason, rather than his volition, which ultimately explains the existence and the goodness of this pattern. This argument is comprehensive and all encompassing, and so extends even to the custom that is common to Christian and infidel—that is, the law of nations. Grotius acknowledges that there are different ways of living, but the authority of usage and custom must be tested against the certain testimony of Scripture. The authority of custom is perfected by the truth of revelation. For Grotius says that the custom which is common to all nations is itself a manifestation of divine reason, because 'the nations disclose the work of the law written [by God] in their hearts' (2004, 105).

Order conceived along these lines leads to a very different conception of the relations of states. Concord, rather than mutual antagonism and perpetual conflict, is the underlying condition of international life. The international realm imparts an intrinsic unity, despite the existence of separate states, which is greater than the sum of its parts. So, states may be judges in their own cause, but do not enjoy absolute liberty to act. Self-interest is conditioned by the good of the whole. While each state is entitled to enforce its right, by force if necessary, the right of war is licit only so far as it is used to remedy disorder that disrupts or impedes this order of concord. Order in this sense consists in an interconnected whole, composed of coordinate parts, the pattern of which is rationally intelligible. Moreover, the pattern of order is hierarchical in character; order is defined in terms of mutual relations of superiority and inferiority, which springs forth from God and, at the same time, comes together for the sake of God.

THEOLOGY AND FOUNDATIONS OF INTERNATIONAL ORDER

This exploration of the theological foundations of Bull's thinking about order prompts two main conclusions. The first concerns Bull's engagement with classical thinkers and what he claims on their behalf. Bull and many of his English School fellow travellers engaged the history of political thought at a time when the rising tide of social science, in America especially, viewed the traditional canon as increasingly peripheral to research programmes aimed at building and testing theory. The attraction of the history of political thought can be explained, at least in part, by a sense of detachment and a desire on the part of English School theorists to achieve some distance from the fury of the present. Evidence of this orientation is present in Wight's insistence (1960, 43) that the character of international relations is one of recurrence and repetition, and that the questions which animated the likes of Hobbes and Grotius, among others, are also our questions. It is also evident in the concluding pages of *The Anarchical Society*, where Bull (1977, 319–20) disavows the pretension of providing 'solutions' and 'practical advice' as to what troubled the world and how it might be overcome. He described his study of international order as an intellectual engagement that afforded no room for what he disparaged as the corrupting influence of practical scholarship. Too often, though, the bid to acquire a longer and more sophisticated view of international relations resulted in distortion and caricature. Many of the insights that Bull gleaned from the history of political thought certainly fall into this category.

This is manifest most immediately in the crude and superficial way in which Bull borrows his central concept from Augustine, namely order, while entirely neglecting the theological context that informs its character. Bull's hostility to religion, encouraged by the unyielding empiricism of his teacher John Anderson, pre-empted any foray into the complex and unverifiable territory of theology (see Jeffery 2006, 130–3). Yet Bull's misuse of Augustine's definition of order set up his subsequent misunderstanding of Hobbes and Grotius when theorizing order in the modern states system. Consequently, Bull's defence of international society, ignorant of its underlying ideational source, is confused and ultimately stunted. Understanding Augustine correctly opens previously unexplored avenues of inquiry which show that Hobbes and Grotius stand for rival conceptions of order, both of which are compatible with the idea of international society. It is in this sense that a theologically shaped key unlocks a richer and more coherent account of international order than Bull otherwise presents. I have argued that the pattern of order he associates with the idea of international society has roots thrust deep in the soil of Ockhamist theology. There is no intrinsic reason to this world; it *is* simply because he willed it into existence. Order is a radically contingent construction when severed from a necessary rational pattern that defines the relations of things; it is an artefact of will and artifice that finds stability and regularity in God's promise and covenant.

Hobbes inherited Ockham's theological worldview and translated it into his iconic political philosophy, and so it is with Bull. When Bull describes and subsequently defends the idea of international society he thinks the thoughts and speaks the language of Hobbes, not Grotius. Order for Bull, as for Hobbes, is a construction, and rules voluntarily instituted and accepted testify to what has been constructed. But the authority of these rules does not issue from the intrinsic reason of their content; they are binding, not because of their self-evident character, but because they are properly enacted. As Bull makes clear, there are no mandatory goals of social life that are true for all human beings as the natural lawyers claim; hence these rules provide no more than contingent guidance as to how contingent goals might be realized. Rules pertaining to the elementary goals of social life—life, truth, and property—can be expressed in any number of ways; what matters most is that they have 'a foundation in the will or consent of political communities throughout the world' (Bull 1984a, 120). There is no universal or transcendent good that determines the way in which states are arranged. Rules of this kind are formal in character—states are associated in respect of common benefit, enjoyed separately, as opposed to a common good that perfects states as parts of a comprehensive whole. In other words, there is no common project of international society, only particular projects, which may facilitate cooperation and assist in the avoidance of collisions.

The second conclusion concerns the extent to which international society rests on a common culture. One of the central concerns of *The Anarchical Society* is the contention that all historical international societies had at their foundation a common culture: 'a common language, a common epistemology and understanding of the universe, a common religion, a common ethical code, a common aesthetic or artistic tradition' (1977, 16). Bull evinced both optimism and uncertainty about the prospects of an international society born out of the dissolution of European empire and the emergence of powerful non-Western states. The future of international society, he argued, having outgrown both its Christian and European foundations, depended on the cultivation and internalization of a cosmopolitan culture that embraced all of international political life. Yet he worried about the shallowness of this culture because it existed mainly at the elite level in many societies. Whatever its merits, this hope for the future is accommodated within, rather than holds out an alternative to, the constructed conception of order that has been attributed to Ockham, and after him, Hobbes. The constructed nature of Bull's cosmopolitan culture is evident when he says 'it is surely the duty of all intelligent and sensitive persons, however conscious they may be of the obstacles standing in the way of the emergence of such a world society or community, to recognise its desirability and dedicate themselves to work for it' (1977, 289). A culture capable of sustaining such a community must reflect consensus on common interests and values of the entire world, and not merely its Christian or European element; it must reflect the collective will of all states on matters of economic and social justice, the redistribution of power, and racial and cultural equality.

But none of this is necessary, much less desirable in itself. For whatever goals are used to arrange the discrepant parts of international society, they have no objective authority, which distinguish right order from disorder. Human rights provide an apt case in point. Bull says that human rights might be included in this cosmopolitan culture, but he is adamant in saying that there can be no a priori demonstration of their objective validity. The idea that human beings are free and equal, and should be treated as such, cannot be shown to exist objectively in the nature of things. There are attitudes and preferences, as well as arguments from convention, but in the end their authority is grounded in nothing more than in what can be agreed (Bull 1979a, 89). Aspects of the historically specific cultural experience of Europe, such as human rights, might survive and, indeed, flourish in a globalized international society. But Bull was quite certain that the Christian religion could be safely subtracted from the future, no matter how it might develop. The international society of the theologians and the early-modern jurists had receded into the background, never to return. The theologians had contributed to the development of international society, after which it was taken over by those invested in a secular outlook that looked beyond the parochialism of culture to a shared, but sometimes fuzzy, notion of modernity.

Bull is certainly correct when he says that with culture we encounter corresponding understandings of the universe; ways of counting and knowing, as well as knowing what to count; values systems, ethical codes, and legal traditions; and, of course, religious institutions and practices. What he does not understand is just how deeply this claim penetrates. Religion consists in something more than an attribute of culture; it has exerted and continues to exert enormous influence on the constitution of reality and how it is known as an object of knowledge. In other words, religion is not just a variable among others, or even a particularly important variable that social scientists ignore at their peril. Religion, and specifically beliefs about the nature of God and the extent of his power, is constitutive of reality as such. Yet Bull seems to be entirely unaware of the fact that in his attempt to dispel the theological odour of natural law he merely pushes the matter on to different theological ground. Invoking Hobbes and Grotius (and others) to describe international order had the effect of assimilating unacknowledged theological presuppositions into his thinking. But, ignorant of his sources, Bull had no way of escaping the distorting embrace of caricature. The voluntarism that is located at the heart of *The Anarchical Society* is deeply indebted to Christian theology. Indeed, Bull's thinking about international order is shot through with Christian ideas of subjective freedom, as well as related ideas of moral autonomy and personal responsibility, all of which are 'engaged, not in Hellenic soil, but in the Biblical doctrine of divine omnipotence and the historically peculiar doctrine of creation that goes with it' (Oakley 1999, 126–7).

Turn this soil over and *The Anarchical Society* takes on a rather different character. Bull never abandoned the idea that an 'actual' international society, as opposed to the theoretical or normative one that existed in the minds of Grotius and other natural lawyers, had to be grounded in what states do, as a matter of fact, and what they agree. He believed that it was state practice that extracted the theory of international society from the dogmatic and ultimately unverifiable thickets of religion. Here, Bull gets entangled in the political analogue of the problem that the nominalist theologians set out to address, namely vindicating God's freedom while accounting for the regular order of the universe. Confronted by a world of independent states, each equal in authority and jurisdiction to all others, Bull reconciles freedom and regularity in acts of will and expressions of consent that parallel the biblical discourse of promise and covenant. He chooses Jerusalem at the expense of Athens. Like the incomprehensible God of Hobbes's *Leviathan*, the God who answered Job's query as to *why* he acted as he did, not with an explanation of his reason but with a reminder of his untrammelled freedom, the ultimate authority of will and consent in Bull's thought is also unknowable. It rests on an assumed rule that serves as a substitute for the rationally intelligible precept of natural law that obliges the keeping of promises. To demand any more than this is to demand what cannot be given, because '[t]o establish validity of these rules we can appeal only to other rules, whose validity is established in the same way: there are no rules that are valid independently of human will, that are part of "nature"' (Bull 2000b, 168). It seems, then, that sustaining international society requires a kind of faith after all.

Uncovering unacknowledged theological presuppositions invites a broad reassessment of *The Anarchical Society* and its continuing relevance. Bull tersely reminded Midgley that the study of international relations affords no place for theology; rational argument, uncontaminated by God, is the only basis of acceptable scholarship (2000b, 168–9). Theology may have had some purchase for practitioners of the subject in the past, but its star had faded, never to return as queen of the sciences. The paradox of *The Anarchical Society* is that it reflects Bull's antipathy for religion, and yet its central argument is an expression of a particular kind of theology. He happily shed the Christian foundations of international society, but as he searched for a cosmopolitan culture to sustain that element of society in the future, it never occurred to him that he looked to intellectual materials furnished by Ockhamist theology. In uncovering this theological inheritance it seems as though important parts of *The Anarchical Society* are no longer serviceable. The pattern of order that Bull associates with Grotius takes its intellectual bearings from the theology that anchors Hobbes's political philosophy. The distinction between system and society, which tracks the distinction between Hobbesian and Grotian patterns of order, cannot be sustained. The Hobbesian state of war and the Grotian idea of society are not in competition with one another, with human vulnerability and human flourishing forever caught in the balance. And the progressive story that Bull tells about international society gradually outgrowing its Christian foundations takes on the appearance of myth. In the end, he merely swaps one theological foundation for another.

But taking account of these theological foundations does not bring to an end *The Anarchical Society*'s run as a classic. Venturing into the world of medieval theology corrects the persistent mischaracterization of Bull, and English School claims for international society more generally, as 'Grotian'. It also corrects the persistent mischaracterization of Hobbes and what his thought holds for international theory. There is a great deal more to Hobbes than caricatured readings of a single chapter of *Leviathan*, relating to the state of nature, which is used to distil all of international relations into that spare and oft-repeated conclusion that life is 'solitary, poore, nasty, brutish, and short' (Hobbes 2012, 192). Hobbes's political philosophy is given to a theory of international society that privileges the language of will and artifice: contract and consent (see Malcolm 2002; Bain 2015). Engaging theology also helps to uncover hitherto unexplored layers of the text. Understanding the complexities of what the idea of order might entail renews historically significant, though forgotten, channels in which to theorize the idea of international community as an articulated whole, the excellence of which is disclosed by the arrangement of the parts. It also illuminates different ways of locating universality and explaining the conditions of solidarity. It is in this sense that *The Anarchical Society* remains, not the last, but the first word on the theory of international society.

5

The Anarchical Society and Human Rights

Christian Reus-Smit

Hedley Bull was a master of taxonomy. Indeed, if there is a distinguishing feature of his theorizing, it is the drive to classify and categorize, to carve up a phenomenon or issue into elements or dimensions, and then compare, contrast, and relate them. He had a penchant for dichotomies and trichotomies: international order/world order, international system/international society/world society, order/justice, international/human/cosmopolitan justice, classical/scientific, and pluralism/solidarism. This penchant gave his theorizing a powerful architecture, an architecture of robust concepts, well ordered and prioritized, deployed in razor sharp analytics. So powerful has this architecture proven, that followers and critics alike have struggled to free themselves from his cardinal classifications and distinctions, proving that artful taxonomy can leave an enduring heuristic legacy.

The problem with taxonomic theorizing, however, is that it is prone to Cinderella syndrome: the squeezing of ugly, ungainly political phenomena into overly stylized conceptual distinctions that crack when pressured. Bull's writings on human rights are emblematic of this problem. He wrote very little on such rights: a dozen pages in *The Anarchical Society*, a chapter in an obscure edited collection, and a five-page review essay pretty well exhaust his oeuvre (Bull 1977; 1979a; 1979d). It was his student, John Vincent, who later wrote the major work in the English School on human rights (1986). What emerges from Bull's limited writings, however, is a powerful, if abbreviated, position on the nature of human rights and their significance in world politics, a position deftly crafted from within his taxonomic architecture. Yet forty years of subsequent research on the politics of human rights, on sovereignty as a practically constituted institution, and on the historical sociology of international society have exposed the limits of this architecture.

This chapter critically evaluates Bull's position on human rights, advancing three key claims. I begin, first, by reconstructing his overarching taxonomy, and showing how he reasoned out from this framework to an internally coherent argument about human rights. The central theme of this argument was that human rights were potentially 'subversive' of international society: that the principle that individuals had inalienable rights threatens cardinal norms that sustain international order (Bull 1977, 83). Second, I argue that reading human rights through this taxonomy distorts both the nature and politics of human rights, and that closer attention to what human rights are and how they shape political life destabilizes key categorical distinctions within Bull's taxonomy. Third, a key failing of taxonomic theorizing is that it does not, in itself, constitute a theory of international social change. I argue, however, that greater attention to the nature and political effects of human rights can help develop such a theory.

THE TAXONOMIC ARCHITECTURE

Bull's writings on human rights appeared in a brief period between 1977 and 1979. This is important for two reasons. First, they were written at the height of his 'anarchical society' phase: they come well after his earlier work on nuclear weapons, his discussion on human rights in *The Anarchical Society* sets the tone for the other two essays, and it is well before the revisionist Hagey Lectures of 1983. Second, he was writing in the midst of President Carter's human rights diplomacy, and Bull referred repeatedly to this context. He saw this as a new phase in the politics of human rights, and he was anxious to counter overly idealistic assessments of its transformative potential. But just as he witnessed this phase, he also missed everything that came later. In following decades, human rights exploded as an issue in global politics, leading some to treat them (incorrectly in my mind) as a post-1970s phenomenon (Moyn 2010; Hopgood 2013). And while Bull noted the burgeoning scholarly analysis of human rights in the late 1970s, he missed the wealth of increasingly rigorous scholarship that followed, particularly after the end of the Cold War. Thomas's *The Helsinki Effect* (2001), Risse, Ropp, and Sikkink's *The Power of Human Rights* (1999), and Simmons's *Mobilizing for Human Rights* (2009) are but a few of the works he would never read.

In *The Anarchical Society* Bull set out to answer three questions: 'What is order in world politics?' 'How is order maintained within the present system of sovereign states?' And 'Does the system of sovereign states still provide a viable path to world order?' In answering these questions, he began by defining order in social life as 'a pattern of human activity that sustains elementary, primary or universal goals of social life...' (1977, 5). He then introduced the first of his taxonomic distinctions, between international order and world order. The former is 'a pattern of activity that sustains the elementary or primary goals of the society of states, or international society';

and the latter is 'those patterns or dispositions of human activity that sustain the elementary or primary goals of social life among mankind as a whole' (1977, 20). Bull held that while international order was a recurrent feature of world politics, world order remained an elusive aspiration. And because international order was the only order within reach, it was imperative that it be preserved.

Embedded within these different conceptions of order are two different kinds of society: international society, and world society. International order is a pattern of activity that sustains the goals of an international society; world order a pattern that supports the goals of human society more broadly. Bull devoted most attention to the first of these, leaving the second to later English School theorists (see, in particular, Buzan 2004). An international society exists, he famously argued, 'when a group of states, conscious of certain common interests and common values, form a society in the sense that they conceive themselves to be bound by a common set of rules in their relations with one another, and share in the working of common institutions' (1977, 13). International societies are not the same as international systems, which are 'formed when two or more states have sufficient contact between them, and have sufficient impact on one another's decisions, to cause them to behave—at least in some measure—as parts of a whole' (1977, 9–10). While not the same, Bull argued that the idea of international society presupposes that of an international system, and held that at any given moment elements of system and society might coexist.

In answering his second question—how is order maintained within the present system of sovereign states?—Bull identified the 'elementary or primary goals' of international society, key rules that instantiate those goals, and institutions to uphold those rules. The goals of international society are preserving the society of states itself, protecting the independence of individual states, sustaining international peace, limiting the exercise of violence, ensuring that promises are kept, and maintaining the stability of possession, the last three of which he considered elementary goals of all social life (1977, 16–19). Meeting these goals depends on the articulation of more or less formal rules of conduct, as rules provide 'guidance as to what behaviour is consistent with these goals, and what behaviour is not' (1977, 54). In particular, the cardinal rules of international society restrict the legitimate use of force, uphold the sanctity of treaties (*pacta sunt servanda*), and ensure territorial integrity and political independence (non-aggression, non-intervention, the right to self-determination, etc.). In the absence of a central authority to enforce compliance with these rules, Bull emphasized the role of international institutions, particularly the balance of power, international law, diplomacy, war, and management by the great powers.

The next taxonomic distinction is between international and human justice. With the first, the domain of justice is international society, and justice relates to the application of the basic rules of interstate conduct. For example, 'Every state maintains that it has certain rights and duties that are not merely legal in character but moral: it contends that its policy is just in the sense of being morally correct ("general justice"), and demands equality or fairness of treatment as between itself and other states ("particular justice")...' (1977, 82). The domain of human justice, by comparison, is world society, and justice in this case relates to 'the moral rules conferring rights and duties upon individual human beings' (1977, 82). As we shall see, Bull locates human rights in this second sphere of justice. The categories of international and human justice are closely related to Bull's oft-used distinction between pluralism and solidarism. For a pluralist, Nicholas Wheeler contends, 'states are the principal bearers of rights and duties in international law, with individuals only having legal rights insofar as the state provides them' (1992, 467–8). International justice thus takes priority. For solidarists, by contrast, individuals take moral priority, and their rights and duties undergird the rights and duties of states (Wheeler 1992, 467–8). Human justice trumps international justice.

The above taxonomic distinctions are nested within a *grund* dichotomy that structures and animates Bull's writings: between order and justice. A cottage industry explores this aspect of Bull's work, so little further is needed here. It is sufficient to note that Bull saw order and justice as competing values in world politics, and sought to understand which, if either, had priority. He wrote that 'Order is not merely an actual or possible condition or state of affairs in world politics, it is also very generally regarded as a value. But it is not the only value in relation to which international conduct can be shaped, nor is it necessarily an overriding one.... I propose to examine the contending claims of order and the other human value most frequently contrasted with it, justice' (1977, 74–5). As we shall see, in his anarchical society phase, Bull famously privileged the former, even if many read the later Hagey Lectures as softening, if not reversing, this position.

HUMAN RIGHTS AS SUBVERSIVE

Bull's position on human rights is a direct product of this taxonomy. As noted, a central theme of his work is the relationship between order and justice. In *The Anarchical Society* he states as a truism that justice 'is realisable only in a context of order; it is only if there is a pattern of social activity in which elementary or primary goals of social life are in some degree provided for, that advanced or secondary goals can be secured' (1977, 86). Since world order is unattainable, he focused on the preservation of international order. And he saw the rules and institutions of international society as the principal, if not only, order-sustaining mechanisms. Basic rules limiting the use of force, ensuring treaty obligations are met, and guaranteeing non-intervention and self-determination are paramount, and the institutional practices that uphold them, however unpalatable, must be seen as essential to international peace and well-being.

For Bull, the only kind of justice minimally compatible with all of this is international justice: justice that concerns the rights and duties of sovereign states. Even then, he held that the preservation of international order frequently involves the violation of state's rights: the 'institutions and mechanisms which sustain international order, even when they are working properly...necessarily violate ordinary notions of justice' (1977, 91). He cites as an example the balance of power, 'which offends against everyday notions of justice by sanctioning war against a state whose power threatens to become preponderant, but which has done no legal or moral injury...' (1977, 91).

If international justice is hard to reconcile with international order, human justice is near impossible. Human rights are Bull's example of such justice, as they involve moral and legal rules and principles that pertain to individual human beings. He acknowledged that by the late 1970s rights talk was everywhere in world politics, and that a battery of international instruments had codified legally binding international human rights. But he threw cold water over idealistic responses to such developments. Behind the talk, and the purported consensus informing the human rights regime, lay markedly different interpretations of what human rights mean, and when rights are championed in international society (1979a, 85), it is selectively and always in the interests of the champions (1977, 90). It was his theoretical critique, however, that was most damning. The idea of human rights—the notion that individuals have inalienable rights, and that other individuals have responsibilities to observe and protect these rights—threatens the jurisdiction of sovereign states and licenses intervention:

> The foundation of this society of states was their mutual recognition of one another's sovereign jurisdiction, and a corollary of this was their acceptance of the obligation not to interfere in one another's internal affairs. In an international society of this sort, which treats the maintenance of order among states as the highest values, the very idea of human or natural rights...is potentially disruptive. For if human rights come to assume not merely a moral but a legal form, and if it comes to be held that one state can interfere within the sovereign jurisdiction of another to uphold the human rights of its citizens, the basic rules of international society may be undermined. (1979a, 82–3)

Added to this, Bull feared that a world in which human rights were taken seriously would undermine the obligations that bind individuals to their states. The 'idea of the *rights* of the individual human being raises in international politics the question of the right and duty of persons and groups other than the state to which he [the individual] owes allegiance to come to his aid in the event that his rights are being disregarded.... These are questions which, answered in a certain way, lead to disorder in international relations, or even to the breakdown of international society itself' (1977, 83–4).

While Bull was sceptical about the universality of human rights, pointing as we saw to disagreements across cultures about how such rights should be interpreted, he admitted one area of consensus. Again, though, this reveals just how much his broader theoretical architecture dictated his position on human rights. Bull's insistence that there are elementary goals of social life, common to domestic and international societies alike, jars with his critique of the universality of human rights. If minimizing violence, ensuring promises are kept, and stabilizing possession are universal elementary goals of all social life—goals that all peoples share, and that must be met if society is to exist at all—then why can we not speak of concomitant universal rights? Bull squares this circle by admitting that rights relating to these goals come as close as we can get to 'natural' or 'objective' rights (without actually getting there): 'There is not a natural right to security of the person, or to have one's property respected, or to have contracts honoured, but because a posteriori we know these rights to enjoy something like universal support, it is possible for practical purposes to proceed as if they were natural rights' (1979a, 90). Here Bull comes close to a recent argument about the universality of human rights, in which universality is grounded not in the moral nature of such rights, or the needs of humans as particular kinds of moral beings, but in their near universal acceptance (Beitz 2011). This matters little, however, when it comes to his general position. Even if all individuals have such rights, with international order it is the elementary goals and attendant rights of states that matter, and any attempt to privilege individual rights, however rooted in universal elementary goals, threatens international order.

UNSTABLE CATEGORIES

In Bull's schema, human rights potentially 'subvert', 'disrupt', 'undermine', 'threaten', and 'disintegrate', a largely 'inhospitable' international society. I want to suggest, though, that human rights are at least as subversive of Bull's taxonomic categories and distinctions as they might be of international order (which I go on to question later in this chapter). My starting point is to probe the nature of human rights themselves. There are two ways to do this. The first is philosophical, where one inquires into the nature of human rights as distinct kinds of moral principles. This is the approach Bull adopts. He defines what a human right is, discusses the relationship between rights and duties, and identifies several bases on which an individual might be said to have human rights: moral, legal, and empirical (1979a, 79–82). In due course,

I too will say something about the philosophical nature of human rights. For the moment, however, my approach is political. Human rights are not just philosophical principles; they are political principles, invoked for political purposes, in political struggles, with political consequences.

As I have argued elsewhere, human rights are power mediators, 'normative principles that materially weak actors can invoke to alter the power relationship between themselves and materially preponderant actors or institutions (empires, sovereign states, etc.)' (2013a, 38). This is what John Locke referred to when he called the natural right to freedom a 'fence against tyranny' (1988, 279), what Henry Shue meant when he wrote that the 'fundamental purpose of acknowledging any basic right at all is to prevent, or to eliminate, insofar as possible, the degree of vulnerability that leaves people at the mercy of others' (1996, 29–30), and what Vincent pointed to when claiming that human rights are 'a weapon of the weak against the strong' (1986, 17). Most commentators ignore this feature of human rights, and when they touch on it, they generally fail to grasp its full significance. Bull himself does just this. He notes that human rights 'are above all rights possessed by human beings as individuals, and are intended to limit the rights of society or the state' (1979a, 81). But instead of grasping this insight, and exploring struggles over rights as vital sites in the constitution of social and political power, he points simply to the challenge rights pose to the statist norms of international society.

Once we see human rights as power mediators, Bull's conceptual categories, and the dichotomous hierarchies in which they stand, lose coherence and begin to collapse in on one another. As we have seen, Bull's taxonomy consists of four principal dichotomies, the last of which is a *grund* distinction overarching the others:

International order/world order
International society/world society
International justice/human justice
Order/justice

All four dichotomies are hierarchically ordered, with the left side always taking precedence. Human rights are located in two of these dichotomies—international/human justice, and order/justice—and in both cases on the right. Yet once we recognize that rights are power mediators, they properly sit between Bull's categories, not on one or other side.

Let me begin with international justice/human justice. A human right presupposes two entities: the rights holder, and a political authority. This comes to the fore in any claim for the recognition and protection of a human right. The claim is made by, or on behalf of, a rights holder, and directed at a political authority, either to observe and protect the right in question, or to cease its violation. Not only does a human right assume a relationship between these entities, its purpose is to mediate that relationship. For Bull, human justice concerns the rights and duties of individuals, international justice concerns the rights and duties of states, and the two stand in fundamental tension. In reality, the idea of human rights entwines these two conceptions of justice. Every argument about the human rights of the individual—whether civil and political rights, or social and economic rights—is also an argument about the rights and duties of states, about the scope and purpose of political authority. The idea of human rights thus has one foot in human justice and one in international justice, and arguments about human rights constitute both.

This is more than a philosophical nicety. For at least five centuries, the politics of individual rights has simultaneously shaped the rights and duties of political authorities (empires and states, principally) *and* the individual as a self-conscious, rights-bearing moral agent. Struggles over liberty of conscience, equal political representation, freedom from persecution, equality before the law and due process, and the sovereignty of the people have profoundly affected the nature and scope of political authority. This has not just involved reconstituting the rights and duties of pre-existing sovereign states, but constituting states themselves as the dominant legitimate units of political authority. When Bull penned *The Anarchical Society* in the 1970s, decolonization had only recently produced a universal society of states. For centuries prior to this a hybrid order existed, in which sovereignty in the European core was tied to empire abroad. Bull and Watson's *The Expansion of International Society* examines the emergence of a universal international society out of this hybrid order, but they fail to recognize the critical role that struggles over individual rights played in driving key waves of this expansion (Reus-Smit 2013a; and for a discussion of the limits of Bull and Watson's account, see Dunne and Reus-Smit 2017).

This connection between the politics of human rights and the constitution, not only of the rights and duties of states, but states themselves, challenges a second of Bull's dichotomies, between international and world society. In the vast majority of cases, the political forces that have mobilized human rights to define and redefine the rights and duties of states have not come from within international society: they have come from world society. For Bull, international society is a society of states, and the rights and duties of its members are generated through their interaction. But in the struggles that eroded the old hybrid order, and that eventually produced today's universal international society, the key agents were subject peoples in the imperial periphery. And, more recently, a wealth of scholarship has shown how transnational advocacy networks have mobilized human rights norms to challenge categorical notions of sovereign jurisdiction, and to pressure individual states to improve their human rights records (Keck and Sikkink 1998; Risse et al. 1999; and Risse et al. 2013). All of this suggests that instead of international society and world society being two distinct social categories standing in a dichotomous relationship, the two are deeply enmeshed. Furthermore, when viewed through the lens of human rights, international society appears more as a political institutional architecture within a broader universe of global social forces.

A word remains to be said about Bull's *grund* dichotomy: order and justice. Bull was correct that these values are often in tension, that very often the pursuit of justice—international, human, or cosmopolitan—can challenge the norms and practices that sustain order. But what the human rights case shows is that international orders can be the product of struggles for justice. Elsewhere I define international orders as systemic configurations of political authority, comprising multiple political units, separated according to some principle of differentiation: heteronomy, suzerainty, sovereignty, etc. (Reus-Smit 2013b). Orders rest not only on a particular distribution of material capabilities, but also on legitimacy. Yet arguments about the legitimacy of an order, and of the units of political authority it comprises, always invoke moral values, very often framed as issues of justice. In the development of the modern international order, the moral values in question have concerned human justice, and more specifically individual/human rights. So while vexed issues such as humanitarian intervention show the tensions between contending values of order and justice, the broader politics of human rights reveals a far more complex relationship between the two.

GENERATIVE THEORY

I have argued so far that Bull's perspective on human rights was a product of his taxonomic mode of theorizing, but that human rights sit uncomfortably within his taxonomy. Instead of fitting neatly within Bull's architecture of categorical distinctions, human rights exist in interstices of these categories, ultimately eroding the dichotomies and trichotomies so central to Bull's theoretical framework. I now turn to a second limitation of Bull's taxonomy: its lack of, and inability to produce, a generative theory of international change. Not only is there no such theory in Bull's work, but his taxonomic reading of human rights impedes the development of such a theory. Closer attention to the nature and function of human rights would have revealed the limits of his taxonomy, as shown above, and suggested avenues toward a more dynamic theory.

This is most clearly apparent not in *The Anarchical Society* but in Bull and Watson's *Expansion of International Society*, a work centrally concerned with understanding international social change. Their purpose, the opening paragraph declares, 'is to explore the expansion of the international society of European states across the rest of the globe, and its transformation from a society fashioned in Europe and dominated by Europeans into the global international society of today, with its nearly two hundred states, the great majority of which are not European' (Bull and Watson 1984, 1). But while the book provides a narrative account of this transformation, along with a distinctive argument about the nature of the 'expansion', it contains no theory of international social change.

Daniel Nexon provides one, usefully encompassing, conception of such theory, arguing that it should identify prevailing social structural conditions, as well as the potential for change, and specify 'what kinds of choices made by agents, and what kinds of adjacent processes, are likely to activate those transformative dispositions and generate new structural arrangements' (2009, 23). While *The Expansion* contains various assumptions about change—like socialization was the principal mechanism for integrating non-Western peoples, and heightened cultural diversity undermines order—no such theory is evident. Instead, a conceptual apparatus is imported from prior writings of the English School, most notably Bull's taxonomic framework from *The Anarchical Society*, and then used to structure the interlinked historical narratives of the volume's contributors. The advantage of this approach is that it gives the book a robust conception of the globalizing social order: the society of sovereign states. The disadvantages, however, are twofold: the narrative is shackled by Bull's taxonomic architecture of dichotomous and trichotomous distinctions (leading contributors to see some things and not others), and there is no theoretical argument about the dynamics of expansion. The account presented in *The Expansion* is clear: a society of states first emerged in Europe, imperialism extended European power across the globe, and as decolonization freed non-European peoples from colonial rule, more and more states were admitted to norm-governed international society. In the end, though, this is a descriptive account: no theory of change undergirds it (see Dunne and Reus-Smit 2017).

Focusing on the politics of human rights, and how this destabilizes Bull's key categories, can aid in the development of such a theory, however. The crucial insight here is that human rights are not confined to a discrete sphere of human justice, isolated and distinct from the sphere of international justice, the realm of states' rights and duties. Rather, because the concept of human rights assumes a rights holder and a political authority, the politics of human rights—the claims made in their name, and the struggles these engender—constitute simultaneously individuals as particular kinds of moral and political agents and the locus and scope of legitimate political authority. Human rights are implicated in change at two levels, therefore: at the level of the individual, and at the level of structures and institutions of political authority.

Human rights are not static phenomena, though: they are dynamic in two senses. Before proceeding, let me shift the terminology to speak of 'individual' rights, not 'human' rights. Individual rights are the rights of sole persons, as opposed to groups or corporate bodies, and they commonly take two forms. Some individual rights are 'special', deriving from particular contracts, customs, or social roles: the rights one gains when signing a contract to purchase a house, for example. Other individual rights are 'general'. An individual holds them not by virtue of contract, custom, or position, but because they are a particular kind of moral being, a being with inherent qualities that the rights are meant to protect or enable. Human rights are the quintessential example of such rights. Individuals hold them not because they are enshrined in national or international laws: they are enshrined in laws because individuals hold them—because they are taken to be inherent and inalienable (Reus-Smit 2013a, 36–8).

The idea of a general individual right is inescapably dynamic, though. Precisely who, among all biological humans, constitute moral beings endowed with such rights has been deeply contested. We take it as axiomatic today that general rights are universal; that all biological humans are rights holders. Yet for most of the history of such rights the assumption has been the reverse: only some biological humans were thought to be the kinds of moral beings endowed with, or deserving of, general rights. Various criteria have been used to define who was inside or outside what Axel Honneth terms the 'zone of application': race, religion, civilization, class, property, and gender have all been invoked to fence off rights holders from subaltern others (1995, 113). These boundaries have proven inherently unstable, though. Any attempt to define who among all biological humans constitutes a moral being endowed with general rights is necessarily subjective, and thus open to challenge. What is more, because rights are legitimate social and political powers, their recognition and codification constitutes relations of superordination and subordination, domination and subjection. Those denied general rights have thus had powerful incentives to challenge established definitions of the rights-bearing human being, and to expand the prevailing zone of application. And this is the history of general individual rights: a history of repeated rights revolutions, in which those denied the requisite standing as qualified moral beings—members of denigrated faiths, non-Europeans, non-whites, unpropertied men, women, indigenous peoples—have struggled to expand the zone of application. It is only as a consequence of these struggles that the zone has come to encompass all biological humans—that general individual rights have become 'human' rights.

Human rights are dynamic in a second sense as well. All political orders distribute rights. Indeed, as configurations of political authority, one could argue that in essence they *are* distributions of rights: the rights of political authorities, and the rights of subjects or citizens, ordered in more or less hierarchical ways. Just as orders differ—some imperial, some sovereign, some heteronomous, etc.—so too do the regimes of rights that hold them together. Some regimes comprise special rights, with rights distributed according to custom, contract, or social position. The heteronomous order of medieval Europe is one example, resting on a regime of hierarchically ordered feudal rights. Europe's nineteenth-century territorial empires are another, where rights were hierarchically distributed between metropolitan citizens and peripheral subjects. Other regimes of rights comprise general rights, rights grounded in the nature of the individual as a particular kind of moral being. Over the past two centuries sovereign states have increasingly distributed rights on this basis, claiming as does the French *Declaration of the Rights of Man and of the Citizen*, that the purpose of all political orders is 'the preservation of the natural and imprescriptible rights of man'. Whether based on special or general rights, prevailing regimes of rights have a profound impact on the nature and scope of legitimate authority in a political order. Not only do they define the limits of such authority—how far it can encroach on the freedoms of the individual—but also the source of that authority (the sovereignty of the people) as well as its fundamental purposes (to preserve the 'rights of man').

Because political orders rest on regimes of rights, their stability depends, in significant measure, on the legitimacy of these regimes: their legitimacy overall, and the legitimacy of the distribution of rights within them. Historically, challenges to rights regimes have been important engines of political change, leading not only to the reconstitution of political authority within orders, but also the wholesale transformation of orders. Challenges that invoke new ideas of general individual rights in orders resting on regimes of special rights have been particularly transformative, as was the case in successive decolonization struggles, where universal rights were mobilized to challenge imperial hierarchies. The idea that individuals have 'natural, imprescriptible, and inalienable' rights, and that the preservation of these rights is the moral purpose of political authority, is fundamentally incompatible with distributions of rights based on custom, contract, or position. And where such rights have been successfully mobilized, orders frequently experience crises of legitimacy, demanding either heightened reliance on coercion and material inducements or the reconstitution of the order itself (Reus-Smit 2013a).

Thinking about human rights in this way offers three ingredients of a theory of international social change. First, it provides an account of the social structural nature of international orders, understood as configurations of political authority, structured by regimes of rights (special or general, equal or unequal), and dependent as much on legitimacy as material might. Second, it suggests an important dimension of potential change: instability generated by challenges to a prevailing regime of rights, or to particular allocations of rights within a regime. One step further, it points to a particularly potent challenge: that posed by new claims to general individual rights in orders based on regimes of special rights. Third, it identifies possible micro-foundations for a theory, agential qualities or dispositions that can, under given social conditions, instigate change. Because regimes of rights distribute legitimate social powers, they empower some and disempower others. Furthermore, the allocation of rights is an act of recognition. This is clearest with general individual rights, where their granting is recognition that certain individuals constitute worthy moral beings, and their denial is, for Honneth, the essence of disrespect (1995). The disempowerment and lack of recognition that frequently attends rights regimes can be a powerful motive for change, a motive accentuated by disjunctures between the legitimating discourses used to sustain regimes of rights, the lived experiences of the disempowered and disrespected, and availability of new ideas about social and political entitlements. These ingredients do not amount to a developed or systematic theory of international social change, but they indicate how an understanding of human rights that is freed from Bull's taxonomic framework might contribute to the development of such a theory.

RIGHTS AND SOVEREIGNTY

I have argued elsewhere that IR scholars think about human rights in a particular way (Reus-Smit 2013a, 1). They assume the existence of a system of states, produced through war-fighting and economic imperatives, and then ask whether the twentieth-century human rights regime has had any impact on the internal or external behaviour of states: whether it has civilized an order otherwise driven by the struggle for power and material gain. Some say yay, others nay, but this is how the debate is framed. Bull's position fits well within this frame, and as noted above, he was a sceptic. He held that order was possible among states, and attributed this to states' mutual recognition of their sovereign rights and responsibilities. But the forces that generated states in the first place, and the system of states in turn, were the conventional ones highlighted by realists: violent conflict and economic competition. Not only were human rights norms unlikely to alter these dynamics, Bull considered them a threat to the statist rights that undergird international order.

This way of thinking about rights is reflected in the silences of the literatures on the development of the international and the history of human rights. The former emphasizes war-fighting, the exigencies of the capitalist world economy, the institutional rationality of the sovereign state, even the epistemic revolutions associated with the rediscovery of single point perspective and cartographic representation, but individual rights are seldom mentioned, and then only as an analogue of sovereign rights. The latter traces the history of human rights as moral principles, their codification in national and international law, and their expression in transformative social movements, commonly citing anti-slavery as a crucial watershed. The role of rights in the development of the international system is largely ignored, despite their prominence in landmark events such as the American and French Revolutions. Readers are presented with two parallel histories, therefore: as though the politics of rights had nothing to do with the generative dynamics of the system of states.

In reality, however, the two have been deeply interconnected, and the ingredients of a theory of international social change outlined above help illuminate these connections. For five centuries the prevailing international order integrated sovereignty in the European (then Western) core and empire in the periphery. IR scholars write as though a system of sovereign states has been the enduring structural condition of international relations, but until the second half of the twentieth century, it was this hybrid order that provided the political architecture of world politics. And while the same scholars have focused on systemic change—change within the system of states (e.g. shifts in polarity)—they have neglected crucial processes of systems change: change from one order to another. Particularly over the past 200 years, the hybrid order gradually gave way to today's universal sovereign order, finally realizing what IR scholars assumed long existed. This constitutes one of the most profound transformations in the social structural conditions of international relations in world history, and many of today's most challenging political issues only make sense in the context of this transformation: debates over intervention, the rise of non-Western powers, the future of multilateralism, the sovereign equality of states, the integrity of Middle Eastern states, the list goes on.

This transformation unfolded through a series of great waves of imperial fragmentation into successor sovereign states: the collapse of the Spanish and Portuguese Empires at the beginning of the nineteenth century, the Austro-Hungarian and Ottoman Empires after the First World War, and Europe's remaining empires with post-1945 decolonization. In each case, individual empires suffered profound crises of legitimacy, and in the last, the institution of empire itself experienced a terminal crisis, never recovering as a legitimate form of rule. Focusing on these crises brings two things to the fore. First, it highlights the glue that holds any system of rule together—legitimacy, the perception that it is 'desirable, proper, appropriate within some socially constructed system of norms, values, beliefs, and definitions' (Suchman 1995, 574). Existing explanations, which emphasize imperial frailty, geopolitical rivalry, or socialization to the norms of a world polity or international society, neglect or obscure this factor. Second, it emphasizes the agency of subject peoples. Legitimacy is an inherently social phenomenon—auto-legitimation is impossible: legitimacy has to be recognized, granted, or ordained by others. In empires those 'others' are diverse, including the broader community of states, metropolitan citizenries, and, crucially, peripheral subjects. With each imperial crisis, a tipping point was reached where subject peoples shifted from seeking reform within empire—'Long live the king and death to bad government', in words of Spanish Americans at the dawn of the nineteenth century (Reus-Smit 2013a, 129)—to struggling for sovereign independence. A focus on legitimacy highlights this critical shift.

Imperial hierarchies are institutionalized in distinctive regimes of rights. These regimes are made up of special rights (rights associated with social position), and these rights are ordered hierarchically: the rights of imperial elites over imperial citizens and subjects, the rights of metropolitan citizens over peripheral subjects. The precise nature of these regimes varies from one empire to another, but some version is essential to the codification of social and political hierarchy, a defining quality of empire as an institutional form. All systems of rule require legitimation, and the principal legitimation challenge for empires is sustaining the legitimacy of these hierarchical regimes of rights. As noted above, historically the greatest danger to such legitimacy has come from new claims for the recognition and protection of general individual rights and the struggles these have animated. In holding that there are certain inalienable rights that all individuals have by virtue of their moral personhood, such claims challenge any attempt to distribute basic social and political rights according to social position. Particularly salient here have been claims to equal enfranchisement, political representation, and standing before the law.

Two examples illustrate this. The first is the crisis that beset the Spanish Empire after Napoleonic usurpation in 1808 (see Reus-Smit 2013a, ch. 4). After Napoleon installed his brother Joseph on the Spanish throne, insurgencies broke out across the empire, driven initially by the goal of reinstalling Ferdinand VII. In 1810, an insurgent 'Cortes' was called in Cadiz, charged principally with negotiating a new imperial constitution to be instituted once Napoleon was defeated. What transpired at Cadiz was critical to the empire's future. Throughout the eighteenth century there had been a series of revolts in the Americas against harsh economic and political reforms instituted by Spain's Bourbon monarchs. Yet in most cases these revolts were reformist, not revolutionary: they sought better imperial governance, not an end to empire. The Cortes of Cadiz was dominated by liberals, and again their impulses were reformist. This changed radically, however, when the Cortes considered the issue of political representation in a reformed empire. As liberals, the majority favoured the representation of individuals, not traditional corporate bodies or estates. The problem was that the peninsula Spaniards and the Americans could not agree on who, among all of those living within the empire, constituted individuals: moral beings worthy of the equal right to political representation. The former held that only those of Spanish blood qualified, whereas the latter insisted that Indians and freed slaves were also worthy. Extended acrimonious debate followed, ending with the defeat of the Americans and the 1812 Spanish Constitution that denied inhabitants of the colonies equal rights of political representation. This was a key factor in radicalizing the American insurgencies, which now turned from imperial reform to sovereign independence, the latter achieved through a decade of anti-colonial wars.

The second example is post-1945 decolonization (see Reus-Smit 2013a, ch. 5). Two things stand out about this period of imperial fragmentation: it was universal—all of Europe's remaining territorial empires disintegrated—and the institution of empire itself collapsed: the norms and discourses that licensed individual empires lost all moral currency. This universality, together with the demise of such a central and enduring institution, stemmed, in significant measure, from the struggles for the right to self-determination that took place in the human rights forums of the United Nations between 1945 and 1970. After the First World War this was a right of ethnically defined nations, and only those within Europe. Not only was this unhelpful for most colonial peoples, who were generally multi-ethnic and always non-European, it was discredited by Hitler's quest for a homogeneous greater Germany, a tragically perverse expression of an ethnic right to self-determination. After 1945, newly independent post-colonial states used the UN's human rights forums to redefine and resuscitate this right, grounding it this time on universal human rights. First they played a central role in the negotiation of both the *Universal Declaration on Human Rights* and the legally binding *Covenants on Civil and Political Rights and Economic, Social, and Cultural Rights*. Contrary to common misperceptions, these states argued consistently for the priority of civil and political rights, and worked with like-minded states to defeat Western efforts to limit the obligations of federal and imperial powers. Most importantly for our purposes, they grafted a new right to self-determination to emergent human rights norms, arguing not only that colonial rule was a fundamental violation of human rights, but that self-determination was an essential prerequisite for the enjoyment of other civil and political rights. It is difficult to find a clearer example of the entanglement, and mutual constitution, of individual rights and states rights: rights Bull separated into the realms international and human justice.

CONCLUSION

The central theme of this chapter is that Bull's perspective on human rights was structured by his taxonomic mode of theorizing, and that this shackled and blinkered his understanding of how human rights function in world politics. His taxonomic distinctions between international/world order, international/world society, international/human justice, and order/justice more generally provide the framework in which he reasons about human rights. Yet a closer look at the nature of human rights, and how they have figured in world politics, destabilizes his conceptual dichotomies: human rights straddle the domains of international and human justice, and the struggles for rights that have reconfigured international society have emanated from world society. More importantly, while Bull provides a taxonomy that enables us to carve up forms of order, society, and justice, he offers no theory of international social change.

Human rights were in this respect a missed opportunity, as greater attention to their nature as normative and political principles, as well as the impact of concrete historical struggles on transformations in international order, can contribute significantly to the development of such a theory. Yet for all of this, Bull's taxonomy has proven useful, perhaps inescapable. While trying to show the limits of Bull's taxonomic thinking, and how it crumbles when put under the pressure of human rights, I have nonetheless used it as a starting point. Like all sites of critique, it has worked as a structured launching pad. I may argue that human rights straddle the realms of human and international justice, and that world social forces penetrate and transform international society, but I use Bull's concepts to make these arguments.

6

Decolonizing *The Anarchical Society*

Mustapha Kamal Pasha

INTRODUCTION

Are claims for redistributive justice reconcilable with the demands for order? Central to Hedley Bull's prescient appreciation of intertwined, yet opposing, logics of order and justice, this question remains as significant today as it was forty years ago. Intrinsic to this question are issues of stability or flux, predictability or uncertainty, recognition of past wrongs or preservation of the international status quo—issues that direct inquiry into the substantive content of international relations, not merely their formal expressions. Despite the demise of the Third World (Berger 1994) with new articulations of global wealth and power, the inherent tension between the claims of the 'have-nots' and the fortune of the 'haves' of the contemporary international order refuse easy discharge. In the context of growing real or perceived disparities between different parts of the international system, the relation between 'order' and 'justice' involves the essential nature of international community that can either be forged or conceived. Bull may not have imagined the centrality of that relation in *The Anarchical Society*, especially in light of his subsidiary reflections on justice in contrast to a more elaborate discourse on order.

The question of justice provides a critical vantage-point to explore the silences and deferrals in the text. These silences and deferrals cast a long shadow on how international relations are perceived in *The Anarchical Society*, but especially divulge the limiting horizons afforded in strategies to domesticate the problem of difference, i.e. the differentiated nature of the international. This chapter explores the aporetic nature of this question against the horizon afforded by spectrality—the ghostlike presence/absence of justice in Bull's account of the international. Underscoring the inadequacy, yet indispensability, of Bull's treatment of justice in conjunction with order, the essay sketches out the lineaments of a decolonial perspective. The problem of justice in this alternative narrative occasions three interrelated components: (1) an acknowledgement of particular (exclusionary) historical settlements that have shaped the contemporary international order; (2) recognition of racially differentiated space (or 'coloniality') as a durable feature of past and present international order; and (3) exposure of some of the more potent effects of this differentiation on the capacity or power of (unequal) actors (sovereign states in Bull's formulation) in the international system.

An acknowledgement of past historical settlements denaturalizes the contemporary international order. It does not merely contextualize it, but helps place into sharp relief the difficulty of fulfilling the promise of decolonization within spatio-temporal horizons set hegemonically. Thus, the relative success or failures of 'weaker' sovereign states can be evaluated less by reference to domestic capacity than the burden of their respective (colonial) history. This perspective does not warrant alibis for domestic malfeasance, but places into context historically produced structural impediments to functionality and state effectiveness. Attention to these impediments also affords better appreciation of the impossibility of disentangling 'inside' from 'outside,' the 'domestic' from the 'international.' Post-colonial state capacity lies at the interstices of both.

In the second instance, notwithstanding the illusion of plurality in international space, hierarchy and (racial) differentiation capture the substantive character of the international. These features (hierarchy and differentiation) may not be readily apparent in the post-colonial universe of independent nation-states, remaining largely peripheral in received liberal stories of modernization, in accounts of the 'civilizing process', as well as in notions of citizenship and immigration, or ideals that inform the idea of 'international community' itself. Insiders and outsiders have neither disappeared nor metamorphosed into cosmopolitan subjects with decolonization. International relations are trapped not only within borders, but embodied. Racial and culture markers condition relations amongst states, but especially amongst peoples and populations within and across borders.

An obvious repercussion of the above is that states and subjects/citizens are neither culturally neutral actors nor mere abstractions. International relations are zones of racial and cultural encounters, often fraught with judgements of otherness. Neither a 'clash of civilizations' nor a 'fusion of horizons' condenses the complexity of encounters. Differentiation and hierarchy channel relations in determinate pathways: prejudice, prejudgement, and stereotype. Differentiation is deeply political, a process to include or exclude, to empower or disempower. Alongside hierarchy, differentiation challenges the flat liberal horizon of pluralism.

Bull has no truck with racial or any other cultural form of differentiation. He fully acknowledges the unequal nature of the international system based on asymmetrical distributions of power and wealth. However, he is unwilling to recognize coloniality as the historical foundation of international order and its contemporary relevance to the consolidation and expansion of international society. Bull can only authorize a partial recognition of Third World demands, captured in the clichéd language of justice. Specifically, he remains uninterested in the coercive inclusion of former colonies into the network of rules and institutions as part of the formation of international society. The process of incorporation appears benign for Bull, betraying few scars of colonial violence in its varied permutations. Marked by racial differentiation and hierarchy/subordination, the process congeals on an alternate register; that of coloniality—a concept that gestures towards the continued and durable effects of colonialism, outliving its formal historical instantiation. The problem of redistributive justice is linked to coloniality, underscoring the exclusionary character of the world order. Hence, attempts to reconcile justice with order without probing the initial terms of exclusion can only be largely a futile exercise. The expansion of international society is likely to enhance order, not justice; the spectre of justice continues to haunt the international order, threatening the stability of international society.

The question of European colonialism is inseparable from the constitution of international order. As W.E.B Du Bois forcefully put it: 'With nearly every great European empire today walks its dark colonial shadow...One might indeed read the riddle of Europe by making its present plight a matter of shadows, speculating on what might happen if Europe become suddenly shadowless' (Du Bois 1925, 385). The language of coloniality implied in these remarks suggests two separate, if linked, historical trajectories: the emergence of European self-identity as a sphere of civilized society (or society of sovereign states) against the backdrop of the age of discovery, including the consolidation of the idea of sovereignty in the process of colonization itself (Anghie 2004); and the colonial roots of the contemporary international order as a consequence of the processes of colonization and decolonization. Whilst both trajectories encompass elements of coloniality, its usage in this essay stresses racial hierarchy and differentiation as defining features of the international order. The positionality of the ex-colonial world in that order is, therefore, not merely defined by asymmetrical vectors of wealth and power, but by the stubbornness of assumed markers of 'civilization' both as process and condition of being. Despite the changing coordinates of 'centres' and 'peripheries', international society to the ex-colonial world is largely an exclusionary zone, more as an aspiration of arrival than an accomplished fact of decolonization. Bull's placement of 'Third World demands' on the periphery of the international order is a concession that simply hides bigger worries about the civilizing divide that characterizes international society. Despite the 'pluralist' nature of the international system, for Bull (as well as for others in the English School), an *international society of difference* is a contradiction in terms; international society is essentially a Europeanized society, personifying particular (cultural) values. Differentiation, hence, is a major hurdle to full membership in international society. The strategy of subsuming difference into sameness in favour of order exacerbates injustice.

A principal effect of the ordering logic of justice and order is that justice cannot be prioritized without calling into question order. Bull's privileging of order over justice is not only contingent upon the uncertain mood that followed decolonization, but a necessary feature of the international society he envisions. This component occupies a prominent place in *The Anarchical Society*, and spills over, although with more determinate answers in *The Expansion of International Society* (Bull and Watson 1984). Exposing international order to historical scrutiny would reveal its illegitimacy. On the obverse side, the legitimacy of international society depends upon how successfully demands of redistributive justice can be incorporated. These conundrums underscore the point that *differentiated* space is an enduring feature of (colonial) international space. The pluralist character of the society of sovereign states simply disguises this basic fact. In the final analysis, Bull is unable to reconcile the irreconcilable: order and justice. His rationale takes the engagement with justice as 'excursions' undertaken 'only because they are essential to the treatment of order' (1977, xiii).

PROBLEMATIZING JUSTICE

Bull's reasoning for prioritizing order above justice takes as its point of departure an a priori commitment to the sustenance of society itself:

> It is true that justice, in any of its forms, is realisable only in a context of order; it is only if there is a pattern of social activity in which elementary or primary goals of social life are in some degree provided for, that advanced or secondary goals can be secured. (1977, 86)

Relying on an Aristotelian formulation, Bull equates justice either with 'right conduct or virtue in general' (1977, 79) but especially a particular kind of right conduct, viz. conduct in which persons are treated fairly, or even given the rights and benefits that are due to them. Justice presupposes treatment based on rules that are fair, neither arbitrary nor non-discriminatory; and rules are deployed with fairness and impartiality. Again, drawn from Aristotle, Bull distinguishes between *arithmetical* justice which necessitates equality of rights or benefits, and *proportionate* justice which privileges distribution of rights and benefits over equality to rectify societal imbalances (1977, 80). Bull's overall strategy is to offer a minimalist framework for problematizing justice. Yet, even this modest aim recedes in the context of the international. His intentions are not in question, since it is order that principally interests him. The main issue is how the relegation of justice to order impairs Bull's vision of international society. To anticipate the point, an international society of difference cannot be conceived with a preferential focus on order.

Bull is fully aware of the unequal and differential make-up of the international system. 'Because states are grossly unequal in power,' he reasons, 'certain international issues are as a consequence settled, the demands of certain states (weak ones) can in practice be left out of account, the demands of certain other states (strong ones) recognised to be the only ones relevant to the issue in hand' (1977, 206). His rationale confirms his Realist propensities when it comes to the question of order: 'The inequality of states in terms of power has the effect, in other words, of simplifying the pattern of international relations, of ensuring that the say of some states will prevail while that of others will go under, that certain conflicts will form the essential theme of international politics while others will be submerged' (1977, 206). However, Bull is not a simple-minded Realist, but someone equally committed to liberalism. In several instances in *The Anarchical Society*, he shows his preference for individuals above states. This preference is quite consistent with his general misgiving about unfettered national sovereignty. Ultimately, it is the quantum of individual benefit that serves the promise of liberal society:

> What is more important than economic justice among nations, is economic and social justice among individuals, whether this is conceived in terms of equality of benefits among all human beings, or in terms of a minimum level of such benefits, that is the global elimination of poverty and social deprivation. Achievement of this goal depends not merely on the transfer of resources to poor countries, but also on the just distribution of these resources or the benefits accruing from them among the citizens of these countries. (1977, 290)

Bull is amply aware that the question of justice is linked to 'a radical redistribution of the world's wealth' (1977, 316), a formulation that suggests his recognition of the potentially destabilizing nature of post-colonial distempers, but he also recognizes the imprudence of ignoring them. The issue of justice raises 'profound questions' about international order and conduct in international relations. 'Ideas of justice' that undergird Third World demands for change in the international order are important. He is interested in the compatibility of those ideas with Western understandings of order. In a prescriptive mode, Bull is also eager to know which desirable conceptions of justice ought to be promoted. Bull is cognizant of the multiple registers on which Third World demands for justice materialize: the question of equal rights of sovereignty or independence; just or equal application of the principle of national self-determination; racial justice; economic justice; and the right of cultural liberation. The riddle is how Bull's awareness of these registers slips into the background in efforts to sustain the international society he envisions. Again, it is the kind of international society Bull pictures that is unsuited to recognizing difference. His misgivings are not unhinged from the wider complex of Western IR in which difference remains a nagging problem, both of recognition and co-evalness (on co-evalness see Fabian 1983).

Third World demands are not divorced from contradictions. The basic contradiction is between sovereignty and international obligation. Bull finds it paradoxical that 'the demand for global central direction', which entails international obligation, 'comes exclusively from the Western countries, and that the countries of the Third World and of the Socialist Commonwealth are vehement defenders of state sovereignty' (1977, 304). For Third World countries, however, 'a move towards greater centralization of power now [promised by sovereignty] would be likely to result not in a redistribution of wealth, resources and power favourable to themselves, but in a consolidation of its present distribution' (1977, 304). Key to Bull's apprehension is the potential tension between national sovereignty that is aggressively promoted by postcolonial states and the requirements of international society. The latter inevitably involve not only compromise and cooperation, but acceptance of extant (Europeanized) rules and norms established *before* decolonization, power arrangements realized in the concert of 'great powers' in earlier and contemporary settings, and modes of conduct that imbibe a 'standard of civilization'. Bull's anxieties relate to the disturbance Third World demands could possibly cause. Hence, it is an international society of sameness, not of difference, that preoccupies Bull.

Bull's international society of sameness is pluralistic: elements of sociability arise from the state-system. His Realist streak dispels any romantic illusions of a one-world cosmopolitanism. In essence, it is *cultural* affinity that constitutes international society, the hegemony of Western habits of thought and practice, sufficiently internalized by nation-states to behave as if same. The liberal streak in Bull is resistant to embracing the darker proclivities of Hobbesian suspicion about human nature and its stubborn features. The international society of states, therefore, serves as a bridging institution to resolve the mutual exclusivity of anarchy and injustice. Bull is neither apologetic nor hubristic in defending the states system, and especially that element in it that goes by the name of international society. A pragmatist, he does not see much vitality in alternative framings. Rather, other arrangements could potentially deprive diverse communities of cultural and political autonomy, on the one hand, or paralyse the possibility of pacific international relations, on the other. Yet, this is a thin pluralism, nominal and wholly resistant to radical difference. On a decolonial reading, Bull's international society fulfils the evolutionary promise of European civilizing institutions, norms, and practices.

Whilst recognizing the above constraints, Bull is a careful thinker disinclined to settle on easy markers of radical cultural divergence unlike civilizational warriors of Samuel Huntington's vintage. For Bull, there is greater affinity amongst seemingly rival understandings of the world than is commonly appreciated. Third World demands for justice, for instance, do not operate in a relativist universe. Bull sees considerable affinity between those demands and Western ideas of justice. Notions of international law, national self-determination, human rights, and cultural independence all had their roots in Western thinking. Whilst the original formulation of these demands reflected the subaltern status of Third World nations in the international order during the colonial period, the post-colonial language of these demands to Bull's dismay, however, suggests a growing divergence between the two perspectives.

Bull notices differences between an absolutist interpretation of sovereignty by Third World states and the Western conception of sovereignty tempered by obligations to the international community. Bull detects inconsistency in the Third World's stance over the question of sovereignty. These states make claims on Western powers for distributive justice, but they do so in the name of international obligation. Stressing the difficulty of reconciling the idea of an international society with claims of distributive justice, political judgement must lean in the direction of international society to avert its potential erosion with limitless claims. Apparently, Bull seeks an international society of sameness; Third World demands present a radical alternative. In time, however, international obligation would eventually construct pathways towards a more potent solidarism, reflected in Bull's later thinking.

In a similar vein, Bull finds irreconcilability between the idea of Third World national liberation, usually taking the form of socialist reconstruction and self-determination as prevalent in the West, which is attached to democratic principles. Bull appears troubled by the presence of violence and disorder in the 'liberation of the African and Asian peoples from European empires' (1977, 95). However, he displays remarkable historical reflexivity in discovering strong parallels in the experience of Western nations and Third World national liberation. Often, though, the Third World experience has been inspired by the attainment of freedom and its legacy in the West. His principal complaint is not in liberation movements themselves but their aftermath, which for Bull is quite disappointing.

The Conclusion to *The Anarchical Society* recognizes the paradoxical nature of the order/justice nexus. On the one hand, 'order in world politics conflicts with goals of justice—international, human and cosmopolitan'. On the other hand, 'while there is a sense in which order is prior to justice, it does not follow from this that goals of order are to be given priority over goals of justice in any particular case...a study of order in world politics, such as the present one, needs to be complemented by a study of justice' (1977, 319). Bull is aware that his treatise does not fully address the question of justice in sufficient depth. This concession essentially disguises the deeper problems with the notion of order itself.

SPECTRALITY AND THE DECOLONIAL GAZE

In a provocative Derridean reading of *The Anarchical Society*, Jenny Edkins and Maja Zehfuss find the idea of deferral 'crucial to Bull's treatment of order' (2005, 458). The sequence of the argument itself betrays a latent hierarchy with considerations of order not only preceding those of justice, but the preponderant attention devoted to order. As Edkins and Zehfuss suggest, 'the postponement of the consideration of justice is not innocent, but provides the ground for an analysis that prioritises order' (2005, 458)—*'justice is a supplement to order'* (2005, 460; emphasis in original). This is how deferral works:

> [A]uthors invariably exclude or defer for later consideration aspects of the issue under consideration that they see as marginal...these deferrals turn out to be central to the argument. In other words...[T]he 'main' argument is always already under threat from that which is excluded as insignificant. This means that our reading is not concerned with what Bull wants to say but with the implications of what he does say. Highlighting what is dismissed as unimportant is a rhetorical move that makes it possible to politically intervene in the discourse; it takes its cue from within the discourse but shifts the perspective. (2005, 456)

A key inference of deferral is depoliticization: 'when Bull excludes contestation over the basic goals of society and defers the consideration of justice to concentrate on order, he is defining away politics' (2005, 461). Two principal aspects of depoliticization are immediately visible. First, the relegation of justice in favour of order pushes post-colonial remonstrations for a more equitable international order to the margins. From the positionality of hegemony, any demand is likely to appear as disruptive of the natural state of affairs. However, more crucially, depoliticization implies a condition in which order becomes detached from history: how it came into being and at what human cost. To be sure, detachment from history in Bull is a necessary feature of Bull's static treatment of order. This entails two concomitant complications regarding order: (1) Bull's deferral of justice depoliticizes because he desists the challenge by justice; and (2) his ahistorical treatment of order silences discussion of the unjust origins of the current order. Ultimately, it is the 'trade-off' between order and justice that interests Bull (1977, 319), not order per se. Against the background of the Cold War and decolonization, excessive concern for justice can corrode the fragile international order (1977, 318–19). Notwithstanding Bull's immediate concerns, his analysis produces an aporia for balancing order and justice, with the only option for escape resting upon sacrificing justice.

Sidestepping deferral, this chapter frames Bull's engagement with the twin problem of order and justice around the notion of spectrality which allows, perhaps, a more concentrated interpretation of his (post-)colonial predicament. Deferral operates strictly with abstract universals without establishing analytical bridges with the concrete. Working with spectrality means to recognize the living presence of the dead, but also the difficulty of exorcising the past without releasing its effects on the present. In Bull's case, it is the haunting presence/absence of coloniality (embedded in his concerns for redistributive justice) that is simultaneously repudiated and embraced. Bull cannot explicitly take coloniality on board without undermining his understanding of both 'order' and 'justice'. On the other hand, he cannot easily repudiate the alterity of Third World demands appearing under the sign of 'justice'. 'Spectrality', as Jameson proposes, 'does not involve the conviction that ghosts exist or that the past (and maybe even the future they offer to prophesy) is still very much alive and at work, within the living present.' According to Jameson, 'all it [spectrality] says, if it can be thought to speak, is that the living present is scarcely as self-sufficient as it claims to be: that we would do well not to count on density and solidity, which might under exceptional circumstances betray us' (Jameson 1999: 39).

From a decolonial perspective, order may itself be a violent settlement based on injustice. The division of the world, for instance, between wealth and destitution, or between the powerful and powerless is the consequence of historical processes involving dispossession, forced labour, and enslavement of the many by the few. Any status quo disguises its prehistory. Yet, considerations of coloniality are susceptible to erasure or silencing. Seen as anachronistic or an irrelevance to theory-construction in International Relations, coloniality rarely presents itself as a problem, an unresolved, unsettled question. Ironically, the English School as an intellectual pursuit is inconceivable without tacit or explicit engagement with the ramifications of decolonization (Callahan 2004). Specifically, decolonization ushers in new challenges to international society: how to 'socialize' ('civilize') new states into Europeanized norms and institutions (Gong 1984). The problem is compounded by postcolonial resistance to an international society that has been historically structured around colonial dispensation of thought and deed. Without entertaining heterodoxy, international society can appear simply as an extension of the European civilizing project (cf. Hall 2002). However, in its mature iterations, the School appears less inclined to advertise its basic commitment to that project as its defining feature, settling instead on endless scuffles between pluralist and solidarist tendencies and their respective potential within international society (Dunne 1998b).

A decolonial perspective on both international order and international society will yield a different narrative. Both international order and international society are inextricably conditioned by coloniality, not only in their respective formation but contemporary functioning. Extending Quijano's concept of the 'coloniality of power', racial and cultural hierarchy is a 'fundamental' axis of that order. 'The racial axis has a colonial origin and character, but it has proven to be more durable and stable than the colonialism in whose matrix it was established' (2000, 533). For Quijano, the racial axis is the product of two historical processes: 'codification of differences in the idea of race, a supposedly different biological structure that places some in a natural situation of inferiority to others. The other process was the constitution of a new structure of control of labor' (2000, 533). To reiterate, Bull avoids the language of race, culture, or civilization altogether in his

Decolonizing The Anarchical Society

magnum opus, but this does not dispel his anxieties about the potential decline of international society with decolonization, especially the problem of incorporating former colonies into international society. Implicit to his thinking is the uneven presence of 'civilizing' elements for right international conduct. Bull's intellectual progenies appear to be less restrained in promoting the 'standard of civilization' as an obvious prerequisite of membership in international society (Buzan 2014). On Quijano's reading, 'the incorporation of such diverse and heterogeneous cultural histories into a single world dominated by Europe signified a cultural and intellectual intersubjective configuration' (2000, 540).

The idea of the colonial construction of the present takes inquiry into different directions pertaining to the genealogy, structure, and functioning of the international order. It refutes the fiction of self-enclosed European processes as the driving logic of modernity (Pagden 1998). On a decolonial reading, it is no longer possible to see modernity in provincial terms, either the flowering of Western Reason, the endogenous rise of capitalism inspired by particular (Protestant) religious settlements, or the expulsion of violence or its taming with 'civilizing processes'. Modernity takes on a *global* character with the expansion of the international not merely as the consequence of post-Westphalian diffusion of rationalities, structures, institutions, and norms from the West to the non-West, but the inscription of coloniality at the centre of order. Despite mutations in that order with the rise and decline of particular Western powers, wars, and decolonization, its differentiated character presents an alternative picture. The defining element of differentiation is racial hierarchy, confronted frontally at Bandung by colonials or ex-colonials. One of the pioneering post-colonial gatherings of new post-colonial states from Asia and Africa, the Bandung Conference in 1955 underscored the living legacy of colonialism, congealed in the dangerous nuclear politics of the Cold War and the unequal structure of the global political economy. The 'Bandung Impulse' (Pasha 2013) continues to reverberate in International Relations, less as a nostalgic moment of 'Third World solidarity' and more as a cipher of persistent racial hierarchy and differentiation. Despite the promise of formal equality enshrined in Westphalian sovereignty, the 'colour line' remains a durable feature of cognition and practice in world politics.

Bull is fully aware of the colonial inheritance of order, but he elects to construct the theoretical architecture of *The Anarchical Society* without archaeological sensibility. The language of justice Bull deploys is quite deliberate. It simultaneously gestures towards history and its erasure. Third World demands carry no scars of coloniality, only resentment as Wight explicitly articulated (Wight 1956). The making of international order predictably follows an Anglo-American pathway, virtually disconnected from the history of empires, colonial entanglements, and the investiture of power in the Centre afforded by colonial adventures in the Periphery. Decolonization arrives miraculously, giving massive annoyance to the consolidation of international society.

Spectrality suggests otherwise. The absence of the dead offers few guarantees that they can be banished from the living. Displaced or sublimated, the dead cast a long shadow on those who imagine that they have no past competitors. Comforted by the certainties of the present, the unsettled past tends to surprise. It is the ghost of colonialism that serves as the Other in *The Anarchical Society*. Bull is fully cognizant of the perils of disclosure. The Third World can potentially metamorphose into something more menacing. However, his acute sense of the pragmatic also suggests that Western norms and practices have travelled far enough and entered non-Western consciousness in ample measure to domesticate anger and resentment. The wellsprings of anti-Westernism do not run as deep for Bull as his fellow travellers imagined. The 'revolt against the West' Bull would return to in his subsequent work is already anticipated in *The Anarchical Society*, but the revolt is necessarily too infirm to change the order of things.

The Anarchical Society is not a self-conscious historical text, but it congeals, first and foremost, a crucial historical moment that functions as a spectre for Hedley Bull's ruminations on world order. To reiterate, it is the spectre of colonialism, or more precisely, its formal demise and aftermath that haunts the text. The spectral effects of that historical moment (decolonization) are neither self-evident nor adequately spelled out in what has arguably become one of the sacred texts in the English School liturgy. Displaced across the entire textual field, the anxieties and uncertainties of a yet-to-become postcolonial order direct Bull's ambivalent and often contradictory pronouncements on the nexus between order and justice. What would later transpire as a 'revolt against the West' is already anticipated, troubling international society or what can be without much imaginative licence read as a Western-inspired 'order' for the conduct of international relations. Claims of justice attached to the presumed revolt must be compromised for Bull to sustain order, and one of its principal elements, international society.

It is no secret to Bull or his readers that international society is a *particular* form of sociability, neither a fusion of rival horizons nor the reconciliation of difference. The mainstay of this form is the consolidation of European-inspired civilizing processes that rest upon the pacification of violence, secular settlements curtailing the power of religion (without depleting religious sensibilities in the expanses of ethics and righteous conduct), individuation and the celebration of a rights-bearing liberal subject, and respect for the sanctity, not only of life, but property. Bull's conflation of fact and value is a necessary mechanism to surreptitiously endorse particular (liberal) values. In this case, he shares the ethos of nearly all Western IR scholars despite factional disputations over the nature of the international.

With decolonization, Bull's confidence in sustaining the normative structure of Western sociability is shaken, not stirred. The West can no longer authorize imperial arrangements, but it can still carry the expectation that only its version of sociability can triumph worldwide despite decolonization. Prioritizing order above claims of ex-colonials for redistributive justice can also create conduits for stabilizing international society. Decolonization and international society can coexist. Unlike Bull's musings on this troubled coexistence in his later writings, in which the expansion of the post-colonial world is potentially deleterious to the expansion of international society, *The Anarchical Society* harbours no such fears. There are no Third World dragons to slay; the incorporation of post-colonial states into international society or their embrace of the normative structure of the West, reflected in the (universal) value of security against violence, and the (bourgeois) values for the observance of contracts and the sanctity of property, would guarantee both the substance of order and the stability of international society. The passage of the colonial into the post-colonial world need not be fraught with unknown unknowns. Yet, Bull also laments that the 'area of consensus has shrunk' due to, among other factors, the 'revolt of non-European peoples and states against Western dominance' (1977, 258). This poses new problems since 'the system of international law that derives principally from European experience has been challenged by non-European states, especially the new states of Asia and Africa, as having been built upon the special interests of European powers, and designed to serve as an instrument of their domination' (1977, 259). Bull clearly recognizes the instrumental nature of European-inspired international law, a key plank of his international society.

It becomes obvious upon closer scrutiny that it is difficult for Bull to harmonize his critique of Third World sovereignty with his pluralist sensibilities. He cannot embrace pluralism, on the one hand, and simultaneously reject the Third World's need for autonomy, on the other. In a solidarist universe, a reconciliation between pluralism and sovereignty would be moot: sovereignty would be subordinated to cosmopolitanism. However, this pathway is not Bull's preference in *The Anarchical Society*. What prevents him from letting the logic of Third World demands play out is his apprehension that they could potentially undermine international society. Bull does not spell out the source of this anxiety, but a possible answer lies in the spectre of colonialism and the (unjust) order it has helped spawn. Yielding to Third World demands would be tantamount to releasing old demons with the questioning of the legitimacy of the international order itself. Built around the logic of coloniality, the order would reveal not merely fractured space, but *differentiated* international space.

International society has enough difficulty dealing with fractured space. The fractured character of the international is implicit in the notion of pluralism. However, it is considerably more onerous to build and consolidate an international society of racial and cultural difference. Bull is not very enthusiastic about alternative paths to world order. A *substantive* acknowledgement of racial and cultural differentiation and hierarchy of the international would only undermine international society. Only a *formal* acknowledgement of difference could allow the stabilization of international society: a society of states, an anarchical society. Although differentiation and hierarchy are historical products, not instantiations of a natural order, it is prudent not to lift the veil and disclose how international order and international society came about. Historical amnesia, instead, offers a more reliable route to establishing international society. Bull is mindful of the ambivalent uses of the past, including Third World states. Despite 'the illegitimacy of colonial sovereignty', post-colonial states have sought legitimation of their claims for sovereign control over their own resources and the 'desirability of transferring wealth from rich to poor states'... 'against the background of acceptance by the new states of the basic structure and tenets of the system' (1977, 259). The veil of ignorance applies more broadly than merely the Western world. Yet, Third World demands pose a special challenge to international society.

A contradiction lies at the heart of *The Anarchical Society*: recognition of Third World demands without a substantive endorsement of any discernible solution to alter the nature of the international order. Bull is insistent that:

> No consensus is possible today that does not take account of the demands of Asian, African and Latin American countries and peoples for just change in respect of the elimination of colonialism and white supremacist governments, the redistribution of wealth and resources, and the ending of relationship of dependence or subordination in which most of them stand to the rich countries. (1977, 300)

A similar sentiment is expressed only a few pages later: 'international order at the present time has to be built upon a strengthening of consensus within the society of states, and that this is unlikely to be achieved without a radical redistribution of resources and power in favour of the weak and poor states of the Third World which constitute a majority of states and of the world's population' (1977, 314). He is even willing to concede that 'the nascent cosmopolitan culture of today... may need to absorb non-Western elements to a much greater degree if it is to be genuinely universal and provide a foundation for a universal international society' (1977, 317). Bull is aware of the fragility of any order 'founded upon the great powers alone' (1977, 315). Yet, the needs of order must always subordinate the claims of redistributive justice. Third World demands cannot be readily accepted without jeopardizing international society.

Like his mentor, Martin Wight, Bull also appears to imbibe misapprehensions regarding post-colonial distempers. Although Bull does not share Wight's religious penchant, a post-Bandung sense of melancholy equally colours his judgement. For Martin Wight:

> The Axis powers were driven by resentment of the territorial empires and deep-rooted stable cultures of France, Britain, and America. The Bandung powers are moved correspondingly by the contrast between their poverty and our

wealth... At its best this is expressed in the demand for equality, and clothes itself in Wilsonian language of natural rights, liberty, and self-determination. But it would be an error to suppose that this language means the same to those whose historical experience and religious premises are totally different from ours as it does to us. Hitler, too, employed it with consummate effect.

(Wight 1956, 249–50)

Bull's main worry is that post-colonial distempers, expressed notably by leading scholars such as Ali Mazrui (1967), are of greater salience than the Third World's instrumental use of the rhetoric of sovereignty. Implicit in Bull's thinking is the real worry that Western societal norms have not been fully incorporated into the ethos of post-colonial international practice. The wider context of extant Western anxieties is the intuition that the spectre of colonialism transmutes as a degraded philosophy of history. In its original formulation, this philosophy presupposes not merely belief in progress but the conviction that the march of time is never detached from European tutelage. What happens when the barbarians at the gates either wish to reject pedagogical dependence or elect to construct alternative spatio-temporal horizons? Liberated from colonial entrapment, both as physical confinement and mental incarceration, received rules may not appear so attractive. Cognizant of peripheral rage, Bull wishes to tame it. Hall (2011) captures the mood of several British intellectuals of Wight's times (including Bull, who broadly shared the Anglo perspective on the world, although from a different—Australian—positionality):

For Carrington and Barraclough, Wight and even sometimes Bull, decolonisation seemed to be eroding the foundations of international order, civilised relations between states, and, above all, the fragile consensus that Europeans had established about what was just and ethical and what was not. The 'revolt against the West' brought into question, in other words, almost all of their inherited traditions of knowledge about world politics and required their reinterpretation.

(2011, 59)

In sum, Bull's solution to a resolution of claims of order and justice is neither theoretically sustainable nor practical. Without an adequate appreciation of the genesis of the claims of justice ensuing from the post-colonial world or the foundations of order itself, the valiant exercise can just be a form of liberal gesturing which rests on a disciplined avoidance of the repressed. To be certain, post-colonial demands for either greater sovereignty or resource distribution are not purely rhetorical. These demands stress absence of what is offered in liberal discourses of freedom and development. The unequal distribution of power that Bull freely acknowledges places the post-colonial states in a condition of vulnerability. During the height of the Cold War, the regions of the Third World were transformed into zones of ideological testing. The experience of colonialism for colonial populations was principally one of violence, dispossession, and dehumanization. Entry into international society was, therefore, not merely a passage into civility, instantiated by a civilizing process, but a ratification of a possible end to sustained brutality. Sovereignty offered a provisional suspension of violence, but especially the dehumanizing regime of coloniality.

The expressed demand for distribution worrying Bull presents a cognate narrative of injustices produced by colonialism. Bull is obviously unaware in *The Anarchical Society* of major Third World intellectual currents (notably Dependency Theory) emphasizing the 'development of underdevelopment' or unequal exchange, but he is not entirely oblivious of the North–South divide. How can this demand be absorbed to prevent the erosion of international society?

A spectre, according to Derrida, 'is always a revenant. One cannot control its comings and goings because it begins by coming back' (Derrida 1994, 11). To stress, the ghost of coloniality is both present and absent in *The Anarchical Society*. It cannot be tamed by Bull nor by other protagonists of the English School. Bull neither favours empire nor wishes its return in other guises. A pluralist world, consistent with Bull's liberal impulses, is perhaps the best arrangement both to dispel the Manichean logic of bipolarity as well as to usher in support mechanisms of an international order potentially under threat with challenges to international society. The post-colonial world is a problem for Bull since it seeks something that is likely to diminish order. However, more wearisome for Bull is normative disobedience. Clearly, claims for redistributive justice exceed the zone of permissiveness.

Implicit in Bull's repudiation of post-colonial claims of justice and his privileging of order is a repressed commitment to Western norms as idealtypical universals. Collusion with these norms in the name of historical injustice could unleash unruly processes that could undermine a pluralist international society, but especially a solidarist formulation as a society to come. Bull does not entertain the possibility that universals can arise from alternate locations. Notions of justice, for instance, can only mirror Western understandings of this category. A prisoner of his times, Bull cannot be faulted for harbouring apprehensions attending decolonization, but especially its implications for sustaining the international order in a world torn by Cold War rivalries. He embodies particular worries that can only attend receding secularized theological commitments. Bull is, however, unable to either escape or transcend the spirit of his setting.

CONCLUSION

A decolonial reading of *The Anarchical Society* does not see Hedley Bull simply as a counterpoint to ahistorical theorizing enshrined in Structural

Realism that emanates from the hegemonic academic entrails of the United States. Bull repudiates the self-evident verities both of Classical Realism, with its deeply pessimistic renderings of the human and the world, and also the celebratory dream-world of liberal cosmopolitanism, yet he does not offer an alternative that would satisfy the post-colonial sceptic. Bull is squarely locatable within strictly Western coordinates. Self-referential, Western IR inhabits the arrogance and illusion of self-sufficiency. As master narrative, it serves and it must serve on this view as universal reference for claims of freedom, justice, equality, or rights worldwide. The non-Western provinces that the empire allows to endure as culture or nation must not entertain delusions of self-subsistent alterity. Otherness can only enter zones of acceptability as a copy of the original, the West as norm, the non-West as peculiarity. This stretches further: the West theorizes, the non-West experiences.

The principal decolonial protest against Bull is his wilful amnesia regarding the colonial roots of the international order he visualizes. *The Anarchical Society* builds a halfway house between an explicit appreciation of Third World demands for a just order and the erasure of their historicity. Over twenty years before the publication of Bull's magnum opus, the Bandung moment placed into plain view both the context and the rationale of post-colonial disobedience to colonial reason. The proponents of international society are well aware of Bandung and its message. The defining feature of colonial reason is the naturalization of racial difference and hierarchy.

A decolonial reading of *The Anarchical Society* does not advocate bypassing Bull's categories, principally those of 'order' and 'justice'. These categories, as well as others in the Western repertoire, can neither be circumvented nor overlooked. The principal task, it seems, is to interrogate their historical origins, deployment, and effects. To be certain, a story of origins cannot be conflated with the logic of these categories. Thought acquires a relatively autonomous character, seeking detachment from its genesis. The main issue is that any story of origins can also be a story of erasure, silencing, or selectivity. In Bull's case, both 'order' and 'justice' subsist in an ahistorical zone, an amnesiac zone. Once their ahistoricity is naturalized, Third World demands can only appear to be anomalous.

Similarly, Bull's deployment of these basic categories cannot don the attire of neutrality. Both 'order' and 'justice' have particular uses, designed to address particular problems confronting a world that is becoming increasingly post-colonial. Whilst the Cold War offers a modicum of predictability, especially under the intimidating canopy of nuclear deterrence, it is not obvious how the ex-colonial states will embrace a weakened (and weakening) European order. By defining 'order' and 'justice' in specific ways, ownership of certain unsavoury features of the Western past can be evaded. This is not to suggest either the necessity or desirability of expiation. The point is analytical.

Can Bull eliminate coloniality from his framework to interrogate Third World demands for a more equitable order?

The effects of historical erasure extend beyond *The Anarchical Society*. Tacitly agreed on particular genealogies and not others; deploying categories in specific ways without releasing them from the bondage of Eurocentrism; and taking the self-referential practice of theorization as norm, gives Western IR invincibility against critique. Other mappings of the international then appear as precisely that: as 'other' mappings. Setting up a permanent hierarchy between norm and exception, natural and abnormal, or universal and particular, IR theory can trudge along in its splendid isolation from the world it presumably endeavours to comprehend. The world, after all, is only what its field of vision permits.

To Bull's credit, the world is not a flat place. He is abundantly aware of diversity and division. It is the fractured nature of the international that guides his quest for international society. Despite his latent cosmopolitanism, however, it is the subterranean structure of Western supremacy that comes more naturally to Bull, even if he elects to be neither its apologist nor promoter. His intellectual honesty prevents him from suspending his critical faculties in the service of a new empire or imperium. The ethos of Western cultural supremacy appears to operate more unconsciously: in the field of hegemony associated with two centuries of European power, its distempers, and Bull's attempt to envision a more stable world in the aftermath of colonialism. It is the spectre of colonialism that directs his concerns, but a spectre evading capture. Both the strengths and weaknesses of *The Anarchical Society* on the nexus between 'order' and 'justice' become more intelligible by recognizing Bull's strategy of denial and coloniality's spectral agency.[1]

---

[1] I am grateful to Hidemi Suganami and Madeline Carr for inviting me to this project. Special thanks to Hidemi for helping me clarify the deployment of the language of 'coloniality' and excellent suggestions on all aspects of the argument. Thanks also to Adam Humphreys for providing important critical feedback. All errors are strictly mine.

Part III

The Anarchical Society and World Politics Forty Years on

7

The Anarchical Society and the Control of Global Violence

Robert Ayson

The control of violence in global affairs is not just one of the several marks of a functioning anarchical society. It is arguably the most essential one if the states comprising that society are to exist, and are to exist in at least tolerably minimal levels of society with each other. This does not mean that the control of *all* violence globally is a necessary condition for the anarchical society. But the deliberate avoidance of the most serious and catastrophic version of that violence is required. Without agreed restraint on the most devastating types of conflict, where one state (or group of states) might obliterate another, the notion of an international system of states (let alone a condition of society between them) itself comes adrift.

A logic of this sort can be noticed in Hedley Bull's work on the anarchical society. Rules about the use of violence in international relations, which were often informally agreed rather than formally instituted, were not just central to Bull's formulation. These were in many ways *the* quintessential ingredients. The quest for rules limiting the extent of violence inhabits each and every one of the five institutions which Bull identifies as component parts of that society (1977, 101–229). Rules on violence are certainly there, for example, in relations among the great powers (which are specifically charged with observing and nourishing them). They play central roles in the institutions of diplomacy and international law. The aim of restricting violence is undoubtedly a leading reason for the maintenance of the balance of power as a further institution of that society. Perhaps ironically, war itself is the fifth of these institutions. But by this, Bull does not mean war in all its untrammelled varieties, but war deliberately managed and regulated. In controlled form, war could be an instrument in the quest for international order.

It is difficult to think of any other condition (save perhaps the recognition of the existence of states itself) which plays such an important role in each one of these institutions. But rules to regulate global violence are not just vital for the practice of Bull's anarchical society in the mature form that he depicts it in 1977. They are also vital in the evolution of Bull's own approach to the study of international relations, reaching back at least as far as his first appointment in that subject at the London School of Economics in 1955. As the first part of this essay will show, the international problem of regulating violence provided the test-bed for Bull as he developed his ideas about the anarchical international society and the forms of international cooperation such a society required. Part of this story is the way that Bull used contemporary examples of efforts to regulate violence (and efforts to avoid any such rules) as illustrations of his evolving theory.

This sets the scene for the second part of this essay: an examination of the fitness of Bull's anarchical society for the international problems of violence that predominate today. It is unfair to expect that Bull would have anticipated these problems in any detail. But it is right to ask how well his ideas travel in a world where the Cold War has been over for a generation, and where questions about global violence by non-state as well as state actors are prominent. Of course the international problem of violence is not likely to be experienced similarly everywhere, and the receptivity of one part of the world to particular rules about violence can be expected to differ from the reaction elsewhere. Hence the third part of this essay will investigate the suitability of Bull's ideas about the control of violence between states in the context of the Asian region, where the distribution of global power, including military power, is increasingly concentrated. A little known fact is that Bull himself spent a good deal of his career considering the requirements for Asia's order. But even so, do his ideas about the control of violence in that conception of Asia's order, adjusted to a period where the relativities of power were quite different from today's, work as well now as they appear to have then?

VIOLENCE AND THE BUILDING OF BULL'S ANARCHICAL SOCIETY

While *The Anarchical Society* is appropriately treated as a work on international political theory, the fact that Bull had spent many of his earlier academic years focused on questions of international strategy is often overlooked. Addressing this deficit was a central motivation for this author's intellectual history (Ayson 2012). A crucial part of that task was to draw attention to Bull's first book, often overlooked by International Relations theorists, including scholars of the English School. *The Control of the Arms Race* (Bull 1961) previews some of the very ideas about international order which one finds in his later writing. Ostensibly based on the findings of conferences held by the newly established Institute for Strategic Studies, it was a study devoted to questions surrounding the regulation of violence in the nuclear age, an issue that its writer could only cover well if he was an expert in strategic affairs.

Quickly becoming a classic in the new genre of arms control studies, this first book establishes an argument that would become familiar to Bull's later readers. Formal rules could play a role in regulating the use of force in international politics, and especially those designed to reduce (or remove) the chances of catastrophic nuclear war. But more important were the informal understandings on the need for restraint, especially among the great powers, without which formal treaties could easily be an unimportant superstructure sitting upon a hollow base. Rejecting the logic of the disarmers who saw a world free of nuclear weapons as the only hope for security, a view he came to after studying the Geneva inter-war disarmament negotiations for Philip Noel-Baker, Bull (1959a) had come to see armaments as part of the infrastructure of international politics. In a system of sovereign states, each of which required armaments for the protection of their sovereign status, the question was not whether nuclear armaments could be abolished. It was whether they could be properly regulated in ways which were designed to produce common benefit.

Because of the nature of the states system, that regulation would not come from a central authority (there was no arbiter of that common interest), but from agreed action among its sovereign members. It meant limits being set on the future spread of the ownership of these weapons (a theme explored by Jan Ruzicka, Ch. 8 in this volume). But it went far beyond this. The crucial rule upon which international security now depended was not a limit on nuclear proliferation. It was instead a rule among the few great powers who already possessed nuclear weapons (and most notably the United States and the Soviet Union) that they must avoid major war between themselves, not least because of the immense cost that was guaranteed in a nuclear age.

This issue was so pressing to Bull that it became the central reference point for his argument that the expanded international system of the post-war (and Cold War) years might come to resemble an international society (1965a). If the superpowers could recognize the common interest they clearly had in the avoidance of major war between themselves, and could act to restrain themselves by observing this rule of the game, then there was some hope for that society. For Bull the agreements between the United States and the Soviet Union limiting nuclear testing were not guarantees of that society, but they could be signs of a deeper understanding (1965a). The restraint that society required need not be met through formal treaty. It could be achieved through tacit bilateral cooperation, and most easily through unilateral measures.

That restraint could also be seen in wider aspects of the Cold War's central relationship. The United States and the Soviet Union, Bull argued, had a common interest in avoiding the spread of nuclear weapons to other members of the states system (1965b). It was this quest for monopoly status that underlay so much of their behaviour towards their allies and their enthusiasm for the Nuclear Non-Proliferation Treaty. Judging that some other major states (including Britain, France, India, and even revolutionary China) might have a good case for their own arsenals, this sometimes made Bull uncertain about the merits of the treaty.

But an even more vexing question was how far that restraint applied to wars short of nuclear annihilation. Bull did not expect the superpowers suddenly to lose all interest in the use of force for political purposes. And yet because of the enormous destructive power of nuclear weapons Bull wondered if that old Clausewitzian formula was actually breaking down (1966b, 46). While never quite resolving this conundrum, he saw the major powers (and especially those who possessed nuclear armaments) as having special responsibilities for setting the standard about the use of force in international politics. If a wider international society was to be established, the great powers at its centre had a crucial role in this respect. Indeed a later jeremiad against the United States and the Soviet Union was aimed in particular at their failure to live up to these expectations in respect of their attitudes towards the use and threatened use of force in the later Cold War years (Bull, 1980). In other words the passage of time had done little to strengthen the embryonic stage of an anarchical nuclear society. Things in some ways were actually going backwards.

But all of these expectations about the control of violence in the nuclear age did not remake Bull into a prohibitionist when it came to armed force. He did not expect the great powers to be pacifists. Moreover, as he increasingly shifted his gaze to other participants in the international system of states, Bull saw in the actual use of armed violence in international politics at least two notable and not wholly unwelcome attributes. One was a sure sign of the capacity of minor powers to resist the domination of the stronger (Bull, 1979a), which presumably might extend the relevance of the balance of power as an international institution. The other, Bull argued (1979b) was the unfolding of the colonial world and the consequent entry into the international system of newly sovereign and independent states. At about the time his best known work was about to appear, the use of violence for political purposes was occurring mainly in the Third World and it is not hard to read into some of the writing Bull was producing on this specific question a fascination, and perhaps even a sense of delight, that this resistance was occurring (1976). At the very least it confirmed his view that no preponderance of power was everlasting.

But that also brought things back to the question of accommodation as preponderant powers recognized the challengers to their dominant positions. And if the successful accommodation of a small number of newly armed nuclear powers was one test of the new international society, then the West's necessary accommodation of Third World countries would be another. And here, for some of the reasons already mentioned, monkish notions about abstaining from violence had little place. Moreover the increasing agency of Third World countries was also a matter of justice, and in this case justice could sometimes outweigh the immediate requirement for order. As a pluralist, Bull saw these values as potentially competitive (1971a). Moreover, just as the quest for order could sometimes involve the resort to force (the European Concert, after all, had been preceded by the violent defeat of Napoleon's hegemonic ambitions) so too might the quest for justice. The role of armed violence and its tense relationship with notions of an anarchical society continued on here, but in different clothing.

At the same time Bull extended some of the very same expectations of responsible behaviour to these newer kids on the block. Those who took up violence, even in the name of a more equal international politics, had to take great care in living up to the standards of the emerging society of states. As this society was anarchical, its quality depended heavily on unilateral and voluntary restraint. The grandiose ambition and petulance that Bull sometimes detected amongst what he referred to as the Afro-Asian states was an enemy of the new standards of civilization that the new international society depended on (a subject treated in greater depth by Andrew Linklater, Ch. 17 in this volume). But that obligation was mutual. The great powers needed to be restrained in the violent interventions they embarked on. Again Bull did not seek a prohibition on armed intervention: he saw it as a tradition that waxed and waned. This was a practice that needed regulation rather than a complete ban, although Bull had observed, 'A world as diverse and divided as ours is more likely to be able to agree on the prohibition of intervention than on formulae for making it legitimate' (1971b, 34).

Force was not anathema to Bull's conception of an anarchical society, either in its general conception where the practices of the European great powers were a common reference point, or in efforts to identify elements of an emerging society in the second half of the twentieth century. Fulsome disarmament was like a transformation of the states system: something conceptually plausible but, for the time being, practically unworkable. Arms control, and the conscious management of organized violence around commonly accepted rules, was the better counterpart to the dispensation of international politics where the state reigned supreme. And even then, Bull could perfectly understand why individual states might wish to bend or break the emerging rules. For example when he got to Canberra in the late 1960s to take up a new chair at the Australian National University, he was quick to advise policymakers that Australia's security circumstances required it to have a clear military capacity to strike Indonesia. And a sharp deterioration in Australia's position might one day require Canberra to embark seriously on a nuclear weapons programme (Bull, 1968). So much, then, for a fulsome accommodation of the Third World.

THE CONTROL OF VIOLENCE TODAY

But in Bull's anarchical society there was no necessary incompatibility between having a capacity to use force against a potential adversary and needing to accommodate that country as an emerging or existing power. Indeed these two factors could be reinforcing: another country's growing military capacity was precisely one of the reasons that made accommodation necessary, and the deliberate fashioning of a stable balance of such power was so often an essential underpinning and sign of that accommodation. Yet having watched so closely the emergence of the superpower nuclear competition, Bull was also concerned that as balances of military power could arise as accidents of history, the great powers might mislead themselves to think that as things changed, they had no need to manage these balances consciously (1961).

That need for conscious management became very clear as he watched Asia's changing order from his new academic home in Australia. Bull was never slow in raising big questions about American power and policy, believing at one stage that after Vietnam, Washington would almost completely retreat from Asia (1971c). At the same time, his analysis did not suggest that the United States would be absent as a conscious and influential presence in the region's diplomatic evolution. There was a noticeable connection between Bull's arguments about the intelligent management of political understandings and the main act of US policy in that period. This was the remarkable, albeit limited, accommodation between Mao and Nixon which signalled Washington's acceptance of China's place as a great power and China's rejection of a more revolutionary (and violent) brand of international politics. Just as this was the main edifice for Asia's order over the last forty years (a point to which I will return in the next section, 'The Problem of Violence in Today's Asia'), it was the détente between the United States and the Soviet Union which allowed at least a temporary escape from the Cold War antagonism. And while many of those tensions returned, a trend which disappointed Bull in the last years of his all-too-brief life, the heavily armed superpowers were still able to avoid a catastrophic war between them. They had therefore held to that most basic common interest.

In the quarter century since the end of the Cold War, the absence of great power war has remained a fact of international politics. This has occurred despite the existence of significant differences of opinion. These have been most noticeable in recent years in the growth in the discord between the United States and Russia, including over the latter's annexation of Crimea as part of the struggle between Russia and Ukraine. Russia, China, and the United States have had very different views on the legitimacy of military interventions to address humanitarian crises in Syria and elsewhere and on the appropriate regulation of cyberspace, to cite but two areas of contestation (see Carr, Ch. 10 in this volume). But major power differences have not resulted in major power wars.

Before this achievement in regards to the control of violence can be considered as a sign of an imperfect but working anarchical society, some deeper factors need to be considered. The first is the common argument, exemplified by Zoellick, that one of the main reasons for the absence of great power conflict in more recent decades is the involvement of all of the great powers in a single international economy and the extensive levels of economic interdependence which can act as an impediment to conflict (1997). Views differ on the extent to which this interdependence is as pacifying as is often believed, and views also differ on the extent of these economic connections. But it is unquestionable that the United States and China have treated the prosperity they derive from growing economic integration in Asia as a common interest, even if they might want to direct that integration in different ways. Moreover, one of the leading instruments available to the West in response to Russia's treatment of Ukraine came in the form of economic sanctions. That option would simply not have been on the table in the same way had Russia not relied heavily on its participation in the global capitalist economy.

This raises a problem for Bull's vision of the anarchical society. Economic intercourse was not one of his five institutions, and he devoted rather little of his time as an academic to questions of economic interdependence. Much of his analysis gave priority to the strategic elements of great power status: the rising economy of Japan was not sufficient for great power status—that, Bull said, required nuclear weapons (1971c). And China was especially pertinent to the United States; its nuclear arsenal would one day offer the prospect of a mutual deterrence relationship. As it did for Thomas Schelling (1960), whose work Bull followed closely, this was the sort of interdependence which struck the latter theorist as the most important.

Another question mark lies in the distribution of power internationally. The post-Cold War period, especially in its early years but even still to some extent today, has been marked by the predominance and preponderance of a single great power, the United States. This raises questions about the role of the great powers (plural) as one of the institutions of international order, as it does about the place of the balance of power as another of the five. It also raises questions about the responsibility of the great powers for agreeing on a set of rules regulating the use of violent force.

If the other great powers (notably China and Russia) are in a militarily unequal position vis-à-vis the dominant United States, it might be thought that their relative weakness reduces the need for these rules in so far as they apply directly to great power confrontations. But that same predominance is at the very least a challenge to the rules relating to the use of violence in other international settings. With its power largely unbalanced, and with the former Soviet Union and post-Tiananmen Square China largely acquiescent, the United States has had a rare freedom to shape some of the rules of the game in its own image and interests, including the informal understanding that armed force should only be used as a last resort and in situations of where international security is grievously challenged.

It is hard to avoid the conclusion that in the last twenty-five years, the United States has been very willing to challenge the political status quo by resorting to the use of armed force. This was most notable in Iraq, when in 2003 the George W. Bush Administration initiated a war to unseat the incumbent regime in Baghdad. But it has also been evident in supporting NATO-led action in Libya, the use of drone strikes in Pakistan, and the use of overwhelming force in Afghanistan to topple the Taliban regime and drive away Al Qaeda. Earlier still, in the first decade of the post-Cold War period, the United States was active in leading NATO military action against Serbia and in a doomed intervention in Somalia. In none of these actions has the United States worked completely alone, but its English-speaking allies, the United Kingdom and Australia, have been especially frequent partners.

Given its actions in Georgia and Ukraine, Russia can hardly be seen as completely inactive in this regard. But these have mainly been limited conflicts on its periphery, including in sovereign states which, not that long ago, were still Soviet republics (see Kaczmarska, Ch. 16 in this volume). Like the United States, Russia has had a preference for air strikes over boots on the ground in Syria, although Moscow has been much more willing than Washington to take risks there. China, for its part, has drawn closer to breaking a tradition of inaction on this score by deploying naval forces to the Horn of Africa, where it has participated in attempts to control the offshore piracy emanating from Somalia. And the increasing reach of its forces in maritime Asia is part of a policy of pressure against other claimants to the South China Sea. But in comparison to the United States, China has been much less militarily active in external settings (and has not fought since engaging Vietnam briefly more than a generation ago). Indeed perhaps the country that resembles the United States the most in its willingness to mount expeditionary armed campaigns, aside from the already mentioned United Kingdom, has been another former great power from Europe. This of course is France, which has come to the assistance of a number of African governments threatened by insurgencies, including through the not infrequent use of force.

At least to some extent the Western enthusiasm for military interventions has become a self-limiting affair. Barack Obama's election in 2008 on a promise to reduce America's involvement in the long and complex internal wars in Afghanistan was a sign that the costs of these ambitious missions had exceeded their initial benefits. It is as if the United States, in its present policy, has come to the same position that Bull depicted over four decades ago about the approach to the management of conflicts in the Third World. 'Western governments', Bull wrote during a particularly prolific year of writing, 'have concluded that the costs of a military presence or of military intervention in these countries now outweighs the risks' (1971d, 457). As a successful candidate for the Presidency, Donald Trump appeared to promise even greater reluctance to intervene, although at the same time he also suggested a preference for using force even more strongly.

Rather than a wholesale rejection of military intervention, these debates are more about the utility of force in certain circumstances. It did not then, and it does not now, reflect a wholesale commitment to a rule limiting the use of force in the management of internal conflicts. The disagreement between the great powers on whether the United Nations Security Council should endorse humanitarian military action against Libya and Syria is further evidence that these rules, or at least their application, are in continual flux. The numerous Chinese and Russian vetoes in the second case (partly out of concern about NATO's exploitation of the first example to help ensure Gaddafi's removal) can be explained partly out of their calculations that an Assad-led Syria is better for them than the alternatives. But it also appears to position China as the champion of very conservative understandings of what the norms of non-interference and sovereignty allow (which helps explain Beijing's unease at Russian action in both Georgia and Ukraine). This championing is no accident given China's resentment at liberal democratic criticism of its internal policies, and a long-standing concern that military intervention elsewhere in the world may create a tradition whose next step is to take Beijing to task over its self-declared 'core interests' in Tibet, Xinjiang, or even Taiwan.

The result is a lack of consensus in 'world opinion', a phrase Bull used in some of his earliest academic publications, about when violence is and is not to be used in response to internal conflict (1958). This disagreement reduces international support for efforts by more adventurous Western nations to launch further such commitments abroad. In consequence a *de facto* (and almost accidental) equilibrium may have been found to the extent that the more conservative views of a rising China have, at least partially, been accommodated. This is certainly what some of China's vetoes (and Russia's) have helped solidify at the Security Council to the frustration of powers wanting more action on humanitarian distress in Syria. By the same token, Russia's decision to mount its own air strikes in that distressed country, involving a degree of intervention that is distinctly uncomfortable to China, and driven by a set of interests that do not coincide with America's, demonstrates the fragility of any such understanding.

The question then is whether the great powers (and their supporters) are able to deliberately shape this situation. Can they fashion out of this mess a common basic position on the management of violence by external state actors in internal conflicts? And can this informal understanding become part of the fabric of the somewhat shallow anarchical society? As few of these conflicts (from Somalia and Bosnia to Libya and Syria) constitute direct threats to the interests of the great powers, and as few of them threaten an escalating crisis which sees the great powers challenge each other militarily, it might be thought that the stakes are not high enough to require them to agree on implicit, let alone explicit, standards of restraint. The contrast with the situation on which Bull cut his strategic studies teeth is an obvious one. After all, it was a common threat of nuclear annihilation that helped remind the United States and the Soviet Union of the basic common interests they had in controlling their bilateral strategic competition in the Cold War: the first test case for Bull's international society in an expanded system of states.

There is one obvious cause of mutual alarm among the great powers today which potentially unites the wider system of states. This is not the harm they can do each other, but the threat posed by a particular constellation of non-state actors who are proficient in the use of terrorist violence. While not a new concern when the nationalist terrorist violence of the 1970s is considered, the shocking violence imposed on the United States in the 9/11 attacks suggested that a new era of catastrophic terrorism had arrived. This particular incident remains unique in terms of the impact a single set of terrorist attacks has had on a great power. But it did provide something of a rallying cry for concerted international outrage and action. Two years before it divided the world with its unnecessary attack on Iraq, the George W. Bush Administration's leadership of military action against the Taliban and Al Qaeda came at a moment of almost universal determination to limit the chances of further terrorist action. Many questioned the 'war on terror' appellation, and many would come to doubt the efficacy of the long-term campaign in Afghanistan once the Taliban had been unseated. But the immediate post-9/11 period revealed the potential for consensus among the states of the international system on the need to control at least one category of violent threats.

It helped no end that these challengers to international security were not states themselves. Few things can unite the anarchical society of states than problems from outside that society. But quite how Bull would see the anarchical society operating in response to this type of problem is unclear. He mentioned terrorism very rarely in his writings: a close study of them by this author (Ayson 2012) revealed but one minor piece of writing dedicated to the subject. But what we can say with some confidence is that the decade and a half since 9/11 is unlikely to be remembered for generating a new set of *formal* international rules against terrorism in general, not least because of the difficulties of agreeing on a definition of the problem. But at the same time there have arisen some relatively well-understood standards in terms of what states may (and in some cases must) do in dealing with particular terrorist actors, including Al Qaeda. Some of these have involved formal rules: states have generally accepted that they have an obligation to work together in seeking to reduce the flow of finances to named groups such as Al Qaeda and Islamic State. Through United Nations Security Council Resolution 1540 they are required to observe prohibitions on the supply of weapons of mass destruction to non-state actors. While this may be the result of exaggerated concerns about Al Qaeda's interest in acquiring nuclear weapons, it indicates a broad interest within the society of states in placing limits on the violent capacities of groups using terror.

Some of these rules have been informal understandings about what states are permitted to do. At least in the days and weeks after the September 2001 attacks, some of these permissions were generous ones. They included the degree of acceptance about the use of force by the United States and its partners in Afghanistan in the immediate response to 9/11. United States drone strikes on Al Qaeda and Taliban targets on the Pakistan side of the Afghanistan–Pakistan border were also tolerated, despite the questions these acts have raised about the sovereign authority of the government seated in Islamabad. This permissive environment has also enabled states of all kinds to enact stronger domestic rules constraining the behaviour of their citizens in the name of national security, including laws which give greater powers to intelligence and police agencies.

Such momentum has allowed for a common cause between liberal democracies (most of whom are now a little less liberal than they once were) and some of the world's leading authoritarian governments. These circumstances have reduced for Russia the chances of being censured for its actions against Chechen rebel groups. China gets something close to a green light for actions against Uyghur separatists whom it designates as terrorists. But whether the measures involve formal rules endorsed by United Nations Security Council Resolutions or informal understandings which open up new possibilities for coercive action, a common threat underlies them all. The actors whose violence is to be restrained by these rules are not themselves direct parties to the rule-making process. There may be a degree of consensus among the rule makers sufficient to suggest an anarchical society is in operation. But this is an effort to impose the consensus on actors who exist beyond the anarchical society and who may have aspirations to overturn the existence of that society in the Middle East and elsewhere.

If there was sufficient agreement within the society of states that these outsiders could be destroyed or rendered inert by unfettered violence, many states within that society would probably support that freedom of action. But two considerations make that unlikely. One is the increasing recognition of the counterproductive effects of doing so, not least because the groups using terror are often difficult to disconnect from the local societies which they pray on but which also in some instances lend them succour. Counterinsurgency strategy, with its emphasis on a population-centric approach, is one response to this challenge, but it requires an almost impossible level of local knowledge and familiarity on the part of any intervening power. More robust and violent responses, including the defeat of terrorizing groups on a town-by-town basis (as seen in Iraq in more than one conflict cycle) can all too easily leave grievances festering which offer a ready platform for later terror. The second is the realization that this may be exactly what some of the groups using terror desire: an unrestricted war where the distinction between civilized states and uncivilized violent non-state actors has completely broken down.

The creation of this situation of unrestricted violence seems to be one of the clear intents of an offshoot of (and successor to) Al Qaeda. The strategy used by Islamic State has in mind the encouragement by brutality of a chaotic environment in which it has the upper hand, and where state authorities, in failing to prevent the bloodbath, have lost their legitimacy and point of difference. And in gaining effective control of a swathe of territory involving large parts of Syria and Iraq, in which a form of government under Islamic State has been established, this group has surpassed Al Qaeda. This achievement, however fleeting it has proven to be, might be taken as evidence of a quest for statehood: if the self-declared caliphate walks and talks like a prospective state, perhaps it deserves to be treated in that way. But, as Toros and Dionigi argue in Chapter 9 in this volume, the beliefs and behaviour of Islamic State are inimical to the norms that even an imperfect international society of states is based on.

Because of its brutality, Islamic State is commonly regarded as not observing any recognizable limitations on the application of violence. But while violating minimal standards in relation to violent conduct (by beheadings, mass executions, and the encouragement of terrorist acts by children), Islamic State has not undertaken the spectacular attack on a distant country that was seen in September 2011. Instead it has relied on giving inspiration to foreign fighters and local groups. But the groups claiming allegiance to Islamic State range far and wide in the developing world, from Nigeria to Afghanistan to Indonesia. And foreign fighters have been attracted to the Middle East from many Western countries including France, the United Kingdom, and Australia. This, along with atrocities in Paris, Brussels, and Nice has helped ensure a deep sense of consensus within the society of states that Islamic State cannot be taken lightly.

Indeed the widespread agreement that Islamic State is an adversary has encouraged some unusual partnerships. While they may view the sectarian issues in the Middle East quite differently, the United States and Iran have come to see Islamic State as the most pressing threat in Iraq and Syria. And even though Russia and the United States differ in their attitude to the Assad regime in Syria, they both have reasons to oppose Islamic State's activities there. Indeed the more Russia takes a long-term role in the Syrian conflict, the more it may find itself on the receiving end of attacks by Islamic State supporters.

But it is not clear that this common interest has been encouraging shared rules on the use of violence among the leading members of the states system. The United States has limited the extent of its military campaign against Islamic State (which has largely been restricted to airstrikes) because of its unwillingness to get fully caught up in another nasty internal conflict. This is restraint through unilateral caution, something Mr Trump has questioned without offering a consistent alternative. It is much more an internal strategic rule than one worked out as part of the strengthening of a wider anarchical society. And it is not restraint in the expectation that other great powers will also be restrained: there is no necessary reciprocal expectation in play here. Washington can act on a reasonably safe assumption that, for reasons which have little to do with the operation of an anarchical society, but which reflect another great power's reluctance to engage too fully in it, China is unlikely to get especially involved in the campaign. However, as noted earlier, the United States and its Western friends have not found the same introspection operating on the part of Russia.

THE PROBLEM OF VIOLENCE IN TODAY'S ASIA

The importance of this specific form of restraint returns us to an issue raised earlier in this essay: the extent to which concerns about global violence should focus on the prospects of a major clash between the great powers. The record of relative peace since the Korean War, where China and the United States fought each other directly, might suggest that there are other problems that demand attention. But, somewhat ironically, it is in Asia where this tradition of great power peace probably faces its sternest test. And it is in the strategic competition between these same two powers where this test is concentrated most heavily.

In the first decades of the twenty-first century, Asia's security is dominated most of all by China's rise. Economic advancement has provided Beijing with the regional influence to dent America's primacy. But while China's growing wealth has also funded a more capable People's Liberation Army, Beijing has continued to focus on economic development as its central aim. This is almost the reverse of the situation that Bull noted at the time when he began watching Asia closely nearly fifty years ago (1967). China was rising, he noted then, but he said rather less about the economic aspects of that power and much more about the degree to which China's nuclear capabilities would pose a counterweight to American and Russian nuclear forces.

As he watched the world from Canberra, Bull argued that China was becoming one of the four great powers of Asia, the security of which region would rest less in the bilateral balance of power between the two superpowers and rely more on a quadrilateral equilibrium between the United States, the Soviet Union, China, and (non-nuclear) Japan (1971c). As with Bull's writing about the balance of power more generally, he stressed that any such equilibrium would require conscious management by the four. Such limited collaboration would not be enough to make for an Asian concert, but if it did occur the four together might provide for a modicum of order in a still volatile region.

It is tempting in the first decades of the twenty-first century to adjust Bull's conception and replace the Soviet Union with a rising India. The idea of a modern Asian concert involving the United States, China, Japan, and India has a certain appeal, and has been invoked by such observers as the Australian strategic thinker Hugh White (2012). But these ideas are often more about what might be than what is. Bull's version of this logic did not survive the rise in superpower competition in the 1980s, to say nothing of the subsequent collapse of Soviet power which left the United States in a singularly predominant position. In different circumstances but with a similar theme, it is clear that India and Japan cannot really compete with today's big two. It is widely recognized in Asia that the bilateral relationship between the United States and China is the defining feature of regional security, although as I have argued, there are many more significant security issues to consider in a rounded view of regional security (Ayson 2015).

The fact that China's rise in Asia is the cardinal challenge to American primacy does not remove the possibility that the two can recognize common interests in the control of violence in interstate politics, and jointly develop rules of the game to make this restraint a constituent element of regional order. Indeed this expectation would be entirely consistent with Bull's argument that it is in such a circumstance when these rules become more important. Moreover, it is when the predominant power recognizes the growing importance of the rising power that these understandings become possible as well as necessary.

While it is forty years since Nixon met Mao to produce an initial accommodation, the United States is not yet in a position where it views China as an equal in Asia. Washington has still been regarding itself as an indispensable leader and balancer in the region, and the gap between American and Chinese military power remains wide. But China's ability to raise the costs of American power projection close to the Asian mainland has been growing, and this factor is proving an unsettling reality for America's close allies. Yet what would be even more unsettling for an ally such as Japan is the prospect that China and the United States may be developing a mutual understanding that the costs of war between themselves are too high for the sake of protecting third parties. Political change in the United States has raised a variation on this concern. Will Trump's America be willing to do a deal with Beijing, which leaves much of the running in East Asia to China and reduces the reassurance that Washington can offer to its regional allies and partners?

Cooperation between the big two is not to be sniffed at in other aspects of regional affairs. China and the United States have shown themselves willing and able to work for the control of violence in some of Asia's flashpoints which, if neglected, might lead to open armed conflict between them. On the Korean peninsula, for example, while they have not been able to achieve the nuclear disarmament of North Korea (which has always been more of a priority for Washington than Beijing), their participation in several rounds of the Five Party Talks can be taken as a sign of a mutual interest in some form of arms control. They also appear to have developed an informal understanding on Taiwan. The United States will not support moves by Taiwan towards independence from China, and Taiwan's leaders know they do not have a blank cheque from Washington should they behave provocatively. China has retained reunification as an eventual goal, but it appears for now to have restrained its willingness to use force across the Taiwan Strait. Indeed twenty years ago, China and the United States were already able to manage a Taiwan Strait crisis where an initial rising of tensions between them was eventually ratcheted down. Trump's initial comments on Taiwan suggest, however, that he may be willing to upset this understanding.

Even before Trump's arrival at the White House, things were more volatile and prone to misunderstanding over maritime territorial disputes in Asia where the United States has accused China of using coercion to challenge the status quo. The stakes are especially high in the East China Sea where China squares off against Japan, whose alliance with the United States is the most important such agreement in all of Asia. Partly because of the paucity of political trust and effective communication between North Asia's two most powerful neighbours, the risk of serious escalation between them is an ongoing problem. This could easily drag the United States into the fray if a Sino-Japanese crisis became especially serious. Such is their enmity at times, it is difficult to argue that Japan and China see each other as part of a society of states. But even here there are signs that informal rules about the control of interstate violence apply. The United States has agreed that its alliance with Japan does cover the disputed East China Sea islands, but it has also remonstrated with Japan to seek some sort of accommodation with China, fearing that the two could easily jeopardize Asia's peace. For its part, China has kept its campaign of pressure on Japan below the level of actual physical force.

This pattern is also evident in China's behaviour in the South China Sea where its grandiose claim overlaps the claims of a number of Southeast Asian maritime countries. But while the United States has drawn closer to Vietnam and its old ally, the Philippines, in neither case has it stepped in militarily. In 2012, for example, when China had sent a number of its vessels to the Scarborough Shoal area, the United States did not intervene militarily in the stand-off which would see the effective control of these features transferred from the Philippines to China. And with the 2016 election of Rodrigo Duterte as the new

Philippines leader, Beijing may have got even more than it could have wished for: the leader of a formal US ally in Southeast Asia who seemed more interested in smooth relations with China than in working with Washington.

However the correlation of diplomatic forces changes, serious problems can still result from a form of restraint where the avoidance of outright violence is the central aim, even if the consequences are peaceful at first glance. On the one hand, any understanding between China and the US that outright violence between them must be avoided raises serious questions among America's allies and partners about the point at which a military engagement from Washington would occur. On the other hand, it allows China to change the facts of the ground without resorting to violent action, but in a way which encourages it to use latent force for bargaining purposes.

If the United States can still deter war in Asia but finds it more difficult to deter coercion short of war, questions are raised about the price of Asia's peace. At the very least it means that informal agreements designed to avoid war need to be supplemented by understandings about the exploitation of force short of armed conflict. The latter could well be crucial to the hopes for an anarchical international society, at least to the extent that this society extends to Asia. But here there are significant disagreements in the way. The United States and China, for example, have very dissimilar views on the freedom of navigation that military vessels should enjoy in the exclusive economic zones claimed by other countries. For the United States there is a premium on maintaining the freedom to project such power. For China, which takes a different view on the application of international law to this problem, and which rejected the legitimacy of the Permanent Court of Arbitration's consideration of and verdict on the case brought by the Philippines government, there is a premium on restricting what it regards as highly intrusive American surveillance efforts.

The fact that both sides understand they have a common interest in the avoidance of war is not enough to provide for a common understanding on this question. This will be tested the more the United States insists on conducting freedom of navigation operations in waters close to features claimed by China, and the more China militarizes those features to signal its commitment to defending its position. Especially if a Trump Presidency means a more uncertain and uneven set of approaches from Washington in its relations with Beijing, the management of violence will become a steeper challenge.

CONCLUSION

In an anarchical international society the control of global violence is very often more a question of informal understandings, underpinned by mutual restraint, than it is of formal agreements, enforced by an international authority. The existence of a set of rules on international conduct suggests a commitment among states to restrain their competition, which is especially significant as the distribution of power among them is shifting. But if these rules do not extend to regulating the most dangerous aspect of that competition—armed violence—then it is hard to argue that any such anarchical society is worth contemplating.

Forty years on since the publication of Bull's most influential work, it is evident that there are at least some understandings in place in respect of this signally important area of statecraft. Unless we can attribute the rarity of inter-state war, and the decline even of intra-state conflict, to a series of complete accidents of history, conscious effort among the powers to restrict their resort to violence ought to be part of the explanation for this phenomenon. For example, even though Asia's security is being challenged by the changing distribution of regional power, there is enough evidence to suggest that the region's largest powers (and especially China and the United States) believe that they have a common interest in the avoidance of inter-state war. That common belief requires them to limit the escalation of crises, something they have shown at least modest skill in achieving. Whether they can continue to successfully do that is another question, not least when the competition between them is increasing in the exploitation of latent force short of actual violence.

But in the last two decades the rules on constraining violence have faced their tougher tests when it has come to the actions of larger states in military interventions against weaker ones. If only because of the extraordinary costs that followed for the United States from its invasion of Iraq in 2003, the era of the most ambitious Western military adventures of this sort appears to have closed. Russia's annexation of Crimea and military campaign against Ukraine shows that without restraint by all of the major powers, any confidence that there is a system of rules on violence can be harmed significantly even in cases where major interstate war is avoided.

If more universally observed patterns of restraint are to apply across the society of states, that society requires its members to enjoy a significant monopoly on armed violence within their sovereign territories. In the Middle East, there have been many situations where this has not been the case. Islamic State has found a freedom to exploit its own form of violent action, and, at least for a time, to turn that violence into areas of *de facto* sovereign control. This is a clear sign that there are serious problems for the anarchical society if non-state actors do not observe its informal rules about the use of violence. In places where the effective sovereignty of states has almost vanished, new rules about the use of violence may in fact be promoted by the non-state actors themselves (who may reject the guiding rules of the states system) or from some more active intervening states attempting to impose a brutal form of stability where chaos has been allowed to develop. The first of these rule-making attempts can be a unifying factor, to the extent that the society of states often regards violent non-state actors as a threat to the entire system. Yet the divided and divisive international responses to the crises in Libya, Syria, and Yemen suggest that there are limits to the unity that can be found from the second.

8

A Plea for Restraint

The Anarchical Society and Nuclear Proliferation

Jan Ruzicka

The purpose of this essay is to reconstruct Hedley Bull's position, which can be identified in *The Anarchical Society*, on the relationship between nuclear proliferation and international order.[1] The link between the two posed an important question that clearly preoccupied Bull. Given the complexity of the book, it will come as no surprise that he probed the question from various angles, but provided no straightforward answer. Bull resisted accepting either of the commonly espoused positions regarding the consequences of the spread of nuclear weapons to international order. He was neither a proliferation optimist in the style of Kenneth Waltz (1981), who believed that states wishing to pursue nuclear weapons should be allowed to do so because they would then act carefully, nor a proliferation pessimist in the mould of Graham Allison (2010), who predicted detrimental changes to international order if the spread of nuclear weapons were not prevented. Instead, and in line with his larger theory of international politics, Bull navigated a path between the two extremes. This is the basis of his plea for restraint when it comes to nuclear proliferation.

The notion of restraint resists mechanistic assumptions underpinning both nuclear optimism and pessimism. Each of these positions supposes a specific, in-built, and directly opposed causal path regarding what would happen when additional countries go nuclear—'international relations will become more stable' vs. 'the world will be a far more dangerous place to live in'. The two

---

[1] I would like to thank the participants of the June 2016 workshop at Cardiff University for their comments on an earlier version of this essay. I also benefited from helpful discussions on the subject with Nick Wheeler. Ken Booth and Kamila Stullerova read and extensively commented on previous written drafts of this essay. I would like to thank them very much for their help and generosity.

positions derive their persuasiveness not from some magical insight into the future, but from their respective beliefs about what nuclear proliferation would lead to. What would actually happen is, of course, unknown to all observers. This inability to know which way things would go is the very reason for the co-existence of the two positions (Sagan and Waltz 1995).

For Bull himself, whether the future with many more nuclear states would lead to a more dangerous or peaceful world was not a foregone conclusion. He allowed that 'a world of many nuclear powers would be most dramatically different from the present one' (1977, 240). How different and in what ways remained to be seen. As Bull wrote nearly twenty years before the publication of *The Anarchical Society*, 'any increase in the number of nuclear powers will increase both the blessings and the dangers' (1959b [1987], 238). The direction would be determined by the ability of states to show restraint in their actions and the willingness to maintain international order. This imposes demands on both the nuclear weapon states and the non-nuclear weapon states. Such demands are differentiated, but nuclear order cannot be achieved unless both groups of states exercise restraint appropriate to their positions in international politics.

Bull held the prospect of an increased number of nuclear armed states as quite likely and the developments of the 1970s, chief among them the Indian nuclear test of 1974 and the reluctance of many states to sign on to the Nuclear Non-Proliferation Treaty (NPT), seemed to suggest such turn of events. Moreover, he was sceptical about the United States' and the Soviet Union's willingness to limit their behaviour in such a way that would allow for the maintenance of international order and the prevention of the spread of nuclear weapons (Bull 1980). Both these prospects led him to consider the implications of nuclear proliferation for the very existence of the states system. In Bull's view, the failure to deal effectively with the pressures brought about by nuclear proliferation opened the possibility of the states system's ultimate collapse.

Developing more fully Bull's position allows us to think through the relationship between nuclear proliferation and international order in today's circumstances. The quality of a classical text should be considered in the light of the ways in which it examines the problems it sets out to address and the extent to which those ways—ways of thinking—can, through our own critical engagement with them, give us insights in addressing our contemporary problems. In order to do that, this chapter outlines how Bull's ideas can help us identify a number of paradoxes arising from the manner in which the problem of nuclear proliferation is treated in current international politics. For instance, and as explained in more detail later in the chapter, preoccupation with the spread of nuclear weapons to new countries is conducive to unrestrained behaviour on the part of some nuclear weapons states towards increasing their own nuclear capabilities. This, in turn, may increase proliferation pressures.

BULL'S POSITION ON NUCLEAR PROLIFERATION

Given the extent to which his scholarship and professional career were preoccupied with arms control (Bull served from 1965 to 1967 as the inaugural Director of the United Kingdom's Arms Control and Disarmament Research Unit), it is remarkable how little attention has been paid to Bull's writing in this particular area. Robert Ayson's excellent study of Bull's oeuvre quite correctly notes the prevailing lack of interest in Bull as a strategic thinker (Ayson 2012, 57; see also Ayson, Ch. 7 in this volume). Interestingly, Ayson reaches essentially the same conclusion as that offered by Robert O'Neill and David N. Schwartz (1987) in their introduction to the collection of Bull's various writings on the subject of arms control twenty-five years earlier. Remarkably, in that quarter of a century, not much has changed in the reception of Bull's works. For example, William Walker's outstanding book on international nuclear order is inspired by Bull's analysis in *The Anarchical Society* (2012). Walker explicitly draws on Bull's conceptualization of order to articulate his definition of international nuclear order. There are also clear resemblances to some of Bull's concerns in Walker's 'logic of restraint'. Nevertheless, Walker's book does not attempt to systematically examine Bull's position on nuclear proliferation or even nuclear weapons more generally. In this regard, Ayson's book is an exception. Since he offers a comprehensive treatment of Bull's writings as a whole, when it comes to nuclear proliferation Ayson looks closely into works other than *The Anarchical Society*. This makes sense. They promise a more fertile ground to understand Bull's position, because they address the nuclear issue more directly. Still, *The Anarchical Society*, in order to examine the key general questions that concern Bull, contains a position with regard to nuclear weapons and their proliferation. The reason is, as Ayson puts it, that 'it is difficult to overstate the centrality here of the problem of managing nuclear armaments to Bull's conception of the shape of wider international politics' (Ayson 2012, 65).

Bull's position has at least three important dimensions that this essay seeks to reconstruct. First, he refuses to reduce the notion of nuclear proliferation to horizontal proliferation. Second, Bull displays a good deal of agnosticism about the potential consequences of nuclear proliferation. Third, he demonstrates concern about implications which nuclear proliferation might have for the continued existence of the states system.

Two Types of Nuclear Proliferation

'Nuclear proliferation' is most often conceived of as the increase in the number of nuclear armed states. Which country is going to be the next one to go nuclear and how it will influence regional and global interstate relations has become, over time, the central concern in debates about nuclear weapons. The concern grew particularly strong in the 1960s, especially after China tested a nuclear device in 1964 and other countries were assumed to follow. If a relatively poorly developed country had managed to master the making of the bomb, there was little reason to assume that others would not follow, particularly as the ability to harness the power of the atom was considered to be the marker of modernity and progress. Extensive lists of states with the adequate resource base, technical skills, and the necessary industrial infrastructure were compiled. This concern persisted and took on new forms in the 1970s, just as Bull would have been writing *The Anarchical Society*. India had detonated a nuclear device, Brazil and West Germany had just signed a large civil nuclear deal that was thought by many to be a cover for a military programme, and suspicions were voiced about countries such as Argentina, Pakistan, and South Africa. It should come as no surprise that, in Bull's judgement, '[w]hether a world of many nuclear powers is taken to represent a desirable alternative to the present form of the international system or not, it must be reckoned an alternative that has a fair prospect of being realised' (1977, 243).

The process of horizontal proliferation is, however, merely one aspect of the spread of nuclear weapons. Bull was well aware that just as important was vertical proliferation, which refers to the increase in the number of nuclear weapons owned by states already possessing them. He aimed quite clearly at the superpowers' huge nuclear arsenals. Bull's emphasis on the role of superpowers is a very useful reminder that while horizontal proliferation may have become a far more prominent issue in various international venues, both types of proliferation have serious potential to influence international society and with it, international order.

The upshot of vertical proliferation and the superpower crises, in which it played a part, is the increased realization of shared interests and the heightened responsibility that the superpowers must carry. In the era of nuclear weapons, the superpowers do not act merely in their own self-interest. Since their mutual nuclear conflict would have catastrophic implications for all other states, they 'act as trustees for mankind as a whole' (1977, 299). To be sure, Bull stressed that the need to act in such a manner has always been part and parcel of being a great power and should not be seen as a by-product of the introduction of nuclear weapons into international politics. As he put it, 'the avoidance and control of crises involving the risk of great power war is a perennial function of the great powers in relation to international order, and not a special feature of the nuclear era' (1977, 212). Nevertheless, nuclear weapons have introduced two very specific, hitherto unseen, concerns; first, nuclear crisis control in relations among the superpowers, because any conflict among them could escalate to the Earth-destroying extreme; and second, the prevention of the spread of nuclear weapons to other states, so that there can only be a limited number of potential nuclear crises. In Bull's words:

> The United States and the Soviet Union, it is true, recognise common interests not only in combating abstract dangers like nuclear war, but also in thwarting particular other powers. They have co-operated against potential nuclear powers within the framework of the Non-Proliferation Treaty. (1977, 226)

The nuclear weapons states, Russia and the United States chief among them, have been far more diligent with regard to the latter aim than the former. They have used the provisions of the NPT to dissuade and prevent states from acquiring nuclear weapons, while largely ignoring the commitment contained in the treaty's Article VI 'to pursue negotiations in good faith on effective measures relating to cessation of the nuclear arms race at an early date and to nuclear disarmament'. Many have interpreted this as a failure of, and potentially a significant threat to the NPT, including eventually, Bull himself in his scathing critique of the superpowers (1980). However, Bull also noted some positive gains stemming from the superpowers' possession of nuclear weapons; it has pushed them towards a degree of cooperation which is not entirely accidental. As Bull pointed out, '[i]t may be argued also that there is a further element of contrivance in the agreement between the United States and the Soviet Union on the common objective of maintaining a balance between themselves, at least in the limited sphere of strategic nuclear weapons' (1977, 114). For Bull such an arrangement was less significant because of the limitations it puts upon nuclear-armed great powers than for the fact that it prevents domination by a single nuclear power that could militarily impose world government (1977, 263). From the perspective of international order, the existence of several nuclear great powers might not represent the best of all possible worlds, but it is, in Bull's view, preferable to a potentially tyrannical world government.

Bull considered horizontal proliferation and the possibility of a world of many more nuclear powers chiefly within the framework of nuclear deterrence. This would be a situation where 'the spread of nuclear weapons proceeded so far as to enable every state to deter every other state from nuclear attack' (1977, 120). For Bull, the important point about such a potential situation is the realization that without a conscious effort to manage it, mutual nuclear deterrence will deteriorate. The balance of power created by the spread of nuclear weapons will not sustain itself mechanically. Instead, its persistence has to be ensured by arms control, which will require mutual restraint on the part of nuclear powers. As he put it, 'left to its own logic or momentum, strategic nuclear competition between the super powers could lead to the undermining of mutual nuclear deterrence' (1977, 121).

The discussion of this phenomenon in *The Anarchical Society* is somewhat obscured by the fact that, as Bull proceeded with his analysis, he switched from a general question—what would a balance of power based on mutual nuclear deterrence look like in a world of many nuclear powers?—to a particular historical manifestation of mutual nuclear deterrence, namely the American–Soviet relationship during the Cold War. Between these two states, and the same would apply to all other bilateral balances, mutual nuclear deterrence is but a part of the overall balance of power among them. In Bull's own words, 'the creation of a relationship of mutual nuclear deterrence is a necessary condition of a balance of power between them. But it is not a sufficient condition' (1977, 121). However, there is a twist. In a relationship of mutual nuclear deterrence, the overall balance of power becomes rather insignificant. All that is needed is the sufficient ability to retaliate in kind, also known as the minimum deterrence. This is an important insight, for it allows states to fend off potential aggressors even when the relationship might be unbalanced (think, for example, about the relationship between North Korea and the United States today).

What does Bull's argument mean in terms of the restraint that must be exercised, if a condition of mutual nuclear deterrence is not to deteriorate? It appears to undermine the reason for restraining horizontal proliferation. Horizontal proliferation might still be limited, however, if a non-nuclear state decided to rely on guarantees from a nuclear power, the so-called nuclear umbrella. But reliance on and the provision of such extended deterrence in turn have implications for vertical proliferation. If a state must hold enough nuclear warheads to ensure a deterrent capability serving its own interests and also those of its allies, limitations on vertical proliferation will be much more difficult to achieve. The state's policy will be subject to pressures arising from questions about the adequacy of an available nuclear arsenal for a task that is much larger in scope than defence of one's own territory. Moreover, these questions will be raised not only within domestic political settings, but also from the states living under the nuclear umbrella. Facing the possibility of being abandoned by their nuclear protector, they will seek additional reassurance. This danger is further compounded by the very nature of mutual nuclear deterrence. As Bull reminded his readers, mutual nuclear deterrence is 'essentially a state of belief: the belief on each side that the other has the will and the capacity to retaliate to a sufficient level' (1977, 123). While he did not spell this out, this subjective quality of mutual nuclear deterrence further exacerbates the difficulties connected with the provision of nuclear deterrence by a nuclear umbrella state, because there is never a clear threshold of how many nuclear weapons are enough. It also generates complex problems for nuclear proliferation: vertical proliferation is, on the one hand, the *sine qua non* of stemming horizontal proliferation, but, on the other, the very fact of vertical proliferation increases the pressures that might spur horizontal proliferation. The two must therefore be considered together, which is not often done as horizontal proliferation dominates agendas time and again.

Proliferation Agnosticism

If a world of many more nuclear powers is likely, questions about what such a world would look like and how order might be maintained in it become inescapable. In discussions about nuclear weapons this has been a recurrent feature. Much of what gets identified as relevant questions about nuclear arms and advocated as appropriate solutions to these questions depends on how authors envisage their respective world of many nuclear powers, specifically its proclivity to war and peace. Accounts tend to oscillate around two main positions, nuclear optimism and nuclear pessimism (Sagan and Waltz 1995).

Bull refused to align with either of these positions. However, because he did not use the language of nuclear pessimism and optimism, his nuanced position has been overlooked. Even authors who have called for an end to the optimist vs. pessimist divide make no reference to Bull's writings (Feaver 1995; Kroenig 2009; Gavin 2012). This is perhaps partly the result of them operating within a specific American setting, but partly also a reflection of the fact that Bull's writings resist a clear categorization. On the one hand, he saw some benefits accruing from nuclear proliferation (the avoidance of the imposition of world government, in particular), and on the other hand, he recognized dangers inherent in the spread of nuclear weapons (the growing potential for accidents). Ultimately, this position, which is here termed 'proliferation agnosticism', is again used to support Bull's advocacy of restraint.

When Bull considered the possibility of a world of many nuclear powers, he went to the full extreme. He envisaged the possibility of nuclear weapons being available to *all* states in such a way as to enable them to inflict unacceptable harm on every other state. This would be the full-blown mutual nuclear deterrence scenario. It allowed Bull to take on Morton Kaplan's assumptions behind the latter's 'unit veto system' (Kaplan 1957). Bull was adamant that from the fact of nuclear proliferation it does not 'follow that the system must be a Hobbesian state of nature, or that it must be marked by extreme tension' (1977, 242) as Kaplan thought. For that to be the case, Bull argued, Kaplan had to smuggle in assumptions that come from outside of his model. Bull thus rejected the premises of nuclear pessimists about the world of many more nuclear weapon states. He even noted the possibility whereby actors could neutralize their nuclear weapons by the disciplining power of fear and 'might eventually discover that the order it [an international system] had achieved could exist independently of that discipline' (1977, 242). Bull emphasized the speculative nature of such an idea. But it is precisely the speculative nature of his idea—which many would consider implausible, yet cannot be easily refuted—that enabled him to stress the equally speculative character of Kaplan's vision of the unit veto system.

Bull's agnosticism about the effects of the spread of nuclear weapons also gave rise to his doubts about the belief that proliferation would in fact lead to the establishment of more stable and orderly international relations. The accounts extolling the stabilizing effects of nuclear weapons simply extrapolate too readily from the experience of the US–Soviet relationship, even though there is little evidence to support such extrapolation. Bull cautioned against generalizing from the experience of the United States and the Soviet Union because their relationship involved many features particular to it (1977, 242). Whether such specifics would travel well into other particular contexts is at least questionable. Even if they did, it would not eliminate other obvious risks associated with nuclear weapons. While the irrationality of nuclear war may be clear to see for all, 'there are still dangers of nuclear war arising by accident or miscalculation' (1977, 125). Such risks simply increase with the growing number of the nuclear armed states. All that still leaves aside the assumption so central to mutual nuclear deterrence, namely that 'men can be expected to act "rationally"' (1977, 125). Bull was sceptical about the validity of this assumption, which further deepened his doubts about the potential stability of a world of many more nuclear powers.

Moreover, even in a world of many nuclear powers there would remain scope for political exploitation of force. Bull showed how 'the persisting utility of force in the nuclear age is not merely a feature of the present imperfect distribution of nuclear weapons among the nations of the world, but could be expected to obtain also were these weapons to become generally available' (1977, 191).[2] In a war between nuclear armed states there remains a possibility that the extent of hostilities would be limited so that it would not reach the nuclear level or the parties would refrain from direct violent confrontation altogether. This is, of course, illustrated by the American–Soviet relationship which saw proxy wars but no direct military confrontations even at the sub-nuclear level of warfare. Once again, however, Bull cautioned that 'we cannot assume on the basis of the Soviet–American stalemate so far that these or other nuclear powers will not be prepared to risk direct military conflict with each other, including limited nuclear war' (1977, 193). All this puts Bull closer towards the nuclear pessimists, but note that while force might still be deployed in a world of many nuclear powers, the use of nuclear force could be tempered partially or even completely.

Bull's preoccupation with international justice amplified his proliferation agnosticism. On the matter of international justice and the possession of nuclear weapons Bull held a clear view. There are only two ways in which international justice can be served. Either no state can have nuclear weapons or all can retain the possibility of acquiring them: 'International justice in the

---

[2] This point was so significant to him that he reiterated it several pages later: 'Thus war is not robbed of its historic political functions merely because of the existence of nuclear weapons and other advanced military technology; nor could these political functions be expected to disappear as a consequence of the spread of nuclear weapons' (1977, 194).

sense of equality... can be met fully only by complete nuclear disarmament, or by a system in which these weapons are available to all states or blocs' (1977, 242–3). The latter option, however, seems to have few supporters. As Bull did not fail to note, even the opponents of the NPT, which at the time he wrote *The Anarchical Society* included two of the five nuclear powers recognized by the treaty (China and France), were not advocating a *laissez-faire* system that would make nuclear weapons available to all states. Instead, they argued over where the line between the nuclear haves and the have-nots 'should be drawn, which states should be within the club and which left outside' (1977, 243). In other words, in a world where proliferation is limited, so will be international justice, whereas a just possibility to obtain nuclear weapons leads to a potentially, but not inevitably, more dangerous world.

The existence of an unjust international order when it comes to nuclear weapons availability may be preferable to alternatives. But, in Bull's opinion, it does not do away with the need to continually seek legitimacy for a privileged position enjoyed by the great powers (1977, 228). Demands for justice, nuclear justice among them, have to be accommodated and 'where the demands cannot be met, at least the motions have to be gone through of seeking to meet them, so as to avoid alienating important segments of international society' (1977, 229). It is not clear whether Bull considered nuclear justice as one of those issues where demands cannot be met, but it would appear to be the case from what he has written elsewhere. He did envisage some expansion of the number of nuclear armed states, but did not endorse the *laissez-faire* position of nuclear optimism (1961).

Bull reminded the readers of two arguments which he put forward in his first book, *The Control of the Arms Race* (1961). The first one concerns the idea of a world without nuclear weapons. Bull clearly treated this as a hypothetical that will be impossible to realize, because nuclear technology cannot be un-invented. As he wrote, 'if it were possible to return to the world that existed before the development of nuclear technology (which it is not), international security would be enhanced' (1977, 126). The other argument goes directly against the optimists' view of nuclear proliferation: 'I have also argued against the notion that international security is enhanced by the spread of nuclear weapons' (1977, 126). Neither of these options exists and therefore some form of accommodation must be achieved (on the crucial place of accommodation in Bull's work see Ayson 2012). Restraint provides the best way forward in dealing with a situation that has arisen and cannot be argued away. We must do the best we can.

While these two arguments could be read as placing Bull more in line with the nuclear pessimists, it is important to realize that Bull shifted slightly, but not insignificantly, the terms of the debate here. Note that in the previous paragraph the problem of nuclear weapons and their proliferation is not discussed with reference to international order, but rather international security. However, it is Bull's preoccupation with international order that enabled him to 'recognise the positive functions performed by relationships of mutual nuclear deterrence among the nuclear powers' (1977, 126). It may well be that international order, as opposed to international security, is better served by some degree of nuclear proliferation. The destructiveness of nuclear weapons presents a clear danger to security of states and individuals, hence their absence would increase international security. At the same time, nuclear weapons contribute to the maintenance of international order. This is what mitigates his leaning towards the stance of nuclear pessimism. Nevertheless, the pitfalls of nuclear proliferation are too obvious to ignore and make it impossible to endorse fully the nuclear optimists' position either. That position, moreover, lacks any demands on actors' exercise of restraint, because moderation is assumed to come about automatically as a basic characteristic of the situation itself. To believe that is not only to deny agency of states and international society, but requires also a giant leap of faith.

Nuclear Proliferation and the Existence of the States System

The ability of states and international society to act in a manner that would be conducive to international order is of course the central tenet of *The Anarchical Society*. As was shown in the previous section, nuclear proliferation has potentially far-reaching consequences for the maintenance of this ability, whether it be the result of instability and violence that could, in theory, follow the spread of nuclear weapons or as a consequence of the belief that restraint no longer need to be achieved through purposive action, because the possession of nuclear weapons will ensure it mechanically. There is at least one more important way in which nuclear proliferation could have significant implications for the existence of the states system.

In Chapter 2 of *The Anarchical Society*, where Bull addressed the question whether order exists in world politics, there is a very brief passage on Clausewitz's definition of war (1977, 49–50). Specifically, Bull was concerned with two aspects of Clausewitz's position, namely the lasting character of results achieved by war and the speed with which war can be conducted. This led Clausewitz to famously stress war's political nature. Bull stated that 'it is only in the context of nuclear weapons and other recent military technology that it has become pertinent to ask whether war could not now both be "absolute in its results" and "take the form of a single instantaneous blow"' (1977, 50). What this means is that potentially the distinction between the powerful and the weak becomes blurred unlike at any other point in the past because even the relatively weak could deliver a decisive and instantaneous blow against the strong. The blurring then is a direct result of nuclear proliferation. As Bull remarked, 'it is only the spread of nuclear weapons to small states, and the possibility of a world of many nuclear powers, that raises the question whether in international relations, also, a situation may come about in which "the weakest has strength enough to kill the strongest"' (1977, 50).

It is highly significant that these remarks appear in the context of Bull's discussion of Thomas Hobbes's idea of the state of nature. While Hobbes himself was not much interested in relations among states (Sovereigns) per se, his text does imply that states are not as vulnerable to violence as individuals. As Hobbes wrote: 'But because they uphold thereby, the Industry of their Subjects; there does not follow from it [the state of war—"condition of warre"], that misery, which accompanies the Liberty of particular men' (1996 [1651], 90). Bull agreed with this in so far as history of modern international society was concerned, noting that 'states have been less vulnerable to violent attack by one another than individual men' (1977, 50; on this point see also Williams 2005, 43–4). States have also been vulnerable in differentiated ways, because of their varying degrees of power and resilience. The great powers have, of course, possessed a far greater capacity to absorb blows than small states for which even a limited military attack could be fatal.

Accurate though the distinction between individuals' and states' relative vulnerability may be historically, Bull raised the possibility that nuclear weapons change this situation in two ways. First, in the nuclear age, states have become vulnerable in a similar way as individuals have long been—they might be put out of existence in a single blow, which is historically unprecedented. Second, in a nuclear world the differences in power, which used to translate into differentiated capacity to withstand attacks, cease to matter. The large and powerful states are as vulnerable to nuclear weapons as the small and weak states.[3] Some early theorists of the nuclear age quickly realized as much and concluded that there is no defence against nuclear weapons and that the use of such weapons can only be deterred by a similar threat of annihilation (Brodie et al. 1946). In other words, Bull suggested that with the onset of the nuclear age, the possibility has arisen that the international system could truly become Hobbesian. Only in the nuclear age may one conceive of states living under the same fear of destruction that Hobbes envisaged in his idea of the state of nature for individual human beings.

---

[3] It is obviously the case that large states, for example Russia, have by virtue of their territorial vastness, a certain strategic depth that is not available to small states like Belgium. This makes an immediate destruction of their entire territory unlikely. It would be a mistake to conclude, however, that this would somehow enable them to survive even a 'moderate' nuclear attack. First, the key political, economic, and social centres offer targets on a concentrated scale that is not significantly different from a small state. Second, and more importantly, general environmental consequences of even a limited nuclear exchange, let alone a massive one, would be catastrophic well beyond the areas directly hit.

The important qualifier here is that it is not the simple existence of nuclear weapons that would bring about the Hobbesian state of nature, but rather the spread of nuclear weapons. So long as nuclear proliferation could be prevented, the prospect of avoiding the Hobbesian state of nature for states remains possible. If nuclear proliferation were to happen, however, all bets could be off. Nevertheless, given Bull's proliferation agnosticism, it is not a foregone conclusion that a war of all against all would follow. As shown in the previous section, the spread of nuclear weapons does not necessarily mean one particular outcome would ensue. It is impossible to know how the situation would play out. The possibility exists, at least theoretically, that the widespread possession of nuclear weapons might result in a set of fairly robust and stable deterrent relationships (as it did in the case of the United States and the Soviet Union), or states might be able to form security communities (Deutsch 1957), as is the case between the United States and Great Britain.

Bull mentioned the possibility of the formation of a security community when he came to consider the prospect of the continued existence of the states system (1977, 283). But because the other option—a war of an unprecedented destructive nature—is at least equally, if not more likely, nuclear weapons pose an unparalleled threat to international society. It comes in two forms. One is obviously the prospect of the very destruction of the states system as humanity manages to annihilate itself in a nuclear conflict. This threat was apparent to Bull who wrote that 'in discussions of strategic and arms control questions, it is not uncommon to speak of a general nuclear war as not simply a disaster for the society of states and an infringement of individual human rights, but also a threat to human life or human civilisation as such' (1977, 84–5). The other threat to the states system stems from the imperative to abolish states along with international society and replace them with world government. If government is the way out of the dangers of anarchy that vulnerable individuals face, it stands to reason that when states have become equally vulnerable as individuals, the idea of world government might present itself as the solution to the nuclear problem (Craig 2003). Just as physical destruction represents one threat to the states system, the establishment of world government would spell out the end of states, international society, and the states system.

Judging from the piercing critique of the idea of world government that Bull offered in *The Anarchical Society* and in *The Control of the Arms Race*, this would not be a very appealing prospect to him. Bull's preference for the continued existence of the states system is unmistakable:

> The system of a plurality of sovereign states gives rise to classic dangers, but these have to be reckoned against the dangers inherent in the attempt to contain disparate communities within the framework of a single government. It may be argued that world order at the present time is best served by living with the former dangers rather than by attempting to face the latter. (1977, 287)

The spread of nuclear weapons poses a very real threat to the states system. The point of exercising restraint in order to prevent nuclear proliferation is thus more than just avoiding the nuclear Armageddon. The point is also the very preservation of the condition that ensures the continued existence of the states system.

Bull, it will be recalled, considered nuclear weapons as a barrier to the military imposition of world government by a single great power (1977, 263). From that perspective, nuclear weapons themselves constitute a restraining factor. However, Bull was far more concerned with the restraint that the nuclear weapon states must exhibit in their actions. He highlighted the possibility that 'states will maintain and develop the prudence and restraint they have so far displayed in relation to nuclear weapons and other weapons of mass destruction' (1977, 287). This is somewhat surprising given the caution which he repeatedly expressed about generalizing from the US–Soviet nuclear experience. Admittedly, in 1977 there was some evidence that the two superpowers were able to work together not only to limit and stabilize their mutual competition, but also to prevent the spread of nuclear weapons to other states. Yet, Bull was sceptical enough to express doubts whether 'these elements of restraint in the policies of the two leading nuclear weapon states are bound to endure, or to be generalised so as to embrace other nuclear weapon states, actual and potential' (1977, 287).

Once again, Bull is navigating between optimism and pessimism. The exercise of restraint is to provide a sustainable course, for '[i]t has certainly to be recognised that if this system of restraint is not maintained and extended, a minimum of peace and security, or of minimum world order, cannot be achieved through the states system' (1977, 288). This analytical conclusion led Bull to an unusually strong normative endorsement of the system of restraint. Indeed, the exhortation is so strong that he expressed his hope (something that strategists always caution against—hope is not a strategy) that the system might last: 'it is reasonable to hope that this system of restraint will be preserved and extended, and it is vitally important for world order to work for this goal' (1977, 288). Bull's writing here cannot be characterized in any way other than as imprecise and vague. For instance, he neglects to specify who should work for the preservation of the system of restraint. The reader is somewhat at a loss as to how to make sense of this, as Bull's argument essentially boils down to a call for order to work for order. There is a whiff of desperation in his defence of the states system and in his plea for restraint.

PARADOXES OF NUCLEAR PROLIFERATION

Bull's analysis of nuclear proliferation and international order offers a notable corrective to the predominant treatments of this important phenomenon. The emphasis he put on both horizontal and vertical proliferation, agnosticism about the consequences of a world of many more nuclear powers, and the preoccupation with the fate of the states system remind us that proliferation is a far more complex issue than just a matter of restricting a single state's access to nuclear weapons.

To stress the complexity of an issue is not a virtue in itself. Nevertheless, it provides for the possibility of making a case for the exercise of restraint. Such restraint goes well beyond simple deterrence or compellence of other states. It entails the support for norms and institutions inhibiting proliferation, the maintenance of agreements whereby states promise to abstain from nuclear weapons, or the evolution of guidelines of responsible behaviour. All of these are fairly standard ideas. Crucially, however, the system of restraint also requires self-restraint in nuclear states' policies. As Bull argued two years before the publication of *The Anarchical Society*, 'the control of proliferation depends, more than it depends on anything else, on the practice of restraint by the nuclear weapon states' (1975, 188). He thought that the nuclear powers could and must demonstrate self-restraint in a number of ways. They needed to avoid using nuclear weapons in their mutual conflicts and thus manifest the weapons' limited utility, show their commitment to arms control, continue to recognize their mutual interests in avoiding nuclear war, and perhaps even reconcile themselves to the fact that some proliferation was inevitable. The application of this fairly broad notion of self-restraint to the nuclear weapon states set Bull apart from the conventional advocates of arms control in his era and is the chief value of his contribution. It also alerts us to some paradoxes of nuclear proliferation in contemporary international politics.

The importance of restraint and the way in which its absence influences the working of institutions of international society is amply manifested by the United States' behaviour in the sphere of nuclear proliferation since the end of the Cold War (Craig and Ruzicka forthcoming). Bull worried that

> a state which is in a position of preponderant power, either in the system as a whole or in a particular area, may be in a position to ignore international law, to disregard the rules and procedures of diplomatic intercourse, to deprive its adversaries of the possibility of resort to war in defence of their interests and rights, or to ignore the conventions of the comity of great powers, all with impunity. (1977, 117)

This rings especially true, as William Walker showed in detail, concerning the US non-proliferation policies in the first decade of the twenty-first century (2012). The lack of restraint on the part of the United States combined with the inability of other states to restrain its unrivalled power led to some truly catastrophic decisions.

Prescient though Bull's analysis of the consequences of power preponderance may be, its actual manifestation alerts us to an obvious paradox and raises an important question. How was the unprecedented American behaviour possible in a world of nuclear armed states? This is truly puzzling, since Bull believed that a world of several nuclear great powers should be conducive to the balance of power. One possible explanation must be that there has not been enough proliferation! The rather different treatment received by Iraq and Libya on the one hand and North Korea on the other seems to support the point. This is no doubt an unappealing conclusion to those who are worried about the threat which nuclear weapons pose to humanity as a whole. But it is also a conclusion that appears to be inescapable. If the dominant power is unwilling to exercise restraint in its actions, there are likely to be growing proliferation pressures in order to be able to restrain it by the means of deterrence. This is similar to the proliferation dynamic that Bull envisaged in the 1970s with the spread of nuclear weapons to countries like India.

Another factor to consider is that in the absence of an ideological confrontation about the future of the world—which is really a competition about the bases of a particular international order—there are, provided that the condition of mutual nuclear deterrence pertains, few incentives for great powers to uphold the global balance of power. The 2003 war in Iraq is a case in point. While there were objections from Russia, France, and China against the American-led invasion, ultimately these were just rhetorical and amounted to no actual balancing behaviour. In a world of nuclear weapons, the nuclear powers need not balance in order to ensure their survival. Bull objected to the ideological confrontation and thought it harmful to international order (1977, 115; 243–8). It is entirely plausible that the price to pay for the lack of ideological confrontation—an occasional war in the name of enforcing international norms, like the war in Iraq—is a comparatively good price to pay, because the potential price of an ideological conflict is far greater. But those writing on nuclear proliferation need to be mindful of the possibility that if they flatten the issue to a concern with horizontal proliferation, their arguments provide a ready-made justification for various military adventures (Craig and Ruzicka 2013).

Finally, there is the paradox of great power cooperation when it comes to the prevention of horizontal proliferation. While some, like Andrew Hurrell, may decry the renewed importance of nuclear weapons which 'has resulted in the erosion of an important element of collective management of security, namely the Nuclear Non-Proliferation Treaty' (Hurrell 2007, 193), the non-proliferation regime actually represents a platform where there has been a good deal of great power cooperation. This focuses chiefly on the maintenance of these powers' own nuclear privilege, which *de facto* means imposing restraint on others but not on themselves. Thus to speak of the erosion of the regime is too one-sided (Ruzicka and Wheeler 2010; Horovitz 2015). In fact, since Bull wrote *The Anarchical Society* in 1977 and dubbed the United States and the Soviet Union as 'the great irresponsibles' in 1980, the NPT has become far more robustly entrenched and is now a nearly universal treaty. The great power consensus has a lot to do with this and the occasional disagreements between the nuclear powers ought not to blind us to the alignment of their interests.

Bull's analysis of international order and the place of nuclear proliferation in it constitutes an insistent plea for restraint. As this essay has shown, there are productive tensions in Bull's work, some of which are ultimately irreconcilable. While it would be easy to criticize Bull for sometimes attempting to square a circle, such criticism would be missing the point. It is precisely the awareness of the need to square a circle and the realization of the impossibility of doing so that, in the nuclear age, should guide states and international society to exercise restraint.

9

International Society and Islamist Non-State Actors

The Case of the Islamic State Organization

Harmonie Toros and Filippo Dionigi

INTRODUCTION

In *The Anarchical Society* (1977) Hedley Bull has proposed one of the most influential modern theorizations of International Relations. His theory, nevertheless, was embedded in a social and historical context that, forty years later, has significantly changed.

The relevance of social and political actors that do not belong to the category of the state or to the group of multilateral inter-state institutions is one of the most significant developments in international politics, which has acquired prominence at least since the end of the Cold War (Buzan 2004). Scholarly literature has highlighted the importance of phenomena such as the emergence of a global civil society (Held and McGrew 1998; Kaldor 2003) and the role of NGOs as facilitators of norms diffusion (Keck and Sikkink 1999; Risse-Kappen 1995). The rise of transnational organizations constitutes another challenge to the state's monopoly of power in international politics (Nye and Keohane 1971). Furthermore, and of relevance to this analysis, armed non-state actors have become increasingly influential, especially after the 11 September 2001 attacks.

The Anarchical Society advances a state-centric conceptualization of world politics and thus may appear ill equipped to account for a context increasingly populated by influential non-state actors. To be fair, in *The Anarchical Society*, Bull considers the possibility that the international system may change, reflecting patterns of increasing transnational integration and the growing importance of non-state actors (Bull 1977, 225–7). He considers various scenarios including a centralized 'World Government' (1977, 252–4); the emergence of a 'new Mediaevalism' (1977, 245–7; 54–66) in which the 'overlapping or segmented authority that characterised mediaeval Christendom' (1977, 264) would re-emerge; and the formation of a 'world political system' whereby state and non-state actors interact in a shift from international society to a world society. His assessment, nevertheless, leads to the conclusion that none of these scenarios essentially challenges the centrality of the state and it is not, therefore, in significant decline.

In an international political context in which the state's monopoly of power is increasingly confronted by the proliferation of non-state actors, has Bull's theory become obsolete? We argue that, although grounded in a statist perspective, Bull's concept of international society still constitutes a useful interpretative framework to account for the discourse and practice of those non-state actors that have the objective of becoming a state or a surrogate for it.

This essay focuses on non-state armed actors. Specifically, we analyse the case of the organization Islamic State (*al-Dawla al-Islamiyya*), which offers an example of how a non-state armed actor can challenge and confront international society, while at the same time engage with and mimic its norms and practices. Indeed, although the identity of IS is based on an ideological foundation remote from and even contrary to the traditional institutions of international society,[1] we observe how its discursive and practical activities cannot transcend fully the influence of international society. IS thus provides an interesting test case against which to confront Bull's conceptualization of the role of non-state actors in international society.

We argue in this chapter that international society constitutes a source of validation for IS. The use of international society's vocabulary, practices, and institutions constitutes for IS a way to attempt to elevate its status from that of informal organization to that of a state. However, once established as a para-state entity,[2] IS has engaged in a process of norm contestation whereby it has confronted the traditional (and mostly Western-centric) conception of order of international society and countered it with the ideal of a 'Caliphate' as a religious supranational order. Thus, IS appears to have used international society's language and attempted to mimic its institutions strategically so as to be able to eventually mount a more credible attack on international society itself.

---

[1] Balance of power, international law, diplomacy, war and great powers. (Bull 1977, 71–4)

[2] As we shall see, the debate on whether IS is a state or not is a crucial aspect of its very existence. We use the term para-state because, however imperfect, it captures the precarious and unstable reality of IS as an organization that simulates certain characteristics of statehood. We refrain from using the term 'quasi-state' because in scholarly literature this term identifies entities which, although not enjoying full statehood in empirical terms, 'have been internationally enfranchised and possess the same external rights and responsibilities as all other sovereign states' (Jackson 1990, 21). This does not apply to the case of IS.

We will initially contextualize non-state actors in the debate on Bull's theory of anarchical society and the English School at large. Subsequently, we provide an overview of the rise of IS. In order to show its interactions with international society, we then analyse discursive and material instances of its use of international society's norms and institutions. Finally, we examine the uneasiness that IS's rise and its state-building agenda have created and how international society has attempted to counter IS strategies to be acknowledged as a state.

NON-STATE ACTORS AND THE ANARCHICAL SOCIETY

For decades, non-state armed actors have engaged in political, social, economic, and military activities to achieve their objectives. As part of this process, they have interacted with international society through multiple channels. Self-determination movements are the most striking example. Groups such as the Palestinian Liberation Organization, the Kurdish groups for self-determination, Hamas, Hezbollah, the National Salvation Front, and the Front for National Liberation in Algeria—to mention but a few examples—have all resorted to the use of force as a means to achieve self-determination.

Bull considers the role of these actors as an emerging phenomenon which he defines as 'the restoration of private international violence' (1977, 268). He observes that these movements challenge the state monopoly of the legitimate use of force but notes that 'the non-state groups which at present assert the right to engage in international violence appear in every case to aim to establish new states, or to gain control of existing ones' (1977, 270).

Indeed, achieving statehood is the main objective of these movements because statehood is the status that guarantees self-determination, sovereignty, and therefore the freedom of peoples to control their lives. In this process, the use of force is only one aspect of their strategy; most of these organizations have engaged also in activities that resemble the typical actions of states domestically and internationally. For example, some of these movements have established diplomatic contacts. The Palestinian Liberation Organization (PLO) has established 'embassies' in states in which Palestine is recognized as a state, and has participated in UN General Assembly activities. Kurdish activists have established lobby groups in parliaments and international organizations, and they have progressively asserted a *de facto* statehood (Voller 2014). Other groups have established their presence operating as paramilitary organizations (as Hamas or Hezbollah) thus raising their status to security providers or border control forces against occupying states (Gunning 2008; Harik 2004). Many of these actors have often contested borders and attempted to demarcate new territorial boundaries. Most of these organizations, importantly, also supply services and welfare including some form of education and social security (Grynkewich 2008; Huang 2015).

Non-state actors that pursue the objective of statehood, then, attempt to legitimize their objectives not only by referring to their own ideological frameworks (such as Nationalism, Anti-colonialism, Socialism, Islamism, etc.), but also by resorting in their discourse to the practices, norms, and vocabulary of international society. Becoming a state is not only a matter of force but also a matter of engaging in discursive and symbolic practices associated with statehood in international society.

Some of these processes have turned out to be relatively successful, and they would not have been as effective in an international normative vacuum. Instead they were dependent on their reference to international society and the recognition that they received from at least some of its members as a source of legitimacy. For example, the transition from the PLO to the Palestinian Authority, and the current process of recognition of the State of Palestine within the United Nations, mark significant developments in the state-building process of Palestine (BBC 2015; UN 2012). The Kurdish question has witnessed new important developments following the US invasion of Iraq in 2003 and during the war against IS (Stansfield 2014).

Bull acknowledged the fact that armed non-state actors can have a degree of success. According to him, '[W]hat is more impressive than the fact that international violence is resorted to by these non-state groups is the fact that their claim of the right to do so is accepted as legitimate by a substantial proportion of international society' (1977, 268–9). International society, therefore, is used by non-state actors as a source of recognition of their legitimacy. The possibility for these non-state actors to succeed is dependent on their capacity to muster a degree of recognition of their cause and status among the members of international society. These actors, therefore, engage in a process of interaction with international society, by adapting, interpreting, or contesting its norms and principles. To some extent this interaction *can* turn into the early phase of a process of socialization defined as 'inducting actors into the norms and rules of a given community'[3] (Checkel 2005, 804). As Bull observed in a later publication, international society expands to include also excluded actors; and 'the coming together of numerous and extremely diverse political entities to form a single international society presupposed that these entities had come to resemble one another at least to the extent that they were all, in some comparable sense, states' (Bull and Watson 1984, 121).

---

[3] Note that we refer to this specific definition of socialization because Zurn and Checkel highlight that by this definition socialization can take place through mechanisms that include not only normative suasion, but also 'role playing'. The latter represents a more *instrumental* or *opportunist* conformity to norms that nevertheless can lead to actor socialization (Zürn and Checkel 2005, 1050).

The emergence of Islamist groups arguably poses a challenge to Bull's understanding of the role of non-state actors in international society. They have become increasingly diffused in the Middle East and North Africa regions and their influence has competed with or supplanted secular, nationalist, or socialist-oriented groups. Furthermore, the more recent generation of Islamist non-state actors such as Al-Qaeda (AQ) differ on how they articulate their political projects as they do not have a strong territorial ambition either materially or ideologically (Mendelsohn 2012, 595). They generally refer to a vague idea of an Islamic land (*Dar al-Islam*), the borders of which remain blurry. Whereas secular self-determination movements aspire to forms of statehood that fundamentally resemble the Western nation-state, Islamist movements, such as AQ and IS, refer to the ideal of the caliphate as their final political objective. Their constituency is not a national group, and instead they consider the Umma (the Muslim community) as the people over which the caliphate legitimately rules.

Such features may appear inevitably to diminish the possibility of interacting with international society. Barack Mendelsohn has argued that groups such as AQ and Hizb ut-Tahrir have as their objective, an international order that is inevitably incompatible with international society as a Westphalian system (2012). But can such groups be integrated in international society? Do they fit Bull's account of the integration of non-state actors? Stephen Walt, with reference to the case of IS, has argued that the international system in the long term tends to socialize even the most challenging cases. 'The new state gradually adapts to prevailing international norms and practices, and it eventually moves from pariah to partner, especially when its interests start to coincide with those of other states', Walt argues (2015).[4] Not everyone agrees. Lawrence Rubin observes that an actor such as IS will never be socialized into international society as the ideological foundations of Islamist movements have the effect of causing an 'ideational security dilemma' that prompts a hostile response from other states whose identity is challenged by the state-building endeavour of Islamist actors (2015).

Of course, the International Relations debate on socialization is extensive and has been central to the English School from its early works, such as F.S. Northedge's *The International Political System* in which he argues that even the regimes most opposed to the international system, such as the Soviet Union, end up being some of its staunchest defenders (1976). David Armstrong furthered this investigation into revolutionary states when he argued that the status quo of international society tends to prevail over the influence

---

[4] Walt's conceptualization of norms and practices of the international system are not the same as Bull's conceptualization of norms and practices of international society, but the debate on IS' future relationship with other states—whether thought of as in an anarchic realist system or an English School system—is the central question.

of revolutionary international actors which are progressively socialized into it, while also being able to shape at least some aspects of international society (Armstrong 1993).[5] Although we argue that arguments made with regard to the socialization of states may only partly be applicable to the case of IS, our focus is less on whether IS will eventually be socialized and more on how the IS ambition to statehood and its efforts to realize this, have been at least in part drawn from international society's conceptualization of a modern state. Indeed, rather than arguing whether or not IS will survive or be integrated into international society, the aim of this essay is to examine how it has positioned itself with respect to international society—at times in line with its material and discursive practices and at times in violent opposition to them—showing the centrality of such norms and practices.

FROM AL-QAEDA TO IS

IS[6] is the most recent addition to a vast group of Islamist non-state actors that have been operating regionally and globally for decades. Its ideological roots belong to a radical interpretation of Sunni Salafist traditions which have their origins in the Arabian Peninsula and which, until recently, was mainly represented by AQ (Bunzel 2015, 9–11).

The organization originates from AQ's Iraqi branch operated by Abu Musab al-Zarqawi who, in 2004, dismantled his militia to establish al-Qaeda in Iraq (AQI) (Hashim 2014, 71). The main objectives of AQI reflected the typical principles of Islamist Salafism, including the removal of the occupying forces from Iraq, the promotion of *Tawhid*,[7] the fight against 'infidels', and the establishment of the caliphate. But the brutality of its anti-Shi'a sectarian violence and the deliberate attacks also against Muslim civilians apparently caused disagreement between AQ's leadership and AQI (al-'Ubaydi et al. 2014; Bunzel 2015).

In 2006, al-Zarqawi was killed by the American forces and a new organization, Islamic State in Iraq (ISI) was founded under the leadership of Abu 'Umar al-Baghdadi. This time the objective of establishing a state entity had more prominence but it failed because ISI was not capable of attracting the

---

[5] A useful conceptualization here is also Jeffrey Checkel's (2005) idea of a transition from a 'logic of consequence' to a 'logic of appropriateness'.

[6] We refer to the present organisation as IS. As examined in detail in this section, it is the latest incarnation of a non-state armed group that originated as al-Qaeda in Iraq (AQI) in 2004, evolved into the Islamic State of Iraq (ISI) in 2006, into the Islamic State of Iraq and Sham (ISIS) also known as the Islamic State of Iraq and the Levant (ISIL) in 2013, and finally into the Islamic State (2014) in June 2014.

[7] *Tawhid* can be broadly defined as the principle of the unity and uniqueness of God, thus confirming the strictly monotheistic nature of Islam.

support of local populations and dignitaries (Hashim 2014, 72). What is important to note is that the ISI's announcement in October 2006 of establishing a state in the short term was a significant departure from AQ strategies and objectives, which have always revolved around the long-term strategy of building a caliphate after having expelled the US and its allies from Muslim lands. As noted by Brian Fishman, ISI had the ambition of resembling a caliphate-state by virtue of control of territory, leadership of an Emir, the implementation of tasks such as judicial services based on Sharia principles, and collection of *Zakāt* (2007). Both within and without the Iraqi community, however, ISI was ridiculed for its incapacity to effectively achieve any of these aspects and thus failed to gain credibility (Bunzel 2015, 17–24).

Nevertheless, ISI re-emerged in 2010. This time the objectives of the organization were more clearly structured and its operations benefited from a number of favourable factors such as the war in Syria, the exacerbation of sectarian divides, and the failure of the Iraqi state to exercise its functions (al-'Ubaydi et al. 2014, 18–26). Another aspect characterizing ISI was the recruitment within its ranks of former Iraqi members of the Baath party with political and military experience who provided know-how in military and intelligence activities (Hashim 2014, 73–5).

In April 2013, ISI officially expanded its range of action to Syria and mutated into the 'Islamic State of Iraq and *Sham*' (ISIS)[8], the latter being a traditional name identifying the Arab land in the Levant region. At this point, ISIS was openly challenging AQ's leadership and eventually in Syria became involved in clashes with the local branch of AQ, *Jabhat al-Nusra*.

In June 2014, ISIS released a declaration, 'This is the Promise of Allah', in which it announced the establishment of the Islamic state in the form of the Caliphate (*Khilāfa*) led by Abu Bakr al-Baghdadi; it was at this point that the organization took on the name 'Islamic State' (anonymous 2014a).

In contrast with AQ, the leadership of IS not only claimed the title of Caliph for Abu Bakr al-Baghdadi, but declared that 'the legality of all emirates, groups, states, and organizations becomes null by the expansion of the caliph's authority and the arrival of its troops in their areas' (anonymous 2014a, 5). Thus, differently from AQ, it attempted to establish a unified authority as a tangible territorial existence of the Islamic State as caliphate, the borders of which are coterminous with its military expansion. Furthermore, the Islamic State not only claimed the control of land but also of people. Indeed, in the declaration document of IS, all Muslims are called to the religious duty (according to IS) of subjecting themselves to the caliphate and to the authority of the caliph giving *bay'ah*[9] to him.

---

[8] Also translated as the Islamic State of Iraq and the Levant, ISIL.
[9] *Bay'ah* is a declaration that establishes the status of submission of a subject to an authority.

Thus, in contrast to its previous incarnation that was ridiculed for its incapacity to establish an effective state in 2006—with some Islamist scholars calling it '"imaginary" and existing only online' (Bunzel 2015, 20)—IS's stronger claim to statehood by the early 2010s led to an increased capacity to establish its broader credibility and effectively challenge AQ's leadership of the global jihadi movement. Most importantly for our argument, aside from boosting hegemonic ambitions within the Islamist fold, territorial control and state-like practices of IS also directly challenged the international society of states. We shall examine more closely how IS has taken on the features of statehood in the next section.

IS AND STATE-BUILDING

IS represents both a confirmation of and a challenge to Bull's understanding of the role of non-state actors in international society. Like most non-state armed groups, it has sought to acquire recognition as a power by engaging with the discursive and material practices of international society, and has partly implemented a state-building process by 'mimicking'[10] the standards and practices of modern statehood. Indeed, from its inception as AQI, IS placed greater importance on state-building than other movements such as AQ had, and attempted to establish the trappings of a modern state (borders, government, armed forces, police, tribunals, social services, currency, etc.).

Three reasons can be identified for this. Firstly, AQI and its successor groups (ISI, ISIS, and IS) had the opportunity to act in an unprecedented institutional vacuum. This has made state-building a strategy that responds directly to needs and opportunities emerging from the context of state failure within which this movement operated in Iraq and then Syria. Secondly, as examined in the previous section (From Al-Qaeda to IS), AQI and its subsequent incarnations were part of a broader project (including some Baathist elements) to reclaim the reins of the Iraqi state from the US administration and the predominantly Shi'a and Kurdish competing groups that were under US or Iranian influence. Thirdly, territorial control, as well as a functioning bureaucracy and economy, were a means to demonstrate to the Western-dominated international society and its regional allies that IS was a power to be reckoned with, capable of accomplishments in the same sectors in which Western powers and their allies had failed in Iraq and Syria. Being recognized

---

[10] We refer here to the concept of mimicking as a socialization mechanism as defined by Alastair Iain Johnston, 'Mimicking is a mechanism whereby a novice initially copies the behavioural norms—including discursive practices—of the group to navigate through an uncertain environment' (Johnston 2005, 1021–2).

as capable state-builders was thus key in the group's positioning with respect to at least three audiences. First of all, it sought credibility with respect to a local audience as a viable alternative to collapsing states. Secondly, it aimed to prove to the transnational jihadist movement that it had supplanted AQ as global leader. Finally, with respect to the international society of states, they aimed to use their alleged state-building success to prove that they are a power to be reckoned with. To achieve these goals, IS engaged in the mimicry of state discursive and material practices. Each shall be examined in turn.

Discursively, the IS leadership clearly stated that state-building was its foremost aim. 'The jama'ah's most important goal would be to revive *tawhid* (the unity of God) especially in matters ignored and abandoned by "Islamic" parties in our times—matters relating to wala' (governing), hukm (ruling), and tashri (legislation)' (anonymous 2014h, 35). Indeed, the first time al-Zarqawi appeared in a video message in 2006, he announced the establishment of the *Mujahidin Shura Council*, hailing it as 'the starting point for establishing an Islamic State' (Bunzel, 2015: 16).

By 2014, when IS was able to demonstrate territorial control, it insisted on the effective existence of a 'state' in *The Promise of Allah* (anonymous 2014a). The document uses the rallying chorus, '[I]ndeed, it is a State!' reiterating the identification of the territory it had control over. Furthermore, it is particularly important to point out how the word used is that of '*dawla*' and not caliphate (*Khilāfah*). IS regards itself as the Islamic 'State' and only subsequently is this state identified as a caliphate. *Dawla* is not a term derived from Islamic theology. It is used only two times in the Quran and never with the meaning of 'state' as IS uses it. In its more commonly used meaning, the concept of *dawla* identifies the bureaucratic, administrative, hierarchical structure of the state entity in a modern sense. This analogy between IS as a political organization and a modern form of statehood is matched also by a hierarchical structure that resembles that of a governmental cabinet. As Charles Lister observes, 'By perceiving and presenting itself as a state, IS has sought to control and govern territory and maintain a cabinet of ministers responsible for a broad range of "ministries," incorporating military, civil, political, and financial duties' (Lister 2014, 21).

This discourse of state-building can also be found in the practices of IS. In its para-state activity, IS has established a presence on economic, security, administrative and education levels (Turkmani 2015, 9–12). For example, the economy of IS is informed by the objective of achieving autarchy (Turkmani 2015, 13). Thus, IS has implemented a taxation and extortion system that has provided economic revenues for the administration (Lister 2014, 21–4). IS has also engaged in the exploitation and trade of local natural resources, above all oil. According to the former vice-governor of the Iraqi Central Bank, Mudher Mohammah Saleh, IS in early 2015 controlled 15 per cent of Iraqi GDP, including numerous oil fields and refineries (Fritel 2014).

The economic organization of IS also began to assume state-like characteristics when it announced the establishment of a gold-pegged currency by a self-appointed Office of the Treasury (Alkhshali and Ford 2014). While the economic viability of the project is, to say the least, questionable (anonymous 2015), what is significant is that IS has tried to shape its international image of itself as a state by claiming to have a role as financial and monetary actor.[11]

Similarly IS depicts itself as an entity capable of administering and implementing basic state-like tasks such as road maintenance and health services. Most reports on activities taking place in IS-controlled areas remain unconfirmed, but it is sufficient to point out how the organization portrays itself as a services provider (Lister 2014, 27–9). In one of its 'reports' published in the English-language propaganda magazine, *Dabiq*, IS claims that it has carried out road maintenance, provided services such as cleaning of public areas, the provision of meals and assistance to the elderly, and even cancer treatment to children through local hospitals (anonymous 2014g, 27–9). In addition to this, an administrative system of *Wilayat* (Provinces) has been put into place, with a structure which, according to IS propaganda, includes a police force (*al-Shurta al-Islamiya*), border enforcement, and other tasks such as tribunals and 'information' networks (anonymous 2014f, 18–20; 2014g, 16–17). There are several testimonies also confirming the establishment of a religious judicial system which relies on both courts and religious police. Furthermore, services such as street cleaning, electricity, water, and activities related to agricultural production are in place at least in the main urban areas under IS control (Turkmani 2015, 9–10).

This insistence in discourse and practice on state-building (which no doubt exaggerates the reality on the ground) has been essential for IS to claim credibility as a state-like organization. Indeed, what these discourses and practices denote is an acceptance of statehood—as understood by international society—as the primary criterion by which power is judged in today's international arena. By making claims about territorial integrity, the monopoly of the use violence, a nascent economic system, and a bureaucratic administrative infrastructure, IS attempts to promote itself as a modern state by Western standards and to gain acknowledgement of its presumed status of state within the region and in international society.

The result is not a state, but a para-state or a caricature of a state. The army is, at least in part, impersonated by thuggish militias, security is largely implemented through extreme displays of violence and arbitrary justice, and the economy relies on extortion and looting. Furthermore, the provision of services (health, transports, road maintenance) is generally based on pre-existing structures where available (Lister 2014, 21–3; Turkmani 2015, 9–11).

---

[11] IS propaganda diffused further images and comments on this activity in 'The Currency of the Khilafah' in *Dabiq*, 2015, No. 5, pp. 18–19.

But IS's goal of state-building nonetheless re-affirms the pattern that Bull outlined with regards to other non-state actors when he claimed that their ultimate aim remains 'to establish new states, or to gain control of existing ones' (1977, 270). The ideal of statehood as it is represented by the standard forms and practices of international society constitutes a mark of credibility for non-state actors such as IS, as they attempt to carve out a place in the map of international society by leaning on the legitimacy that these forms and practices confer when properly implemented.

STATE VS. CALIPHATE

IS's objective of establishing an Islamic state, however, is not only about the idea of 'state' but also about its 'Islamic-ness'. The organization needs, on one hand, to find its place in international society, and on the other hand, to live up to the expectations generated by its Islamist identity. In other words, its institutions cannot be simply a police organization, a social security service, a taxation system, and a military force. Instead, to be consistent with IS identity, the police has to be an *Islamic* police, services have to be *Islamic* services, citizenship has to be Muslim citizenship, its army has to be an Islamic army of *mujahidin*. Otherwise its credibility in the eyes of its Islamist supporters will inevitably be affected.

Thus, in its progression from organization to para-state entity IS has increasingly framed this process in the concept of the caliphate, because this is the only polity that Salafism can justify as legitimate in its own religious terms. The IS declaration of the caliphate in 2014 is a milestone in this process of Islamic branding of IS's alleged statehood. Indeed, IS has presented its pre-caliphate state-building strategy as merely a stepping stone towards its real goal of establishing a caliphate. Baghdadi, in his first public sermon after being declared caliph in June 2014, said that declaring the establishment of the Caliphate is a duty for all Muslims (al-Baghdadi 2014). The 'Islamic State', then, was merely a 'condition' towards the creation of the caliphate (anonymous 2014e), with the former status seen as a means to be recognized as worthy and capable of being entrusted with the latter. Whether this is the organization's intention or not, this discursive move ensures that IS cannot be accused of having been socialized and accepted into Western-dominated international society as they claim that their engagement with the latter's understanding of the state and state practices has been solely instrumental.

Thus, whereas the adoption of discourses and practices of statehood have the effect of producing an analogy and therefore a connection between the IS para-state and internationally accepted forms of statehood, the Islamic branding of the state as a caliphate produces a gap, or even a clash, between international standards and IS. The declaration of the caliphate, in fact, amounts to an open challenge to the commonly accepted forms of statehood in international society (Mendelsohn 2012).

The first aspect that sets apart the caliphate promoted by IS from more common forms of statehood is that its political leadership is entirely centralized in the figure of the caliph. According to the traditional understanding of the concept, the caliph should be a descendant of the Prophet Muhammad and a Muslim willing to fully implement the principles of Islam in its political leadership. In the 2014 declaration of the caliphate, this is clearly stated when it is claimed that a *majlis al-shura* (a consultative assembly) has appointed Abu-Bakr al-Baghdadi as caliph. Baghdadi is identified as *Amir al-Mu'minin*, 'the commander of the faithful' and IS also attributes him with ancestry related to the family of the prophet (anonymous 2014a; Lister 2014, 11). According to this view, the Caliph acts as the worldly 'vicar' of god's sovereignty following the steps and examples of the prophet's experience. Sovereignty therefore is fully embedded in a conservative interpretation of Islam that sharply differs from the Westphalian origins of sovereignty that we find in the English School tradition.

Secondly, the caliphate is professed by IS as a transnational and potentially universal political institution to which all Muslims are called to submit. Thus, IS not only contests the legitimacy of borders that were established in the region by the end of the First World War, it rejects the idea of nation and national borders. This has been the result of a gradual transition. As discussed above, IS was initially delimited and contextualized within the borders of Iraq, then later within Iraq and Syria (*al-Sham*), and only in 2014 did it drop national demarcations completely in order to articulate its supranational ambitions. Baghdadi in his address as caliph, states that 'indeed the world today has been divided in two camps and two trenches, with no third camp present: The camp of Islam and faith, and the camp of *kufr* (disbelief) and hypocrisy' (al-Baghdadi 2014).

This rejection of nationalism creates a concept of sovereignty that directly challenges that of Bull's international society. Fishman analyses in detail an essay written by Sheikh Utham al-Tamimi who conceptualizes this meaning of sovereignty and territoriality. According to this view, a previous incarnation of IS was a sovereign state in the sense that it would exercise its sovereignty over anyone who swore allegiance to it. Thus, the state rules over any territory in which its 'citizens' were dwelling, beyond the limits of officially recognized borders (Fishman 2007, 7). IS has adopted this interpretation and the institution of the caliphate entails the submission of all Muslims to its authority and that of the caliph as a religious duty through the act of *bay'aa*. As the declaratory document of the caliphate states, 'He [the caliph] is the *imam* and *khalipha* for the Muslims everywhere' (anonymous, 2014a, 5). As Mendelsohn notes, this configuration of political order entails a subversion of an international system based on separate sovereign states (Mendelsohn 2015).

IS therefore presents an idea of the caliphate as antithetical to the principles of a society of sovereign states as it deems this kind of order to be an embodiment of an idolatric cult in which the sovereignty of god is replaced by the sovereignty of the state. The caliphate, in its accomplished form, is supposed to constitute a global polity replacing the nation-state order with a universal regime ruled by IS's interpretation of Islam.

Finally, the branding of the Islamic para-state as caliphate was matched with a military and media campaign that purposely provoked shock and revulsion from those actors who have even the least deference for international normative principles. In an issue of *Dabiq* and through other media channels, IS has made public its use of children as soldiers as part of its strategy. In another issue, IS condoned slavery, and in particular sexual slavery of women, as a morally acceptable practice when implemented towards non-Muslims, and even argues that it is sanctioned by its interpretation of Islam as 'humiliation and degradation for the Kafir' (al-Muhajirah 2014, 46). Another activity provoking media attention and public dismay concerns the destruction of UNESCO world archaeological sites explained as the destruction of idols and cults left by infidels' civilizations (anonymous 2014d, 22–4).[12] Here too the objective seems to be one of clearly opposing a presumed Islamic identity and values against principles and norms that have enjoyed international legitimacy.[13]

The announcement of a caliphate, as well as the practices that followed its establishment, have been explicitly in tension with the attempt to realize a state structure that resembles the idea of statehood more commonly found in international society. The para-state entity that IS has attempted to create, especially at an early stage, has not only been complemented but also contradicted by its specific branding as a/the caliphate. Whereas IS's ambition to statehood has encouraged it to emulate 'states' in the sense accepted in international society, the announcement of the caliphate embodies a rejection of international society's principles to be replaced with Islamic principles as interpreted by IS.

IS's identity is, therefore, caught in a contradiction whereby it is trying to build its credibility and reputation of state-like entity but, at the same time, is engaged in a contestation of the sources and principles upon which such recognition can be acknowledged. Once again, this begs the question of

---

[12] Note that later investigations have highlighted that IS has only in part destroyed the heritage site.

[13] In *The Expansion of International Society* Bull described a process of international norm contestation that resonates with the claims of cultural and religious authenticity that IS makes in its bid for international statehood. Although he did not refer explicitly to the case of Islamism, his discussion of a 'revolt against the West' resembles the process that we describe herein with regard to IS (Bull 1984b).

whether IS will follow the fate of past revolutionary states which were eventually integrated into international society while also impacting on its form and functioning (Armstrong 1993). Indeed, Soviet legal scholars, such as Korovin and Pashukanis, struggled with similar problems in the 1920s and 1930s, questioning how the Soviet state could engage with 'bourgeois' states, and understood any interaction as an occasion to attack the capitalist system (Chakste 1949). Armstrong notes, however, that 'Soviets adjusted their approach, opting for a general observance of the conventional norms of diplomacy in their formal relations with other states, while continuing to support the cause of world revolution through Comintern' (Armstrong 1993, 264).

One way in which IS may be less open to socialization than revolutionary states is that unlike them, it has not taken over a pre-existing bureaucracy with long-established practices that include engagement with international society but has rather attempted to build its own bureaucratic structures.[14] Furthermore, as a non-state armed group shunned by other states and international organizations, IS has less occasion to interact with international society, potentially reducing its chances of socialization. It is difficult to predict whether IS, if it succeeds in maintaining some degree of territorial control, will eventually move further down the confrontational route or instead show signs of socialization. This will also depend on how international society engages with it.

THE POLITICS OF THE 'SO-CALLED'

We have seen that the name of IS has gone through several mutations reflecting an evolution from an AQ-related organization to an autonomous Islamist entity claiming to constitute a caliphate. The correspondent evolution of the organization's name is more than symbolic. As discussed above, the act of identifying the organization as 'state' (*dawla*) has been a means to pursue the objective of being acknowledged by international society as such. As mentioned earlier, Bull pointed out that non-state actors consistently rely not only on the use of force but also on processes of recognition and external support in their attempt to establish their status of 'state'. IS is no exception: acknowledgement as a state is a key aspect even though it is entirely hostile to the source of this acknowledgement, i.e. international society.

IS demonstrates a keen interest in showing how it is acknowledged as a state entity. In the caliphate announcement document, IS tells other Islamist groups

---

[14] Although IS has taken over the provision of public services from previous administrations, IS has attempted to build a new bureaucratic structure.

that they too must acknowledge the Islamic State, since *America, Britain, and France acknowledge its existence* (anonymous 2014a, 9 emphasis added).

This is further corroborated by another strategy of IS in which it attempts to put 'into the mouth of its opponents' the acknowledgement of its statehood. Here we refer to the series of articles in *Dabiq* entitled, 'The Islamic State in the Words of the Enemy', which appears in all nine issues analysed by the authors. It selects and highlights declarations from analysts, politicians, and journalists which, IS claims, recognize the status of IS as a state. For example, Douglas Ollivant, former Director for Iraq at the US National Security Council, and Brian Fishman of Westpoint are quoted as saying: 'The group [IS] does not have safe haven within a state. It is a de facto state that is a safe haven' (anonymous 2014c, 32). Indeed, this is accurately quoted from Ollivant and Fishman's blog (Ollivant and Fishman 2014). The journalist, Patrick Cockburn for *The Independent*, is quoted as saying: 'Neither the Iraqi nor the Syrian armies, its chief military opponents, are strong enough to over-run the jihadi state' (anonymous 2014f, 52).[15]

Western and other states hostile to IS have struggled to counter this process. The fact that IS has called itself 'Islamic State' makes it difficult to avoid acknowledgement of its status whenever its name is mentioned. As a result, various alternative forms of naming IS have emerged. One of the most common is the use of the locution 'so-called' preceding IS in order to avoid ambiguity. For example, Barack Obama referred to 'so-called Islamic State of Iraq and the Levant' in a letter to the Congress in 2015 and elsewhere explained that he did not consider IS either Islamic or a state (Obama 2015a; 2015b).[16] The regional opponents to IS have coined the word D'aesh originating from its acronym in Arabic. This term has progressively gained a pejorative connotation and is used by those who are disinclined to call IS by its own name.

The list of examples could continue, but what we shall note here is that alongside the military battle to defeat IS, there is also a clear discursive conflict being fought on whether IS can be referred to as a 'state'. IS has deployed all of its media capacity to present itself as a state in the eyes of its supporters and of its enemies. Against this, the opponents of IS have countered this attempt by trying to avoid any implicit or explicit verbal acknowledgement of IS as a state. We consider this war of words as a significant indicator of how seriously both sides—IS and its opponents—treat statehood as understood by international society.

---

[15] Original text is http://www.independent.co.uk/voices/isis-hostage-crisis-militant-group-stands-strong-as-its-numerous-enemies-fail-to-find-a-common-plan-10009151.html.

[16] For a telling example of how problematic the question of naming IS is in order not to lend it credibility over its status, see also the statement of US Secretary of State John Kerry in a public hearing on the matter (Kerry 2015).

CONCLUSION

Four decades ago Bull may have underestimated the power of non-state actors to contest not only the borders but also the norms and practices that define state actors. What he did not underestimate is the enduring power of international society as capable of granting the status of 'state'.

Non-state actors may be able to put up an ideational challenge against international society, but it is still *from* international society that they need to wrangle legitimate power. It is international society that recognizes non-state actors as either enemies worth reckoning with or as actors worthy and capable of socialization. Power and authority remain closely attached to the entity of the state. Non-state actors aspire to statehood because they recognize that it is only by being acknowledged as a state by international society that their power can effectively be substantiated.

The case of IS is particularly interesting. Whether or not IS remains in control of territory and whether or not it is socialized in the international system, the case shows how even an actor that is, in theory, opposed to the institutions and practices of international society, inevitably had to engage with its discursive and material practices in order to establish its relevance.

As we examined here, IS has engaged in a state-building campaign—both discursive and material—in order to be seen as a valid and viable state. Its strategy capitalizes on the state-centric nature of international society and on the institutional vacuum that has been left by the crumbling of the Iraqi and Syrian states. Interestingly, once established as an organization that could claim some semblance of statehood—a 'para-state'—IS chose, alongside its state-building practices of governing the territory under its control, to also challenge international society's norms and practices declaring the founding of a caliphate and displaying practices designed to shock and provoke international society. Thus, IS used what it claimed was an acknowledgement of international society to gain prominence as a significant international actor. Having felt that it had achieved this, IS was confident enough to directly challenge the very norms and practices that it had used to achieve its position.

Western-led international society could not ignore the rapid rise of IS and its role in Syrian and Iraqi territories but any statement stressing the danger of IS and its state-building strategy became a discursive win for IS. This led to what we have named the 'politics of the so-called' in which state actors have insisted that IS is certainly a threat to international society, but one characterized by its 'non-state' or 'so-called' status.

The complex and contradictory nature of this process, which on one hand is about state-building but on the other hand is about international society norm contestation, brings us to the conclusion that a sharp dichotomy between socialization and alienation can hardly be drawn. IS remains an actor with a two-pronged strategy which, in phases of expansion exploits the discursive and material practices of international society to implement a state-building project, but subsequently attempts to contest and possibly subvert its norms while continuing to engage in state-building practices on the ground, i.e. the building of a caliphate. How and whether these two contrasting directions will be reconciled we have yet to see.

In this chapter, however, we have shown that Bull's concepts still constitute an important explanatory framework to understand the dynamics of contention and adaptation with which a non-state actor such as IS has engaged in its bid to be acknowledged as an international actor. Whether IS succeeds or not, the norms and practices of the anarchical society remain the central criteria upon which the power and authority of all actors—state and non-state—continue to be based.

10

Cyberspace and International Order

Madeline Carr

INTRODUCTION

When *The Anarchical Society* was published in 1977, the world was on the doorstep of seismic technological change. Telephones were still attached to a cord, letters were a mainstay of private and commercial communication, and computers were housed in universities and military research facilities. Hedley Bull's ideas about how social processes between actors mitigate the anarchy of international politics were developed within the context of industrial age technology and he speculated only briefly on how emerging information and communications technology (ICT) might impact on those social processes in the future. Forty years of extraordinary development in technology—both in terms of scope and scale, have raised many questions, but fewer answers, about how emerging technologies reinforce or contradict what we thought we understood about international relations.

In fact, for most of those forty years, policymakers (but less so IR academics) have been attuned to the imperative of trying to make sense of these technological shifts for conceptions of global security, power, and order. There are too many significant policy implications to enumerate here but protecting critical infrastructure from cyber security vulnerabilities has been one of the more enduring concerns. Connecting critical infrastructure like energy plants, financial institutions, and transport systems to a global computer network comes with many opportunities for increased efficiency and lower costs which developed states have raced to exploit. But the relatively insecure nature of the Internet also introduces a range of vulnerabilities for those systems to be penetrated, manipulated, and damaged. The potential for such interference to lead to large-scale destruction and loss of life, coupled with speculation that state or non-state actors may pursue that potential in lieu of, or in addition to, conventional kinetic force, has led to a focus on cyber security in domestic and international politics. This has manifested in a number of ways, including the development of national cyber security strategies, the establishment of dedicated cyber security military units and doctrine, and in discussions on international cooperation on cyber security at head-of-state level. States are clearly concerned about the implications of digital technology for violence and conflict in international relations. They are preparing both to respond to it and, one must surely conclude, to utilize it in order to pursue their own national interests.

Considering the very broad implications of this technology, there have been surprisingly few attempts to employ International Relations theory, concepts, and ideas for understanding the landscape of cyber (in)security. Most of the existing work on this emerges from scholars working on military doctrine or strategic studies with a particular (and somewhat repetitive) emphasis on the writings of Clausewitz.[1] In fact, a useful starting point for trying to systematically think through continuity and change brought about by the information age can be to return to some of the other enduring IR thinkers to consider how their ideas may help. In doing so, of course, one may also observe ways in which those ideas, useful and enduring as they might be, may also come under challenge from novel circumstances. With that in mind, this essay draws on several of Bull's ideas on international order to look specifically at the problem of *attribution* in cyberspace—the persistent difficulty of tracing activities in cyberspace back to a conclusively identifiable actor.

This problem of attribution presents a unique problem for international relations because it removes an important element of the social structure that has been part of what creates order, as Bull understood it. Bull's ideas about the states system, international society, and, therefore, international order, all rest on the (previously sound) assumption that state actors are readily and accurately identifiable and that, barring some exceptions, their actions are attributable to them. This is integral to states' ability to engage in practices like diplomacy and international law. The problem of attribution, then, introduces a new dimension of anarchy—of *disorder*—to the social practices of international relations.

Although attribution may have implications for all five of Bull's institutions of international society, I focus here predominantly on international law—specifically the laws of armed conflict and international humanitarian law—because this is a particularly active site of state cooperation and contestation about cyber security.[2] Bull's ideas about the goals of minimizing violence and promoting

---

[1] Notable exceptions include Joseph Nye (2010), Johan Erikkson and Giampiero Giacomello (2006), Mary McEvoy Manjikian (2010), Nazli Choucri (2012), and, most recently, Daniel McCarthy (2015) and Lucas Kello (2013).

[2] In fact, great power relations, diplomacy, and war are all central to the debates about international law and cyberspace and the essay offers some observations about them, but only in relation to international law. Each one of them (and possibly the balance of power as well) could be the focus of further study.

peace are helpful here because both of them are major themes in debates about international law in cyberspace. This essay makes several observations about the rather mixed implications of the problem of attribution for international order. First, not only does attribution render international law difficult to apply in cyberspace, it also means that the reasons why actors tend to adhere to international law are weakened, and that the transition from informal international norms to customary law may be much slower than otherwise expected. At the same time, the challenges of this additional dimension of anarchy have been a catalyst for considerable progress in negotiations over norms of responsible state behaviour—an outcome that Bull himself might have anticipated. Finally, the potential for anonymity means that some unexpected and uncertain avenues for non-violent resolution of political tensions are developing.

The chapter is organized as follows. The first section, 'Bull on Technology' outlines what Bull had to say about what was then emerging technology in order to put his views into context and to delineate where and how his ideas fit in with the arguments put forward in this chapter. Following that, 'The Problem of Attribution' touches on why conclusive attribution of cyber attacks can be challenging and how scholars have dealt with this to date. The chapter then moves to explore the implications of attribution for international order. It does so through two substantive sections of analysis: the first, 'The Goal of Minimizing Violence', engages with Bull's ideas about political violence and maintaining peace as goals of international society which helps to establish the relationship between violence and cyberspace; the second, 'International Law and Cyberspace', deals with states' recourse to international law. The conclusions here are that the problem of attribution generates both opportunities and challenges for international order. If we are to maximize the first and minimize the second, it will be important to fully understand how they intersect with (and sometimes challenge or contradict) conventional ideas and concepts about international relations that developed in the context of industrial age technology.

BULL ON TECHNOLOGY

It is perhaps more surprising that, in *The Anarchical Society*, Bull delved into the implications of what was then very nascent technological change to the extent that he did, rather than that he did not develop this aspect more fully. He was, after all, explicit that his inquiry into order was confined to 'enduring issues of human political structure' rather than the 'substantive issues of world politics' at that time (1977, xiii). In addition, the development of information and communication technologies (ICTs) in the mid-1970s, when he was writing, pre-dated any real speculation on what networking technology would mean for international relations. And finally, there was very little movement elsewhere in the discipline of IR with which Bull might engage on these issues.

Bull's thoughts on the potential for ICTs to have a transformative effect on international relations are contained in Chapter 11 on the decline of the states system. His starting point is to engage with the debate of the late 1960s about the unifying or fragmenting influence of 'electronic' communication and media. Bull cites scholars like Brzezinski (1970, 3) who were arguing that the world remained fragmented despite the 'shrinking of the globe' while others (like McLuhan 1962) envisaged the future as a 'global village'—more united and, consequently, more peaceful. Bull explains that he finds the fragmentation argument more compelling because closer contact can generate new tensions and because he anticipated the benefits of new technology would be most pronounced at a national or regional level rather than an international level (1977, 273–4).

This debate about whether ICT's will bring us closer together, thereby rendering us more tolerant of one another's perspectives, or whether that proximity will exacerbate our differences and heighten tensions between us, continues well into the second decade of the twenty-first century. However, it is no longer the driving question at the heart of debates about technology and international relations. Nor, really, is the somewhat over-simplified question that Bull poses of whether emerging technology spells the decline of the state. There are many ways in which states are choosing, or being forced to accept, further compromises of sovereignty that may eventually combine to significantly reshape our conception of what a 'state' is. On the other hand, despite the considerable role of US-based transnational private organizations, and the many ways in which civil society has been empowered, the states system continues, 'for the time being' as Bull would qualify it, to be the key mechanism for governing cyberspace (Carr 2016b). Today, scholars are more cautious about attributing deterministic outcomes to technology that not only evolves and changes very rapidly, but which is also no longer regarded (as industrial age technology was, to a large degree, in the twentieth century) as a force for change that is divorced from human agency (Carr 2016a, 17–32).

Bull's analysis was narrowly confined to 'communications' technology and premised upon the *benefits* that he thought might derive from this technological shift. Neither he nor most other IR scholars at that time had any conception of the threats that would later come to be perceived as woven through so many aspects of politics, civil society, commerce, and military practice. Essentially, Bull regarded ICTs as another 'awkward fact' for the view of world politics as simply relations between states. But this, he pointed out was only consistent with a long list of anomalies and irregularities that had previously arisen and failed to bring about the decline of the states system (1977, 274). He also acknowledged, however, that 'a time may come when the anomalies and irregularities are so glaring that an alternative theory, better able to take account of these realities, will come to dominate the field' (1977, 275).

After forty years of extraordinary technological change, it is clear that Bull's question about the impact of emerging digital technology on the states system was really a question too broad to be explored through such a narrow aperture. Engaging with a question like his in 2017 requires first addressing a whole field of constitutive issues that arise from what we now understand to be the complex interplay of politics and digital technologies. However, while Bull's analysis of technology may not have been particularly useful, his ideas about the social nature of international relations can certainly help us to begin working through those many granular questions that it is necessary to address in order to build understanding about international relations in the information age. Indeed, the problem of attribution is one such granular question and Bull's work facilitates an approach that brings in the social dimension of what has generally been regarded as an explicitly technical problem.

THE PROBLEM OF ATTRIBUTION

It can be difficult (sometimes impossible) to conclusively attribute cyber activity using technical methods (Wheeler and Larsen 2003). The skill of the attacker, the sophistication of the target's security architecture and practices, and the time between detection and investigation of an attack all present challenges to attribution. The fact that attribution is neither always *possible* nor always *impossible* has generated disagreements in IR about its significance. We can only speculate on whether, in the future, technological solutions will be found to completely eliminate the attribution problem, or whether advances in shielding identities and masking actions online will keep pace with detection and tracing capabilities—such that the problem persists. The current state of play is one in which, for sophisticated actors (both state and non-state), it remains possible to avoid detection and conclusive attribution. For highly skilled security investigators, it is often possible to trace attacks to regions, states, or even neighbourhoods but not usually to make substantiated claims about the actor's identity or the motivation or intention behind an attack—a point I return to in the discussion of the application of international law.

Much of the literature on the attribution problem focuses quite narrowly on its implications for deterrence. Rid and Buchanan point out that attribution is 'at the core of virtually all forms of coercion and deterrence'. They regard it as impacting on a state's 'credibility, its effectiveness, and ultimately its liberty and its security' (2015, 4). Clark and Landau write that '[a]ttribution is central to *deterrence*, the idea that one can dissuade attackers from acting through fear of some sort of retaliation. *Retaliation requires knowing with full certainty who the attackers are'* (2011, 25 italics in original). The challenges of deterrence in cyberspace coupled with the capacity for less conventionally powerful actors to exploit cyber vulnerabilities has caused concern in many quarters (while clearly being recognized as an opportunity by others).

In *The Anarchical Society*, Bull's arguments on deterrence, its role in balancing power, in rendering war irrational, and in preserving peace, all rest on the premise that states are identifiable (1977, 117–26). He considers two technological developments that might upset mutual (nuclear) deterrence: the acquisition of perfect defence and the capacity to disarm an opponent's retaliatory forces (1977, 124–5). In the context of cyber security, the first development is an ongoing pursuit in which operators of computer systems and networks maintain a regime of constantly updating and patching their systems and improving practices so as to minimize the likelihood of penetration. However, at this stage, there really is no expectation that *any* network is impervious to intrusion and exploitation. Bull's second development, of course, returns us to attribution—because we need to know *who our opponent is* in order to disarm them.

Deterrence is not always effective in the physical world. When dealing with security threats from non-state actors, for example, the kinds of coercive mechanisms that work on state actors have failed to change the behaviour of those who feel they have nothing to lose or who actively seek martyrdom. In the context of cyber security, however, it is proving particularly frustrating for many states that they are unable to deter other *state* actors that are able either to hide their actions completely or to mask them behind proxies (by contracting private hackers). Frustration with the limitations of deterrence in cyberspace, where even great powers seem unable to have their way, has led to perhaps one of the more troubling developments in the literature on attribution. Some analysts have suggested that evidentiary standards for the attribution of cyber attacks be reconsidered so as not to require conclusive technical proof (Healey 2011; Knake 2010)—another proposal that I return to in the discussion on international law.

This literature on attribution and deterrence is important because it points to the challenges of continuing to rely upon a mechanism that has been important throughout the industrial age (and before) but which, it appears, may have limited utility in the information age. It is also important because it is by far the dominant approach of social science scholars interested in the political implications of the attribution problem. At the same time, however, this persistent linkage of attribution to deterrence has tended to limit the parameters of the debate to strategic issues rather than the broader social and political factors that make attribution attractive or desirable in the first place. By continuing to focus so specifically on how attribution can or cannot be reconciled with deterrence, we risk missing the broader implications of anonymity in cyberspace for international relations.

ATTRIBUTION AND INTERNATIONAL ORDER

As pointed out in the introduction, this essay focuses on international law not because it is the only one of Bull's institutions for which the problem of attribution has implications, but because it is the site of much of the current international cooperation and contestation around cyber security. Since this analysis is concerned with the laws of armed conflict, and since the potential for cyber attacks to result in physical violence has been quite vigorously disputed, it is necessary to establish the connection between the potential for violence and cyber security. Bull's holistic approach to the goal of minimizing violence—one that transcends but also incorporates international relations—helps us move away from strategic questions about attribution (How can we develop deterrence? How can we solve the attribution problem?) to think more clearly about what causes different actors to perceive the threat of violence in cyberspace differently. It also opens up space for considering other approaches to cyber capabilities including one that promotes peace by allowing for non-violent solutions to political tensions.

The Goal of Minimizing Violence

Bull argues that all societies seek to (a) ensure that 'life will be in some measure secure against violence resulting in death or bodily harm', (b) 'ensure that promises, once made, will be kept, or that agreements, once undertaken, will be carried out', and (c) ensure that the 'possession of things will remain stable to some degree, and will not be subject to challenges that are constant and without limit' (1977, 4–5). In Bull's view, these goals, 'life, truth and property', are *elementary* goals. Without them, he suggested, we could not call a group a 'society'. He argued that they are also *primary*, because all other goals that societies may have presuppose these ones, and that they are *universal* because all societies seem to 'take account of them' (1977, 5–6). The extent to which the elementary, primary, and universal goal of minimizing violence is relevant to cyberspace is by no means settled in the scholarship. Some regard the potential for large-scale devastation and loss of life as very worrying while others feel that this is a remote and unlikely threat. While these debates are quite polarized (and somewhat stagnant), they both offer important observations and conclusions.

Violence Matters—the 'Cyber Pearl Harbor' View

Since the mid-1990s, policymakers have been concerned about the prospect of a large-scale and violent cyber attack on *critical infrastructure*—those systems like power, water, and communications that we regard as essential to the smooth functioning of society. They have consistently expressed concern that decades of privatization of critical infrastructure combined with reliance on insecure networked systems is a dangerous development, pregnant with the potential for physical destruction and loss of life (Carr 2016b; Legrand 2014). In 2012, Leon Panetta spoke about the threats to US critical infrastructure as he perceived them. He explained that as 'director of the CIA and now Secretary of Defense, I have understood that cyber attacks are every bit as real as the more well-known threats like terrorism, nuclear weapons proliferation and the turmoil that we see in the Middle East' (2012). The 2014 NATO summit declaration stated that '[c]yber attacks can reach a threshold that threatens national and Euro-Atlantic prosperity, security, and stability. Their impact could be as harmful to modern societies as a conventional attack' (NATO 2014).

National cyber security strategies tend to focus on the threat to critical infrastructure and the potential for interference in their command and control systems to have catastrophic effects—the release of water from a dam to flood a populated valley, for example, or the interruption of power supplies in a dangerously cold winter. These scenarios are sometimes referred to as a 'Cyber Pearl Harbor', reflecting political leaders' anxieties about being taken by surprise by a devastating attack and being underprepared. Despite these strong views and persistent concerns, it must be noted that there are others who argue that digital technology is not able to deliver violence and is therefore much more limited in its utility and threat.

Cyber is not Violent—the Sceptic View

When arguments are made to the effect that the threat of violence from digital technologies is inflated, they are very often framed in terms of a belief in the continuity of the relationship between technology and global affairs—the status quo. This argument rests on the premise that despite the vulnerabilities to critical infrastructure, the reliance of civilian and military systems on the Internet and other networks, and the occasional intent of actors in international relations to cause physical destruction, loss of life, and/or large-scale disruption, we have yet to experience a cyber attack with these effects. Therefore, some scholars argue, there is no basis upon which to expect that we will experience one in the future. Thomas Rid has written extensively (and sceptically) about violence and cyber attacks. He recognizes that the kind of critical infrastructure attack about which others are so concerned is possible, but emphasizes that, 'so far, no such scenario has ever happened... Not a single human being has ever been killed or hurt as a result of a code-triggered cyber attack' (2013, 13).

The status quo argument required clarification in the wake of the Stuxnet operation, revealed in 2010, in which a nuclear enrichment facility in Iran was damaged by a computer worm (Clayton 2010). Although this incident did not result in any loss of life, the implications of an actor penetrating a highly secure facility using cyber tools and causing physical destruction to critical infrastructure is the very scenario that keeps policymakers awake at night. There are a number of ways in which scholars sceptical about the destructive potential of digital technology have responded to this important example. They argue that: (a) the attack was very expensive and consequently beyond the reach of, or unattractive to, most actors (Rid 2012; Lindsay 2013, 388); (b) the attack was limited in its effects because it did not destroy the Iranian nuclear facility and therefore is unlikely to lead to more widespread use of similar exploits (Lindsay 2013, 390–2); and (c) that cyber weapons like Stuxnet are 'use and lose' capabilities which must be deployed in secrecy and so have little to offer in terms of compellence or deterrence (Gartzke 2013, 60).

There are weaknesses in all three of these assertions. Costs are not static, limited efficacy in one attack is no indication of future developments, and claims about the limited appeal of cyber weapons need to be substantiated by some kind of empirical research. However, if this line of argument—that digital technologies *are* limited in their potential to cause violent acts—were more robust, then we might assume that attribution matters less for sustaining the goal of limiting violence and, by extension, international order. Unfortunately, the flaws in these arguments aside, a determinist approach to technology like the sceptical one has little utility in international relations because it fails to take into account human agency and it also discounts the extent to which international relations itself shapes technology (Carr 2016a).

Although cyber security fears (like any other fear) are no doubt overinflated by some actors in some circumstances and for some purposes, that does not calm the nerves of policy makers who are alert to the potential for technological vulnerabilities to be exploited by those who might wish to pose a serious challenge to international order. These two dichotomous positions are unlikely to be reconciled in the near future. Sceptics would only be convinced by a proliferation of devastating attacks, while few policymakers are likely to feel easy about ignoring the potential of these threats just because they have not yet eventuated. There is a third possible approach that moves beyond both of these positions: that digital technologies can also provide much less violent solutions to political conflict.

The Potential for Maintaining Peace

In addition to pointing out the possibilities of ICTs for physical destruction, the 2010 Stuxnet attack also precipitates consideration of the potential for digital technologies to be employed to address political tension *without* violence. This therefore has implications not only for the future of political conflict, but also for the maintenance of peace, Bull's third goal of international society. Although this is a less widely held view than either the 'Pearl Harbor' or the 'Sceptic' approach to violence and ICTs, it is worthy of some consideration here and especially in light of Bull's point that he was referring not to a 'universal or permanent peace' but rather to the absence of war as a 'normal condition' (1977, 18). Once again, Stuxnet provides a useful example through which we can explore this but with an important caveat.

Despite the wide coverage of this event in academic literature and in the media, it is important to keep in mind that our knowledge of the politics of the Stuxnet attack remains largely anecdotal and unconfirmed (a key problem for scholarship in this field). There has been one dominant narrative to develop after Stuxnet became public knowledge and this is based on the work of an award-winning American journalist, David Sanger, who has based his account on interviews with many high level (but anonymous or unattributable) sources. For many reasons, relying upon 'evidence' like this is deeply problematic. For the purposes of this essay, I do not engage with it as 'truth' but rather as a useful hypothetical. It does not matter for the purpose that it will be used here, whether Sanger's account is completely, partially, or not at all accurate. What his account offers this essay is a platform to think through possible implications of similar attacks.

According to Sanger, Israel's growing concerns about the Iranian nuclear programme were edging the state toward plans for a kinetic attack on Iran's Natanz nuclear facility. In an effort to prevent action that they felt may lead to a catastrophic conflict in the Middle East, Sanger suggests, the US worked with Israel to develop the 'Olympic Games' program, of which the Stuxnet worm was a central component. The program ran for several years, not destroying the nuclear facility but delaying progress sufficiently to slow down Iran's transition into a nuclear state. In this way, then, with no loss of life and no escalation to a kinetic conflict, the Stuxnet worm potentially delivered a non-violent solution to an extremely dangerous, volatile, and potentially devastating political crisis in the Middle East.

Although there has been widespread conjecture (supported by Sanger's story) that the US and Israel were behind Stuxnet, neither state has claimed responsibility. This ambiguity possibly left a wider range of response options open to Iran. If it were conclusively attributed, Stuxnet may have forced a different response not only from Iran and its supporters, but also from the rest of the international community that opposes, at least in principle, such overt militarization of cyberspace. It is difficult to address (and therefore, possible to avoid) the issue when there is no conclusive identification of the actors behind Stuxnet. In that regard, the problem of attribution may have provided a pressure valve for Israel and the US as well as for Iran and for the rest of the international community. It is possible that Stuxnet represented a very creative approach to promoting peace (or the absence of war) and that cyber capabilities have much more potential to do so than those who argue about their (non-)violent properties acknowledge.

Bull's rationale for the goal of minimizing violence is that unless people enjoy some 'measure of security against the threat of death or injury at the hands of others, they are not able to devote energy or attention enough to other objects to be able to accomplish them' (1977, 5). This is reflected in comments about cyberspace by the Russian Foreign Minister, Igor Ivanov, to the UN in 1998. Ivanov wrote to the Secretary General to express Russia's concerns about the potential for ICTs to undermine international order. He wrote that, in Russia's view, the international community must not 'permit the emergence of a fundamentally new area of international confrontation' that would 'divert an enormous amount of resources that are so necessary for peaceful creativity and development' (in Tikk Ringas 2015). Tikk Ringas cites this as the first instance of a state actor linking ICTs to international law in the context of global security and suggests that Ivanov's letter was the genesis of significant discussion amongst the great powers about international law and cyber security (2015).

International Law and Cyberspace

There has been a debate about whether international law conceived of in a different technological age, could be readily applied to cyberspace. On the one hand, the International Court of Justice states that the laws of armed conflict apply to 'any use of force, regardless of the weapons employed', and on the other, the Permanent Court of International Justice states that acts not forbidden in international law are generally permitted (Schmitt 2013, 3). Although both Russia and China have argued strenuously for a treaty to address global cyber security concerns, the US view that no new law is necessary has thus far prevailed.[3] The focus of international negotiation and discussion has, instead, revolved around two axes: first, establishing whether and how existing international law applies in cyberspace; and second, negotiating norms of responsible state behaviour. The expectation is that some or all of these may one day crystallize into customary law. As Bull noted in regard to the different problems of his time, the value of international law lies not in its capacity to dictate rules that states must adhere to and to stipulate consequences for the violation of those rules. Rather, the value of international law lies in its capacity to provide a mechanism or a channel through which agreed interests may be institutionalized, acknowledged, and organized. In doing so,

---

[3] One exception is the Council of Europe Convention on Cybercrime, but this does not address global security concerns beyond criminal activity.

international law provides some measure of predictability and reassurance about state behaviour. It allows states to signal their 'intentions with regard to the matter in question' (1977, 142).

When thinking through the implications of the problem of attribution for international law, there are three important questions that Bull's conception of this institution of international society raises. First, how can the law be applied to anonymous actors? Second, how does the problem of attribution impact on the motivation for actors to abide by the law? And finally, how useful is international law, as Bull conceived it, for signalling states' intentions and for promoting predictability? Before engaging with these questions, there are some definitional issues that produce real impediments to applying international law to cyberspace. Understanding these is essential to comprehending the complexity of these three questions.

Applying International Law in Cyberspace

Although states agreed in 2013 that existing international law *does* apply in cyberspace, the problem of *how* to apply it has yet to be resolved. Questions persist about the interpretation of Article 2(4) of the UN Charter, which prohibits states from the 'use of force' unless granted authorization by the UN Security Council or unless (as stipulated under Article 51) responding to an 'armed attack'. Exactly how to define an 'armed attack' and what exactly the threshold for 'use of force' should be has confounded legal scholars in the context of ICTs. These concepts, upon which the laws of armed conflict and international humanitarian law rest, were developed prior to the advent of modern ICTs and, consequently, they have proven exceptionally difficult to map onto the complex nature of cyber incidents. Boothby et al. point out that an armed attack should be 'grave in scale and effects', though there is no test to distinguish 'grave' from 'non-grave' consequences (2012, 83). Most legal experts, they suggest, agree that an armed attack will result in 'death or a significant degree of injury to persons or physical damage to property' (2012, 83).

On the one hand, this returns us to the arguments of the cyber sceptics who will point to the fact that there has never been a cyber attack that resulted in death or injury on such a scale. But what, then, of the Stuxnet attack, of which former CIA director Michael Hayden has said 'you can't help but describe it as an attack on critical infrastructure' (cited in Farwell and Rohozinski 2011, 111)? Unlike kinetic weapons, cyber tools can be designed to cause large-scale physical damage to critical infrastructure *without* killing people. That is a unique capability that one could argue avoids traditional interpretations of 'armed attack', but it is not necessarily a practice that states would regard as permissible. In arguing that some of our ideas about violence and war may require rethinking in the information age, Chris Demchak has called attention to what she calls 'wars of disruption', in which the focus is no longer *lethality* but organizational *disruption* through information systems (2011). Some certainly feel that there is a gap here between what was intended in *lex lata* and what current circumstances call for and this has been at the heart of these debates about definitions.

It is reasonable to expect that, sometime in the future, these questions will be satisfactorily resolved—that we shall see some consensus on how to define the 'use of force' and 'armed attack' in cyberspace. However, as long as they are defined by *consequences* (i.e. loss of life, large-scale disruption), the problem of attribution will still act as an impediment to the application of international law. Consequences themselves are not adequate because it is the actor and their motivation that combines with consequences to allow us to classify and make sense of any kind of violence. Without a clear identity of the perpetrator, it can be very difficult to separate criminal activity from politically motivated activity, or to separate politically motivated activity undertaken by a non-state actor from that of a state actor. And that in turn raises questions about what type of law applies and what kind of penalty is appropriate or legal.

Even if we put to one side the current challenges of interpreting international law in this context and focus again on the problem of attribution, a second question arises: what will motivate states to adhere to the law if they may violate it in anonymity? If it is possible to carry out illegal acts such as attacks on critical infrastructure without those actions being conclusively attributed and, therefore, without eliciting the usual consequences of violating international law, what might restrain states from exploiting the opportunities that ICTs present?

Why Obey the Law?

Bull articulates three reasons why states obey international law. First, because the law may be regarded by them as 'valuable, mandatory or obligatory'; second, because of the threat of coercion; and third, in the hope that doing so may prompt reciprocal behaviour from other states (1977, 139–40). He draws these social factors back to the self-interest (or national interest) of states by pointing out that the 'importance of international law does not rest on the willingness of states to abide by its principles to the detriment of their interests, but in the fact that they so often judge it in their interests to conform to it' (1977, 140).

Certainly, political actors may abide by international law in cyberspace so as to signal that their state upholds its obligations, so as to avoid coercion, and in the hopes of fostering reciprocity. However, this conception of the social nature of international law is predicated on a clear understanding of who is acting and who is being acted upon and this is deeply problematic in an anonymous environment. States may very well have a shared interest in protecting critical infrastructure from cyber attacks, but if anonymity is an option, Bull's motivations for adhering to the law are no longer as compelling an explanation of state behaviour as they might otherwise be. For example, there has been speculation that the attacks on the Ukraine power grid in December 2015 were state-initiated or state-sponsored. If that were true, it may not indicate that the offending state had little interest in a prohibition on critical infrastructure attacks. It may instead indicate that although they shared that interest, there was some expectation that by avoiding conclusive attribution, they could also satisfy other foreign policy interests without cost. The problem of attribution complicates these notions of obligation, coercion, and reciprocity that Bull sees as fundamental to the motivation of states to adhere to the law.

International Law in the Information Age

Given the challenges that attribution introduces to *applying* international law and given the ways in which it may reduce actors' motivations for *adhering* to the law, we must ask the following question: how effective is international law as a mechanism to promote predictability and reassurance about state behaviour? At this point, it is useful to consider some of the progress that has been made around agreeing on cyber norms.

In response to Ivanov's 1998 letter to the UN, the UN Disarmament Committee established the *UN Group of Governmental Experts on Developments in the Field of Information and Telecommunications in the Context of International Security* (UNGGE). Since 2004, this has been the primary site of global political debate about international law and cyber war and it has resulted in progress on establishing some norms of responsible state behaviour in cyberspace. The 2015 UNGGE meeting produced a consensus report that acknowledged that 'the use of ICTs in future conflicts between States is becoming more likely' (United Nations 2015, 8). The report proposed eleven voluntary, non-binding norms, rules, or principles of responsible behaviour for all states (including abstaining from attacks on critical infrastructure) (United Nations 2015, 8). These norms, the report explained, are aimed at 'promoting an open, secure, stable, accessible and peaceful ICT environment' (United Nations 2015, 6).

It is not always the case that norms make the transition to customary law (and nor is it necessary for them to do so in order to be effective in shaping state behaviour or expressing shared interests) (Erskine and Carr 2016). However, within and around the UNGGE process there is some expectation that these norms of responsible state behaviour in cyberspace will become sufficiently embedded in, and representative of, state practice that they will eventually be recognized as customary law. Bull is very clear that in assessing the efficacy of international law it is not necessary to find that states always adhere to it and never violate it. Indeed, he makes the observation that 'in cases where conformity between actual and prescribed behaviour can be regarded as a forgone conclusion, there can be no point in having rules at all' (1977, 136). Rather than evaluating the extent to which actors' behaviour is shaped by laws, Bull suggests that the question should be whether international law is observed to a sufficient degree to be regarded as a means of preserving international order (1977, 137). Here, the problem of attribution raises a unique problem in that it can be difficult to determine whether states are, indeed, exhibiting some generality of practice which might then be considered to be indicative of customary law or whether they are *claiming* to do so while in fact regularly violating those norms without being detected. This, Boothby suggests, could mean that customary law in this context is very slow to develop and we face an extended period of uncertainty about how effectively international laws of cyberspace contribute to international order (2016).

What this UNGGE process *has* done, however, is provide a mechanism for states, especially the great powers, to express their views, articulate their interests, and negotiate both the common ground upon which they agree and also those divergences that are so fundamental as to prevent further progress on the questions discussed above. One of these divergences is certainly approaches to attribution and this comes through clearly in the 2015 UNGGE report.

In addition to articulating state concerns that 'the misuse of ICTs may harm international peace and security' (2015, 6), the report also makes two important statements that reveal the great power tension around the problem of attribution. One of the proposed norms reflects the (largely Western) view that technical attribution is too difficult and uncertain to be considered essential to retaliation. The report therefore proposes that, '[i]n case of ICT incidents, States should consider all relevant information, including the larger context of the event, the challenges of attribution in the ICT environment and the nature and extent of the consequences' (2015, 7).

This view reflects the frustration of some states that have been unable to deal effectively with ongoing cyber attacks that they believe are state sponsored or state supported. Neither technology nor the law has proved adequate for protecting state assets—a particular frustration for the US. Jason Healey has argued for avoidance of the trap of 'attribution fixation', by which he means 'the belief that [analysts] cannot assess which organization or nation was behind an attack until technical forensics discovers the identity of the attacking machines'. He suggests that 'attribution becomes far more tractable when approached as a top-down policy issue with nations held responsible for major attacks originating from their territory or conducted by their citizens' (2011, 1).

Essentially, this approach to attribution is one that avoids the difficulties of the accurate forensic analysis of cyber incidents through technical means and relies instead upon judgements about who one feels was *most likely* behind the attack, given a whole range of other factors like capability and motivation. The momentum behind this position in the US and its expression in the UNGGE norm signal the somewhat concerning potential for states to talk themselves out of the necessity of the burden of proof, or of establishing lower evidentiary standards for attributing cyber attacks, thereby opening up the way for unsubstantiated accusations, allegations, and even misdirection of blame for malicious actions.

Recognition of these dangers is noted later in the same report, reflecting the views of other states including Russia and China. In the discussion on how international law applies to the use of ICTs, the report states that 'the indication that an ICT activity was launched or otherwise originates from the territory or the ICT infrastructure of a State may be insufficient in itself to attribute the activity to that State. The Group noted that the accusations of organizing and implementing wrongful acts brought against States should be substantiated' (United Nations 2015, 13). This is likely a response to US allegations of illicit behaviour on the part of particularly the Chinese and Russians that have not been accompanied by convincing attributory evidence. Examples of these include the 2014 indictment of five serving Chinese military officers over charges that they had been responsible for a sustained campaign of Chinese industrial espionage (Department of Justice 2014) and the 2015 imposition of (additional) sanctions against North Korean officials in response to the alleged attacks on Sony Pictures (Obama 2015c). Some regard these US responses as an effort to send a message that they will not continue to tolerate violations of their 'sovereign' cyberspace.

This tension between the great powers over attribution is one of the major fissures that prevents more forward momentum on the applicability of international law in cyberspace. It also raises questions about the efficacy of international law, not as a means of enforcing rules (it is clear that attribution is necessary for that), but, as Bull suggested, as a mechanism for institutionalizing shared interests, for signalling state intentions, and for promoting predictability. This may slow down or arrest the development of further much-needed clarity in customary law.

CONCLUSION

There are a number of conclusions to be drawn from this analysis, both for how we think about the problem of attribution in international relations and for how Hedley Bull's ideas about international order stand up in the information age. His work is particularly useful for discussing attribution because it helps us to consider it and to analyse it as a *social* dimension. Engaging with his ideas about international order opens up a whole new landscape for thinking about an issue that has previously been considered almost exclusively through a technical or a strategic lens. Recognition of actors and the presumption that states are clearly identifiable is central to so many aspects of international relations that the inability to do so adds as a new dimension to the anarchy that (to some extent) shapes global politics. Perhaps most significantly, Bull helps to redirect the focus from looking for solutions to looking for the right questions.

In addressing the long-standing question of whether or not cyber attacks can be violent, Bull's work allows us to break out of the rigid confines of the dominant debate about whether cyber tools can result in violence or not. Instead, by taking into account his views on peace, we might look instead at the potential for ICTs to be employed in resolving political tensions in cyberspace and the potential for unattributed actions to further minimize confrontation.

In terms of international law, the implications of attribution are mixed. Fundamentally, it makes the applicability and the motivation for actors to comply deeply problematic. It also means that it will be very difficult for us to *recognize* customary law if and when it does develop out of the proposed UNGGE norms. On the other hand, confronted with these challenges, with this new dimension of anarchy, we see states responding very much as they have in the past, by balancing opportunities to exploit the potential of new technologies to pursue their national interest with participating in social practices like negotiation, diplomacy, cooperation and, however slowly, agreements on responsible state behaviour in cyberspace. And this would possibly be more or less as Bull might have expected.

Finally, having weighed up these factors of continuity and change, one would have to say that ICTs could no longer be regarded as simply another 'awkward fact' for international relations. Rather, if Bull were working now, he might come to regard them as a central 'issue of human political structure' (1977, xiii). They are an integral element that is woven inextricably through many aspects of our civil, political, military, and commercial existence and they have as much—but quite possibly more—potential to impact upon international order as industrial age technology did. It is impossible (and unwise) to make predictions about how this technology will be deployed in the future, and about what the long-term implications for international order will be, and I think that if Bull were writing now, he would widen his lens to explore the intersection of technology and international relations much more carefully. Instead, it falls to us to conduct further work that engages with ideas, concepts, and methodologies from international relations and other fields in order to better understand the massive technological shift that we are now living through.

11

The Anarchical Society and a Global Political Economy

Louis W. Pauly

INTRODUCTION

In *The Anarchical Society*, Hedley Bull highlighted the centrality of the states system in the quest for global order, but he did not dismiss system-changing developments underway both below and above the authoritative governing institutions of the state. If he were with us today, he would undoubtedly have much to say about the consequences of such developments within the world economy. For in the decades since 1977, the cross-border mobility of goods and services, people, ideas, and capital has transformed our world. The crises associated with that transformation, moreover, have posed dramatic challenges to order on a global scale. It would be incorrect to state that Bull failed to anticipate that transformation. It is true, however, that he was quite sceptical that it would any time soon bring about effective and legitimate global governing institutions transcending the states system.

This chapter focuses on integrating financial markets, a prominent feature of the contemporary global economy and a phenomenon at the core of the 'anarchical society of states' before 1914 (Frieden 2006). The integration process went partially into reverse during the inter-war period. As the Second World War was ending, moreover, post-war planners doubted the wisdom of allowing capital to flow freely in the context of either a regime of floating exchange rates or a restored gold standard. Before Bull died, however, capital controls were loosened and global finance had begun to recover its Janus-faced systemic role. One side helped to carve measurable risks out of the myriad uncertainties confronting humanity and to manage them through cross-border market mechanisms, while the other periodically threatened to spin those markets entirely out of control.

Bounded polities face great challenges in harnessing the benefits and limiting the costs of financial openness. In hindsight, this was quite obvious before

1914. It remains so today. The difference is that we are now witnessing the development of a global capacity to govern more open financial markets. It is emerging even as its legitimacy remains in question, and it will remain fragile as long as that question is open.

Bull would have had no trouble recognizing the self-interested interaction of great powers in building a collaborative governing capacity, but his basic perspective would likely not have led him to expect the degree of solidarity that has regularly if grudgingly manifested itself in the financial policy arena ever since the breakdown of the Bretton Woods arrangements in the early 1970s. A hierarchical state-centred system continues to provide the foundation (Lake 2009). The dynamic energies released when inevitable political conflicts manifest themselves in large, open markets provide the impulse for policy change and development. The resulting order, as Bull would have expected, results mainly from the policies of the powerful that limit ever more strictly the fundamental choices of the weak and, more modestly, their own future options.

Bull would not have been surprised that justice is the lagging variable. There is no obvious reason, though, to doubt the existence of a widening sense that justice cannot be forever denied. The gradual emergence of a capacity to govern a global financial order has already put a spotlight on the legitimacy deficit. The political energies either to address it or to destroy that order are evident. Bull gave us reason to make the more optimistic bet.

My objective here is to outline and assess the politics behind the emergence of global financial governance in the full light of Bull's perspective and intellectual legacy. Although his own empirical depiction of international society may have been limited by his less than comprehensive attention to an economic and especially financial transformation then beginning, his central political insight remains timely. Even in a globalizing society centred on but not limited to an increasing number of states, a society now marked by the staggering mobility of information, goods and services, human beings, and financial capital, the desire for order precedes the search for fairness. Especially obvious at points of systemic emergency, dominant states still underwrite the emerging global order. If it is to endure, however, it must eventually rest upon an expanding sense that the basic interests of the many and not just the few will be met. In his most famous book, Bull himself aptly concluded:

> If our analysis has led us to reject the view that the states system is in decline, it should also lead us to notice one of the cardinal features of its present phase. This is that there is now a wider world political system of which the states system is only part. By the world political system we understand the world-wide network of interaction that embraces not only states but also other political actors, both 'above' the state and 'below' it (1977, 276).... [W]orld order, or order within the great society of all mankind, is not only wider than international order or order among states, but also more fundamental and primordial than it, and morally

prior to it. The system of states has constantly to be assessed in relation to the goal of world order. (1977, 319)

The challenge is not to deny the ultimate necessity of order on a global scale, but, like Bull, to use our powers of practical reasoning and empirical observation to discern the evolving pillars upon which its governance must rest if it is to persist. Bull's analytical method and moral sensibilities continue to help us examine those pillars, including the pillar today supporting global finance.

BUILDING A GLOBAL SOCIETY

Within the 'English School' of international relations, Barry Buzan has long been the most forceful advocate of a more thorough treatment of the causes and political consequences of transnational economic deepening. A decade ago, he noted:

> My inclinations lean toward the strategy of Rosenau (1990) and Bull (1977), which is to find the point of interest in the balance between the state and non-state worlds.... In some ways, they are profoundly antagonistic, both in concept and in practice. In other ways, they are heavily interdependent, again both in concept and in practice. (Buzan 2005, 133)

Bull himself did not miss the contemporary phenomenon of deepening economic integration across the borders of states. He simply noted that it was not unprecedented, and he warned against exaggerating its near-term implications. Moreover, his notion of a 'world political system', within which states and other actors 'above' and 'below' construct a 'world-wide network of interaction', circumscribed the arena where such interdependence might be expected to encourage a movement toward rules and institutions capable of underpinning a stable social order on a global scale. Such rules and institutions would be instruments of collective governance, but Bull did not predict the emergence of 'world government' anytime soon. Formal political consolidation on the basis of either contract or conquest seemed to him implausible in the near term, and he devoted Chapter 11 of *The Anarchical Society* to explaining why.

In that same chapter, though, he did wonder whether non-state actors were pushing the states system towards a 'new mediaevalism' that would 'deprive the concept of sovereignty of its utility and viability' (1977, 264). He focused on the pressures leading some states toward regional governance systems and others toward internal disintegration. He noted the expansion of 'private' international violence, and he assessed the impact of expanding transnational organizations and multinational corporations. Finally, he took account of rapid technological change. With this in mind, he addressed directly the essential framing by Robert Keohane and Joseph Nye (1977) of what was becoming the mainstream American approach to the field of international political economy.

> There is no doubt that there exists among all societies today a high degree of interdependence or mutual sensitivity in the pursuit of basic human goals. However, we have also to recognise that the term 'interdependence' has become a cant word that serves to rationalise relations between a dominant power and its dependencies, in which the sensitivity is more one-sided than it is mutual.... [Interdependence also] does not in itself generate a sense of common interest, let alone of common values.... Some transnational relationships are of global and not merely regional importance, but their effect is to promote not the integration of world society as a whole, but rather the integration of a dominant culture, which as it draws closer together at the same time draws farther apart from those social elements that are left outside.... [Still] the world political system of whose existence we have taken note in no way implies the demise of the states system.
> (1977, 280–1)

In the end, though, Bull held that the 'future of international society is likely to be determined, among other things, by the preservation and extension of a cosmopolitan culture, embracing both common ideas and common values, and rooted in societies in general as well as in their elites' (1977, 317). Durable systemic order, then, would eventually come to rest on a basic sense of solidarity and a shared sense of what some of his intellectual precursors termed an irreducible awareness of the common good.

Bull himself emphasized ideas and values rooted in the dominant societies with which he was most familiar. For this reason, Stanley Hoffman (1986, 179–95) noted the tension in his thinking between defence of a system organized around great powers and his observation that coherence and stability even among them remained marked by uncertainty, despite the facts of deepening interdependence. As Buzan and Lawson (2015, 46–7) point out, Bull and others within the English School were fully aware of the great industrial transformation that opened the era of globalizing capitalism. An obsession with Westphalia and intra-European struggles to establish a state-led order, however, may have led them somewhat to downplay the import of that transformation. To re-emphasize the idea of underlying uncertainty, nearly forty years after Bull's opening, Buzan and Lawson (2015, 4) proposed a framework that depicted industrialization, rational state-building, and the advance of ideologies of progress in the nineteenth century not only as generating a tension-filled core–periphery global order but also as destabilizing great power relations by exposing the balance of power to rapid technological and social change.

While Bull was still alive, Susan Strange's ruminations on structural power in a dynamic capitalist system moved along a line of practical reasoning similar to that of Buzan and Lawson. Although she criticized the state-centricity of the early English School, Strange shared Bull's concerns about the distributive and normative implications of 'woolly' concepts like 'interdependence' and 'international regimes' (Tooze and May 2002, ch. 15). At the same time, she took Bull and many other IR theorists on both sides of the Atlantic to task for misunderstanding the complex structural effects of several dynamic global forces, especially those associated with 'international finance' (Tooze and May 2002, 104; Germain 2016, ch. 1).

It is precisely here where we may begin more precisely to trace the delicate interplay Bull was beginning to sense between the continuing evolution of a society of states and the potentially destabilizing deepening of a global society of all humanity. Theorists of globalization have, in fact, recently focused directly on this theme. For example, Jan Aart Scholte (2005) draws a line between straightforward processes of internationalization and interdependence, on the one hand, and, on the other, the expansion and proliferation of supra-territorial connections that transform the basic social geography within which political agents at all levels make decisions. Martin Shaw (2010) and others (e.g. Albert, Buzan, and Zürn 2013) do not deny that such spatial restructuring is underway, but they suggest the need for deeper sociological and psychological exploration, since the empirical phenomena associated with globalization appear to be forcing a widening sense of the holistic nature of life on the planet. Reus-Smit (Ch. 5 in this volume) supports an analogous claim in the field of human rights, while others similarly treat issues arising from the natural environment and military security arenas. Together, these scholars are calling for a deeper awareness of common values constitutive of a society that has begun to recognize itself as worldwide in nature.

Without abandoning Bull's insistence on the practical utility of the doctrine of state sovereignty in the historical evolution of world order, his student Andrew Hurrell (in his 2007 book) anticipated that such a recognition would spawn reactionary impulses. The hunch that they would be likely be frustrated lies in the background of Hurrell's robust defence of an expansive sense of solidarism in global order and his warning against the siren song of a return to a pluralist system that never really existed in its ideal-typical form. In a much-cited article, Alex Wendt similarly defended the associated teleological argument and predicted an inevitable movement from a system of states, to a society of states, to world society, to collective security, and finally to a world state (2003).

Recent developments in financial markets hardly take us all the way there, but they do suggest powerfully that profound structural change is underway and tending in the same direction. A reborn Hedley Bull would be unlikely to find himself lost in an era of globalizing markets and an emergent global society, for his own thinking accommodated just such a development. But he would surely urge us to discipline our hopes, remember the human capacity for self-destruction, and ground our contemporary assessment of political probabilities in historical evidence. Without denying the long-run importance of an expansive sense of justice and fairness, Bull's empirical observation of order preceding justice in actual human societies continues to inspire a pragmatic and realistic moral sensibility. The aim of the next sections, admittedly brief and suggestive, is to imagine how with a little nudge he might have interpreted the recent evolution of a globalizing financial system at the heart of a world political economy.

TOWARDS GLOBAL FINANCIAL GOVERNANCE?

In principle, Bull would likely have expected integrating markets both to strengthen bonds of global solidarity in the long term *and* reinforce fissiparous pressures in the short term. Just such a complex political dynamic, indeed, was foreseen by other thinkers as ideologically diverse as Polanyi (1944) and Hayek (1944). It is the political consequence of this interaction of many contingent factors exerting themselves on the states system in a necessarily uncertain global setting to which we must turn our attention.

In the face of the special risks generated when capital can move more freely across contemporary national borders, as Bull would have asserted, there still exists no unambiguous global authority to assess them, to prevent periodic crises, or to resolve emergencies. Nevertheless, we can observe that nascent governance capacities in each category are today becoming visible. Legitimation grounded in solid claims of global social justice may someday render those capacities more durable, but their current emergence is the straightforward result of yesterday's decisions by great powers to manage internal and external distributive struggles through the instrument of more open markets. Those capacities thus necessarily reflect sometimes convergent and sometimes conflicting interests, heightened competition among states and market actors, and unavoidable policy spillovers. Conceptualizing their political implications requires underlining an essential distinction, one Bull well understood, between authority (the right to govern) and capacity (the ability to govern).

A transformation in political authority arguably occurs in three steps: the building of political capacity (or coercive power as it is commonly understood), the effective deployment of that capacity (or the actual solving of problems), and then the legitimation of that deployment (through wide-enough social acceptance to render it sustainable). Here, we can take a helpful cue from the political philosopher Thomas Nagel (2005, 147) who, like Bull, rejects the common view that legitimation needs to come first. Cross-border problem-solving can occur in an imaginable policy space that ranges from autonomous and simultaneous national action to intergovernmental coordination to supra-territorial governance. When actual problems are definitively addressed by whatever means, effective capacities may be said to be developing, even if their legitimacy may remain problematic. Such capacities appear now, in fact, to be evolving quite rapidly in the policy arena defined by systemic financial risks. They are, moreover, changing the very meaning of state sovereignty as it was widely understood in Bull's day.

Measuring, reducing, and pooling risks *ex ante*, as well as providing compensation *ex post*, describe the basic principles of insurance systems, including the system we conventionally call government (Pauly 2014). At the heart of such systems are practices of burden sharing. Robinson Crusoe's survival would be most improbable in any non-fictional world. Only communities reliably sustain human life, and over time many human communities have observably expanded the bonds of solidarity required for group survival. Where fires once wiped out whole cities and left bankruptcy in their wake, insurance and reinsurance firms now spread the risks of catastrophe far beyond city limits. When such firms lose their bets that disaster will not occur, the markets they and their overseers have developed spread their losses globally and provide external resources for local recovery. In the modern era, indeed, states have encouraged such markets and regularly intervened to stabilize them.

When conventional market-based insurance schemes reach their limits, the nation-state has sometimes proved successful in expanding the boundaries of what might accurately be termed 'risk communities' (Faure and Hartlief 2003). It has sometimes done so *ex ante* through mandatory risk pooling and public subsidy, and sometimes *ex post* by covering losses actually incurred from national fiscal accounts. Its own limit, then, has historically been defined by its fiscal capacity (James 2014). Even such limits, however, have in the contemporary period sometimes been exceeded through intergovernmental arrangements (Goodhart and Schoenmaker 2006). Although modest in scale and scope, for example, agreements are in place among some national and now regional governments to share the potential costs of disasters at nuclear power plants.

As noted above, Bull was well aware that a 'world-wide network of interaction' already embraced many state and non-state actors. Against this background, restricted intergovernmental arrangements for global financial risk management cannot be the end of the story for anyone other than closed-minded ideologues unable to perceive the existence of an emerging global system undergoing dynamic development. In truth, it would take a fair dose of hubris to believe that human social evolution has somehow reached its end in our own day. On what ground is it reasonable to assume that human ingenuity exhausted itself in the political construction of the nation-state, of functioning federations, or of entities like the European Union? On what ground is it reasonable to assert that although human beings can obviously continue to manufacture global risks in the financial arena and elsewhere (Beck 1992), they absolutely cannot design accommodating instruments for managing them, not least by conceiving the means necessary reliably and routinely to exceed the fiscal limits of separate and autonomous polities? In the light of history, as Bull would have understood, there is no good reason to accept any such assertion, even if we recognize that consequent political dilemmas would remain formidable.

At this point, disciplined imagination in the direction of the global must be called upon. Bull certainly invited such speculation, even as he cast doubts on the near-term feasibility of an actual global polity. If the threats global financial risks suggest are serious, however, and if states, elites, and parties with interests in the success of private firms and markets continue to seek the benefits of capital mobility, it is not enough for Bull's descendants to cherish such doubts and simply hope for the best.

In short, at the centre of attention across a range of contemporary policy arenas like the arena of globalizing finance lies an undeniable awareness of tomorrow's potential catastrophes. An impulse towards 'preventive governance' thus may reasonably be seen as driven by the shared imperative of disaster avoidance. In fact, repeated near-disasters have recently heightened the realization that discrete preventive policies are futile unless they are pursued jointly by 'sovereign' political authorities and ultimately unless such authorities can reliably be transcended during future emergencies.

Preventive financial governance in a collective sense today already depends upon the ability of those 'in authority' to determine pre-emptively how much systemic risk is acceptable to societies no longer separated in practical terms by clear borders. It is complicated by the fact that in a still-decentralized governmental setting, characterized by different degrees of regulatory capture by non-governmental actors, some authorities may be unwilling to accept high preventive costs, while others may be unwilling to accept anything less than strong *precautionary* measures entailing high opportunity costs. (The global debate on regulating financial derivatives in the wake of the 2008 crisis, for example, featured characteristic differences between states favouring clear rules and well-supervised trading on organized exchanges and others willing to let freer markets innovate and absorb the risks of failure.)

The challenge of governing global financial risks thus spans two observable dimensions, namely, the identities of key actors and the scope of their aspirations. Given the residual authority of the state and the historic political bargains underpinning specific states that were emphasized by Bull, we might therefore expect *transnational* prevention practices in the financial arena to emerge through opaque processes full of conflicts. Decisions would likely remain fluid and informal, that is, not necessarily embedded in fixed treaties. The locus of actual decision-making would likely be dynamic, multilayered, and bureaucratic (Black 2008). Central bankers, regulators, and industry associations would be expected to play key policy development roles, with political executives and legislators standing by to ratify collective decisions if necessary and often after the fact.

The occasional denial of political responsibility for such decisions, especially when they have serious distributive consequences, may actually help preserve and even strengthen preventive governance capacities. The instrumentality of impersonal markets, informal collaborative fora, and diverse standard-setting associations may in a wider sense come to be seen as reasonably responsive to a functional, order-preserving, logic. Under conditions of complex interdependence, political conflicts and policy spillovers just might be expected to force significant innovations in governance. Ideological commitments to 'sovereignty' and 'democratic legitimacy' may remain, but governing instruments may become increasingly effective even as they continue to fall short of conventional expectations of legitimacy. A discrete policy problem may lead to a partial and imperfect solution, contested but convenient. In the end, of course, political conflicts and underlying legitimation dilemmas may themselves lead to systemic crises. As policy spillovers and conflicted decision-making processes interact, however, they may also provide the spark for new political capacity building beyond the nation-state and even beyond the states system.

With these logical possibilities in mind, the next section, 'Three Policy Arenas', looks more closely at contemporary financial governance and separates out the *distinctive politics involved in cross-border risk assessment, in crisis prevention, and in transnational emergency management.* As we shall see, the practical reasoning and moral sensibility modelled by Bull remain helpful in drawing out systemic implications. Likewise, a Bull-inspired dose of scepticism promises to keep that effort well-grounded.

THREE POLICY ARENAS: RISK ASSESSMENT, CRISIS PREVENTION, AND EMERGENCY MANAGEMENT

At the frontier of financial risk management is speculation, which stimulates the pooling instinct and finds its footing in the law of large numbers (Pauly 2014). Global financial risks again suggest the idea of 'insurance' structured at whatever scale is efficient for what are commonly termed 'orderly markets'. As financial markets were opened after the early 1970s and allowed to become more integrated across the political boundaries of both developed and developing countries, ever more apparent became a basic deficiency in systemic risk assessment and management. A decade later, the main arenas within which still mainly national overseers sought to cooperate in their risk assessment and measurement activities were easy to identify.

After the 1974 failure of Germany's Herstatt Bank destabilized markets around the world, supervisory interaction became ever more clearly multilateralized through a central bankers' club hosted by the Bank for International Settlements (BIS). Originally established to manage reparations payments after the First World War, the BIS had by then developed a profitable business managing central-bank reserves. That business funded a convenient venue as well as staff support for regular informal meetings of central bank governors, mainly but not exclusively from advanced industrial countries. Upon this foundation gradually developed a series of related technical clubs. The Basel Committee on Banking Supervision (BCBS) was the first (Goodhart 2011).

The BCBS from the beginning focused primarily on the micro-level, and specifically on the task of ensuring that large banks operating across national borders were properly supervised, with an agreed division of responsibilities between home and host country governments. Their 'concordat' never worked perfectly, but it did reflect converging approaches to risk assessment. It soon led the BCBS to experiment with minimum standards for the loss-absorbing reserves of banks, thus reducing the likelihood that national monetary and fiscal resources would be called upon during periods of instability (Kapstein 1998). The so-called 'Basel I' agreement also nudged forward collaborative work by other national and some regional bodies aimed at better prudential oversight within and beyond the banking sector narrowly defined. An informal, collaborative insurance system thus began to emerge in embryonic form.

Intergovernmental organizations like the International Monetary Fund and the World Bank tried to adapt their own surveillance and financing functions to accommodate changes in capital markets, but they were hampered by their macroeconomic and developmental mandates, by the treaties upon which they were based, as well as by their scale. In 1999, in the aftermath of the Asian financial crisis, leading governments under the rubric of the G20 chose to establish the Financial Stability Forum (FSF) to concentrate on the systemic effects of the expanding operations of financial institutions crossing borders and business lines in increasingly complicated ways. Those effects became undeniable in the midst of a broader systemic crisis ten years later, when the G20 reconstituted the FSF as the Financial Stability Board (FSB). Other sectoral bodies had by then also begun convening with assistance from the BIS (McKeen-Edwards and Porter, 2013). They included the International Association of Deposit Insurers, the International Association of Insurance Supervisors, and the International Organization of Securities Commissions (IOSCO). The often-overlapping activities of the FSB and such technical clubs came to be called the 'Basel Process'.

Much of the initial technical work of these clubs focused on *cross-border risk measurement and analysis*. What differentiated them was their internal composition and near-term interests. Aside from private firms trying to influence policies in various ways, mainly back home in national capitals, they were composed of supervisors located within central banks, government officials, representatives of independent agencies, public and private managers of financial exchanges, and formal industry associations. The bank-centred Institute of International Finance perfectly represented the latter kind of political actor, which combined special-interest lobbying, globally-minded sectoral assessment, and the capacity to directly engage in policymaking, especially in the United States, where the dividing line between the public and the private is famously (and arguably intentionally) unclear (Farrell and Newman 2014).

As Bull might have said when he penned the passage on non-state actors quoted at the outset of this chapter, it is noteworthy that by then the process of risk measurement and analysis could no longer adequately be encompassed by the term 'inter-state'. Too many players were involved, no legal treaty was expected, and the evolving standards at issue crossed many neat boundaries—political, functional, public-private, and technical. The result was not chaos, but it was more complex. It also began to hint at an order inaccurately characterized as 'international'.

Although technical clubs did clarify the systemic risks associated with dynamic financial markets, they were not equipped to stop regional crises—from Latin America to Asia to North America and Europe—often from roiling those markets. Specific crises, in turn, began to stimulate a new kind of deepening political interaction aimed at *crisis prevention*. One key objective remained enhancing the capital adequacy of international active financial intermediaries. But other instruments were tailored to domestic circumstances and designed to foster self-discipline by the managers of those firms. In 2006, the most extensive and detailed effort to increase the equity bases of more diversified financial conglomerates came in an accord commonly dubbed Basel II. Under its terms, intermediaries were encouraged to bring sophisticated internal risk-models and a nuanced risk-weighting system into capital adequacy calculations ultimately and collectively agreed to by their home supervisors. Notwithstanding the increasing prominence of non-state actors, the politics of policymaking here reached a traditional limit, not least because underlying risk cultures and enforcement practices across major regions remained distinctive.

The fact that the implementation of Basel II left much discretion with national supervisors was only the most obvious source of future trouble. The reliance on internal risk modelling served to expand the competitive advantages and leverage available to large money-centre banks. Astute observers pointed out that the impact might be 'pro-cyclical', that is, the new standards might encourage intermediaries around the world to excessively restrict lending during recessions and to imprudently expand lending during booms. Others noted that the Basel Process still depended too much on national institutions more responsive to diverse and often conflicting domestic policy priorities than to global understandings (Singer 2007). Bull might have recognized here the continuing importance yet inadequacy of great-power collaboration in the production of a sustainable order.

More than a common language of risk assessment continued to be required to stabilize markets when disorderly conditions arose and safely to extend the experiment in financial integration beyond the core of the system. In the absence of a global regulator and complete convergence on enforceable accounting standards, and in the context of intense competition for market share, other kinds of *crisis preventive practices* were needed. One tangible consequence of this broadening realization was the development of payment-settlement systems that automatically promised to limit cascading cross-border defaults. Less immediately successful were various proposals to align executive compensation with long-term firm profitability, to limit pure financial speculation, and to rein in the implicit public subsidies underpinning the operations of firms likely in a crisis to be deemed too-big-to-fail. In practice, the Basel II regime—still working mainly in and through national authorities who were both cooperating *and* competing with one another—increased the fragility of the integrating system as a whole.

The larger systemic question ever since the breakdown of the Bretton Woods system focused on precisely how open and integrating markets would and should force constructive adjustments in national macroeconomic policies and discourage excessive national payments imbalances. Their most common effect in practice was to accommodate such imbalances and postpone necessary adjustments. By the turn of the twenty-first century, for example, it was clear that the United States was importing too much, saving too little, and depending for its financing needs on vast inflows of capital from China, Japan, Germany, and many middle-income and developing countries. For a time, the situation looked like a happy one for all concerned, not least for the cross-border firms handling the requisite, if arguably perverse, capital flows from relatively poor countries to a relatively rich country. Instead of encouraging macroeconomic adjustments, expanding capital markets actually permitted such imbalances to grow. Spillovers from one policy arena to another, moreover, were much in evidence. Loose monetary policies, lax regulation, remarkably high leverage in key financial intermediaries, illusory financial innovations, a broadly under-appreciated turn in the business cycle, and the reliance on the housing sector to sustain national prosperity in the United States and elsewhere—are now all commonly blamed for what happened next.

Real-estate related bank failures were not new in American history, but after 2007 staggering numbers occurred (from less than two dozen in 2007 to almost 500 by 2011). In their wake, the capacity of existing multilateral arrangements to pre-empt contagion across the markets to which those banks were now directly or indirectly connected proved inadequate. Expanding reliance on poorly equipped and informally constituted technical clubs failed to prevent a systemic financial emergency that threatened to bring on the second Great Depression.

The attention of policymakers now turned to *emergency management*. Indicative of a rapidly broadening sense that more countries needed to be involved in the task was an expansion in the membership of the BCBS and other BIS-hosted clubs. By March 2009, the number of countries around the BCBS table grew from thirteen to twenty-seven, with the inclusion of emerging-market countries from the G20. At the same time, a refurbished FSB and its staff (mainly borrowed from the BIS) were mandated to accelerate an ambitious work programme to identify the constituent elements of more stable and resilient financial markets, including but not limited to higher capital buffers, minimum liquidity ratios, and maximum leverage requirements for banks and other financial institutions deemed to be 'systemically significant'. Although this accelerated project in preventive governance appeared quite consistent with earlier technocratic efforts led by central banks and supervisory institutions, it actually masked the reassertion in the face of an emergency of great-power finance ministries, especially that of the United States.

Aiming to restore order, regardless of immediate considerations of justice or fairness, governments around the world intervened heavily and directly in global markets in the fall of 2008 and for many months afterwards. The United States in particular lent and invested monetary and fiscal resources—the resources of its own citizens—lavishly. Beneficiaries, however, now included not only its own large financial institutions but also many foreign institutions operating within and across its borders.

In the immediate aftermath of a US decision to let the Lehman Brothers investment bank fail outright, banks around the world had confronted a drastic shortage of liquidity. In coordinated operations, the Federal Reserve and other central banks pumped billions of dollars into money markets. With reluctant congressional authorization, the US Treasury soon established funds to purchase troubled assets from American and foreign banks, and ultimately to make a massive capital injection into a large insurance company, AIG, some of which was used to pay AIG's obligations in full to major domestic and foreign counterparties. Fearing economic collapse, central banks around the world together also slashed short-term interest rates and initiated novel monetary expansions.

In circumstances where illiquidity and insolvency were not easy to differentiate, between 2007 and 2010 nearly 200 domestic and foreign firms benefited from US Federal Reserve liquidity facilities. Their total extra earnings attributable to those operations topped US$13 billion, a figure that must be set against estimates of US$21.6 billion in total losses during the crisis period. There is nothing unique about this effect, for that is what is often meant by recapitalizing institutions at the core of vital payments systems. This one slice of data, however, is illustrative of the impact of a massive set of programmes put in place by the US central bank and Treasury to support markets now intricately linked around the world. Other Federal Reserve actions aimed at restoring global order are worth a deeper look.

Currency swaps between central banks to manage liquidity pressures are hardly unusual. The novelty during this particular crisis came in the unprecedented scale and speed and extent of such operations, and later in the rendering of some new reciprocal swap facilities permanent. Leadership was certainly required and the Fed provided it, but important followers did not need much convincing. In essence, mutually self-interested and informally coordinated actions by key-currency central banks activated and significantly deepened three swap networks centred on the Fed and the dollar, the European Central Bank and the euro, and the Swiss National Bank and the Swiss franc. Additionally, the kinds of regional swap arrangements put in place during and after previous crises in Asia and Latin America were again activated. From 2007 onwards, nearly half of all potential foreign-currency demand from local financial institutions around the world was for US dollars, including demand originating from US bank subsidiaries and branches whose parent banks had pulled liquidity home as US markets were contracting. Swap facilities from the Fed, therefore, played a crucial role, directly by keeping US dollar markets liquid and indirectly by reassuring market participants that funding risks would remain limited. In all, fourteen countries negotiated swap lines with the Fed. All but four eventually drew on those lines, but each benefited from the market-calming influence of their very existence. In October 2013, the Fed, the European Central Bank, and the central banks of Canada, the UK, Japan, and Switzerland agreed to convert their temporary swap facilities to permanent lines.

Central banks were not alone in their emergency management activities. Between September 2008 and June 2009, the United States and advanced-economy governments around the world announced some thirty-four systemic or institution-specific programmes involving bank recapitalization, debt guarantees, asset purchases and guarantees, and increases in deposit-insurance limits (Panetta et al. 2009). As Bull might have predicted, *systemic emergency management* was clearly led in this instance by the United States. Its success, however, depended on informally coordinated assertive action by all national authorities at the core of the system as well as by the regional authorities of the Eurozone (Drezner 2014).

Gradually, market turmoil subsided. Policymakers and market participants then found themselves once again in the arena of crisis prevention. By late 2015 in the context of a new Basel III effort, the members of the FSB had agreed in principle to impose a rule on global systemically important banks that would see their 'total loss-absorbing capacity', including capital and subordinated debt, increase over time to 18 per cent of total risk-weighted assets. Deadlines varied, with banks based in emerging markets given until

2028 to meet the new standard. New rules were designed to reduce bank leverage ratios, and work continued on other measures intended to provide bank management with disincentives to speculate with taxpayer-backed deposits. Contentious debates also resumed on the appropriate deployment of the capital bases of global financial intermediaries across home and host markets.

Plus ça change... noted much sceptical commentary. But who could miss the underlying political trajectory involved? Finance ministries had again retreated to the shadows. Despite the near-catastrophe of 2007–9, there was no serious momentum behind the idea of reverting to the tightly controlled and relatively closed national markets of the post-1945 era. Competition for global market share began rising again in the aftermath of the crisis, yet the lessons of the past could not easily be ignored. The moral hazards introduced to financial markets by crisis-driven government interventions had to be reined in but could not be eliminated. Collaborative and binding regulation was logically required, but it still could not formally be guaranteed at the global level.

Informal *preventive governance* returned as the most feasible objective in a policy arena now rendered more complicated by the entrance of emerging-market economies and even more players from the private and public sides of the rapidly changing landscape of global finance. The demand for order in a more globally integrated environment retained its priority, even as nativist resentment of 'bank bailouts' rose around the word and broader demands for social justice became louder. If he were around to observe this situation, Hedley Bull may well have remained conflicted about the necessity and the difficulty of designing practicable measures to meet those demands after order was restored. His moral sensibility, though, would surely have encouraged him to address that conflict directly.

GLOBAL BURDEN SHARING?

Despite the dimensions of the 2008 crisis, and despite some limited moves toward national 'ring-fencing' by host countries demanding, for example, that foreign firms hold more capital locally, dynamic political interaction inclined the system toward deeper integration. Revived competitive pressures to allow national champions to operate globally, the costs of actually limiting capital inflows and outflows, the reluctance to move back to a pegged exchange-rate system—all impelled financial markets back to the *status quo* before 2007 (Helleiner 2014). Even in the wake of the simultaneous rise of nativist reactions in the United Kingdom, the United States, and elsewhere, only the most pessimistic analysts or market participants were betting that the era of global finance was over. Surely any student of Hedley Bull would remind them that the only serious, if still temporary, retreats occurred in the last two centuries in the context of catastrophic systemic wars.

The true dimensions of the structural dilemma posed by global finance after the crisis of 2007–9 were partly obscured by the arenas within which underlying political conflicts were played out. The *technocratic politics of risk measurement and assessment* were again more obvious right after crisis conditions subsided, and they appeared more tractable. When it came to improving feasible *prevention strategies*, moreover, hopes were also then raised, even as the cooperative politics of loss-avoidance gave way to the more difficult politics of sharing the economic gains delivered by recovering markets. At the same time, the task of designing and rendering legitimate durable *emergency resolution* instruments became more contentious. The ultimate sustainability of a global financial order thus seemed to hinge on whether the experience and prospects of repeated systemic crises could incrementally contribute to a broadening sense of solidarity and co-responsibility—beyond national and regional borders. And here is where policy spillovers come back in.

Financial crises in the past certainly did painfully promote solidarity *within* many civil societies. Something akin to this kind of development sometimes appeared to be occurring within the Eurozone, as financial and other stresses forged just enough of a grudging realization of 'shared fate' to sustain an evolving regional capacity, with a modest and necessary fiscal foundation, for emergency management (Schimmelfennig 2014). The European System of Central Banks coordinated by the European Central Bank was clearly engaged in this drama, while finance ministries once again tried to limit their fiscal responsibilities. But state-based regulatory instruments hardly signalled the only imaginable pathway towards adequate if not optimal financial governance. Within Europe, the most palatable included variants of collective insurance programmes which served to cloak ultimate fiscal guarantees, especially market-focused programmes directed at undergirding a regional banking union. Analogous global plans for reliable and collaborative financial governance beyond the limits of Europe are hardly unimaginable. Before the crisis of 2008, crucial policy debates on the key issue of emergency resolution revolved around the theory and practice of sovereign bankruptcy (Brummer 2012). The crisis of 2008 dramatically raised the stakes.

The ad hoc collaboration of great powers during the crisis stopped short of establishing definitive resolution mechanisms, even if it did provide new impetus to the Basel Process to improve systemic risk assessment and policies designed to prevent future crises (Aquanno 2015). The way the crisis was actually managed did, nevertheless, highlight the underlying issue of justice. As an IMF (2014, 104) study put it, 'In dollar terms, if applied at the total liabilities of the banks [designated by the FSB as global systemically important] net of equity, the implicit subsidies in 2011–12 represent around $15–70 billion in the United States, $25-110 billion in Japan, $20–110 billion in the

United Kingdom, and up to $90–300 billion in the euro area.' Those subsidies may once again encourage imprudent risk-taking and render global markets more, not less, fragile. They also appear increasingly widely to be perceived as unfair and as exacerbating social inequalities around the world.

Bull's observation that order precedes justice was suggested once again during the crisis of 2007–9. Likewise, well worth recalling was his reminder that justice nevertheless remained vital for the long-run persistence of an order destined to be global in nature. Despite much domestic political noise, and despite wilful blindness by some electors and their nationalist champions, the issue of global justice became a prominent theme in post-crisis policy debates. It could not seriously be ignored in the United States and other great powers, in emerging-market economies, or in an array of international financial institutions. The path ahead was filled with moral hazards and significant political complexity, but the path back from a financial order stubbornly eroding national boundaries was obscured by the political consequences of prior policy decisions.

CONCLUSION

The credible prospect of catastrophic loss was enough to motivate just-adequate systemic governance in 2008. The promise of future joint gains seems a less reliable motivator of authoritative systemic regulation. But a modicum of global governance capacity is now logically required by the continuing existence and expansion of systemically significant financial institutions around the world (Gallagher 2015). That capacity is evolving differentially across the spectrum of risk assessment, crisis prevention, and emergency management. Shaping arrangements and future expectations in each of these three arenas are different kinds of politics. Within each arena, as Bull would have explained, order takes priority over justice, but demands for justice have not disappeared and are not being ignored.

The politics of risk assessment involves social learning, common knowledge, and technical coordination by experts, and it is leavened by competitive market dynamics. The *politics of crisis prevention*, awkwardly but necessarily, involves trying to combine local-level incentives for private managerial self-discipline with system-level efforts to build insurance-like arrangements. However masked, risk pooling, portfolio diversification, burden sharing, and converging regulation to reduce moral hazards—all are gradually emerging in cross-national practice. Finally, *the politics of emergency management* still revolves around the power of assertive governance by leading states and self-interested collaboration by followers, all forced by policy spillovers and the spectre of systemic catastrophe.

At a time when systemic power is shifting underneath a globalizing economy, the logic of functionalism here meets the hard politics of establishing robust governing structures, structures that reliably promise order responsive to broader demands for justice, structures, in short, that are widely-enough perceived to be legitimate. The system inclines towards more complexity and more intense political conflict. Nothing is certain, but uncertainty does not preclude faith in the future. As elsewhere in human life, uncertainty rather provides the wellspring for such faith.

Solidarity emerges not from rhetorical appeals but from functional necessity, political struggle, and what Gramsci famously called 'optimism of the will'. The political impulses that gave rise to the regulatory and fiscal capacity of the modern state itself suggest the emergence of its successor (Grande and Pauly 2005). The analytically separable political logics of risk assessment, crisis prevention, and emergency management open pathways to imagining its variegated organization.

If government still ultimately involves the authoritative allocation of values, then actual governments today continue partly to meet their responsibilities through the instrument of integrating financial markets in a global economy. Reactionary responses are today evident throughout the world. They are likely to be frustrated in the absence of a more feasible collective plan for sustaining prosperity, peace, and the capacity for global problem-solving.

Until some form of fiscal authority moves decisively to the level implied by their evolving scope, the collaborative policy instrument of border-spanning and well-functioning markets will rest on uneasy foundations. Institutional experiments like those associated with the Basel Process, the Financial Stability Board, central-bank networks, and, within Europe, a nascent banking union, may for a time help us to assess and live with irreducible systemic risks. The actual deepening of cross-national risk pools in public and private insurance systems, systems that can engender a sense of shared fate within and across politically bounded societies, provide the grounds for some optimism when it comes to designing reliable and politically balanced mechanisms for crisis prevention. Furthermore, although straightforward *ex ante* burden-sharing agreements across diverse societies may remain rare for a time, repeated ad hoc burden-sharing arrangements during systemic emergencies do certainly give rise to reasonable expectations of future cross-national regulatory, monetary, and fiscal coordination. In the language of debates still inspired by Bull, the logic of solidarism still promises to overwhelm the logic of pluralism.

The reconstitution of social boundaries, nevertheless, remains a profoundly political project. The global experiment in financial integration is part of that project. In the absence of deepening confidence that an adequate degree of transnational solidarity will exist before and during future emergencies, it could fail. Associated global risks, however, would not then disappear. As they have in the past, they would simply spill into other policy arenas, including the arena of security policy. Avoiding that scenario and fostering solidarity now necessarily means attending to the demands of justice. As Bull himself put it, 'The states system will indeed prove dysfunctional if states are not able to preserve and extend the sense of common interests, common rules, and common institutions that have moderated their conflicts in the past' (1977, 295).

A process of deep social re-ordering on a global scale anticipated by Bull's own practical and moral reasoning is underway. The transformative moment in industrial capitalism sparked within the states system but now driving governance capacities beyond the sovereign confines of existing states, a moment highlighted by Buzan, Lawson, and many others, has already occurred. As predicted and critiqued by many theorists from many different perspectives, global finance is now a fact of life. Notwithstanding the rage of nativists, a widening array of states and powerful non-state actors has apparently concluded that stopping the evolution of integrating markets is less desirable than trying collectively to steer it and to stabilize its foundations. The long-run acceptance of systemic governance delivered partly through the expansion of orderly global markets will depend upon limiting the unequal outcomes those markets produce. Bull's analytical and moral sensibilities remain relevant. Order retains its priority, even as it increases demands for greater justice that must eventually be met.

In the face of some future disaster on a scale never experienced in recent centuries, we may nevertheless find ourselves for a time moving in the opposite direction. If so, we will be lucky indeed to retreat to Hedley Bull's anarchical society. So we must hope for the eventual reassertion of hard-won wisdom. Hyperbolic nationalists, scowling finance ministers, and libertarian financiers should not confuse us. The political capacity to govern global economic and financial risks is emerging, albeit unevenly across distinct policy arenas. Its ultimate legitimation is possible, functional, and necessary. The global society that Bull glimpsed, and to which he assigned moral priority, is on the horizon.

12

The Anarchical Society and Climate Change

Robert Falkner

INTRODUCTION

Hedley Bull's *The Anarchical Society* is the first English School text that addresses, albeit briefly, international environmental politics. Bull's interest in environmental issues is motivated mainly by his desire to refute claims that 'the states system is an obstacle to the attainment of man's ecological objective of living in harmony with his environment' (1977, 283). The book does not discuss climate change as such. Published in 1977, five years after the first UN environment conference but two years before the first World Climate Conference, *The Anarchical Society* conceives of environmental issues as a set of distinct problems that require international scientific cooperation and environmental management. By contrast, climate change has emerged today as an all-encompassing global ecological threat that requires the wholesale de-carbonization of the global economy. It is, as Hoffmann suggests, 'perhaps *the* global challenge of modern times' (2013, 3). Had Bull lived to observe the rise of international climate politics since the 1990s, would he have arrived at a different assessment of the environmental agenda? Would he still view global environmental politics through the same pluralist, state-centric, lens that is at the heart of *The Anarchical Society*?

This essay offers a close reading of Bull's classic text in an effort to apply his theoretical perspective to the international politics of climate change. My objective is to explore what contribution pluralist English School theory can make to our understanding of how international society can respond to global warming, and what its limitations are. After reviewing Bull's discussion of environmental issues in *The Anarchical Society*, which can be found in a brief passage on 'Man and the Environment' in Chapter 12 and a few short comments that are dispersed throughout the book, I explore the core tenets of pluralist English School theory and how they apply to climate change. This is followed by a discussion of the possibility of a transition towards a solidarist response to environmental threats, which Bull briefly hints at but never fully explores, and a concluding assessment of Bull's overall argument.

BULL ON 'MAN AND THE ENVIRONMENT'

Man-made climate change, which is caused by emissions of CO_2 and other greenhouse gases (GHGs) such as methane and nitrous oxide, is one of the major environmental threats that the world faces today. The increase in GHG concentrations in the atmosphere has already led to an average warming of global temperatures of around 0.8°C since the late nineteenth century and, if emissions continue unabated, we are likely to experience a warming of at least 4°C or more over the course of this century. While global average temperatures have fluctuated in the past, the rapid increase in temperatures to a level that has likely not been seen for the last ten million years will irrevocably change the human geography of the planet. Melting ice caps and glaciers, rising sea levels, shifts in weather patterns and precipitation, further desertification, acidification of oceans, and the destruction of entire ecosystems will bring about fundamental changes to the way human societies are organized and sustain themselves (Stern 2015, 3–32). Given the massive cost of adapting to a changing climate and the distributional conflicts that this will cause worldwide, climate change is emerging as a major disruptive force in international political and economic relations. Clearly, climate change is no longer just a scientific or environmental issue. Increasingly, climate change ought to be an integral part of any study of the foundations for order in world politics.

Bull's *The Anarchical Society* does not mention climate change as a threat to international order. This is not surprising, given that Bull was working on the book at a time when climate change, although attracting growing scientific attention, had not yet been recognized by policymakers as a major threat. In the 1970s, the scientific community was still debating whether rising GHG emissions would lead to global cooling or warming, and the international environmental agenda was dominated by other environmental concerns, such as resource scarcity, marine pollution, and acid rain. Evidence of a warming climate was mounting during the second half of the 1970s, however, and by the time of the first World Climate Conference, convened in February 1979, global warming was beginning to emerge as an issue of global concern. Still, it took until the late 1980s for multilateral negotiations to commence on the United Nations Framework Convention on Climate Change (UNFCCC), which was adopted in 1992.

Although failing to address climate change, Bull was the first English School theorist to write about international environmental politics. While the earliest efforts to create an international environmental agenda can be traced back to the time before the First World War, it was the UN environment conference in Stockholm in 1972 that formally established international society's responsibility to protect the global environment (Falkner 2012). Curiously, Bull does not mention the Stockholm conference or subsequent developments, such as the creation of the UN Environment Programme (1973) and various environmental treaties; nor is he interested in investigating the reasons behind the sudden emergence of global environmentalism. Instead, he takes it as given that environmental protection is one of the 'advanced or secondary goals that are a feature of an international society in which a consensus has been reached about a wider range of objectives than mere coexistence' (1977, 70).

For Bull, the interesting point about environmentalism is that it gives rise to a discourse that challenges the existing international order. In a brief section of not more than three pages, which appears in Chapter 12 on 'The Obsolescence of the States System' (1977, 293–5), Bull considers—and dismisses—the suggestion that the states system has become obsolete because of its inability to deal with global environmental threats (see also Linklater and Suganami 2006, 68–70; Paterson 2005, 164–7). The 1970s had seen the first wave of writings on environmental matters by International Relations scholars (for an overview, see Stevis 2014, 18–22), many of which viewed state-centric politics with scepticism and argued for an alternative world order. Such proposals either proceeded along cosmopolitan lines of empowering centralized international authorities, regional authorities and transnational actors (Falk 1971) or opted for more authoritarian solutions (Ophuls 1977). At the time, Richard Falk's book *This Endangered Planet* (1971) was particularly influential in shaping environmentalism's anti-statism, and it is this text that Bull uses as a foil to his own argument in defence of the state-centric international order.[1] Arguing against the then widespread notion of the 'spaceship earth' (Ward 1966) that requires 'global unity and global planning' (Bull 1977, 293) to steer it safely towards environmental sustainability, Bull makes three specific points.

His *first* point is the classic pluralist argument that humanity and the society of states are characterized by a profound diversity of values and interests, and that this prevents sustained international cooperation on global challenges, including ecological ones. In Bull's words, it is not the division of the world into sovereign states as such but 'human disagreement and conflict in the ecological realm' (1977, 293–4) that stands in the way of a common global approach. In a concession to Falk and other environmental writers, Bull goes on to acknowledge that human society may have to tolerate certain restrictions

---

[1] Bull knew Falk well and counted him as a friend. Although setting out to dismiss the core of Falk's argument, Bull was careful to acknowledge his friend in the preface to *The Anarchical Society*, referring to Falk's views as 'one of the most significant points of departure in the study of world politics today' before remarking that 'the attention I devote to refuting him should be taken as a compliment' (1977, ix).

on population growth and resource consumption, to avert a universal 'tragedy of the commons' (1977, 294). This is the closest that Bull comes to accepting the then widespread, though controversial, theory that the global expansion of human societies and economic activity was close to breaching ecological boundaries (Meadows and Meadows 1972). But instead of thinking through the consequences of this neo-Malthusian logic, Bull merely notes that a system of sovereign states is indeed dysfunctional insofar as it could never impose such limitations—but neither could alternatives to international society, unless they were to curb human freedoms to stay within ecological constraints. Having seemingly accepted the need for certain limits to growth in the future, Bull's point is merely to argue that all global political responses, whether they are found through international society or an alternative world order, suffer from the same structural problem of value and interest plurality. Environmentalists are thus wrong to assume that an institutionally reorganized international system with a central authority could bring about the global unity and solidarity that is needed to address the ecological crisis.

In his *second* point, Bull develops the pluralist argument further by highlighting the importance of international order as a precondition for tackling ecological problems. A society of sovereign states can make a valuable contribution mainly because it creates stability and order against the background of normative pluralism: 'Without such a basis of minimum order it is scarcely possible that common issues of the environmental can be faced at all' (1977, 294). Bull does not explore whether the pluralist logic of coexistence in international society alone could give rise to coordinated environmental action and how far this would go in meeting the global environmental challenge. He merely takes it as a given that states are the only actors capable of delivering an emergency response: 'It is undoubtedly the case that effective action in the short run to limit population growth, to control economic development ... or to limit and justly apportion the consumption of resources, depends primarily on the action of states' (1977, 294). It is interesting to note that Bull qualifies his defence of state-centric international politics by referring only to 'effective action in the short run' (1977, 294), leaving open the question of the nation-state's long-term viability as an environmentally sustainable form of political organization. Environmentalists such as Falk may be right after all—but only in the long term.

The *third* argument takes Bull away from a strictly pluralist interpretation of global environmental politics and hints at a solidarist perspective. Bull concedes that '[i]n the long run it [is] unlikely that action at the purely state level will be sufficient to cope with environmental dangers' (1977, 294–5), before going on to suggest that in order for humanity to tackle environmental threats, there would need to be 'a greater sense of human cohesion than now exists' (1977, 295). Having so far defended pluralist international society against the vision of 'post-Westphalian' world politics, Bull now appears to suggest that the pluralist logic of coexistence may eventually have to give way to a solidarist project of creating greater political cohesion and human solidarity. But instead of explaining the implications of this concession, Bull returns to his initial starting point that it is the states system through which 'a greater sense of human solidarity in relation to environmental threats may emerge' (1977, 294) . Rather than consider a cohesive world society as an alternative to the current system of states, we should see its emergence as being dependent on the preservation and development of international society itself. In short, world society-based solidarism can only ever grow out of a pluralist international society that gradually takes on more solidarist characteristics. For the time being, only international society can give adequate expression to the common interests and values that might lead to a more cohesive and globally coordinated response to the ecological crisis.

How do these arguments relate to the international politics of climate change, and what relevance does *The Anarchical Society* have in an age of runaway global warming? In the next section, I explore what insights Bull's analysis yields for the study of climate change politics and whether pluralism could give rise to an effective international response. The subsequent section then examines the possibility of a solidarist project of creating climate governance and explores whether Bull's state-centric perspective still provides an adequate framework for understanding the emergence of an ever-more complex system of global climate governance.

PLURALIST INTERNATIONAL SOCIETY AND CLIMATE CHANGE

As we have seen, it is the inherently pluralist nature of international society that leads Bull to reject environmentalists' arguments for a transformation of world politics. While Bull does not discuss the challenge of climate change as such, I will attempt to construct from his brief remarks on environmental matters a pluralist perspective on climate change. I am particularly interested in understanding what contribution English School pluralism can make to the study of international climate politics, but also what its shortcomings are. There are four aspects to Bull's pluralism that need to be considered in this context: the plurality of values and interests, which is said to prevent global solidarity in the battle against global warming; the pluralist logic of co-existence as the basis for (limited) international cooperation; the centrality of the state system and the role that states play in the search for an international solution; and the special role played by great powers and the primary institution of great power management.

Value Pluralism and Conflict

Starting from the pluralist premise that conflict over individual and societal values is an inevitable condition of humanity, *The Anarchical Society* takes a sceptical stance on the possibility of deep international cooperation. Bull notes that only a minimal consensus exists across societies on the need to protect the common primary goals of international life: life, promises, and property (1977, 19). Beyond this, pluralists do not expect a deeper sense of global solidarity to emerge, let alone form the basis for sustained international cooperation. As was noted, Bull argues, contra Falk, that 'what inhibits a common global plan for action in relation to the environment is not the existence of the system of states but the fact of human disagreement and conflict in the ecological realm itself' (1977, 293–4). It is for this reason that 'in the present condition of world politics... ideas of cosmopolitan or world justice play very little part at all' (1977, 85) and this applies to international environmental politics as much as to the realms of peace and economic justice.

Does Bull's pluralist scepticism apply to climate change as well? Is not the threat of runaway global warming reason to believe that humanity would unite in a global effort to avert such a catastrophe? Average temperatures are set to rise by between 2°C and 4°C by the end of this century according to conservative scenarios, but could also reach much higher levels if certain ecological tipping points were reached. Would not the expected impacts—rising sea levels, more extreme weather patterns, acidification of oceans, and greater ecological stresses in arid regions—force a reorientation of societal values and interests towards greater global solidarity? If climate change were to threaten the survival of humanity, should we not expect the fight against climate change to become one of the primary goals of social life on the planet—goals that Bull believes form part of international society's value consensus?

It is telling that in his discussion of the rise of environmental politics, Bull treats environmental issues as discrete problems of international management, most of which concern

> behaviour that is appropriate not to the elementary or primary goals of international life, but rather to those more advanced or secondary goals that are a feature of an international society in which a consensus has been reached about a wider range of objectives than mere coexistence. (1977, 70)

However, in one brief passage Bull hints at the possibility that, if the ecological crisis turns out to be more severe, then more drastic international restrictions would need to be imposed. Arguing in the context of the 'limits to growth' debate, Bull refers to human freedoms with regard to population growth and economic development that may need to be curbed in order for humanity to stay within its global ecological boundaries (1977, 294). When seen in the context of the contemporary debate on global warming, this passage can also be read as a concession that if ecological problems such as climate change pose an existential threat to humankind, then a business-as-usual response involving international cooperation in the pursuit of secondary goals will not suffice. The fact remains, though, as Bull notes, that the international states system offers the only realistic means for a collective response, and that no other global political system could provide a viable alternative (1977, 294). In other words, climate change could indeed become the globally unifying threat that brushes aside societal differences in values and interests, but international society would remain our best bet for organizing a global rescue.

How close has the world come to such a scenario? Despite the widespread expectation that a warming climate will harm humanity overall, specific climate impacts are, in fact, unequally distributed around the world. Rising sea levels will inflict damage on coastal areas and may submerge low-lying island states, but not inland territories. Changes in weather patterns will lead to greater droughts in some regions, and more extreme rainfall in others, but increases in precipitation and a rise in land temperatures is already benefiting farming in Greenland and may lead to greater agricultural productivity in other countries too (e.g. Canada, Russia) ('Greenland reaps benefits of global warming', 2013). And even though the majority of countries will suffer adverse effects, the degree to which societies will perceive climate change as an existential threat is bound to vary considerably around the world. Furthermore, countries will also differ with regard to the value they attach to ensuring global climate stability through mitigation measures, as compared to pursuing other policies that either focus narrowly on economic growth or adaptation to a warming climate. In other words, even where climate change poses a common threat, the willingness to act against it will be unevenly distributed.

Bull's value pluralism thus remains an important starting point for thinking through an appropriate and realistic international climate strategy. Despite the growing perception of climate change as a universal threat to humankind, the difficulty of agreeing common principles for reducing emissions has not gone away. Indeed, Bull's pluralist scepticism towards the idea of global solidarity is borne out by the agonizingly slow progress that has been made in over two decades of multilateral negotiations under the auspices of the UNFCCC. Even after the 2015 Paris Agreement (Falkner 2016b), Bull would not be far off the mark with his claim that states have 'only the most rudimentary sense of the common good of the world as a whole' (1977, 81).

The Pluralist Logic of Coexistence

In Bull's conception of a pluralist international society, the behavior of states is primarily driven by a logic of coexistence (Jackson 2000, 178-82; Buzan 2004, 143). The rules of coexistence—limits to violence, establishment of property rights, and sanctity of agreements—provide a basic set of constraints that allow sovereign states to live together in relative harmony while pursuing their self-interest. But does such a pluralist society of states have the capacity to deal with as complex a problem as climate change? Can a pluralist logic of coexistence on its own give rise to an internationally coordinated response to global warming?

As we have seen, Bull sees the rise in international environmental rule-making primarily as part of the creation of rules of cooperation, on issues that go beyond the primary goals of coexistence. International environmental governance signifies the expansion of regulatory international law (1977, 153) and involves largely solutions to 'a technical problem of maximizing the interests of the human species rather than as a problem of reconciling different interests' (1977, 177). What if ecological problems posed an existential threat to states and the maintenance of international order? Bull did not consider such a scenario, but runaway global warming could pose a direct threat to national sovereignty, e.g. where it threatens the existence of low-lying island states or coastal regions. It could also pose an indirect threat to international security, e.g. where global warming acts as a threat multiplier by exacerbating distributional conflicts over scarce resources, undermining weak or failing states and setting off trans-boundary migration flows (German Advisory Council on Global Change 2008; Gemenne et al. 2014). Irreversible global warming could thus undermine the peaceful coexistence of sovereign states, making it increasingly difficult for international society to guarantee the 'limitation of violence resulting in death or bodily harm, the keeping of promises and the stabilization of possession by rules of property' (1977, 19). Would a pluralist international society be able to achieve the level of cooperation that is required to avert such a threat?

As Buzan argues, there is nothing in the pluralist logic of coexistence to prevent states from establishing some minimal level of international cooperation on environmental issues (2004, 145). Particularly where core state interests are at stake and effective measures to deal with the ecological problem are available, states may choose to act collectively to prevent global environmental danger. This was the case with international cooperation to protect the ozone layer, and major GHG emitters could conceivably be compelled to take similar action to protect themselves and international society against runaway global warming. In this view, Bull's pluralist stance would be entirely consistent with a modicum of international environmental cooperation to tackle dangerous climate change.

But despite recent moves to view climate change as a security threat (Busby 2008; Scheffran and Battaglini 2011), securitization has not changed the underlying logic of international climate politics. This is partly because climate change will play out over a long period and does not pose an imminent threat. Its impacts will vary around the world, with the heaviest burden falling on poorer and weaker developing countries. By comparison, the major powers face only weak or uncertain security threats, with some potentially benefiting from rising temperatures. Given that the costs of mitigating climate change are also unequally distributed, it is unlikely that the great powers will arrive at similar cost–benefit calculations that would compel them to act together to reduce future global warming. Given the high upfront costs of taking action, uncertainty about future impacts and pervasive free-riding incentives (Keohane and Victor 2011), it is far more likely that the pluralist logic of coexistence will prevent deep forms of international cooperation and will drive great powers towards predominantly national response strategies, mainly in the form of adaptation to climate change. And even if mitigation was in the interest of some great powers, they may find it preferable to take unilateral action, e.g. geo-engineering (Victor et al. 2009), rather than contribute to a collective mitigation effort. Either way, it is reasonable to conclude that if states follow a pluralist logic it is unlikely that they will produce the comprehensive and timely response that is needed to prevent dangerous climate change.

State-centrism

A further implication of Bull's pluralist stance is his insistence that any global response to climate change will need to be channelled through the society of states. Bull is adamant that the nation-state is the sole legitimate representative of individual societies, and the states system is the only viable form of global political organization that can resolve differences in interests and values between societies. It is this unequivocal state-centrism that is perhaps Bull's most widely noted contribution to the study of international environmental politics (Paterson 2005; see also Hurrell and Kingsbury 1992, 5). Indeed, as was noted earlier, Bull set up the debate on environmental issues as one between two diametrically opposed camps: environmentalists who advocate the creation of supranational authorities or a world government and representatives of the state-centric international society tradition. Bull makes two arguments contra the supranationalists: first, the states system is a necessary condition for organizing a global ecological response, and second, even if it becomes necessary to achieve a 'greater sense of human cohesion' as the basis for international environmental cooperation, the path towards such a solidarist future runs through the state-centric system (1977, 295). In other words, the states system already performs vital functions in the pursuit of global environmental goals, and any improvement on this would have to build on, rather than replace, international society.

The history of international climate politics lends some support to Bull's position. For over two decades, the multilateral regime of the UNFCCC has been the central forum for negotiating international climate policy, hosting annual Conferences of Parties (COPs) that have also become a magnet for climate activists and lobbyists (Hjerpe and Linnér 2010). It has spawned a number of innovative climate governance mechanisms (e.g. Clean Development Mechanism, emissions trading) that engage a wide range of actors, including business and NGOs. Despite efforts to replace it by smaller minilateral forums, the UNFCCC remains the only international forum that commands universal legitimacy, including among all major polluters (Falkner 2016a). If anything, the successful outcome of the Paris climate summit in 2015 has allowed the UNFCCC to reassert its role as the central platform for coordinating national policies.

At the same time, however, the limitations of Bull's state-centric approach come into focus when we consider the changing nature of global climate governance. For one, although the UNFCCC regime has retained its central role, it has little to show for in terms of creating an effective response. The climate regime is undergoing a process of fragmentation as new sites of authority are emerging and various non-state actors pursue their own strategies (Biermann et al. 2009). The growth of a multilevel and multi-actor network of transnational climate governance is indeed one of the most remarkable developments in recent years (Bulkeley et al. 2014; Hoffmann 2011). Rather than rely solely on the regulatory authority of the nation-state, more and more municipal authorities, cities, regional governments, businesses and NGOs are taking the initiative in setting climate norms, disseminating low-carbon solutions, and establishing private governance mechanisms. The field of climate governance has become crowded, with state and non-state actors engaged in a dense web of interactions, reinforcing each other's efforts but also acting independently from each other. As will be discussed below, Bull's state-centric perspective, held back by a simplistic binary distinction between the realms of international society and world society, offers little analytical purchase when it comes to advancing our understanding of this growing transnationalization of climate governance beyond the intergovernmental regime.

Great Powers and Great Power Management

Although Bull's state-centric perspective no longer captures the transnationalization of global climate governance, his notion of great power management has, if anything, gained prominence in international climate politics. This may appear to be an unlikely outcome given the climate regime's strong multilateral tradition that has tended to deny great powers a privileged position in the negotiations. Decisions in the UNFCCC's annual COPs are taken by consensus, and the negotiation process has been highly inclusive even by multilateral standards, allowing smaller powers to play an unusually influential role. Most significantly, when agreeing the UNFCCC and the Kyoto Protocol, the Western powers accepted an unprecedented level of differentiation that completely exempted developing countries from the regime's emission reduction targets. This has begun to change more recently, however. While the UNFCCC continues to apply the consensus principle as an implicit procedural norm, the Kyoto-style burden-sharing arrangement has been successfully challenged, first by the United States and later also by other industrialized countries. Ever since the Copenhagen conference in 2009, Western powers have put pressure on emerging powers to take on a climate change mitigation burden that is proportionate with their fast-rising emissions and emerging great power status (Hurrell and Sengupta 2012). This process of rewriting great power responsibilities came to head in the Paris Agreement of 2015, which includes for the first time mitigation pledges made by all major emitters.

The great powers are also more strongly in control of the negotiation process itself. At the 2009 Copenhagen summit, after diplomats tried but ultimately failed to create a post-Kyoto successor treaty, a select group of influential heads of state convened informally at the end of the conference to forge a short political agreement (Falkner, Stephan, et al. 2010). The so-called Copenhagen Accord was eventually rejected at the COP plenary in Copenhagen, but its principles were later integrated into the Cancun COP agreements in 2010, thus laying the foundations for the shift in the regulatory approach that underpins the Paris Agreement. Ever since, the major powers have taken a more proactive role, agreeing the broad outlines of mitigation burden-sharing among themselves as part of the overall multilateral agreement. Both the EU and US engaged in bilateral talks with China and India on how to promote low-carbon technologies in emerging economies (Torney 2015), and in a sign of the gradual convergence of US and Chinese positions the two powers signed a bilateral agreement in November 2014 that established the mitigation pledges that both countries made as part of the Paris Agreement (Vogler 2016, 127–8).

Bull's account of the primary institution of great power management offers a useful starting point for investigating the changing role of great powers in international climate politics. Great powers are a simple fact of international life that 'cannot be wished away' (Bull 1977, 298), and Bull would expect them to have a decisive influence over outcomes in international climate politics. Somewhat counter-intuitively, this was not the case in the early phase of the international climate regime, when the G77 succeeded in exempting developing countries from mitigation obligations. Tony Brenton, a British negotiator at the 1992 Rio Summit, is not alone in noting that 'it is difficult not to be struck by the imbalance in these commitments between the developed countries and the developing countries' (Brenton 1994, 195). Concerned with healing the North–South rift, many Western powers were willing to make this concession in order to get universal support for the UNFCCC. As the political salience of climate change increased in subsequent years, however, the United States and other Western powers gradually rolled back earlier commitments and eventually forced a reinterpretation of the UNFCCC's common but differentiated responsibilities (CBDR) norm. At least since the 2009 Copenhagen conference, great power politics has returned to leave its mark on the climate change regime (Brenton 2013).

However, Bull's understanding of great powers adds an important dimension that sets it apart from standard realist interpretations. For Bull, great powers are as much a social construction as they are the result of material power asymmetry. Great powers perform certain functions in international society—maintaining the balance of power, forcing cooperative solutions—and in doing so they assert not only their power but also aspire to a privileged position that is legitimate. Great powers often act against the immediate interests of smaller powers, but their role can be considered legitimate where they pursue the collective interest in maintaining international order. As agents of a collective hegemony, great powers are 'recognised by others to have, and conceived by their own leaders and peoples to have, certain special rights and duties' (1977, 202). Legitimacy and hegemony are thus closely intertwined in Bull's and the English School's notion of power asymmetry and international hierarchy (Clark 2011). In this sense, the need to gain and retain international legitimacy constrains great powers. Bull is unequivocal that 'when the great powers appear to be undermining order as well as denying justice, the legitimacy of their position is eroded' (1977, 229).

Bull's approach highlights two central issues in the way the great powers have engaged with the global climate challenge. First, by sheer size of their economic might and emissions profile, great powers are inevitably at the heart of the global warming problem. As major polluters, they are largely responsible for climate change and also possess *de facto* veto power in international climate politics. Any regime that is to produce viable solutions needs to reflect the reality of power asymmetry and accommodate the special interests of the great powers. At the same time, great powers themselves need to be concerned about the wider legitimacy of their international role and the outcome they promote within the multilateral regime (Eckersley 2007; Bukovansky et al. 2012). For great power management to operate as an institutional feature of climate politics, great powers need to promote collective solutions that do not ignore the demands for international justice made by smaller powers. Thus, despite experimenting with potentially more effective minilateral solutions, none of the great powers have as yet walked away from the multilateral regime. The return of the United States to the multilateral effort under President Obama and the growing acceptance of mitigation responsibilities by the emerging powers of Asia suggests that, as Bull asserts in *The Anarchical Society*, great powers' 'freedom of manoeuvre is circumscribed by "responsibility"' (1977, 229). But Bull would have warned against exuberant expectations when it comes to great powers' concern for the global common good. The fact that they proclaim to be acting in the global interest does not turn them into 'great responsibles' or 'great indispensables' (1977, 51), and the election of US president Trump, who has called global warming a 'hoax', underlines the fickle nature of great power support for global environmental protection. The need for legitimacy exerts some pressure on the largest emitters to contribute to the collective mitigation effort, but we are still far from effective great power management in the interest of a stable global climate.

TOWARDS A SOLIDARIST RESPONSE TO GLOBAL WARMING?

As we have seen, there are good reasons to suggest that the pluralist logic of coexistence alone cannot generate the kind of internationally coordinated response that could prevent dangerous levels of global warming. It is unsurprising, therefore, that analysts and policymakers have focused on how a solidarist response to climate change, built on strong international institutions and redistributive policies, can be constructed. *The Anarchical Society* implicitly acknowledges the possibility that the transition from a pluralist to a solidarist form of international cooperation might be necessary (1977, 294–5).[2] Bull is not interested in thinking through how this transformation could come about, beyond noting that the states system is the means through which this can happen. But it is clear that Bull opens the door to a solidarist transformation of international society. To achieve the 'greater sense of human cohesion', states would need to 'extend the sense of common interests, common rules and common institutions that have moderated their conflicts in the past', and this concerns not only matters of peace and justice, but also 'environmental management' (1977, 295). This brief passage is the closest that Bull comes to endorsing a solidarist answer to the global ecological crisis, even if he does not believe that this can be realized in the short run.

How could a solidarist solution for climate change be found? As we have seen, Bull notes at various points that international society has already expanded the scope for international cooperation on environmental matters, through the creation of legal rules that advance 'secondary goals' based on an international consensus on international objectives that go beyond 'mere

---

[2] Later in life, Bull became more disillusioned with the pluralist perspective on international order, hinting more strongly at the need for solidarist solutions, especially in the context of North–South justice (see Dunne 1998b, 146–52).

coexistence' (1977, 70). But the expansion of the scope of international law has not led to a strengthening of the rule of law in international relations (1977, 153). International environmental law exists within a state-centric system based on the rule of consent, i.e. the sovereign right of states to accept or reject international environmental regulations, and the unavoidable logic of pluralism holds back an expansion of international law beyond its state-centric limitations.

Bull's expectation that solidarism would be built through state-centric means certainly corresponds with the early phase of international climate politics in the 1990s. The underlying approach of the UNFCCC negotiations closely resembled the putative transition from a pluralist to a solidarist logic of cooperation. Starting out with establishing a broad consensus on the threat of global warming (UNFCCC), subsequent negotiations would then agree specific regulatory commitments and instruments that would move the world closer to a low-carbon future. In this sense, the 1997 Kyoto Protocol can be considered the high point of state solidarism in climate politics. The first and only treaty with quantitative and legally binding targets for emission reductions, it also contains strong elements of interstate justice, with developing countries exempted from legally binding emission reductions and entitled to benefit from new redistributive instruments.

Despite these achievements, subsequent efforts to implement and build on Kyoto have not lived up to solidarist expectations. The US never ratified the treaty, Canada withdrew from it, and other major industrialized countries declared they would not be bound by it beyond the first compliance period. At the same time, the emerging emitters of the developing world resisted pressure to accept Kyoto-style emissions restrictions for themselves. The result of this impasse, clearly visible in Copenhagen in 2009, was the unravelling of the Protocol's top-down regulatory approach. Instead, Copenhagen paved the way for the Paris Agreement's new approach that turned legally binding commitments into voluntary, nationally determined, contributions. Paris thus marks the completion of the shift from the top-down and centralized regime of the past and to a more de-centralized, bottom-up logic of national pledges. Viewed through the lens of Bull's pluralist perspective the Paris Agreement demonstrates both the persistence of deep rooted differences between the great powers and their reluctance to subject themselves to a solidarist framework of mandatory emissions reductions that are framed in a legal context. The great powers may have collectively acknowledged their special responsibility for climate change but they have retained a high degree of flexibility in how they intend to discharge this responsibility. In this sense, the Paris Agreement marks the persistence of pluralism in international climate politics.

What is missing in Bull's account is the possibility of a different kind of solidarist response, one that is rooted in cosmopolitan thinking and that builds on greater involvement of world society actors. Bull's state-centric framework offers little analytical purchase on transnational climate governance, which has gained in prominence more recently. Bull was certainly aware of the possibility of such a development. Indeed, he acknowledges that environmental discourses in the 1970s were infused with cosmopolitan ideas of planetary justice. Environmentalists, he noted, appeal 'to the solidarity of all human beings in facing certain ecological or environmental challenges that face them as human beings' (1977, 85). But he is quick to dismiss the possibility of a political project that builds on cosmopolitan solidarism, merely noting that such ideas 'play very little part at all' in present conditions (1977, 85). No agent exists to bring about this cosmopolitan vision. The self-appointed spokesmen of 'spaceship earth' have no representational legitimacy, just as environmental NGOs do not have the authority to define the interests of humankind (1977, 85–6). It thus falls upon states to find a consensus on the pursuit of environmental objectives as the only hope for developing a deeper level of cooperation on environmental matters.

What if states were not the only actors to build global climate governance? What if the intergovernmental process was an important, but no longer the central, driving force behind current efforts to de-carbonize the global economy? A great deal of recent environmental scholarship has focused on precisely this question, highlighting the growing transnationalization of climate governance, with a variety of nonstate actors experimenting with novel forms of climate governance (Hoffmann 2011) and filling governance gaps that state authorities have left (Bulkeley et al. 2014). It is this remarkable shift in climate politics that Bull's pluralist perspective, with its focus on the centrality of the states system, fails to anticipate or account for.

To be sure, the nature of this complex climate governance field, as well as its relationship with international society, remains contested. The transnationalization trend can be seen to signal that the problem of climate change exceeds the problem-solving capacity of an international political system based on national sovereignty and non-intervention. In this perspective, the climate change challenge lays bare the dysfunctional nature of state-centric international regulation, as Falk had argued in the 1970s. But it should be noted that the case for the emergence of a cosmopolitan solidarism is less clear-cut. States continue to play an important role in encouraging and steering transnational climate governance. At a minimum, international society actors are 'orchestrators' of transnational climate governance, and non-state actors continue to orient their activities on the signals and incentives that the intergovernmental regime sets (Hale and Roger 2014). Private environmental governance is, therefore, never entirely 'private' (Falkner 2003).

Still, it remains the case that *The Anarchical* Society has little to say about these trends. This is of course partly a reflection of the fact that transnational governance only became a more widely noted phenomenon from the 1990s onwards. Transnationalism may have been discussed since the late 1960s

(Keohane and Nye 1971), but its analytical significance was only fully grasped once scholars had moved from depicting the phenomenon to accounting for its impact on policy outcomes (Risse-Kappen 1995). But Bull's account in *The Anarchical Society* also suffers from the binary logic that he unhelpfully imposes on the relationship between states and non-state actors. Rather than conceiving of transnationalism as an evolutionary force that can change the terms of engagement between international and world society, Bull casts transnational actors narrowly as disruptive forces that pose a direct challenge to the state-centric international order. Environmental activists are either 'private individuals' whose views 'are not the outcome of any political process of the assertion and reconciliation of interest' (1977, 85) and thus have no authority in international relations (1977, 86), or they are 'inherently revolutionary' (1977, 88) due to their demands for global justice which requires a complete transformation of the international order. Having set up the discussion in these terms, Bull cannot but fail to recognize how political interventions originating in world society serve to complement and expand international governance, and how they end up redefining rather than undermining the legitimacy of nation-states in an era complex global governance. Not least for this reason, Bull's pluralist vision is a poor guide to the complex reality of global governance that has grown around the UNFCCC regime, and that is likely to gain in significance.

CONCLUSIONS

After over two decades of UNFCCC negotiations, the world is still awaiting an effective international response to the threat of global warming. If he were with us today, Bull would not be surprised at the meagre results of climate multilateralism. As he had argued in *The Anarchical Society*, the plurality of values and interests is holding back international society from developing a sense of common purpose in the fight against global ecological dangers. Climate change may be posing an ever-greater threat to the wellbeing, and even survival, of humankind, but it is unlikely to induce the kind of global solidarity that would push aside distributional conflicts and normative differences between nations. As Bull stated in his last chapter, there are no easy 'solutions' for 'the way ahead' (1977, 318–20).

Bull's pluralist scepticism provides a powerful antidote to the exuberant expectations of an imminent transformation of world politics in the face of the global ecological crisis. The division of the world into sovereign states, blamed by environmentalists for preventing a collective response to global warming, is the unavoidable context in which global environmental policies have to be agreed. In the absence of a viable alternative to the 'Westphalian' states system, intergovernmental negotiations remain the only means with which interest conflicts in environmental protection can be resolved. Bull would have expected the great powers to play a leading role in forging a global response to climate change. Given their economic clout and leading contribution to the global warming effect, they are both effective veto powers and potentially legitimate leaders in international climate politics. When claiming special rights and responsibilities, great powers may be trampling over the interests of weaker states and violating principles of international justice. However, as long as they collectively maintain international order and pursue global objectives, their dominant role in climate politics may have to be tolerated to get the world closer to a viable climate solution.

Although setting out to defend a state-centric international system characterized by power inequality, Bull was not blind to international society's limitations. As he acknowledges in *The Anarchical Society*, the society of states may have started to create international regulatory mechanisms, but it remains woefully weak when it comes to imposing constraints on population growth, resource consumption and industrial pollution. Bull hinted at the need to move towards a solidarist form of international environmental cooperation, although he did not explore how this could come about. Nor did he have much faith in humanity's ability to move in this direction. To some extent, the Kyoto Protocol can be seen as an experiment in creating a solidarist response, based on the UNFCCC's climate protection norm, strong global equity principles and legally binding emission reductions. However, state-centric solidarism did not get very far in climate politics. The Kyoto Protocol's top-down regulatory approach has been replaced by the Paris Agreement's more decentralized system of nationally determined pledges. Bull would most likely agree with Buzan in his assessment that 'environmentalism still represent[s] the aspirational more than the empirical side of solidarism' (Buzan 2004, 150).

But Bull's pluralist and state-centric perspective is less convincing when it comes to the transnationalization of global climate politics. As the states system has struggled to find an appropriate response to global warming, other actors that are operating across scales, sectors, and boundaries are adding their own contributions to an increasingly diverse and complex field of climate governance. With civil society, business and sub-national state actors increasingly performing governance functions that no longer fit into established state-centric notions of authority and power, Bull's binary distinction between inter-state and world society fails to capture the transformative potential of the new climate transnationalism. Of course, Bull would rightly warn against taking the state and pluralism out of the equation—after all, states continue to perform an important role by initiating, supporting and steering private governance, and even world society is characterized by deep-seated conflicts over values and interests (Hurrell 2007, 307). But by framing transnationalism as a revolutionary force that seeks to overcome the state-centric system, he misses out on the subtler changes in international environmental politics that are redefining, rather than undermining, national sovereignty and international authority.

Still, it is unclear whether transnational solidarism can succeed where state-centric solidarism has failed. Despite the remarkable growth in transnational governance networks, the UN climate regime remains an important anchor for developing private climate initiatives and setting non-state actors' expectations. Given the severity of the global climate challenge that the world faces today, both international society and world society have been found wanting as sites of global governance. If Bull were to comment on the recent history of climate politics, he would therefore have good reason to feel vindicated in his view that 'the spaceship earth' still lacks a voice that can speak with legitimate authority in international politics and that 'human unity or solidarity' is in short supply (1977, 85 and 295).[3]

---

[3] I would like to acknowledge the very helpful comments provided by Hidemi Suganami and the participants of the workshop on *The Anarchical Society at 40*, which was held at Cardiff University in July 2016.

13

The Anarchical Society and Indigenous Peoples

Paul Keal

This chapter relates *The Anarchical Society* to the role of indigenous peoples as agents in contemporary international society. The book does not mention indigenous peoples and so this inquiry requires identifying and considering concepts and themes both relevant to and challenged by indigenous peoples. This raises the question of whether there are elements of Bull's conceptual framework that cannot accommodate indigenous peoples and their concerns. Addressing this could, in turn, run the danger of projecting present-day thinking back onto an earlier era. Obviously Bull wrote before more recent debates about indigenous issues that might have prompted him to engage in locating the particular concerns of indigenous peoples in international society and the analysis of it.

The argument of this chapter is that realizing world order, defined as order among 'mankind as a whole', needs to include the specific goal of just relations between indigenous and non-indigenous peoples and that this would require both mutually agreed settlements of historical injustices and engagement with indigenous notions of sovereignty that challenge traditional conceptions of it. Coupled with this is the further argument that Bull's notion of a cosmopolitan world order could have led him to defend the group rights of indigenous peoples. He did not do this because he was a liberal individualist and did not see that group rights were important for world justice. Similarly his conception of sovereignty as a property of states is one that does not comprehend indigenous notions of sovereignty.

The chapter is in three sections. The first identifies the key themes and concepts that inform the development of the argument concerning indigenous peoples in the remaining two sections. These include the idea of a cosmopolitan great society of mankind, sovereignty as a fundamental condition of order, the relationship it has with self-determination, and cultural pluralism. The second section discusses the nature of indigenous sovereignty, and the third deals with the notion of a just world order in relation to indigenous peoples.

WORLD ORDER AND THE ANARCHICAL SOCIETY

Fundamental to the conception of order laid out by Bull in *The Anarchical Society* is the mutual recognition, by states, of sovereignty. International society is a society of states, which depends on mutual recognition. Through articulating and establishing norms and rules of behaviour, which may be written or unwritten, formal or informal, states understand how to maintain order in their mutual relations. Cardinal among these rules is the right to sovereign independence. As part of his account of international order Bull adopted the conventional distinction between *internal* and *external* sovereignty over a bounded territory and the population within it. Internal sovereignty conferred 'supremacy over all other authorities within that territory and population' and external sovereignty was independence from authorities beyond the state (Bull 1977, 8). The society of states and the conditions necessary for international order, as they are conceptualized in *The Anarchical Society*, is one in which states, though not being the only actors, are clearly the most significant. Bull defined international order in that book as 'a pattern of activity that sustains the elementary or primary goals of the society of states, or international society' (1977, 8). Given that it was written in the context of the Cold War, in which there were periods of an imminent danger of nuclear war, it is not surprising that this was his primary concern. Nevertheless, five years prior to publication of *The Anarchical Society* Bull recognized the importance of non-state actors and a broader range of issues.

In a 1972 paper titled 'International Relations as an Academic Pursuit', Bull asserted that the role of 'actors other than the state' in world politics was such that the 'central focus of the subject embraces much more than strictly interstate politics' (2000c, 249). He argued that a global political system had emerged 'of which the "international system" or states-system is only part (even if it is the most important part), and that many of the issues that arise within this global political system... cannot be satisfactorily dealt with in a framework that confines our attention to the relations of sovereign states' (2000c, 252). To deal with these issues, he continued, it was necessary 'to consider, alongside states, not only organizations of states global and regional, but non-governmental organizations, transnational and subnational groups, individual human beings, and *in posse* if not *in esse* that *magna communitas humani generis* which in the writings of the founders of international law was always both historically and logically prior to the idea of a society of states' (2000c, 252).[1]

The idea of a great society of mankind is central to the notions of world society and world order exposited in the first chapter of *The Anarchical Society*. Consistent with his definition of international order as 'a pattern of activity that sustains the elementary or primary goals of the society of states' (1977, 8), Bull defined world order as 'those patterns or dispositions of human activity that sustain the elementary or primary goals of social life among mankind as a whole' (1977, 20). 'Order among mankind as a whole', he explained, 'is something wider than among states; something more fundamental and primordial than it; and also, I should argue, something morally prior to it.' 'World order', he continued, 'is more fundamental and primordial than international order because the ultimate units of the great society of all mankind are not states (or nations, tribes, empires, classes or parties) but individual human beings, which are permanent and indestructible in a sense in which groupings of them of this or that sort are not' (1977, 22). He then closed this chapter by first repeating the claim that world order 'is morally prior to international order' and proposed 'that if any value attaches to order in world politics, it is order among all mankind which we must treat as being of primary value, not order within the society of states' (1977, 22). Of particular note the final sentence asserts that: 'If international order does have value, this can only be because it is instrumental to the goal of order in human society as a whole' (1977, 22).

Implicit in this is that international order, which is coupled with international society, is a foundation of world order. What is important about this is that the evolution of international society involved the dispossession and subordination of indigenous peoples and other non-European peoples. On the basis of ideas about the nature of civilization, indigenous and other peoples were excluded from the rights and obligations 'civilized' peoples expected of each other in their mutual relations. For an indeterminable number of indigenous peoples, the expansion of international society meant death and the destruction of their cultures, resulting in unresolved historic injustices and questions concerning the moral foundation of particular states. Historically, then, the nature of international society has been antithetical to the notion of a just world order, which would respect the rights of all people. A further concern is Bull's contention, stated above, that the ultimate units of world society are individual human beings. His point here is that states come and go, but that individuals have an existence beyond membership of a nation or tribe. The problem with this is that it appears to represent a version of liberalism

---

[1] *In posse*: in the condition of being possible; *in esse*: in actual existence; *magna communitas humani generis*: the great society of 'mankind'.

that detaches individuals from the social structures, which define their identity and give meaning to their life, and which might not accommodate the group rights of individuals. In that case Bull's conception of world order may be one that does not address the historic injustices from which indigenous peoples in settler states continue to suffer. More generally there may be an unexamined inconsistency between his recognition of the importance of cultural diversity in world politics and the goal of a just cosmopolitan world order. These are concerns taken up in the section 'Indigenous Peoples and a Just World Order'.

Significantly, the third part of *The Anarchical Society* is titled 'Alternative Paths to World Order', the penultimate chapter of which canvases 'the conditions under which the states system might continue to provide a viable means of sustaining world order' (1977, 315). Bull argued that 'the states system can remain viable only if the element in it of international society is preserved and strengthened' and that 'the prospects for international society are bound up with the prospects of the cosmopolitan culture that at present underlies its working' (1977, 316). He recognized that the cosmopolitan culture he discerned at the time he was writing was no more than 'nascent' and was 'weighted in favour of the dominant cultures of the West' (1977, 317). Tellingly, he concluded his discussion of this by saying that the cosmopolitan culture underpinning world international society 'may need to absorb non-Western elements to a much greater degree if it is to be genuinely universal and provide a foundation for a universal society' (Bull 1977, 317). In the first of his 1983 Hagey Lectures on 'Justice in International Relations', Bull returned to this theme and declared that there had 'occurred, at least in the advanced countries, the growth of a cosmopolitan moral awareness, an extension of our capacity to empathize with sections of humanity that are geographically or culturally distinct from us' (2000b, 221).

SOVEREIGNTY AND INDIGENOUS PEOPLES

In 1982 the United Nations Economic and Social Council established the Working Group on Indigenous Populations (WGIP). It was tasked with reviewing 'developments pertaining to the human rights of Indigenous populations and to give attention to the evolution of standards concerning the rights of such populations' (Pritchard 1998, 41). For this purpose it adopted the definition formulated by Special Rapporteur Jose Martinez Cobo in a 1986 report in which he identified [i]ndigenous communities, peoples, and nations as

> those... having a historical continuity with the pre-invasion and pre-colonial societies that developed on their territories... and are determined to preserve, develop, and transmit to future generations of their ancestral territories, and

their ethnic identity, the basis of their continued existence as peoples, in accordance with their cultural patterns, social institutions and legal systems.
(Pritchard 1998, 43)

'Indigenous' is thus a term historically linked to the colonization, dispossession, and subjugation of peoples as part of the globalization of the international system.

The working group brought together diverse indigenous peoples with the purpose of seeking rights based on the recognition of shared common experiences. Professor Mick Dodson, who was then Aboriginal and Torres Strait Islander Commissioner, recalls his experience of this when he went for the first time to a session of the WGIP and found himself among people sharing the same stories and sufferings.

> We were all part of a world community of Indigenous peoples spanning the planet; experiencing the same problems and struggling against alienation, marginalization and sense of powerlessness. We had gathered there united by our shared frustration with the dominant systems in our own countries and their consistent failure to deliver justice. We were all looking for, and demanding justice from a higher authority. (Dodson 1998, 19)

Thus through the experience of sharing a common sense of frustration, of having been marginalized politically, legally, and materially, diverse indigenous peoples joined together in creating the global movement Niezen refers to as 'indigenism' (2003). Land rights, self-determination, and sovereignty are at heart of indigenous rights. The latter two, in particular, are what explains why it took more than twenty years for the United Nations General Assembly *Declaration on the Rights of Indigenous Peoples*, which became the central concern of the WGIP, to be negotiated and finally adopted by a majority of states.

The sticking point for governments of key states with indigenous populations in this drawn out process was Article 3 of the Declaration. It proclaims that 'Indigenous peoples have the right of self-determination. By virtue of that right they freely determine their political status and freely pursue their economic, social and cultural development.' The problem with this was that states with indigenous populations framed the right to self-determination in terms of the process of decolonization, which enlarged the states system.

It was long assumed by states that the right to self-determination implies the right to form a separate sovereign state. In that case it represents *ipso facto* a challenge to the territorial sovereignty of states against which it is claimed and cannot be recognized in international law. Rights for 'peoples' are achieved 'only within the existing system of state sovereignty' (Irons 1992, 285). Generally speaking indigenous peoples seeking the right to self-determination have not had the aim of carving out a separate sovereign territorial state. Indigenous self-determination has thus been about securing the right within state structures to determine the conditions of their existence and to reproduce their particular culture. It means the 'entitlement of... indigenous groups [within states] to make decisions about their economic, social and cultural development without... unwarranted interference by the state' (Brennan 1995, 148).

In an earlier publication, I argued for the importance of recognizing the right of self-determination for indigenous peoples (2003). At that time I leaned towards the traditional conception of sovereignty and was sceptical or dismissive of the less precise conceptions of indigenous sovereignty. My position now is that 'sovereignty' has implications that go beyond self-determination and is more important in achieving a just relationship with indigenous peoples as part of a just world order. Indigenous claims to sovereignty and the notion of indigenous sovereignty have challenged the conventional understanding of state sovereignty that underpins both the argument of *The Anarchical Society* and the actual states system. Discourses of indigenous sovereignty have opened up not only the conceptualization of sovereignty but also the scope of inquiry into world politics.

Indigenous sovereignty requires moving away from the Hobbesian notion of territorial states, in which sovereignty is vested in a single authority and is indivisible. Indigenous peoples in this scheme are divested of political authority and are subjects of the states in which they are located. Recent discussions have unsettled this by arguing that indigenous peoples constitute a polity that either already does or otherwise has the capacity to share authority. Essentially the concept of indigenous sovereignty involves engaging with a different, more expansive notion of sovereignty; one that loosens or rearranges the links between nation, territory, and state and expresses sovereignty as a property of entities other than the state.

Commenting on an ongoing debate about Constitutional recognition of Aboriginal peoples of Australia, Duncan Ivison argued that while sovereignty served to provide 'the conditions for politics, and thus the provision of justice' (2015, 3), this should not be 'at the price of relinquishing all to a singular, sovereign authority' (2015, 3). 'Instead of effective, absolute control, it's about the coordination of different sources of normativity and legal orders, none of which can be reduced to the other' (Ivison 2015, 3). Sovereignty, he continues, 'is a conditional good: one justified in part, just insofar as it enables the well-being of diverse peoples that make up that territory to flourish on the basis of reasonable terms of cooperation' (2015, 3). The reference here to different sources of normativity and legal orders, and diverse peoples, thus leads Ivison to cite Noel Pearson's assertion that 'indigenous people are a polity' (2015, 3). In other words, part of a more 'complex legal and political reality' (Ivison 2015, 3) than is encapsulated in the conventional version of sovereignty underpinning international society. Actually they constitute, Ivison says, more than just *a* polity, 'they are a bundle of polities. *This* is the fundamental challenge to our current conceptions of sovereignty that will reveal and in the process, hopefully, prefigure new forms of community for us all' (2015, 4).

Conceiving of indigenous peoples as polities is also central to Jessica Shadian's argument concerning the contribution of Inuit peoples to reconceptualizing sovereignty (also see Shaw 2002). Shadian writes that the Inuit Circumpolar Conference (ICC), which brings together Inuit peoples from the United States, Canada, Greenland/Denmark, and Russia has been misrepresented as merely an NGO rather than, as she sees it, a polity (2010, 486). She points out that the ICC includes 'local government and political representatives' and that rather than being simply 'a contemporary NGO attempting to influence international politics... [it is] an Inuit polity seeking to attain a degree of sovereignty as a political collectivity, able to endure within, through and independent of four state borders' (2010, 490).

Shadian explains that the Inuit peoples have 'established a form of Inuit sovereignty defined through political rights to territory and resource development, cultural autonomy as well as the continuation of being citizens of Canada, the US and Denmark' (2010, 489). As part of this they have gained shared authority that is a departure from the supreme authority conferred on states by the traditional conception of sovereignty. According to the *Inuit Declaration on Arctic Sovereignty* released by the ICC in 2009, '[o]ld ideas of sovereignty are breaking down as different governance models, such as the European Union, evolve. Sovereignties overlap and are frequently divided within federations to recognize the right of peoples' (cited by Shadian 2010, 490).

Crucial to Shadian's account of polities is that they 'engage in politics. Sovereignty as a concept, therefore, does not diminish nor does the state disappear. Instead, sovereignty exists as the process by which being political is possible'. She argues that non-state political entities 'such as the ICC, highlight the need to abstract, relocate, and re-conceptualize sovereignty altogether' (2010, 494), and have contributed to remaking 'the traditional political architecture upon which international politics has played out' (2010, 502). In closing her discussion, she reiterates that collective polities such as the ICC are 'neither left outside the state system nor possessing a state of their own. Rather, the sovereignty of the ICC depends on its ability to maintain the legitimacy of its myth, which over time has evolved, adapted and changed' (2010, 504).

The concepts of shared authority, overlapping sovereignties, and old ideas of sovereignty breaking down bear a close resemblance to Bull's conception of 'A New Mediaevalism' (1977, 254–5) as a form of political organization that might conceivably replace the states system. His argument was that in Western Christendom in the Middle Ages, there had been a form of universal political organization in which 'no ruler or state was sovereign in the sense of being supreme over a given territory and a given segment of the Christian population. Each had to share authority with vassals beneath and with the Pope (in Germany and Italy) the Holy Roman Emperor above' (1977, 254). All authority in this political order 'was thought to derive ultimately from God' (1977, 254).

Bull thus conceived of a neo-medieval order as one that would represent 'a modern and secular counterpart of... [the] mediaeval model that would embody its central characteristic: a system of overlapping and multiple loyalty' (1977, 254). From this it is easy to see both how ideas of indigenous sovereignty can be associated with the idea of a new-medievalism and why Andrew Linklater has been thought to have drawn on Bull in developing his conception of the post-Westphalian state (Falk 2000, 110). Linklater characterizes the post-Westphalian condition as one of 'multiple political authorities and allegiances' (1998, 200). He proposed that states in post-Westphalian arrangements

> do not only break with the traditional habits associated with state sovereignty but also relinquish many of their sovereign powers entirely. The principles of international governance which are integral to this framework of action no longer presuppose the commitment to sovereignty, territoriality, nationality and citizenship which differentiates the modern form of political community from all previous forms of organization. (1998, 167)

Despite the common themes in the discourses of indigenous sovereignty, a new medievalism, and the post-Westphalian condition, each discourse is directed to a different end. The new medievalism should be seen in the context of the debate about the possible decline of the sovereign state and what might replace it. Indigenous sovereignty is not about this but rather about redefining the relationship between indigenous peoples and the states in which they are located. Linklater's concern was the idea of breaking 'up the union of sovereignty, territoriality, citizenship and shared nationality' as a means of reconciling 'the claims of universality and difference' (2000, 203). Indigenous sovereignty is about eliminating 'state-imposed projects of assimilation and development' (Kymlicka 2007, 269) and the 'strong desire' [of indigenous peoples] to regain political control over themselves, their institutions, and their territories'. This, Kymlicka points out, has been a focus of United Nations norms on indigenous rights (2007, 271). In the end indigenous sovereignty is nevertheless a call for shared if not divided sovereignty. This does appear to be incompatible with the orthodox sovereignty embedded in the international society of states and begs the question of whether sovereignty is divisible.

Edward Keene has argued that 'there have always been two patterns of modern international order' and that Bull 'almost completely ignored one of them'. The first of these, which is the focus of *The Anarchical Society*, is 'the pattern of order that developed in the European states-system, through relations between European rulers and nations' (2002, xi). It corresponds to the 'Grotian' conception of international society (Bull, 2000a) and is animated by 'the pursuit of peaceful coexistence between equal and mutually independent sovereigns, which developed within the "Westphalian" system and the European society of states' (Keene 2002, 5). More specifically, in Keene's words, 'its ultimate purpose... was to promote the toleration of cultural and political differences between civilized peoples so as to allow them to live together in peace' (2002, 6). In contrast, the parallel second pattern of order, largely ignored by Bull, encompassed those outside the civilized order, stretching back to the beginning of modern history. It was not based on a states system but instead 'colonial and imperial systems' founded on 'the division of sovereignty across territorial borders and the enforcement of individuals' rights to their persons and properties' (Keene 2002, 6). Its 'central purpose was to promote the civilization of decadent, backward, savage and barbaric peoples' (Keene 2002, 7; Keal 2003, 67–73). But for indigenous peoples in particular this meant the dispossession of their lands, the denial of their sovereign rights, and their subordination to colonial administrations—processes involving, in W.E.H. Stanner's words, losing their identity and 'unlearning' being indigenous 'in mind, body and estate' (Stanner 2009, 154, 164).

The denial of sovereign rights was justified in three interconnected ways. First, the law of nations laid down the conditions under which it was permissible to appropriate 'unoccupied' lands. In the particular case of Australia it was deemed to be *territorium nullius*. In other words, that it was 'not subject to any sovereignty... either because it never had been or had been abandoned' (Lindley 1969, 10). Second, clearly places named as *territorium nullius* were occupied by indigenous peoples, but sovereignty was denied to them on the specious grounds that they did not constitute a political society subject to a central authority. This amounted to the failure by colonists to recognize Aboriginal forms of government. In the case of North America the 'typical form of Aboriginal Government was a nation governed by a council or longhouse of chiefs (sachems) drawn from clans. Each nation had a clearly demarcated and defined territory, a decision-making body, a consensus-based decision making procedure, and a system of customary laws and kinship relations' (Tully 1994, 163; Crawford 1994). It is not the case that indigenous peoples had no government, rather that it did not take a form acknowledged by Europeans. Thirdly, Locke and other theorists developed an argument from agriculture, which held that sovereign rights to land derived from its cultivation and occupation as exemplified by the example of rural England. Hence it was claimed that 'Indians' merely roamed across, rather than cultivated their ancestral lands, and therefore forfeited any rights to them (Keal 2003, 76–8). Taken together these methods of denying prior ownership and sovereignty raised still unresolved questions about the moral legitimacy of settler states with indigenous populations that emerged from colonization (Keal 2003, 1–2).

Sovereignty remains central to debates over how to reconcile relations between indigenous and non-indigenous citizens in settler states. As a general rule advocates of indigenous sovereignty are not pleading for statehood or secession. Indigenous sovereignty is instead framed in terms of recovering rights and agency in the construction of indigenous identity and the reproduction of culture. And for many indigenous peoples this is inseparable from having land rights. There are however, differences between indigenous scholars and leaders over the value of using the term 'sovereignty'. Three examples of these differences are firstly, accepting the meaning of 'sovereignty' inscribed in constitutional and international law but doubting the efficacy of appealing to it as a means to advancing indigenous rights. For example, Noel Pearson accepts the possibility of 'local indigenous sovereignty' existing within state structures but doubts whether the concept of prior sovereignty can be properly comprehended in terms of the conception of it that informs international law (Pearson 1993, 15) and has thus argued that the language of sovereignty is more likely to hinder than help advance Aboriginal aims.

Secondly, there are those who accept a less defined and formal notion of sovereignty. Aboriginal Professor of Law Larissa Behrendt, for instance, argues that the recognition of indigenous sovereignty is 'a crucial starting point for the achievement of rights; including the right of self-determination' (2003, 99). In support of this she cites a statement issued by the National Aboriginal Health Organization.

> Sovereignty is not a vague legal concept: sovereignty is a practical and achievable goal and, for Aboriginal people, can be defined as recognition of our rights. Sovereignty can be demonstrated as Aboriginal people controlling all aspects of their lives and destiny. Sovereignty is independent action. (2003, 100)

Thirdly, Canadian First Nations scholars, Dale Turner and Taiaiake Alfred, are prominent among those who reject discourses of sovereignty as alien to indigenous peoples. Turner argues that Western European discourses of rights and sovereignty belong to 'intellectual traditions that have created discourses on property, ethics, political sovereignty, and justice that have subjugated, distorted, and marginalized Aboriginal ways of thinking' (2001, 325). In the history of contact with settler societies very little attention was given to Aboriginal conceptions of sovereignty. Aboriginal peoples were co-opted or coerced into adopting 'Western European discourses of rights and sovereignty' and so were denied the capacity to talk about their place in the world in their own terms, which would have expressed a different conception of sovereignty (Turner 2001, 327). In the same vein Alfred regards sovereignty as an 'exclusionary concept' that is inappropriate both as a model for indigenous governance and as a political objective for indigenous peoples' (2005, 38). His argument is that 'Acceptance of "Aboriginal rights" in the context of the state represents the culmination of white society's efforts to assimilate indigenous peoples' (Alfred 1999, 59). For him, 'the classic notion of sovereignty' has stood in the way of peaceful coexistence between indigenous and non-indigenous peoples. 'The discourse of sovereignty has effectively stilled any potential resolution of the issue that respects indigenous values and perspectives' (2005, 42). He continues that 'until sovereignty as a concept shifts from the dominant "state sovereignty" construct and comes to reflect more of the sense embodied in Western notions such as personal sovereignty or popular sovereignty, it will remain problematic if integrated within indigenous political struggles' (2005, 43). In this way Alfred is making a case relevant to rethinking the way sovereignty is understood in the lexicon of international relations and by Bull in *The Anarchical Society*.

Clearly indigenous peoples do regard recognition of some form of indigenous sovereignty as essential to just reconciliation between them and non-indigenous peoples within state borders. That would also result in giving them a more definite role in determining the conditions under which they wish to live. It would also be at least a partial realization of Andrew Linklater's vision of post-Westphalian community in which 'the nexus between sovereignty, territoriality, and citizenship' can be broken to allow the development of 'more complex associations of universality and difference' (1998, 60). It might similarly find a place in a neo-medieval order should one ever emerge. To the degree to which indigenous peoples have already achieved shared authority the international indigenous movement can be said to have had an important role in both reshaping ideas of the state as a container of community and the place of transnational polities in contemporary world politics. Yet it has still to be recognized that indigenous sovereignty probably inevitably involves claims over which reconciliation will be very difficult if not impossible to negotiate.

INDIGENOUS PEOPLES AND A JUST WORLD ORDER

The first section of this chapter singled out Bull's conception of a cosmopolitan world order as being relevant to the circumstances of contemporary indigenous peoples around the globe. More particularly I have suggested that a just world order would be one that respects and defends indigenous rights and in which there is progress on satisfactorily resolving the historic injustices perceived to have resulted from the dispossession and subjugation that accompanied the globalization of international society. And a necessary part of this is engaging with indigenous conceptions of sovereignty.

This section focuses more closely on the cluster of justice, world order, and cosmopolitanism in *The Anarchical Society*. My particular concerns are firstly, Bull's repeated emphasis on individuals in ways that appear to either neglect or alternatively are oblivious to group rights in relation to justice, order, and rights generally. Secondly, contrary to the characteristic care he gave to defining the terms and concepts he built into his writing, it is surprising that he did not pay more attention to clarifying either cosmopolitanism or the scope of cosmopolitan culture. His discussion of both of these overlooks or even excludes indigenous peoples and his notion of cosmopolitan culture may be one that would not contribute to a just world order for indigenous peoples.

In *The Anarchical Society*, Bull identified three categories of ideas about justice in international politics: international or inter-state justice, individual or human justice, and cosmopolitan world justice. He defined international justice as 'the moral rules held to confer rights and duties upon states and nations' (1977, 81). These include the equal entitlement of all states to rights of sovereignty and the idea that all nations are equally entitled to the right of national self-determination. But he points out that these two entitlements can conflict, which is demonstrated by cases where 'the principle of national self-determination has been invoked to destroy the sovereign integrity of states and even now [in 1977] threatens a great many of them' (1977, 81–2). This harks back to the objection key settler states initially had to writing the right of self-determination into the United Nations Declaration on Human Rights.

Individual or human justice refers to 'the moral rules conferring rights and duties upon individual human beings' (1977, 82). In relation to this Bull shows how the rights and duties of the individual can conflict with duties to the state and may involve 'questions which, answered in a certain way, lead to disorder in international relations, or even to the breakdown of international society itself' (1977, 84). He reasons that if individual humans, as citizens of states, have 'rights, which other states or international authorities may champion, there are limits to their own authority; and if men have duties, to causes or movements beyond the state of which they are citizens, the state cannot count on their loyalty' (1977, 84). This reinforces the point that Bull's focus is individual rights, but at the same time it suggests that these need to be subordinate to the wider interests of the state if there is to be international order.

Cosmopolitan or world justice, he thought, is concerned with 'what is right or good for the world as a whole, for an imagined *civitas maxima* or cosmopolitan society to which all individuals belong and to which their interests should be subordinate' (1977, 84). He continues:

> This notion of justice as the promotion of the world common good is different from that of the assertion of the rights and duties of individual human beings all over the globe for it posits the idea that these individuals form or should form a society or community whose common interests or common good must qualify or even determine what their individual rights and duties are. (1977, 84)

What is important about this, with regard to indigenous peoples, is the proposition that the common good must qualify or even determine the common rights and duties of the individuals that would be the constituents of world society. The problem about this is that the common rights and interests of indigenous peoples have historically not meshed with those of the cultures of the dominant peoples who colonized them. It might thus be anticipated that indigenous identities, cultures, and special rights would be endangered and eventually subsumed by non-indigenous conceptions of the common good in a world society. Of course this will all remain conjecture so long as world society or community 'does not exist except as an idea or myth' (Bull 1977, 85).

In the first of his 1983 Hagey Lectures, Bull identified the concepts about justice in international relations that he believed should be embraced. Parts of his argument can be readily related to the complexity of the relationship indigenous peoples have with international society and the rules and norms that constitute it.

He first argues that 'whatever rights are due to states or nations *or other actors* in international relations, they are subject to and limited by the rights of the international community. The rights of sovereign states, and of *sovereign peoples* or nations, derive from the rules of the international community or society and are limited by them' (Bull 2000b, 219; emphases added). The problem with this regarding indigenous peoples, is that, to reiterate a previous point, in the history of globalization of the states system, they were systematically denied sovereignty. They were dehumanized, subjected to violence and even genocide, lost their traditional lands, and had their cultures disrupted. Or, citing Kymlicka once again, they were 'the victims of the construction of European settler states in the New World' (2007, 267).

Bull continues in the same paragraph by saying that because of the interdependence of 'politically separate communities' in the matters of their security, prosperity, and control over their environment, 'the idea of sovereign rights existing apart from the rules laid down by international society itself and enjoyed without qualification has to be rejected in principle' (2000b, 220). If by 'politically separate communities' Bull meant states, which is a reasonable assumption, the rules laid down by international society have been, and in important ways continue to be, problematic for indigenous peoples seeking recognition of their 'sovereignty'. In Bull's conceptual scheme sovereignty is inescapably a property of the state, regardless of its political system. Thus in her discussion of *Indigeneity and the International* Karena Shaw makes the telling point that in *The Anarchical Society* 'Bull quietly excludes all those who have not achieved the Western state form from discussion' (Shaw 2002, 62).

Secondly, Bull contends that 'the rights and benefits to which justice has to be done in the international community are not simply those of states and nations, but those of individual persons throughout the world as a whole. The world in which we live is . . . a system of independent states. But within this system, the idea of the rights and duties of the individual person has come to have a place, albeit an insecure one, and it is our duty to extend it.' The 'question of justice', he argues, 'concerns what is due not only to states and nations but to all individual persons in an imagined community of mankind' (2000b, 220). Once again it seems abundantly clear that Bull is referring to human rights conceived of as essentially the rights of individuals. And as he rightly observed, individuals gained a much greater place in international law in the second half of the twentieth century—as indeed the rights of minorities and indigenous peoples have through the international human rights regime. But while Bull recognized that there is a lack of consensus in international law over the 'rights enjoyed by the individual person as opposed to the rights of groups' (2000b, 221), he neither engaged with this issue nor appears to have given serious thought to what group rights might mean for world order.

The right to self-determination, for example, is a collective right that cannot be claimed by an individual. Implicit in the idea of indigenous rights is an affirmation of the existence of collectivities that have a distinct identity linked to their particular culture and place of belonging. A compelling reason for rights specific to indigenous peoples is, therefore, that the rights of individuals do not give legal expression to the existence of unique groups or cultures. If there are just individual human rights then groups of indigenous peoples have no legally defined rights that set them, their culture, and place of attachment apart from others. Without safeguards for collective or group rights, cultural identity is at risk (Keal 2003, 137).

Human rights attached to individuals are regarded as universal. Group rights, such as indigenous and minority rights, are particularistic and arguably incompatible with universal norms. In that case they might be seen as inimical to realizing order in human society as a whole. Indeed, Kymlicka has shown that, when the United Nations and post-war regional organizations were being formed, it was

> assumed that minority rights were not only unnecessary for the creation of a viable new international order, but indeed destabilizing of such an order. Today, however, it is widely asserted that the accommodation of ethnic diversity is not only *consistent* with, but in fact a *precondition* for, the maintenance of a legitimate international order. Indeed, it is increasingly asserted that virtually all of the goals and values of the international community... whether it is human rights, peace and security, democracy, or economic development... depend on the recognition of minority and indigenous rights. (2007, 45)

In another publication, I argued that 'moral legitimacy requires recognition and mutual agreement between indigenous peoples and the majority settler societies in which they are located'; and further, that 'moral legitimacy with regard to indigenous peoples depends on accepting difference, [and] the recognition of cultural rights' (Keal 2003, 174). It is commonly thought that liberals believe any proposals that would limit individual rights in favour of group rights should be opposed. Many liberals argue that measures meant to protect communities, such as granting land rights, are in fact unjust because they perpetuate 'ethnic and racial inequality' (Kymlicka 1989, 150). Kymlicka, however, is one who has been prominent in defending cultural rights from a liberal standpoint. Part of his defence is that members of cultural minorities may be disadvantaged in ways that both justify and require granting them collective rights. Membership in a cultural community, he argues, 'may be a relevant criterion for distributing benefits and burdens which are the concern of a liberal theory of justice'. Thus the fate of cultural structures matters because it is only through them that individuals are able to fully gauge 'the options available to them, and intelligently examine their value' (Kymlicka 1989, 165).

I now turn to the notion of cosmopolitan world order and my starting point is Bull's assertion, noted earlier, that '[i]f international order does have value, this can only be because it is instrumental to the goal of order in human society as a whole' (1977, 22). In the final pages of *The Anarchical Society*, Bull assessed 'the prospects for international society' and argued that these 'are bound up with the prospects of the cosmopolitan culture that at present underlies its working' (1977, 316). It follows from this that a cosmopolitan culture is necessary to realizing world society. The cosmopolitan culture that he has in mind is one in which there has been

> [o]n the one hand... some element of a common *intellectual* culture—such as a common language, a common philosophical or epistemological outlook, a common literary or artistic tradition—the presence of which served to facilitate communication between the member states of the society. On the other hand, there has been some element of common *values*—such as a common religion or a common moral code—the presence of which served to reinforce the sense of common interests that united the states in question by a sense of common obligation. (1977, 316)

It is fair to say that all of this refers to the system of largely European states in which the commonalities he iterates were able to bridge local cultural differences. The absence of commonalities among diverse indigenous peoples and between them and non-indigenous peoples however is precisely what excluded them, for so long, from attaining international personality. Bull moves to the end of his discussion of the importance of cosmopolitan culture with the suggestion that, to the extent that there is one, it needs to be extended to embrace 'both common ideas and common values, and rooted in societies in general as well as in their elites'. And he closes by saying 'that the nascent cosmopolitan culture of today, like the international society which it helps to sustain, is weighted in favour of the dominant cultures of the West. Like the world international society, the cosmopolitan culture on which it depends may need to absorb non-Western elements to a much greater degree if it is to be genuinely universal and provide for a universal international society' (1977, 317).

Exactly what he means here by 'non-Western elements' is not spelt out and this is of fundamental importance to the goal of world order. I take it to mean, in essence, states representing non-Western cultures. In that case it once again overlooks, or is perhaps even dismissive of, the crucial cultural differences between indigenous peoples and the dominant populations of the states in which they are enclosed. The problem for so many indigenous peoples, particularly in key settler states, is that their cultures, belief systems, and sovereign rights have been regarded as incommensurable with those of the peoples who dispossessed them. For indigenous peoples encased within state structures the nature of the order they have been and continue to be subjected to within states is what has driven 'indigenism'.

A further concern about cosmopolitanism in relation to indigenous peoples is the key element of individualism shared by all cosmopolitan positions. According to Thomas Pogge, individualism in this sense refers to the idea that 'the ultimate units of concern are *human beings*, or *persons* ... rather than, say, family lines, tribes, ethnic, or religious communities, nations or states' (Pogge 1994, 89). The problem with this, and with Bull's contention that the ultimate units of world society are individual human beings, is that family lines and tribes are critical to what it means to be indigenous. To the extent that the identity of individuals is defined by membership of family and tribal structures, this is not necessarily inconsistent with individualism; but it is not clear that this element of cosmopolitism is compatible with the aspirations of indigenous peoples.

Regardless of this, Bull's conception of world order does extend international order to include the need to deal with order in relations between civil society and the state. World order, he argued, 'is wider than international order because to give an account of it we have to deal not only with order among states but also with order on a domestic and municipal scale, provided within particular states, and with order within the wider world political system of which the states system is only part' (1977, 22). Even though Bull almost certainly did not have indigenous peoples in mind, the issues which concern them, including the historic injustices to which they were subjected, are very much related to order on a domestic and municipal scale. His contention that world order is morally prior to international order is telling us that order in relations between peoples within and across state borders should have precedence over preserving states that fail to promote and safeguard the rights and wellbeing of their citizens.

With respect to indigenous peoples my own position is, to reiterate, that world order understood as order among 'mankind as a whole' needs to include the specific goal of achieving just relations between indigenous and non-indigenous peoples. Such relations would necessarily be founded on reconciliation and the mutually agreed settlement of historical injustices which, in some cases, may require a treaty. In saying this, it is not my intention to put justice in front of order by proposing justice for indigenous peoples, come what may. My purpose is instead to make the more modest proposal that resolving historical injustices would reconcile order and justice with regard to one small but important part of world order understood as order among all mankind. In other words justice for indigenous peoples would contribute to the sum of a more cosmopolitan, just world order.

Clearly a just world order of this kind is much more of an aspiration than a reality, but the achievements of the indigenous peoples movement over the past forty years, demonstrated by acceptance of the *Declaration on Indigenous Rights*, have been significant. Indigenous peoples have organized the agency needed to effect change in attitudes and policies within states. Even so, we should recognize that world order might equally involve homogenization and the demise of distinctive identities and cultures, thus resulting in a less culturally plural world.

CONCLUSION

During the intervening years since publication of *The Anarchical Society*, non-state actors have multiplied in number and become increasingly important agents in shaping the norms and rules of state conduct. Thus, indigenous peoples have been instrumental in establishing norms of behaviour that affect the moral status and political legitimacy of particular states. The role of indigenous peoples and the issues concerning them reveal some of the fundamental difficulties in establishing a world order that is just for the culturally diverse great society of mankind.

Among these issues, sovereignty remains a central concept, but, as discussed above, it is not the traditional sovereignty in the theory and practice of international society. Indigenous sovereignty is conceptualized in various ways and lacks any settled and agreed definition which, I believe, would have irritated Bull. Regardless of that, the different expressions of it stem from unresolved historic injustices resulting from the conquest and subjugation that accompanied the globalization of international society. Thus at the heart of indigenous discourses of sovereignty are the denial of prior sovereignty and especially indigenous peoples wanting control over the construction of their identities and the reproduction of their cultures. Indigenous sovereignty is critically connected to the relationship between order and justice and to the analysis of it in *The Anarchical Society*, which is discussed by Hidemi Suganami in Chapter 2 of this volume.

With regard to international society and justice, the activities of indigenous peoples over the last forty years can been seen as contributing to the creation of morally prior world order among the 'great society of mankind'. To the extent that there is an emerging world society, albeit one characterized by conflict and division, the international indigenous movement, or to use Niezen's term 'indigenism', has been part of this process. Realizing the normative goal of a just world order would, however, require states to resolve the outstanding issues animating the drive for indigenous sovereignty.

14

Anarchy and Patriarchy in World Politics

Jacqui True

In *The Anarchical Society*, Hedley Bull wrote that 'it is always erroneous to interpret international events as if international society were the sole or the dominant element' (1977, 51). International society, he argued, is 'no more than one of the basic elements at work in modern international politics, and is always in competition with the elements of a state of war and of transnational solidarity or conflict' (Ibid.). This tension between three logics of international politics (the 'Hobbesian', the 'Kantian', and the 'Grotian') discussed in *The Anarchical Society*, now forty years old, provides a crucial opening for alternative theories. By contrast with neorealists and Marxists, Bull's approach recognizes that there is not a single or overarching logic of international politics and moreover, that international politics is fundamentally a social enterprise. Other actors and structures are acknowledged to coexist with states, sometimes consolidating and at other times challenging them.

This essay argues that feminist approaches, though entirely neglected in *The Anarchical Society* (with its unreflexive, consistent use of the male pronoun throughout), help us understand change and continuity in the cultural foundations of international society. The domination of masculinity over femininity is a structural pattern that may have existed prior to the development of the anarchical society. However, the gender division of masculine public and feminine private spheres submerged within civil society in the historical formation of modern European states is one of the foundations upon which the international society among these states was built and subsequently expanded beyond Europe. Patriarchal relations take particular forms with specific manifestations in different Western and non-Western contexts. Diverse challenges to these social relations in contemporary world politics have implications for the stability and the transformation of international order. Bull did not anticipate the relationship between struggles against local and global patriarchies and international relations despite his recognition of world society as a realm of human interaction distinct from international society. However, the struggles against Western domination, that he argued in the 1970s affect the legitimation of international order, must be seen as interconnected with the struggles against masculine domination and for gender justice today.

There are four parts to the argument presented in this chapter. The first part compares the concepts of anarchy and patriarchy and describes how they operate and increasingly intersect as social relations. The second part considers how patriarchal relations are an historical feature of state identities, diplomatic practices, and thus, the maintenance and expansion of the society of states. The third part considers the current situation where patriarchal structures and norms in many parts of the world are unravelling. The fourth part of the essay explores the implications of these changes for order and justice in international society, recalling Bull's concerns in *The Anarchical Society*. If we take patriarchy seriously as a constitutive part of the evolving world order, then it is possible to see both positive and negative effects of the unravelling of local and global patriarchies on international society. It is also possible to see that a stable world order will not be constructed without gender justice, together with social and economic justice, for all subordinated groups.

STRUCTURES THAT WE CANNOT SEE

Anarchy and patriarchy both structure the political norms of state and non-state actors in international and world societies. Sovereignty is a structuring principle of international order—and one of the most enduring features of modern world politics. Patriarchy is also a structural relationship—defined as the gender hierarchy that privileges masculinity over femininity, creating and reinforcing the divisions between public and private (family/home) spheres, reason and emotion, men and women. Feminist and IR scholars both seek to theorize these globalized structures that are hidden or not visible per se but are revealed when we analyse patterns of behaviour across many interactions. Because violence is patterned along gender lines, with men historically fighting wars and women largely supporting their efforts on the home front (across diverse states and social formations), examining the gender social order is essential to international relations theorizing.

Bull describes order as a 'pattern that leads to a particular result, an arrangement of social life such that it promotes certain goals or values' (1977, 4). That order may not be formalized in treaties or customary international law but is constituted by the shared understandings among states with respect to goals of, for example, *life* or security from violent death, *truth* or trust in agreements, and *property* or stability in ownership. Order or social life among states, Bull argues, is possible without centralized power above states and states are more capable than individuals of forming an anarchical society because of common interests, values and the capacities to carry them out (1977, 46–51).

Not dissimilarly, patriarchy is a pattern of social arrangements that are grounded in women and men's negotiations or 'bargains' set within institutional and structural contexts that reinforce gender hierarchy (Kandiyoti 1988; Hunnicutt 2009; Mies 1986). Like international order, patriarchal relations are readily obscured precisely because masculine domination is so pervasive and taken for granted. For example, the everyday practices of chivalry, some of which still thrive today in Western societies, such as opening doors for women to go through first and shaking hands among men (but not with women), effectively entrench masculine protection and women's status as the weaker sex. No one dictates them from above or coerces individuals to follow them. They are, rather (or were once), appropriate standards of behaviour. A photo depicting Russian President Vladimir Putin placing his coat around the shoulders of China's First Lady at an Asia Pacific Economic Cooperation (APEC) dinner made headline news all around the world in November 2014 (Allen-Ebrahimian 2014). Putin's act was reported as both outmoded and overbearing. Chivalry is a harmless act, though historically it served to symbolize and cement a social order that involved limited rights and mobility for women. In an ephemeral moment, the world media merely captured an instance of interpersonal relations within high politics. But the image also tells us something important about international society and its evolving cultural foundations. Putin's chivalrous act personifies the connection—and the more recent disconnection—between the figure of the male provider which is at the heart of the global economy at meetings like APEC, and the figure of the male protector (of 'womenchildren') which is at the heart of state security politics.

Of course, *The Anarchical Society* is a theoretical defence of the purpose and the normative value of international society, whereas no feminist scholar intends to defend patriarchal relations but rather to understand their specific patterns of domination in order to undo them. Bull promotes the value of order rather than any particular substantive values that should be supported by states. He argues that if life, truth, and property are humanity's goals, then it is rational for states to do what needs to be done to protect them (1977, 20–2). However, the patriarchal relations within international order can be made visible if we interrogate the content of these goals, the primacy of *life, truth, and property*. For example, the goal of stability in possession of things, such as property held privately (1977, 5–6) can be understood, historically, as having been secured through the patriarchal institution of marriage in modern European states. The marriage contract shores up the intergenerational maintenance of property and accumulation of wealth. As Friedrich Engels observed in *The Origins of the Family, Private Property and the State*, bourgeois marriage rendered a wife both materially and legally dependent on her husband (2010 [1884]). The marriage contract ensures her fidelity and the legitimacy of the children born to her, as heirs and inheritors of the husband or father's property, essential to the goal of 'stability in the possession of things'.

Importantly, patriarchal relations and international society may not always require violence to uphold them—to the extent that their practices are self-reproducing (Hunnicutt 2009, 9). Those who are not the architects of these institutions and/or do not have access to systems of law and justice may use violence because legitimate or institutional means are not available or effective (though this is clearly not the case for the most part with women). Violence may be needed especially when consensual, hegemonic orders break down (Gramsci 1971), that is, when international and patriarchal societies no longer appeal to their weaker members and confront contending goals and values.

PATRIARCHAL FOUNDATIONS OF THE ANARCHICAL INTERNATIONAL SOCIETY

The Anarchical Society conceptualizes international politics not exclusively as the relations between states but rather as a field of social power constituted by non-state actors as well. However, Bull does not provide an account of how the element of international society came into being nor does he consider the possibility that social relations, such as those based on gender, constitute the meaning of sovereign statehood historically and in the present.

Although the last section emphasized similarities between anarchy and patriarchy as structural principles, they are hardly ever seen as mutually relevant or intersecting. As with the concept of gender, patriarchy is commonly interpreted as a structural pattern that affects only the social relations among individuals rather than among institutions. Yet patriarchal structures have historically played a crucial role in the constitution of state identities, diplomatic practices, and the expansion of international society. Specifically, the gender hierarchy that privileges subjects which accord with masculine, competitive, rational, and autonomous attributes over feminine, caring, emotional, and relational attributes is manifest in the relations between states within international society.

The myriad ways in which patriarchal relations affect the governance of international order are not appreciated within Bull's account of world politics. Underpinning the anarchical society is an implicit gender hierarchy among states, from strong to weak, rational to irrational, powerful to powerless, dominant to subordinate, manly to fragile or deviant (Sjoberg 2012). For instance, one of the ways of determining membership in international society or 'governing' states on the margins of international society is to categorize them as 'weak or fragile states' and/or to refer to them with feminine or nonrational qualifiers, such as *rogue* or *deviant* states and so forth. The lack of recognition of the gendered dimensions of international order is revealed plainly by the sexist language of Bull's 1977 book. Mankind, statesmen, and spokesmen for states are not just archaic mannerisms; they reflect an unconscious way of thinking about world politics that is 'gendered', in that it uses masculine proxies for states and political action and excludes political agency within and across states associated with women, emotion, and the private sphere.

Patriarchal relations have contributed to shaping the anarchical international order as pre-existing, shared informal institutions that have facilitated the consensus among states. Carole Pateman argues that the problem of patriarchy is repressed within the structure of the state and state-system (1988, 1; 1989, 2). In her major work, *The Sexual Contract* (1988), Pateman substantiated, how modern European states emerged from absolutist patriarchal states and were founded on a 'fraternal sexual contract' that upheld the equal rights of male individuals in the public sphere, while relegating wives and daughters as property to the private family household sphere. Patriarchal relations within the households of modern European states were both created and reinforced through the material changes that ensued with the industrial revolution, which, in turn, enabled capital accumulation to fuel the war and gender-making capacities of states-in-formation (Mies 1986; Tilly 1985; Peterson 1992). That order within states was extended and diffused across states. As such, the state system and international society has been made possible by normalised gender divisions of labour that have produced and reproduced the identities and war-making capacities of states. These gendered relations have further helped to cement the sovereignty principle shared and diffused by modern states, which has upheld the prerogative of individual states to determine the distribution of power and resources among individuals, maintaining unjust and unequal gendered relations of domination.

Though patriarchal relations have been 'repressed' or hidden in international society as in the modern state they are fundamental. Indeed membership in international society has been based on conformity with modern standards of civilization that include gender-appropriate conduct. Ann Towns recounts the directive in the nineteenth-century European society of states to officially exclude women from politics and public life, consistent with bourgeois notions of respectable behaviour at the time (2010). As such, Japan and China through legislation 'barred women from political participation for the first time upon formally entering the civilized society of states' (Towns 2010: 187). It was then seen as a progressive feature of Western civilization. The struggle against this norm has involved more than a century of transnational politics. Only recently, in the last two to three decades have we seen gender justice or formal equality become part of the practices of diplomacy and war, being stated as a condition for international recognition and legitimacy of a state, and as a justification for international intervention. Though gender and state identities are not fixed, what has remained constant is the notion that women's political status is linked to the progress of a state, their international ranking, and to the 'othering' of poor performing states. That is, the division between states belonging to international society and those state and non-state actors outside or on the margins of international society reflects a gendered ordering (Ling and Agathangelou 2004).

Hedley Bull acknowledges when men 'are grouped into states, they are grouped in other ways also' and 'there are deeper questions, of more enduring importance [than the order among states] about order in the great society of all mankind' (1977, 20). This statement provides an opening for conceptualizing multiple sites of patriarchal power that work together with hierarchies based on race, ethnicity, nationality, sexuality, class, age, and so on. Patriarchal relations are bound up with other systems of domination, cross-cutting and aligned—which is why some women, men, and states behave to maintain the system of gendered power even when it ensures their subordination. In detailing some of the transformations in international society in the next part of the chapter, Bull's comment regarding the inclusion of post-colonial states in international society could be adapted to address the inclusion of diverse women within and across states and societies: 'No consensus is possible today that does not take account of [their] demands' (1977, 300).

CONTEMPORARY CHANGE IN INTERNATIONAL AND WORLD SOCIETY

We can imagine how *The Anarchical Society* might be fit for purpose in understanding contemporary international politics given the shifts in power—beyond Europe toward a more global international society, and from the West to the East and North to South with respect to economic power. But the visible transformations of patriarchal relations in the forty years since *The Anarchical Society* was written are hardly telescoped in the book. Hedley Bull probably could not have imagined the changes in the role of women, the rise of women's movements and women leaders given his 1970s worldview. What implications do these changes have for international society and to what extent are they shared beyond the West? Bull would likely have been sceptical that such changes in gender relations had major implications for international order.

His book is after all an argument for the unique situation of international society and the fallacy of the idea that the order within states can be extended to international politics.

Theorizing the relationship between social relations and international order is crucial to understanding change in world politics, change which is not likely to come from within existing institutions of international society: the balance of power, great power diplomacy, and international law. Bull well understood that struggles for justice have implications for order. His later work pays significant attention to the revolt against the West, in particular the struggles of decolonization, for racial equality, economic justice, and cultural liberation exploring how they might affect the deepening and expansion of international society (Bull 1984a, 1984b). He also appreciated the multiple logics of change and continuity in international politics; what he called the 'Kantian' element of world politics, promoting transnational solidarity and the universalization of rights; and the 'Hobbesian' statecraft element, promoting great power politics; alongside the 'Grotian' element of society and cooperation among states. I argue that patriarchal structures are unravelling in many parts of the world due, in part, to the material changes wrought by globalization. When viewed through 'Hobbesian', 'Grotian', or 'Kantian' prisms of international thought, however, this unravelling has different implications for the future of international society.

With a 'Hobbesian' lens we can see how powerful states may promote the cause of gender equality because it is in their national interests to do so. A key source of the competitive advantage of states today is their capacity to harness the talents and potentials of their population in tradable economic activity and in the defence of the state *via* the military and broader security apparatus. Even states like Japan are becoming advocates for gender equality and major supporters of the UN women, peace, and security agenda, which promotes women's participation in peace and security institutions and national and international decision-making. The achievement of state goals requires them to close gender gaps in the public and market-based participation of men and women and in so doing, increase the numbers of women available for these activities. Powerful states may also be able to shore up the legitimacy of their position at the top of the international hierarchy by pointing to the gender equality or 'gender inclusiveness' in their society. Through visible women leaders serving as their representatives, they may justify coercive policies vis-à-vis state or non-state actors that actually violate norms of gender equality and women's rights (Hunt 2002; Shepherd 2006). This is a not a new phenomenon. What is new, however, is that gender-inclusion increasingly contests other values in international society. In this way, state promotion of gender equality can be seen to facilitate the maintenance of power rather than a power-shift. It is certainly an advance on earlier assumptions that the rise of women leaders would destabilize the international order because they make weak and feeble foreign policy chiefs (Fukuyama 1998). Though increasing the numbers of women in the public sphere may advance the cause of one state over another, it does not alter the relational aspect of power wherein masculine attributes, ways of governing, and values are ascendant.

The Grotian lens provides a different insight into how states may be motivated to respond to claims for gender justice. Gender equality and justice is an area for win-win cooperation among states—where international norms and policy borrowing can advance relative and absolute gains. Global trends in gender and class inequality are ultimately shaped at the national level through regulations, policies, and laws that remove discrimination and provide incentives for equality. The political and economic gains from addressing these inequalities will be shared among states—albeit some more than others. An example of cooperation in international society on this goal is the creation of the W20 (Women in the G20) within the G20 institution, aimed at closing economic gender gaps (Harris-Rimmer 2015). Turkey founded the W20 in 2014 during the year it hosted the G20, showing its credibility as a state power willing to address a point of weakness in its own economic and society relative to European states. The following year Australia hosted the G20 and established a target for members to close the economic participation gap by 25 per cent, thereby demonstrating its diplomatic capacity as a 'middle power' to provide an international good. In 2016, China, hosting the G20 and W20, used the opportunity to showcase its leadership and state strength in this area. This example illustrates how states can pursue, and even share, interests and values regarding global equality, although the outcomes of their cooperation typically address the struggles for gender justice only in a limited way. International society redistributes the sources of power—enabling greater access for women to education, employment, business, etc.—while not shifting power per se (Arat 2015). For example, gender parity in secondary education enrolment has virtually been achieved in almost all parts of the world as a result of the Millennium Development Goals, but that has not changed the realities for many minority girls and women in accessing education (they may enrol but are prevented from going to school due to threats of harassment, violence, and conflict) nor the lesser returns to investment in education for women and girls globally due to the discriminatory attitudes, barriers, and hierarchies within the global economy and across societies. Addressing that discrimination would require unravelling all, not just some, patriarchal power relations.

Last, a Kantian lens highlights an inexorable process of inclusion driving the push for integration of women in militaries, diplomacy, and international policymaking. That process is the expression of transnational solidarity and the removal of barriers to achieve that solidarity. Here we can see how quickly arguments drawing on evidence made in one realm of international politics— for instance, the global investment returns from women's participation on corporate boards (Credit Suisse 2012; McKinsey and Company 2007)—quickly travel to influence other realms—the greater sustainability of peace when women are present at peace negotiations (O'Reilly et al 2015; Paffenholz et al. 2016). The universalization of rights while often initiated by non-state actors, may also be internalized by states who increasingly advocate for human rights and gender justice as integral parts of their domestic and foreign policies (Bull 1977, 292). This normative change thus affects the quality of international order. An example of this is the international diffusion of norms promoting women's human rights and prohibiting various forms of violence against women. That diffusion has set in motion a dynamic of universalization. However, the process also prompts localization responses, which may involve rejection, denial, or non-compliance with the intended gender equality norms, potentially undermining international society.

Bull reminds us that a cosmopolitan culture that is 'rooted in societies', not only in their elites, may need to 'absorb non-Western elements' to be genuinely universal and able to serve the purposes of international order (1977, 317). The UN and the provisions of international law cannot alone achieve this basis of order (1977, xiv). A genuinely universal, global approach to gender inequality and injustice therefore would need to go beyond addressing gender domination or patriarchal relations as a binary system that is reflected in the male/female international indicators of equality. It would assess the empowerment of women based on an understanding of how gender inequalities intersect with other social hierarchies and forms of oppression (such as race, ethnicity, sexuality, class, age, nationality, immigrant status), and it would regard global migration and multiculturalism as salient in both Western and non-Western states.

How could such a universal approach address the persistent and egregious violence against women and girls which is in seeming contradiction to the unravelling of patriarchal structures? The causes of this violence are rooted in the political economy of power (True 2012). Importantly, with respect to international society, states have diminished their own sovereign power in some respects by expanding capitalist markets and strengthening the freedoms of the 'haves' over the 'have-nots', the latter group which disproportionately includes women. As they compete for resources and investment, states have opened themselves to the productive as well as the destructive forces of capital, just as Marx foretold. These forces undermine existing social contracts and deepen inequalities and tensions within and across societies. When social contracts break down between the state and civil society, so too does the prior 'fraternal sexual contract'—the normative prohibition on perpetrating violence against another man's wife or daughter. That prohibition, of course, did not apply to violence in marriage or the family and has only been institutionalized in some parts of the world.[1] Attention to violence in the

---

[1] According to UN Women (2011) there are 127 countries that do not explicitly criminalize rape within marriage.

family only became a political issue in Western societies in the 1970s when women began exercising their political and economic rights to higher education, to vote, to be employed outside the home, and to control their own bodies. As Chris Reus-Smit argues, the notion that all biological humans have human rights is very recent, even more so, the notion that women are humans and therefore have equal human rights (2013a). The underlying politics of human rights are still at work in international society.

When patriarchal social contracts break down as states facilitate economic globalization, men and masculinities are affected as much as women and girls. Some men's capacity to achieve recognition *as men*, an identity historically linked to dominant breadwinner or head of household status, is challenged and/or weakened by the global restructuring of production. Violence is one response when you cannot achieve the desired status or provide for your needs in a legitimate way. Men's loss of economic status combined with residual patriarchal ideologies that support their rightful dominance and aggressive behaviour, fuels a backlash of gendered violence and/or male suicide in some contexts, especially those affected by rising unemployment, poverty and inequality, displacement, conflict, and disaster (Hozic and True 2016).

Traditional patriarchal structures extended protection to some women concomitant with their non-participation as equal citizens. But that protection came with a major risk; to the extent that women stepped outside of the patriarchal order (the social boundaries of their family-household), they could expect no protection from men; and states and the international order have historically provided limited protection for non-citizens. As Bull notes, '[u]nless men [sic] enjoy some measure of security against the threat of death or injury at the hands of others, they are not able to devote energy or attention enough to other objects to be able to accomplish them' (1977, 5). This is indeed the case for many women and girls worldwide, one third of whom are likely to experience some form of violent injury in their lifetime because they are women (Carter 2014; Ellsberg et al. 2015). Today, though women have the protection of 'international law' extending beyond the family and the state to which they belong, that law does not prevent the gender-based violence they experience. Rather, improvements in women's status and the rise of political women (including women's human rights defenders), frequently provoke explicit targeting of women and girls for sexual and gender-based violence. This violence is the product of unresolved class, religious, and race/ethnic grievances as well as gender ideologies and aggressive masculinities that are directly and indirectly supported by states. We can see this process at work across the world but particularly clearly in those states recently subject to war and Western intervention such as Afghanistan and Iraq. Feminists agree with Bull that the causes of violence or of economic and social injustice are deeper than the existence of the states system (1977, 291); they lie also in the complex overlaying of patriarchal domination across social relations. But that is not to let the society of states off the hook when it is complicit in creating the very material and ideological conditions that fuel gendered and other types of pervasive, global violence.

RESOLVING THE CONTRADICTIONS OF PATRIARCHY WITHIN ANARCHY

If patriarchal relations once consolidated the anarchical society of states in Europe, then they now also challenge that society from within and without. The implications of the unravelling of patriarchal relations for the preservation and expansion of international society are threefold. First, because patriarchal relations have shaped the formation of states, their undoing also undoes a significant cultural foundation of European-based international society. However, the unravelling of patriarchal relations may mean the adoption of a less hierarchical order of nation-states based on gendered distinctions and masculine domination. Second, the unravelling of patriarchal relations in the West has led to challenges to non-Western patriarchies and contemporary responses to those challenges are taking reactionary forms, threatening the stability of international society. Thus, to the extent that states have played a positive role in the unravelling of patriarchal relations, it is incumbent upon them to address these negative effects of that unravelling. Third, although patriarchal relations underpinned the European international society of states, Eurocentric international society is waning, as Bull observes (1977, 319). Moreover, the diminishing of Western forms of patriarchal relations and contemporary challenges to non-Western forms of patriarchy through new networks between world society and domestic societies suggest the potential for the evolution of international society in the present and future.

With respect to the first implication of patriarchal unravelling, cultural norms and practices will have to replace patriarchal relations and they will need to be broadly shared across societies but also diverse in their expression. With the lesser influence of patriarchal norms in domestic societies, it should follow that in international society states are less likely to be ranked and perceived based on hierarchical gender distinctions. To take one example from recent research in West Java, Indonesia, gender equality and women's empowerment may be locally articulated within the Koran and Islamic teachings by male as well as female religious leaders with meaningful impacts on community understanding and support of social change (Muhummad et al. 2007; Rinaldo 2011). If international society, and therefore order, are to be sustained, they will require cultural consensus across societies about values like gender equality, and not merely consensus among diplomatic and policy elites.

Bull argues that the 'decline in the consensus about common interests and values within states system' began in 1914 with the descent into World War (1977, 257). This is an interesting coincidence given it is only after the First World War that women's struggles for political rights in Europe begin to pay off with the extension of the suffrage. In 1915, moreover, 1200 women leaders from twelve countries across Europe and America, some of them suffragists, met in The Hague at a Congress for Peace to put forward their own detailed plan based on twenty resolutions to end the war. Some of the resolutions looked very similar to Woodrow Wilson's Fourteen Points. Woodrow Wilson himself did raise women's suffrage with fellow political leaders, but they rejected the inclusion of women's rights in an 'international' agreement. Though the women peace activists achieved no recognition from state leaders, they formed the now century-old Women's International League for Peace and Freedom with two members receiving the Nobel Peace Prize in 1919 for their efforts at The Hague (Confortini 2012).

While Bull did not recognize these early efforts by women activists to create a new cultural underpinning for international society, one could hardly ignore them today. Women leaders are proving to play crucial roles in bringing consensus in major areas of international cooperation notably in this decade in nuclear disarmament talks, climate change negotiations (Ivanova 2015; Robinson 2016), and sustainable international peace agreements (Paffenholz et al. 2016). They are a corrective to the shallow roots of diplomatic culture Bull bemoans (1977, 317), a culture where gender, ethnicity, and class have been constitutive of the hierarchies within diplomacy (Neumann 2008). But it is not just a matter of deepening diplomatic culture, as Bull suggests. Rather, diplomatic culture needs to engage more widely with society and non-state actors and in building coalitions of unlikely allies around shared global challenges. In so doing, common values upon which international diplomacy is based need to become more clearly articulated and debated. William Hague's efforts to establish an international norm prohibiting the use of sexual violence in conflict at the core of UK foreign policy illustrates what is possible when a foreign policy leader within a powerful state promotes such a transformation of diplomacy and national interests to accord with human rights values (Davies and True 2017). As Foreign Secretary Hague argued contemporary global politics demands greater not less focus on Britain's core values and standards: '[t]he networked world requires us to inspire other people with how we live up to our own values rather than try to impose them' (2010).[2]

---

[2] Hague echoes Bull's recognition of the world political system as a 'world-wide network of interaction that embraces not only states but also other political actors, both "above" the state and "below" it' (1977, 276).

Despite the challenge of achieving genuinely, universal international society through cultural interaction, *The Anarchical Society* provides no insights on how the process of cultural interaction works, or who or what the agents of cultural change might be, at the global level. Forty years later we can observe that women leaders and activists are notable agents of cultural change transnationally and at the global level, significantly increasing the chances of achieving international consensus on a range of global issues as research and practice is beginning to show. After a series of eight male Secretary-Generals, the 2016 campaign for a woman United Nations Secretary-General, which was promoted by fifty-eight member states, is just one indication that without women today's international society lacks moral authority or legitimacy.[3] Swedish Foreign Minister, Margot Wallström took this movement for transformation in the culture of diplomacy even further when she announced in 2015 that her government would pursue a 'feminist foreign policy' (2016).[4] Among powerful state and non-state actors, that statement of foreign policy has received scepticism comparable to men's dismissals of suffragettes campaigning for the right to vote over a century ago (see, for an example, Dangerfield 1996 [1935]).

Albeit incipient and uneven in its progress, the empowerment of women around the world is gradually having an impact on diplomacy. Wallström, like Hague, is determined that the exclusion of the views and perspectives of women in foreign policy will gradually become more unacceptable in this century due to its morality and pragmatism.

With respect to the second implication for international society, the unravelling of patriarchal relations in the West has increased the challenges to non-Western patriarchies, as well as prompting a backlash against the West and against norms of gender equality. Contemporary responses to this gender transformation are taking especially reactionary forms in some parts of the world, provoking conflict and threatening the values upon which international order rests. A visible contemporary illustration of this is the assault mounted by the so-called 'Islamic State' armed non-state group that is currently fighting for territory in Syria and Iraq, and for hearts and minds worldwide, to constitute itself as an alternative to the current state system (in so doing,

---

[3] See http://www.womansg.org/.

[4] The official Swedish government statement of feminist foreign policy considers 'equality between women and men' to be 'a fundamental aim of Swedish foreign policy' in itself, as well as a prerequisite for reaching Sweden's broader foreign policy goals on peace, and security and sustainable development. It seeks to 'strengthen women's rights, representation and access to resources' by implementing systematic gender mainstreaming, based on knowledge and analysis, throughout the foreign policy agenda. In 2016, the focus areas towards these long-term objectives are; strengthening the human rights of women and girls in humanitarian settings, combating gender-based and sexual violence in conflict and post-conflict situations, and highlighting the potential of women and girls as actors within the framework of peace processes, peace support operations, and sustainable development efforts (Wallstrom 2016).

though, replicating many aspects of the sovereign state—as discussed by Toros and Dionigi, Ch. 9 in this volume). ISIS addresses its message of 'the Caliphate' world society to men and women from Western and non-Western, Islamic majority and multicultural states. In particular, it provides a gender-specific, if not gender-inclusive, vision of a society where no one wants for anything. In the Caliphate, women's roles in the family and home will be fully recognized and appreciated and no woman will have to work a double shift to provide for the needs of her children. Men can be warriors and heroes and are guaranteed a wife and sexual partner as well as privileged status as head of household. Moreover, both women and men have a moral purpose and a place in heaven according to ISIS (Quilliam 2015). International Relations commentators have mostly missed the gender dimensions of ISIS, likely because the ISIS death cult trumps and obscures the ISIS rape cult in global media depictions.

It is clear, however, that ISIS's recruitment strategy has deliberately targeted the weaknesses and contradictions of the contemporary world order. The targeting of women and girls for sexual violence and slavery that has accompanied the transnational rise of extremism is not incidental, but premeditated, systematic, and strategic. Importantly, sexual and gender-based violence is both a *push* and *pull* factor for violent extremism. In the case of ISIS, it is being used to recruit men as (foreign) fighters with the promise of sex slaves and wives—and all their sexual needs being met. This political strategy is also being used to take over territory and resources by displacing populations who flee for fear of rape and the shame that accompanies it within traditional societies, and by expelling religious and sexual minorities and non-conformists. In this way, ISIS aims to recreate society as a 'Caliphate' with parents from various nationalities and cultures but all faithful to a global Umma. ISIS is thus not merely an insurgency; it is a counter-cultural movement *for* patriarchy and *against* international society and its anarchical form. It is also a counter-material movement against neoliberal capitalism and the way it subordinates both women and men especially in non-Western states.

To the extent that states have played a positive role in unravelling patriarchal relations (cf. Bull 1977, 292), it is incumbent upon them to address the contradictory effects, such as violent extremist backlash, and the residue, such as ongoing discrimination in practice, of that unravelling. This will require much more concerted international cooperation to create the structural conditions of gender justice and equality that enables the exercise of freedoms, not merely access to them, for the groups of women and men most at risk of gendered violence. Women's rights, including demands for the elimination of systemic discrimination and violence, may be marginalized in the inter-state consensus and may even be traded-off for seemingly more pressing priorities—as we have seen with the withdrawal of ISAF troops and negotiations with the Taliban during the transition in Afghanistan in 2014–15. However, if women's human rights are not addressed, this will be a lost opportunity for strengthening international society and thus for the realization of the basic human goals of international order. Like non-Western peoples and post-colonial states, women's rights movements worldwide will not be 'assuaged by token gestures'—because they ultimately seek the redistribution of wealth, resources, and power (Bull 1977, 301).

The third implication of change in gender relations for international society is that immanent within this change (and the reactions to it) is the potential for the evolution of international society in the present and future. The unravelling of Western forms of patriarchal relations and the potential to challenge non-Western forms of patriarchy through emerging transnational feminist networks across both world society and domestic societies could redefine the normative and cultural consensus required to sustain international order. However, such a consensus would involve pursuing justice alongside order. This, in a way, is Hedley Bull's conclusion to *The Anarchical Society*. Bull concludes that the study of order should be complimented by the study of justice (1977, 319). This is a crucial point given his acknowledgement that while the system of states has generated international order, that order is underpinned by an international society based on shared rules and institutions, which are in decline. That decline is due to the expansion of the states system as well as challenges to it from within and outside, many of which, as I have argued, take patriarchal forms undermining the universalism of common values and norms supporting international society.

However, Bull posits that justice requires order, although he argues it does not follow that order is automatically prioritized over justice in every case (1977, 88–90). I argue the obverse, that today, order requires justice given the extent of anti-systemic struggles within and across states and given the perceived lack of legitimacy in the current international order that does not reflect the diversity of political identities. Order-generating consensus can only be produced to the extent that greater economic and social justice is realized by marginalized groups in world society. Justice not only provides the legitimacy for international order, it generates the constituency who can activate and reinforce the values and norms of the society of states. In that respect, the realization of justice for half the world's population—as part of global movements for women's rights to bodily integrity, to equal participation in decision-making, to equal economic opportunity, and recognition of domestic care labour—is essential to the prospects for strengthening the fabric of international society. Important here is not merely that justice cannot take second place to order, but that we need to rethink our conception of justice—as feminist scholars and women's rights activists have demonstrated in their efforts to address the intersections of gender and racial oppression. Gender justice, Nancy Fraser (1997) has argued, involves not merely *redistribution* or redress for past wrongs but *recognition* of difference, and substantive political *representation* for diverse groups in situations where patriarchies are simultaneously becoming weaker and more resurgent (Fraser 2005). Such a vision for justice goes beyond Bull's additive approach to international order, which seeks merely to include non-western perspectives in international political culture but not to transform it (1977, 317).

CONCLUSION

At a time when international institutions like the United Nations are barely able to mitigate problems of war and conflict, let alone stem them, *The Anarchical Society*'s approach to international order is refreshing. Bull reminds us that the institutions of the balance of power and diplomacy cannot be replaced by international administration—and moreover that international law should not be confused with international morality or progress (Bull 1977, 38). However, the idea that the states system, whether or not it constitutes an international society, is the best means to secure the control of violence, economic and social justice, and protection of the environment is one that should be subjected to rigorous, critical scrutiny.

This essay has argued that patriarchy and patriarchal values privileging masculinity over femininity, reason over emotion, men over women, are constitutive (albeit hidden) foundations of the anarchical society of states. That international society is undergoing significant change, from social forces both within and without. Those social forces include capitalism and its power to break up existing social relations, social movements for the universalization of individual rights set in motion during the Enlightenment, and the agency and resistance of diverse groups of women to masculine institutions and norms, the reach of which extends across all boundaries of nation-states, race, class, geography, caste, and culture. Periods of change and transition are frequently also periods of violence and upheaval. Thus we can see connections between the breakdown of patriarchal social contacts and the heightening of gendered violence cut across various sites of conflict and change with implications for world order. Observing the resurgence of patriarchal movements and challenges to the current international system must lead us to rethink the cultural foundations of international order rather than to incorporate the contested, patriarchal aspects of societies in efforts to accommodate broader interests and values. States have a responsibility in their domestic and foreign policies to counter the violent backlash against women's human rights by promoting and upholding feminist principles that recognize gender differences within a framework of equality that empowers women to participate in decision-making, and to realize their full social and economic potential.

A more just international order, and one that can effectively respond to common global problems, must involve a deepening of inter-state diplomacy to include and engage with significant non-state actors and representatives from all levels of domestic and world societies. In *The Anarchical Society*, Bull argues that a conception of the national 'interest' is a vacuous guide as to how states do or should behave (1977, 66) and that any notion of common interests depends on prior ends and values that are desired or shared (1977, 67). Herein lies a point of agreement between feminist scholars and Bull on the conduct of international politics. Feminists in the academy, in social movements and now in positions of state power argue, for both pragmatic and moral reasons, that foreign policy and international society should be more centrally guided by values of human rights and social justice. Indeed, globally connected women's movements seek to transform international values and to hold states and international society accountable for institutionalizing and enforcing these new norms locally and globally (True 2004: 160). In this way, world society and international society may be mutually reinforcing. Bringing women into foreign and international policymaking would not just add new voices into cosmopolitan diplomatic and international political culture undergirding international order. Bringing diverse women *as women* and *as feminists* engaged in struggles against local and global patriarchies into the debate about common values is crucial to averting the decline in international order as well as to redressing globalized, gendered injustices.

Part IV

Augmenting *The Anarchical Society*

15

The Anarchical Society as Futurology

Heikki Patomäki

INTRODUCTION

The final part of Hedley Bull's *The Anarchical Society* is dedicated to the exploration of possible future world orders. First, Bull maps the space of possibilities in conceptual terms and then investigates trends towards various possible world-historical ends. He continues by normatively assessing alternatives to the states system and especially to what he calls the international society. Finally, Bull considers a range of transformative ideologies and their plausibility.

The mapping of future possibilities follows logically from Bull's theory of world politics and its conceptual distinctions. Isolated states can exist without forming a system. Bull's reading of Rousseau comes close to this picture of isolated states. States may also interact and be part of a system without forming a society. In this case states and their representatives lack intersubjectively shared rules, norms, understandings, and institutions. The third possible alternative to the current international society is a world state. Bull's perhaps most original insights concern the case of overlapping authority and multiple loyalty. He calls this future possibility 'a new mediaevalism'. Bull also argues that there are many possible variations within the order of international society. The world could become disarmed, ideologically homogeneous, and/or based on 'Grotian' solidarity. Alternatively, a large number of nuclear powers could emerge, generating a universal deterrent system.

In 2017, we may ask, with the benefit of hindsight, whether Bull's interpretations and expectations succeeded in foreseeing the next few decades of world history and, moreover, whether he remains an opportune guide from now on. While Bull represented himself as a methodological 'classicist', he did not avoid causal language (1966a). From a scientific realist viewpoint (Patomäki and Wight 2000; Patomäki 2002), we should also enquire whether Bull had an account of the causal powers, mechanisms, and processes capable of generating the trends he either observed or anticipated. Can Bull be read as a philosophical realist or did he, after all, consider causation in empiricist terms? Can we explicate and then assess his implicit premises? What were his typical argumentative schemes?

An interesting thing about *The Anarchical Society* is the way it situates normative discussions in the context of real world historical developments. The problem with conventional Western normative theory is the tendency to either disconnect values from the real, geo-historical world or see them in empiricist terms as something that is actually shared (Patomäki 1992a; cf. Patomäki 2002, 143–63). Given this, normative theory vacillates between irrealist utopianism (when values are sometimes seen as transcendent, i.e. other-worldly) and mere justification of the present (typically when values are conceived in terms of actual tradition or consensus or something similar).

Bull's approach is different. His normative judgements are based on a mixture of considerations, in which actual, possible, and likely world-historical developments play a crucial role. This does not mean, however, that his judgements are always correct or even plausible. I will evaluate critically the factual and normative premises of his arguments (the two are intertwined but not inseparable). My main argument is that because of his omission of political economy, Bull would have been puzzled about the causes of the re-emergence of great power conflicts. For the same reason, he also underestimated the importance of building better common institutions.

WORLD-HISTORICAL TRENDS AND TENDENCIES

How did Bull's interpretations and expectations succeed in foreseeing the next few decades of world history? At first look, Bull seems to have done much better than most in terms of anticipating the future. At the general level of systemic transformations, Bull was markedly right about the continued existence and prevalence of the international society. The most obvious omission was that Bull did not anticipate the end of the Cold War, yet we know that it came as a surprise to most IR scholars, Deutsch (1954) being a rare exception (see Allan and Goldmann 1992, including Patomäki 1992b, for an *ex post* evaluation of IR theories in this light). It is also noteworthy that in the post-Cold War era, the world has both avoided disasters such as a large-scale nuclear war and eschewed systemic changes.

International society has not degenerated into a Hobbesian system of interactions. Ideological tensions were reduced, at least at first, by the unexpected end of the Cold War, although new tensions have risen since then. In Bullian terms, the world has experienced a return to a pre-First World War situation of largely shared liberal or liberal-authoritarian values, although various fundamentalisms have risen to challenge the secular, science-based, and materialistic values of the (il)liberal and globalizing capitalism (Ruthven 2007). The rules and institutions of international society have not disappeared but evolved; yet a world state proper is not in sight. Some of the trends towards a new medievalism have continued, but while they may constitute anomalies and irregularities from the point of view of the states system, these trends have not outdone the institutions of international society in the post-Cold War era, rushed accounts such as Ruggie (1993) and Friedrichs (2001) notwithstanding.

It may be countered, however, that the European integration process has brought about a qualitative change in Europe. In the 2010s, the European Union is a complex hybrid of an international organization and a state (Caporaso 1996 is a well-known attempt to theorize this ambiguity in terms of different forms of state). Despite the British exit from the Union (due by 2019), which reinforces the institution of state sovereignty in Europe, a real doubt persists both in theory and in practice as to whether sovereignty lies with the national governments or with the organs of the EU. This ambiguity was demonstrated in a particularly authoritarian way by the Greek debacle in the summer of 2015. Bull maintained that from a global perspective, the EU's hybrid nature would not make any major difference:

> But such a state of affairs, if it existed in Europe, would not mean that the global states system had been eclipsed, only that in this particular area (as, in the early centuries of the states system, in Germany), there was a hybrid entity which did not conform to the prevailing norms. (1977, 266)

One could further argue in Bull's favour that since the breakdown of the Soviet Union and Yugoslavia, the disintegration of states has halted and the number of states has stabilized. In the 2010s, non-state groups engage in violence and state-violence is privatized to a significant degree, but from a Bullian point of view, there is nothing radically new either in 'freedom fighting' or 'terrorism', or about mercenaries and trading companies that command armies. Trends towards new medievalism have spawned counter-trends. States have continued to try to limit and regulate non-state violence. This dialectic has also generated new—even if only limited—forms of global governance. (Avant 2016; for a critical discussion, Patomäki 2016).

What goes somewhat against the expectations of Bull is that since 1977 transnational organizations have further proliferated. Bull seems to have underestimated both the sway of globalizing forces (Scholte 2005) and ignored the possibility of the emergence of at least some elements of world statehood (cf. Albert et al. 2012; Albert 2016). Transnational corporations, banks, and financial investors are arguably more powerful than ever (as pointed out already by Gill and Law 1989). New free trade and other international legal agreements have consolidated the privileged position of private megacorporations. Globalization may not be as new or discontinuous as sometimes depicted, but qualitatively novel features and properties have emerged, from investment protection clauses and just-in-time systems of global production to computerized derivatives markets and aggressive tax planning. These trends, strengthened further by processes of technological unification, are perhaps the clearest sign of the world system moving towards Bull's new medievalism.

Bull did not fully acknowledge that the line between neo-medievalism and a world state is necessarily blurred. Concepts are not containers with clear-cut insides and outsides. While no proper world state may be in sight, it can be maintained that at least some elements of world statehood exist already, involving the possibility of making binding collective decisions and creating new law. When the state is understood as a trans-historical universal notion, there is no reason to reduce it to one particular instance such as territorial nation-state. Different overlapping forms of modern state authority can coexist within the same space. True, we may concur that the processes of global constitutionalization may be legitimized only partially and are mediated through established territorial states.[1] They are also best understood in terms of functionally specific global constitutions, in plural, rather than in terms of a single overarching formal constitution, even when these processes have deep historical roots in pre-modern moral and legal developments. The relevant legal rules and principles concern especially human rights and private property rights, but involve other tenets as well. (Albert et al. 2012; Albert 2016; Brunkhorst 2012).

Their inherent limitations notwithstanding, processes of global constitutionalization are real and qualitatively different from Bull's categories of different systems. It is also important that the emergence of elements of world statehood has given rise to new forms of agency and politics. At least rudiments of global public sphere and an outline of global civil society have evolved from the 1980s through to 2010s, as a critical response to global problems and, ever so often, in opposition to the evolving neoliberal world order. Sometimes civil society organizations advocate liberal human rights and democracy across the world, thus contributing to the on-going processes of global constitutionalization. Recurrently civil society actors react to global problems and contest the dominant systems of global rule, suggesting alternative steering powers, rules and principles, and sources of legitimation, in their stead (O'Brian et al. 2000; Scholte 2011; see also Patomäki 2011 on the idea of a world political party).

Hence, while Bull may have been right about the continuing existence and prevalence of international society, he seems to have underestimated the

---

[1] Jessop argues that a world state is unlikely to become the dominant scale within any system of multi-spatial metagovernance, especially in a networked, asymmetrical, and still hierarchical world of states (2012). At the same time, Jessop also maintains that the problematic tendencies, antagonisms, and contradictions of the capitalist world markets—which are now 'ecologically dominant'—well justify various political efforts to build a world state. The point of these transformative efforts is to 'limit the ecological dominance of capital accumulation (including its increasingly damaging environmental footprint) and provide other ways to steer the overall development of world society' (2012, 202).

sway of deep-seated globalizing forces. The increasing power and reach of transnational organizations and the emergence of elements of world statehood appear to be to a degree at odds with Bull's expectations concerning possible transformations of the states system.

What about possible changes *within* international society? After the end of the Cold War, the world became ideologically more homogeneous and, subsequently, there were attempts to build systems of collective security or, beyond that, even elements of world statehood in the functionally differentiated sphere of security (United Nations 1992). In the absence of consensus at the UN Security Council, however, the US and its NATO allies have oftentimes resorted to unilateral wars of intervention. As Bull stressed in *The Anarchical Society*, the problem with the accounts of just war is that just causes may and often do clash, whether in the public sphere or on the battleground (1977, 30, 132–3, 157–8). This has clearly been the case in the Middle East and Central Asia. Bull also stressed that attempts at collective security may weaken or undermine 'classical devices for the maintenance of order' (1977, 231). If one great power can resort to war unilaterally, why not the others? The conflict between Putin's Russia and the West can be seen from this perspective as a possible and likely consequence of the unilaterally executed version of collective security by the post-Cold War US and its allies; this unilateralism has amounted in effect to the revival of the just war doctrine. In the Syrian civil war (2011–), too, conflicts over the just cause are interwoven in complex ways, with potential not only for some cooperation but also for further escalation of antagonisms and conflicts.

The world has become neither disarmed nor characterized by a universal deterrent system. The 'peace dividend' of the end of the Cold War turned out short-lived. By 1997–99 it was over and not only in Europe but globally. In the 2010s, world military expenditure exceeds Cold War levels in absolute terms, with East-Asia playing an increasingly prominent role (military spending in Asia and Oceania rose by 64 per cent between 2006 and 2015; Perlo-Freeman et al. 2016). Nuclear proliferation has nonetheless been slow, slower than what many anticipated in the 1960s and 1970s. Underneath sensational media events and the daily drama of world politics, and in spite of some gradual changes and persisting potential for a global catastrophe, the overall situation in 2017 appears to be mostly that of business as usual within the international society setup. This is in line what Bull expected forty years ago.

BULL'S ACCOUNT OF CAUSATION, SOCIAL SCIENCES, AND FUTURES STUDIES

What explains the prevailing or future order or disorder of world politics? Bull's own analyses and anticipations rest on a limited set of argumentative schemes. On occasion he made an explicit connection between explanation and causation. Bull (1977, 74–6) clarifies that his claims about connections between rules, institutions, and order are *causal* rather than functionalist. He even tries to formulate an account of efficient causation in terms of necessary and sufficient conditions:

> A central theme in this study is that the rules and institutions to which reference has been made carry out positive functions or roles in relation to international order. In this study what is meant by statements of this kind is simply that these rules and institutions are part of the efficient causation of international order, that they are among the necessary and sufficient conditions of its occurrence.
> (1977, 74–5)

Beyond this there is little about causation in *The Anarchical Society*. In the 'case for a classical approach', Bull explicates his methodological stance. He gives several reasons for the claim that 'the practitioners of the scientific approach are unlikely to make progress of the sort to which they aspire' (1966a, 369–70).[2] Thus instead of relying on quantitative world order modelling or any other approach trying to test causal claims in a systematic empirical fashion, Bull tries to understand large-scale world-historical developments and their implications in qualitative-historical terms.

Primarily, Bull studies world politics through discussing the relevant literatures. He (re)constructs and assesses other scholars' arguments concerning large-scale developments. He acknowledges the limitations of making such indirect observations and arguments, stressing that our 'general propositions cannot be accorded anything more than the tentative and inconclusive status appropriate to their doubtful origin' (1966a, 361). The key notion here is judgement. Bull relies explicitly on the exercise of judgement, noting that the most important questions are as often moral as empirical-historical. He also makes some logical, political theoretical arguments. For instance, he points out that any argument for a world state that starts with a Hobbesian description of the states system is incoherent:

> But if states are indeed in a Hobbesian state of nature, the contract by means of which they are to emerge from it cannot take place. For if covenants without the sword are but words, this will be true of covenants directed towards the establishment of universal government, just as it will hold true of agreements on other subjects. (1977, 262)

Bull adds rather categorically, however, that there is no empirical evidence that states would be willing to subject themselves to the rule of a world state. Bull

---

[2] It is worth comparing Bull's proclamation with Vasquez's (1996) devastatingly critical assessment of the main claims and hypotheses of political realism (and to a degree liberalism as an IR theory too). Vasquez reaches the conclusion that 93 per cent of political realist hypotheses have been falsified and only about 2 per cent passed the test of high association, including those derived from the most central realist claims (power, alliances). Those not-yet-falsified will be soon falsified.

did not have the opportunity to hear Gorbachev in the late 1980s advocating solutions to global problems by means of establishing a world government; neither did he see the literature on global democracy that resurged after the end of the Cold War (the debate had of course begun during the world wars; see Held and Patomäki 2006). Bull might counter that even if we may now see some weak signs of a world state, there is no credible basis for such a global transformation. Wishful thinking is not a good basis for rational judgements or actions. Rather, what appears particularly important today, in 2017, is that the world is sliding back to nationalist statism and conflicts.

Whether Bull would dismiss the argument concerning overlapping forms of modern state authority within the same space, implying that at least some elements of world statehood have evolved, is more uncertain. Bull's scepticism about a world state is based to an important degree on normative considerations. At times Bull resorts to conservative remarks along the lines of 'haven't we already tried all this consciousness-raising stuff' (1977, 303–4). His main argument is, however, that a world state in itself would not solve the problem of collective violence—or any other global problem. In an argumentative scheme that is characteristic to *The Anarchical Society*, Bull points out that if we can imagine utopian possibilities in relation to a world state, we can also imagine them in relation to alternatives such as international society:

> Of course we can imagine a world government which would not lend itself to civil or internal violence, at least on a large scale, because in it there were institutionalised procedures for the peaceful resolution of conflicts that allowed for change and were generally accepted as legitimate. Under such a world government, as within some modern Western states that have a high degree of political stability and a relative absence of violent internal conflict, large-scale violence might be avoided for long periods. But if we are free to attribute to our imagined alternative form of universal political organisation these utopian features, we are also free to think of the states system in these utopian terms, as a system in which the conditions of a 'pluralistic security-community' are generalised. (1977, 285)

Deutsch and his associates introduced the notion of security community (1957; Lijphart 1981; Patomäki 2002, 193–209). Deutsch argued that the existence of the state is neither a necessary nor a sufficient condition for peace; nor is the non-existence of the state a necessary or a sufficient condition for the prevalence of the acute threat of political violence. These connections are contingent. The imposition of a common government, with its capacity for violent enforcement of norms, may well decrease rather than increase the chances of peace. The real difficulty lies in building a community within which conflicts can be resolved by institutionalized peaceful means and procedures.[3]

---

[3] Neither Deutsch nor Bull explored connections between the possibility of peaceful changes and democracy. I have argued elsewhere that democratization of social contexts (including trans- and supranational contexts) and the development of security community can be mutually

In this Bull agrees with Deutsch. He also uses the same argumentative scheme in the contexts of economic and social justice and the environment. In each case, for Bull a world state is neither a necessary nor a sufficient condition for tackling a global problem.

Bull's standard scheme of argumentation is thus abstract and mostly negative. In social sciences it is rather easy to say that X is neither a necessary nor a sufficient condition for outcome O, because strictly speaking nothing ever is (conditions function only as part of a geo-historical context). The level of abstraction is too high. Apart from the Deutschian mechanism of resolving conflicts peacefully, Bull does not specify any causal powers, mechanisms, or processes that we should take into account in analysing specific global problems. For instance, he mentions 'deeper causes' of economic and social injustice but does not explain them (1977, 291).

Bull was not a positivist, except probably in the sense of legal positivism (following Hart 2012). On the other hand, whether he can be read as a philosophical or scientific realist seems open to doubt. Bull did not have the conceptual resources to resolve the *aporia* of general causal statements vs. historical changes and idiosyncrasies. He criticizes positivism (behaviouralism, scientism) in terms of open systems ontology and double hermeneutics of social sciences, but at the same time he is rather vague about his own ontological assumptions and existential hypotheses.[4] Many of his methodological statements are formulated in an imprecise and at times ambiguous manner (see also Bull 2000d). Bull did not develop a systematic methodological stance. Kaplan's criticism of 'traditionalism' as 'undisciplined speculation devoid of serious substantive or methodological concerns' is not entirely unfounded (1966, 20).

ON THE LIKELY CONSEQUENCES OF THE STATES SYSTEM: A POLITICAL ECONOMY PERSPECTIVE

Despite the limitations of his approach, it is fair to say that often Bull's arguments remain sound, and many—although not all—of his judgements

---

supportive (Patomäki 2003). This is not always the case, however. Since the development of a security community is a long and complicated process of institutionalization of mutual acceptance, trust, and procedures and practices of peaceful change, and since it is always vulnerable to the escalation of conflicts, an inconsiderate attempt at global democratization may turn out to be counterproductive.

[4] It seems likely that he had not heard about the arguments of Harré and Secord (1972), Keat and Urry (1975), and Bhaskar (1975), although they were developed and widely discussed in philosophy and social theory at the time when Bull was writing *The Anarchical Society* in the 1960s and 1970s.

about possible and likely futures have been at least somewhat on the mark. This is in contrast to the bulk of political observers who fail miserably with their anticipations and are often bad at updating their beliefs on the basis of evidence. Tetlock (2005) uses Berlin's (1953) metaphor of foxes and hedgehogs[5] and argues, on the basis of large-scale empirical studies on expert judgements, that foxes over-predict fewer departures, good or bad, from the *status quo*. Yet foxes do not mindlessly predict continuity from the past. In market terminology, they 'are hedging their bets' by rarely ruling out anything as impossible. Their strength lies in open-mindedness and cautiousness.

The assumption of business-as-usual works only until things change. A self-critical, dialectical style of reasoning can spare experts from many mistakes. Foxes are usually better at learning from mistakes. The problem is that too much open-mindedness can amount to mere old-fashioned confusion (all possibilities are covered and thus whatever happens seems compatible with one's anticipations). I would characterize Bull as a fox rather than a hedgehog, indicating that he was capable of balancing his judgements. Foxes are especially sensitive to how forces drawing to different directions often cancel out and result in relative stability.

Bull was less good at explicating how absences and contradictions drive political changes.[6] It is difficult to analyse the historical dynamics of a system without a sufficiently deep account of its underlying structures and mechanisms, or the logics and patterns of its evolvement. The mere absence of necessary or sufficient conditions for a particular outcome does not explain much, nor does it give a genuine basis for anticipating possible and likely futures. Knowledge about history and some casual observations about prevailing trends and tendencies may give more substance to one's judgements, but they are not sufficient for building systematic scenarios about possible and more or less likely and desirable futures. The fact that there is no organized account of underlying causal powers and mechanisms, of relevant contradictions (problems, lacks, etc.), and of related geo-historical processes, means that judgements about possible futures must be made in part in darkness. What is more, Bull's analysis excludes political economy considerations almost entirely.

A particularly pertinent question for Bull in 2017 is this: why was the post-Cold War moment of cooperation, shared values, and solidarity so

---

[5] Foxes are those who 'know many little things', drawing from an eclectic array of traditions. Foxes accept ambiguity and contradiction as inevitable features of life. Bull was a fox in this sense. Hedgehogs are those who 'know one big thing', toil devotedly within one tradition, and reach for formulaic solutions to ill-defined problems (Tetlock 2005, 2).

[6] Bhaskar (1993) develops multifarious dialectical categories and schemes for understanding change at all levels of reality, but focusing especially on contemporary world history. I apply some of these categories and schemes to the analysis of dialectics of global governance in the twenty-first century, initially understood in terms of a simple Polanyian double movement, but then developed into new and more open-ended and normative directions (Patomäki 2014).

short-lived? Why is the world sliding, again, back to nationalist statism, militarized conflicts, and arms race, notwithstanding the sway of globalizing forces and emergence of elements of world statehood? Perhaps the answer can be found, in part, in the dynamics of global political economy, which forms a complex process in which actors and issues are actively interwoven.[7] Politico-economic interconnectedness applies to developments in every region of the world, as the dynamic processes of the world economy shape conditions everywhere. The whole is more than the sum of its parts; but the whole does not work without its parts. Actors do participate in bringing about and steering global political economy processes in various ways, but often in short-sighted or contradictory ways (Patomäki 2008; Patomäki 2013).

How does the world economy work from a Bullian point of view? It is well-known that there is hardly anything about the political economy of peace and security in *The Anarchical Society*. In this rare passage on political economy Bull seems to be committed to the logic of economic liberalism:

> The states system, it may be argued, obstructs realisation of the goals of economic and social justice in two main ways. Because it imposes barriers to the free movement of men, money and goods about the earth's surface—and also to their movement according to a putative global plan of economic development—it inhibits world economic growth. (1977, 289)

Bull does not go so far as to say that free trade is good for peace. Rather he is either ignorant or agnostic about the debates that concern the institutions and mechanisms of capitalist market economy and their internal and external relations to processes such as expansion, securitization, escalation of conflicts and preparedness for war.

Consider the case of the major mid-2010s conflict centring on Ukraine. The immediate background for this conflict has to do with NATO and EU expansion eastwards. Russian leadership has been progressively more determined to draw a line, especially at NATO, but also at EU expansion.[8] This is connected to a particular interpretation of political changes in the former Soviet Union and the Balkans during the early 2000s. The Russian

---

[7] To qualify my earlier remarks on political realism (n. 2), it must be acknowledged that classical political realism can illuminate some of the key causes for this regression in world politics in the 2000s and 2010s. Morgenthau's systematic critique of the temptation of universalism (1961, 11, ch. 7, ch. 20, 560–70), and Carr's (1946, ch. 4.) equally forceful critique of economic liberalism's utopia of harmony of interests, can shed light on the deep structures of meaning that have, once again, turned out counterproductive. In a telling phrase, Carr talked about 'the paradise of laissez-faire'.

[8] There is a long-standing dispute about whether NATO's expansion into Eastern Europe violated commitments made during the negotiations over German reunification. Russian leaders have accused the West of breaking promises made after the fall of the Iron Curtain. *Der Spiegel* argued in 2009 that 'newly discovered documents from Western archives support the Russian position'. For a discussion of these documents, see Klußmann et al. (2009).

state-leaders have been disposed to interpret the so-called colour revolutions as a deliberate strategic means of the expansion of the West and its particular values eastwards. In the words of Foreign Minister Sergei Lavrov: 'The US and Europe use the "Color Revolution" to serve their own interests, impose their own values, and end in creating new global tensions' (Cordesman 2014).

The precise extent to which uprisings in the early 2000s in Serbia, Georgia, Ukraine, and elsewhere were in fact supported, encouraged, funded, or even systematically planned by the US and the EU (or its member states) remains disputed. What we know for sure is that the securitization of these uprisings on the Russian side have triggered at times rather exceptional countermeasures,[9] which in turn have led to unintended counterproductive effects, not the least in Georgia and Ukraine (Delcour and Wolczuk 2015). In this process of step-by-step escalation of conflict, the universalizing inner grammar of Western neoliberalism—manifesting itself through various free market arrangements, neighbourhood policies, and programmes of democracy and human rights promotion—has come to be contested and geopoliticized, even though Russia itself combines elements of state capitalism and neoliberalism in its economic policies and institutional arrangements.

It is evident that many corporate and state actors benefit (or would benefit) from an easy or privileged access to raw materials, cheap labour, industrial capacity or markets in the Eastern Europe, former Soviet Union, and the Balkans. Constructivists are right, however, in stressing that interests are not separate from beliefs but constituted by them (Wendt 1999, 119–38). Interest-constituting beliefs are frequently disputed. For instance, EU's democracy-promotion is built on the neoliberal model of market society. It allows for some pluralism and exploration of extra-liberal ideas, and this is what civil society actors often do. And yet, there are reasons why 'all such ideas are swiftly returned to the magnetic field of (embedded neo)liberal core assumptions' (Kurki 2012, 172). Particular beliefs may come to be selected and pushed because they accord with the already-constituted powerful interests. Yet political economy explanations are not reductionist. They take the

---

[9] Already before the 2007–8 elections, there was much public talk in Russia about the danger of a 'colour revolution'. Academic analysts have been torn between two different interpretations. Some argue that securitization has served Putin's regime in domestic politics; whereas others think that the anxiety of leading Russian politicians is genuine. Duncan (2013) concludes his analysis of 2007–8 that 'fear of a coloured revolution was, it seems, not fabricated with the intention of being used instrumentally to preserve the regime'. The fear seems genuine, but do the dominant beliefs in Russia conflate concerns about ruling elite's position and the interests of society at large? While a nuanced answer to this question lies beyond the scope of my paper, it is worth noting that White and McAllister (2014) consider the possibility that Russia only scarcely avoided a 'Facebook Revolution' in 2011. Given Putin's popularity in Russia, a 'revolution' in 2011 was unlikely. Yet a new phase in securitization was reached in 2013–14. Since Ukraine's Euromaidan, Russia has framed mass anti-regime protests at home and abroad as a military threat (Bouchet 2016).

concept-dependency of social beings seriously. Interests are only moments in social processes.

Once a particular institutional arrangement is in place, it affects the structuring of mechanisms that subsequently tend to bring about particular characteristic causal consequences, shaping the processes of global political economy in which actors are active and issues are interwoven. Thus the conflict in Ukraine was precipitated by a global crisis. The worldwide process of financialization has deepened cycles of boom and bust and made them synchronized across the world. The financial crisis of 2008–9 was the most serious crisis of the world economy since the Great Depression and the Second World War (Patomäki 2010). As a result of the crisis, Ukrainian GDP collapsed by almost 15 per cent in 2009, ending a decade of high economic growth and decreasing poverty. Following a short-lived, half-way recovery in 2010–11, recession and then depression continued. Soon Ukraine faced a situation of mounting debt and rapid loss of currency reserves. The current account in Ukraine reached a record low of –6 USD billion in the third quarter of 2013. At the same time, foreign currency reserves were rapidly approaching an all-time record low of 5 USD billion.

European and North American lenders started to assume, or directly demand, austerity. The problem is that austerity and financial problems easily become self-perpetuating and translate into high levels of unemployment, uncertainties, and economic troubles of everyday life. A further problem is that unemployment and economic uncertainties can aggravate social antagonisms. Unemployment is an issue of existential security and thus creates room for securitization of political issues; this applies to socio-economic uncertainty more generally.[10] In the Ukrainian context, economic hardship is easy to associate with corruption and concentration of wealth.

The Euromaidan protests started in November 2013, when the Ukrainian president Viktor Yanukovych began shying away from an association agreement that had been negotiated with the EU. Instead, he chose closer ties with Russia. The EU had offered a relatively small loan, with conditions similar to the austerity conditions imposed by the Troika upon the euro

---

[10] The unemployment rate rose to about 10% by early 2014. Unemployment has never been the most important source of poverty in independent Ukraine. On the other hand, in 2015–16 the unemployment benefit is only about 50 USD per month. While the insecurities related to the threat of unemployment are never just economic but also moral and social, this aggravates the threat of unemployment. In terms of GDP growth, there was a half-way recovery of the Ukrainian economy in 2010–11, but from 2012 to 2015 Ukraine's GDP contracted again first modestly and then sharply. These developments preceded the political crisis associated with the demonstrations and riots of late 2013 and early 2014. By the end of 2015 the GDP of Ukraine had contracted back to the 2005 level. (World Bank data available at http://data.worldbank.org/indicator/NY.GDP.MKTP.CD.)

crisis countries.[11] Criticism of those conditions fed into the East–West and other divides in Ukrainian political economy and society.

In February 2014, Ukraine appeared to be on the brink of civil war, as violent clashes between protesters and special police forces led to many deaths and injuries. Yanukovych fled to Russia. He was removed from office by the parliament of Ukraine in a manner that violated the then-current constitution. In March 2014, in response to the illegal ousting of Yanukovych, the Supreme Council of Crimea organized a referendum in Crimea. The majority of Crimean people seemed to favour joining Russia. Hastily, Russia made Crimea a part of the Russian federation—against international law according to a number of UN member states—arguing that the unilateral Kosovo declaration of independence in 2008 had set a precedent. At this time, pro-Russian movements, involving Russian citizens, were protesting against Kiev in Eastern and Southern parts of Ukraine. In the East the situation soon escalated into an armed conflict between the separatist militia supported by Russia and the new Ukrainian government. The war in Donbass started in April 2014 and continues as a low-intensity conflict in 2017.

The lessons from the Ukrainian conflict can be generalized from a global Keynesian perspective.[12] Processes of politico-economic expansion and uneven growth in the context of a contradictory and unstable world economy can (co-)generate, (re-)trigger, and escalate conflicts that are always embedded in specific geo-historical settings, with complex backgrounds. After a point, escalation may start to follow its own logic. A number of mechanisms and absences contribute to this outcome. There is no automatic mechanism balancing trade, or supply and demand, or synchronizing diverse economic processes. Increasing inequalities is an important reason why there may be not only a lack of legitimacy but also of inadequate overall demand in the economy. Insufficient demand at home is a problem that states can try to export to other states, for instance by means of pushing for maximal or privileged access to geo-economic spaces, or by resorting to internal or currency devaluation (which lowers the price of exports, making them more competitive in markets, but other states can respond in kind).

---

[11] Austerity tends to depress the economy. These packages also impose retrenchment on public services and distribution policies, wage and pension cuts; and impel changing labour laws under the euphemism of 'flexibility' or 'flexicurity'—typically, also implying wage cuts, thereby lessening citizens' purchasing power and further reducing overall effective demand. (On the effects of the Euro crisis and austerity, see Patomäki 2013, 57–81.)

[12] Already Keynes' own experiences in the 1910s convinced him that economic theories cannot adequately be applied solely at national level; a holistic world-perspective is needed. This implies that issues of the economy and international relations are tightly interconnected (Keynes 1920; Markwell 2006). Global Keynesianism is an approach that frames questions of public economic policy and politics on the world economic scale (Köhler 1999).

When states commit a fallacy of composition in their external policies (i.e. try to improve their situation or position by non-generalizable means), they not only reduce aggregate demand in the world economy but also risk potential conflicts with other states, which may be simultaneously engaging in similar projects. Typically, inadequacies in the overall efficient demand translate into the under-utilization of production capacity and thus unemployment. Since the 1980s, various forms of precarious work have also become more common. High levels of unemployment and uncertainty tend to generate existential insecurity among the citizenry, forming fertile ground for the rise of antagonistic self–other relations and exclusive nationalism. Capitalist world markets and the states system involve plenty of conflict potential.

Many politico-economic processes are self-reinforcing, including processes of (de)industrialization and accumulation of wealth and privileges.[13] States' attempts to intervene in processes that facilitate or prevent (de)industrialization may be blocked by other states, often in the name of free trade. In the 2010s, the principles of free trade are neo-constitutionally secured (Gill 1998). Attempts to block forms of state interventions in the economy can be, and often are, in accordance with the interests of those actors who currently benefit from cumulative causation in the world economy (this is the classical, but contested Listian argument).

Also inequalities of income and wealth among individuals and social classes tend to accumulate. A key argument of Piketty's (2014) is that there is a tendency for $r > g$, where r is the average annual rate of return on capital and g is annual economic growth. Past wealth becomes increasingly important and inherited wealth grows faster than output and income. If this is combined with the inequality of returns on capital as a function of initial wealth, the result is an increasing concentration of capital. Moreover, this process is likely to lead to the accumulation of political privileges and hence de-democratization. Thereby the concentration of capital also shapes the production and distribution of knowledge in society. The selection mechanisms for dominant beliefs, narratives and discourses become skewed towards reinforcing the appropriate beliefs and societal interests as defined by the wealthy and powerful or those representing them. At worst, anything perceived as threatening to basic beliefs and stories may come to be securitized; and anyone disagreeing with the established direction may be constructed as a potential or actual enemy.[14]

---

[13] On the concept of cumulative and self-reinforcing causation in economics, see Kaldor (1972, 1237–55); and on positive feedback loops and self-reinforcing processes in politics, Pierson (2004). For a similar recent analysis of the role of technology gap in trade and uneven growth, see Cimoli and Porcile (2011). In Patomäki (2008, 124–55) I analyse the role of positive feedback loops in the political economy of global security developments.

[14] Also NATO's eastward expansion has been premised on particular but shifting forms and objects of securitization. Meanwhile in Russia and Ukraine, the initial private wealth distribution that resulted from shock therapy and privatization of the state assets in the early 1990s have been

These processes matter from the point of view of international and global security. They strengthen the relative power of actors predisposed to disregarding those rational economic policies needed to ensure full employment and steady economic developments. For instance, growing inequalities tend to reduce overall demand and encourage financialization. Thereby the likelihood of major economic crises and shocks increases. Moreover, de-democratization, securitization, enemy-construction, and inverted totalitarianism (Wolin 2010) are likely to generate and aggravate antagonistic relations with different others. The real problem is that this trend towards increasing inequalities is difficult to reverse. Historically, only major shocks, (especially world wars), interwoven with processes of democratization, have been sufficient for invoking progressive taxation and other causally efficacious measures to reduce inequalities (Piketty 2014, 18-20, 41, 141, 287, 471, 498–500; Piketty's argument finds support in the history of modern taxation, Scheve and Stasavage 2016).

It is time to return to *The Anarchical Society*. Bull participated in the problematical functional differentiating between domains of security and political economy by focusing on diplomacy and statecraft and by ignoring political economy. The progressively ever more institutionalized division of labour between security studies and political economy makes it difficult, if not impossible, to give an adequate account of the causal powers, mechanisms, or processes that underlie world-historical trends and tendencies related to peace and war. The separation of politics from economics affects one's judgement about the potential for new crises, antagonisms, and conflicts. It also affects our normative judgements about future possibilities. The system of states in the capitalist world economy seems increasingly dysfunctional. It is widely acknowledged that political economy contradictions are best overcome by means of collective actions and institution-building. The process of institution-building has potential for transforming the very nature of world politics.

CONCLUSIONS

In the conclusions of *The Anarchical Society*, Bull states that the overall argument of his book 'is an implicit defence of the states system', and this

---

causing turmoil and counter-reactions. In most of the OECD world the Pikettyan 'law' seems to hold and inequalities have been rising gradually. In Russia in the 2000s, Putin's regime reversed the worst excesses of the 1990s and stabilized the socio-economic situation, in the context of solid economic growth benefiting also ordinary citizens. Now the Gini index in Russia is roughly on a par with those of the US, China, and Mexico. See n. 9 for a discussion on how this may have affected processes of securitization in Russia. In Ukraine, the Gini index has been lower, but the wealth concentration more extreme.

concerns especially the elements of international society, which should be preserved and strengthened (1977, 218). Going beyond mere 'Grotian' thinking and international society, Bull also expressed his commitment to critical cosmopolitanism:

> World order, or order within the great society of all mankind, is not only wider than international order or order among states, but also more fundamental and primordial than it, and morally prior to it. The system of states has constantly to be assessed in relation to the goal of world order. (1977, 319)

Normative and empirical claims are interwoven but not entirely inseparable. Despite being (usually) a critical cosmopolitan in moral terms, Bull also maintained that claims about the actual historical decline of the states system are unconvincing. This is not the end of Bull's story about the future of world politics, however. Bull stressed that 'such a conclusion stands in need of continual re-assessment' (1977, 319).

In this chapter I have provided reasons for a reassessment of Bull's main conclusion about our future possibilities. Bull not only underestimated the sway of globalization and the power of transnational organizations but, perhaps even more importantly, his classicist methodological orientation kept him away from explicating systematically those causal powers, mechanisms, and processes that generate events, episodes, and trends of world politics. Moreover, Bull took for granted the division of labour between security studies and political economy and thus underestimated the explosive potential of the states system within the capitalist world economy.

In the 2000s and 2010s, diplomatic discourse has, once again, gradually declined while a new geopolitical orientation has gained ground. Both nationalism and military expenditures have risen. The problem is that many social processes, also when they originate from contradictory rules, principles, and effects, are self-reinforcing. After a critical turning or tipping point, the dynamics of a self-reinforcing process, characterized by positive feedback to at least some actors, tends to support and institutionalize the original choice or choices. Dynamics triggered by particular events or processes at one point in time may reproduce themselves or accelerate, even in the absence of the recurrence of the original events or processes (Pierson 2004). If positive feedback loops dominate, as they tend to do in global political economy, the world may now be heading towards a global military catastrophe.

Both world history and critical-cosmopolitan normative judgements point towards overcoming the states system. Bull's international institutions have nothing to do with economic governance. Political economy contradictions are best resolved by means of collective actions and institution-building. We need adequate mechanisms for world economic policy and new, well-functioning elements of world-statehood.

The Bullian perspective makes it difficult to think about forms of agency and strategies that could lead to such fundamental transformations. What is more, institutions cannot be built without considering their legitimacy. Thus we have to go beyond Bull in engaging with world political theory, by opening up questions about global democracy—bearing in mind that democracy involves argumentation and debates over the meaning and substance of democratic self-determination itself.

16

International Society Encounters the Russian World

The Role of Representations in International Relations

Katarzyna Kaczmarska

INTRODUCTION

Over forty years ago, Hedley Bull posed a significant question: 'If the theories that are available are almost exclusively Western in origin and perspective, can they convey an adequate understanding of a world political system that is predominantly non-Western?' (1972b, 55). Nevertheless, rather than this query, it was the representation of the international realm Bull outlined in *The Anarchical Society* that has inspired and guided a significant part of IR study in Britain and beyond for decades following the volume's publication.

Ever since the idea of international society was proposed, scholars have been pondering the place of Russia in this representation of world politics. Russia, depending on historical circumstance, was seen either as a member of international society, as an apprentice undergoing a process of adjustment, or as an outright non-complier. What has tended to be neglected is that Russian scholars, too, have been producing interpretations of world politics. This chapter does not follow the well-established trend of looking at Russia through the international society perspective with the view to evaluating how well it fits the scheme. The 40th anniversary of the publication of Bull's book gives us an opportunity, rather, to rethink how the framework of international society has been employed and how it has worked as a representation of international politics.

Taking Bull's concept of international society as the point of departure, I show how specific representations of world affairs, despite their strongly voiced claims to universality, are always situated in a social and political setting. As products of social relations and historical contexts, these representations are perhaps more useful in understanding their authors and their origins, than they are for explaining the world political system. A closer look at Russia in that regard helps to de-familiarize Western practices of knowledge production and denaturalize representations which we have become accustomed to treating as self-evident. Their situatedness notwithstanding, some representations are capable of wielding significant power: first, as they are afforded the status of theory, they obtain the aura of objective knowledge; second, as they become taken for granted, they come to be regarded not as interpretations, but as really existing or as the accurate reflection of reality. In both instances they shape the discipline of IR, often contributing to closing it off from other perspectives and viewpoints.

Shedding light on the role of world representations is important, especially now that Russian scholars point to the lack of common methodological and ideological ground for the study of international politics, and also at a time when the Russian ruling elite places the country firmly outside of what it calls 'Western order'.

INTERNATIONAL SOCIETY AS *THE* REPRESENTATION OF INTERNATIONAL POLITICS

According to Bull, the states system, with an element of international society in it, covers the whole world. Bull regarded the Soviet Union, along with the US and China, as great powers in the international society of his time. This assessment was based on three criteria for great powerhood: status (meaning the acceptance of pre-eminence by other great powers and by international society at large), military strength, and special rights and duties recognized by others as well as that state's own leaders and peoples (1977, 200–2).

The Soviet Union posed a serious challenge to the concept of international society at the time of Bull's writing. As Bull himself openly admits, Soviet official rhetoric does not engage with the notion of international society. Rather, it 'subordinates these ideas to the conception of the Soviet state as the centre of global revolution and of an expanding Socialist Commonwealth destined to engulf the rest of international society' (1977, 204). This was certainly not a welcoming background against which to argue the case for international society. Rather than embracing the difficulty, Bull decided to brush it aside and disregard the rhetoric altogether. Claiming that practice trumps theory, Bull dismissed Moscow's proclamations and advocated a focus on practice instead. The Soviet Union behaves as a great power, claimed Bull, for it displays a sense of rights and duties mainly through its role in the United Nations, in arms-control negotiations, and its contribution 'to the settlement of political issues beyond its immediate national concern—in Europe, Asia and the Middle East' (1977, 205).

The way that Bull dealt with this obstacle continues to have a profound influence on the discipline of International Relations. Inadequate attention to the power of discourse prompted Bull, and many of his followers, to dismiss official statements as having insignificant bearing on actions undertaken in the international realm and little power in terms of the construction of international relations. Certainly there has been a mismatch between what Soviet authorities have claimed and what they have done. But a disregard for officially stated goals weakens the argument for international society. In the foreword to *The Anarchical Society*, Bull acknowledges that the concept was inspired, among others, by C.A.W. Manning's thinking. For Manning, the mutual understanding and consensus among statesmen was fundamental as it enabled states to play the 'game' of international social interactions (Manning 1962). It is difficult to voice claims about consensus, common interests, and order if the alleged participants of the game *talk* past each other. Bull's move constituted a departure from Manning's clear thesis that the society of states is notional, that it makes sense only as an idea shared by statesmen and guiding their decisions (Manning 1962, 190).

Bull's interpretation of Russia, which exaggerates the commonality of interests and the sharing of values between Russia and the West, has helped create a false impression that international society and its rules and institutions cover the whole world. In Bull's thinking, it was essential for states forming a society, that they accepted (to some degree, at least) common rules and institutions (1977, 233). Since the states system was presented as a 'universal political organisation' (1977, 233, 249) or 'universal political order' (1977, 248), it follows that international society is a feature of that universal political order. Bull admittedly emphasized that he was not interested in the totality of inter-state relations but just with those interactions which pertain to the society of states (1977, xi). Yet the way he used the term 'universal' throughout the book and his aim of providing an explanatory framework accounting for order in world politics, created the impression that he was describing the world at large.

Bull's approach was ambitious and comprehensive and he employed specific intellectual strategies and rhetorical devices in order to build a convincing case. In *The Anarchical Society*, he presented international politics through wide-angle lenses. The resulting representation has the appearance of being exhaustive; it looks like a complete picture. Even though Bull agreed with Martin Wight that there are three competing traditions of thought that could be employed to understand world politics, his discussion was most elaborate and persuasive with regard to what he called the 'Grotian' tradition of rationalism (1977, 38–9; see, however, Bain, Ch. 4 in this volume, with regard to this much-used label). Here, Bull argues forcefully and does not allow the consideration of counter-narratives to distort the overall argument. Towards the end of *The Anarchical Society*, and particularly in Chapters 10 and 13, Bull writes about the domination of Western powers and their culture (1977, 243), the 'subordination' to rich countries of most of the world's states as well as the great majority of the world's population (1977, 300) and the 'domination' by superpowers (1977, 307). Rather than taking all of these examples as potentially undermining his own definition of order and the goals that international society allegedly helped bring about, Bull situates the inequalities, dangers, and the 'lack of moral authority' of the states system in the future (1977, 310). To maintain consensus about common interests states must, *from now on*, take into account the demands of Asian, African, and Latin American countries (see Pasha, Ch. 6 in this volume). Finally, aiming to justify his interpretation of international politics, Bull employed evaluative nouns, such as *cooperation* or *consensus*, endowing the presumed-to-be existing international society with affirmative meaning.

With *The Anarchical Society* Bull provided a *specific* view of international politics but, despite the caveats present in his narrative, Bull's concept of international society was taken up as a useful starting point for the analysis of particular states, regions, and policies. *The Expansion of International Society* (1984), co-edited by Bull and Watson, relies heavily on his definition. It approaches international society as an account of international politics *as it actually is*, the history of which can be retraced. A specific world map has emerged as a result of these scholarly engagements with Bull's idea of international society. It reflects the assumption that the world's history and geography should be written in terms of their relation to Western Europe. This reinforced the perception of international society as covering the whole world and helped to 'naturalize' the idea of international society.

Today, Bull's volume is mostly remembered for providing a succinct definition of international society (see, for example, Dunne 1998b). *The Anarchical Society* thereby continues to encourage a specific mode of conceptualizing international politics.

RUSSIA AS VIEWED FROM THE PERSPECTIVE OF INTERNATIONAL SOCIETY

International society has been used in subsequent scholarship as a framework through which to assess Russia. It became the language in which to speak about Russia—even in Russia itself. For instance, Russia's leading commentator and scholar, Dmitri Trenin, in the opening words of his book published by the Moscow Carnegie Center, states bitterly that the hopes for Russia 'joining international society', still vivid after the fall of communism, had promptly dissipated (Trenin 2006, 1).

Authors associated with the classical English School took the view that Russia had become Westernized in the course of the eighteenth century and that this Westernization enabled Russia to join European international society (Watson 1984, 61).[1] Contrary to an argument put forward by several Russian and Western scholars (Tlostanova 2014; Malia 1999) that Western Europe never regarded the Russian empire as its equal, the English School placed Russia either inside its understanding of European borders or compared it on equal terms with other European powers. Hedley Bull reiterated this view: 'Like the maritime expansion of the Western European states, the expansion of Russia by land proceeded by the subjugation of indigenous communities and immigration and settlement by metropolitan peoples' (1984b, 218). Yet, this affirmative stance with regard to Russia's role in international society did not prevent Bull from asserting that Russia in Europe 'has always been perceived as semi-Asiatic in character... it was, until recently, a relatively backward and under-developed country, vulnerable to the Western great powers as Asian countries have been' (1984b, 218).

This line of thinking, which cast doubt on Russia's membership in international society, was followed by the English School writings in the post-Cold War period. Iver B. Neumann argued that the differences in Russia's governance, meaning its inability to meet Europe-wide standards, undermined Moscow's credentials to great powerhood and gave rise to doubts about Russia's status as a European and civilized state (Neumann 2007, 37–8). The break-up of the bipolar world and the emergence of a new state, the Russian Federation, however, triggered a wave of interpretations that stressed 'the return' of Russia to international society. Post-Cold War Russia was described variously as; integrating into the 'community of civilized states'; striving to 'adapt' to global Western-led institutions (Buzan 2004, 238); being involved in a 'quest' for international society and recognition as a great power (Aalto 2007, Neumann 2007); adopting to norms of international society (Sakwa 2011b, 959); or undergoing a 'slow and uneven process of adjustment towards the acceptance of common rules' (Averre 2008). The main question for scholars was to what extent Russia could be integrated into Western-led international society and how quickly and easily it could adjust, signifying Western expectations of Russia's adaptive role (Browning 2008).

From within this perspective, the more assertive stance on the international scene espoused by Russia since the early 2000s was interpreted as Moscow's preference for the pluralist vision of international society (Aalto 2007, 199–201). Pluralism, with its stress on institutions of sovereignty,

---

[1] The classical English School is usually associated with the members of the British Committee on the Theory of International Politics. There are, however, differences with regard to specific authors, e.g. Tim Dunne (1998b) considers E.H. Carr—though not a Committee member—as one of the English School's founding fathers.

non-intervention, and great power management, was deemed well suited as a description of Russia's redefined role on the global stage. Moscow was seen as a fierce opponent to any broadening of the rights of international society to interfere in domestic politics, including by way of humanitarian intervention. Nonetheless, its place in international society was not questioned. Russia continued to be seen as partaking of the 'thin' version of this society (Sakwa 2011a, 197).

By the late 2010s, however, Russia came to be characterized as a challenger to the interests and ideas of liberal-democratic states. It has been suggested that Russia has never been a fully-fledged member and remains 'suspended somewhere in the outer tier of international society' (Neumann 2011). Russia's own interpretation of international relations remained largely unaccounted for by this strand of literature which focused instead on providing its own narrative of events, guided by the master concept of international society.

RUSSIA AND THE PROBLEM OF REPRESENTING WORLD POLITICS

Undoubtedly, Russian IR scholarship has often adapted Western theoretical approaches, slightly adjusting them to Russian 'circumstances' (Achkasov and Gutorov 2008; Tsygankov 2008). For example, it is not uncommon to see Martin Wight's three traditions of interpreting international politics (realist, rationalist, and revolutionist) employed to account for Russian post-Soviet politics (Sergounin 2000; Morozova 2009). But significant scholarly effort has been invested in constructing unique representations of the international, rather than applying IR theories stemming from the English-speaking world. Andrei P. Tsygankov, who defines IR theory as a system of analytical and culturally embedded representations of the world and the state (2013, 11), groups Russian IR scholars into three categories. Westernizers (*zapadniki*) see the world as a Western universal project based on Western liberal values. State-centrists (*derzhavniki*) interpret it in terms of states' struggle for power, whereas the advocates of a Third Rome concept (*tretyerimtsy*) see international politics as defined by competition for values and cultural influence (Tsygankov 2013, 15–17).

Without necessarily following Tsygankov's classification, here I wish to draw attention to interpretations which pose a direct challenge to Bull's 'international society' vision. The Russian IR discipline has drawn extensively from geopolitics in order to account for developments taking place between Russia and the West or to explain Russia's place in international politics (Timermanis 2015). The post-Soviet space, for instance, has been presented as an object of 'geopolitical bargaining' between Western states and Russia (Vasilenko 2014, 318–19). But some authors have gone beyond geopolitical concerns with territorial power and engaged to a greater extent with the problem of norms and values. A 2014 textbook issued under the auspices of the Moscow State Institute of International Relations, the leading IR academic institution in Russia and the training centre for state diplomatic cadres, argues that the international realm is guided by 'ad hoc' norms elaborated by the West, rather than by a set of commonly agreed international norms. The ultimate goal of the application of such ad hoc norms is the preservation of unipolarity under the primacy of the United States. The world is unable to agree on main security challenges. Ideological approaches of particular states trump any possibility to articulate a common view (Shakleina and Baikov 2014, 76–7).

More recently the many strands of the idea of the Russian World (*Russkii mir*) have galvanized into a coherent representation of international politics. This idea, rising to prominence in policy discourse during Vladimir Putin's third term (beginning in 2012) and accompanying the conservative turn in Russia's foreign policy, has had multiple links to the academic world. The concept of the Russian World figured in political writings since 1997 (Ostrovsky and Shchedrovitskiy 1997). Since early on in the twenty-first century institutional structures supporting and developing the idea emerged and the concept started to be taught at universities in 2011 (Omarova 2011). Though it may seem novel, the notion has important precedents dating back to the Tsarist and Soviet eras. Notions contributing to the idea of the Russian World, such as 'the Eurasian great power' or 'Russian civilization', have long been present but never dominated Russian discourse (Pavlova and Romanova 2014).

Several features of the Russian World as the representation of the international realm can be distinguished. It implicitly divides the international realm into a broad Russia-centred polity and the remaining world, where the West plays a particular role. Contrary to the purported inclusiveness of the idea of international society, *Russkii mir* ostensibly divides the international realm between 'us' and 'them'.[2] 'Us', however, does not necessarily mean the Russian Federation. The idea of the Russian World transcends the borders of the Russian state in two somewhat contradictory ways. Firstly, it is based on the perception of the Russian nation scattered across the post-Soviet space following the dissolution of the Soviet Union. Secondly, it is the belief in Russia as a distinct civilization that cannot be limited to the borders of the

---

[2] A similar attempt at dividing the world between 'us' and 'them' was undertaken by European elites in the nineteenth century, who regarded themselves as civilized, while classifying non-European political entities as 'uncivilized' and therefore best subordinated. See Linklater, Ch. 17 in this volume.

Russian state. *Russkii mir* is composed of concentric circles where ethnic and orthodox Russians reside at the heart and are surrounded by linguistic and/or historical-territorial identification with Russianness (Naumkin 2014).

The discussion of the Russian World is interwoven with the claim for the existence of a unique Russian civilization.[3] In this context it is usually said to encompass Russian culture, nation, language, and the Russian Orthodox Church (Fomenko 2009; Guseinov, Kara-Murza, et al. 2011; Omarova 2011; Aseev, Kants, et al. 2014). Irina Vasilenko refers to civilizational identity—understood as shared cultural code and norms—as the key integrating factor (Vasilenko 2014, 21–3). Ivan Ivanov argues that the Russian civilizational code embraces 'the primacy of the moral principle, priority of spiritual values over material ones, rejection of inequality and injustice, community of being, commitment to one's duty, patriotism, dedication to the ideal' (Ivanov 2012, 21).

The Russian World concept feeds on several currents in Russian political thought which stress Russia's distinctive *nature* and incompatibility with the West.[4] It is nourished by a specific understanding of authority, under which a leader unconstrained by rules (*samoderzhaviye*) has a moral obligation to act in the interest of *his/her* people (Tsygankov 2013, 19–37). The idea also draws on the conviction of Russia's moral superiority and that Russia constitutes a world of its own (Fomenko 2009, 153, 159–60). *Russkii mir* transcends the traditional understanding of a sovereign state. According to some interpretations, the state and the Russian civilization become one (Naumkin 2014).

The reading of the international in terms of the Russian World became particularly pertinent during Russia's conflict with Ukraine. Since the crisis, the interpretation of the international realm in confrontational terms has gained momentum. Confrontation with the US, or the West more broadly, became the defining feature of the international realm. This confrontation includes the objection to the imposition of the West's cultural code under the guise of 'universal values' (Kosachev 2012). Losing this conflict would inevitably mean Russia losing its position as a 'pole' in international politics. Competition in the international realm is regarded as transcending state borders. Both the Orange revolution in Ukraine in 2004 and the Euromaidan revolution in 2014 were interpreted in Russia as instances of a global competition for spheres of influence (Efremenko 2014). Russian discourse repeatedly accuses the West of shamelessly creating the impression that the period of 'spheres of influence' ended, while *de facto* continuing to broaden its own sphere of interest and denying this right to other powers, including Russia (Karaganov 2014).

---

[3] On the question of what constitutes Russia's civilizational identity, see e.g. Zagladin (2004) and Zhade (2014).

[4] These cannot be easily subsumed under a conservative label for it would suggest that the meanings ascribed to conservatism in Russian and Western political thought converge. For a much broader recent discussion of this issue, see Chebankova (2016).

ON THE ORIGINS OF REPRESENTATIONS

Knowledge of society is structured by the confines of social worlds contributing to its creation (Bourdieu 2004, 113), which is why any book or piece of research must be considered in its own context. Bull's *The Anarchical Society*, as the author states in the *Acknowledgements* section, takes stock of discussions among members of the British Committee on the Theory of International Politics. These debates thrived at a time when the British World was still a part of the popular perception and the Empire featured heavily in British culture (Nicholas 2003).[5] Self-confidence in the Western civilization was strongly present in the British Committee and among some of its key members, which paved the way for drawing largely on the Western European experience. The Committee exploited the idealized narrative of Western European history, its particular and contingent development, and its specific power formations.

In Russia, as in the West, a representation of international politics is a product of social relations unfolding in a particular historical context. This section explores some of the elements affecting Russian worldviews and contributing to the construction of idiosyncratic narratives of international relations: firstly, the interpretation of historical experience and geography; secondly, Russian political thought and questions important for the construction of Russian identity; and finally, approaches to and objectives of studying international politics, which continue to be influenced by the heritage of the Soviet IR scholarship. Although interrelated, these elements can also differ fundamentally in terms of their approach to knowledge, i.e. the possibilities, limitations, and sources of knowing. While the strand discussing Russian identity allows for a more reflexive approach to knowledge, IR scholarship, particularly the strand following the Soviet School, aims at scientific accuracy and claims to be revealing truth.

Historical narratives are crucial for the production of specific contemporary representations of the international realm. The historical development of Russia and the West, though connected in many ways, cannot be claimed to have followed the same trajectory. The experience of certain historical events, as well as narratives developed to explain them, differ starkly between Russia and the West. There are also differences in the approach to historical knowledge. In Russia, history remains the privileged source of truth which speaks not only to the past but also to the present. The elevated status of historical knowledge coexists with an emotional attachment to historical events developed among the general public. As Sergei Oushakine put it, Russians 'create

---

[5] The trans-oceanic British World is a concept I borrow from Bridge and Fedorowich (2003: 11).

some sort of an emotional relation with the past' and live in the past instead of learning from it (Oushakine 2015).

One of the most striking contemporary examples of disjuncture in the interpretation of historical events is the dissolution of the Soviet Union, which left a legacy of resentment in Russia and a sense of triumph in the West. For Russians, the fall of the Soviet Union was hard to accept: 'what seemed impossible became a reality. The USSR fell apart... few people realized how truly dramatic those events and their consequences would be' (Oushakine 2015). Russian academic textbooks refer to the fall of the Soviet Union in terms of an event that drastically altered the geopolitical situation 'on the planet Earth' (*na planete v tselom*) (Timermanis 2015, 650). This attitude is broadly shared by the Russian elite, which considered the dissolution of the Soviet Union as disastrous and inexplicable (Borko 1997, 205). Vladimir Putin famously called it 'the greatest geopolitical catastrophe of the century' and an 'outrageous historical injustice' (Putin 2005; Putin 2014).

The distinct interpretation of history is supplemented by differences in Western and Russian geographical depictions of the world. Geography, rather than being a product of scientific reasoning, is very much subject to interpretation. Terms such as 'Asia' or the 'East' become described or mapped onto the world in specific ways depending on who does the mapping. In addition, seemingly purely geographical (and therefore presented as 'scientific') denominations, such as the East and the West of Europe, usually acquire symbolic meaning in the course of their employment. While in Western European cultural depictions, the East can receive negative connotations, in the Russian culture, the East tends to acquire a positive meaning. The former Soviet republics of Central Asia, in turn, tend to be depicted in Russia not as parts of Asia but as components of the post-Soviet space (*post-sovetskoye prostranstvo*) or Eurasia (Lo 2014, 78). Particularly in the 1990s, these states tended to be described with a politically loaded term of 'the near abroad' (*blizhnee zarhubezhe*). The term did not fall into a complete disuse and returned in the official names accorded to associations gathering Russian compatriots.[6] Russian discourse stretches the conception of Europe extending it 'from Lisbon to Vladivostok' (Menkiszak 2013). The malleability of geography is perhaps best illustrated with the positioning of Ukraine, which is depicted as occupying the post-Soviet area, or as part of Russia, as a key component of Eurasia, or as belonging to the 'broader European space'. Especially following the Euromaidan Revolution there has been an upsurge in specific geographical depictions of Ukraine. Yevgenii Satanovskii, the president of the Middle East Institute of the Russian Academy of Sciences, wrote in 2014 that Ukraine has

---

[6] For instance in June 2015 Rossotrudnichestvo, Russian federal government agency for the Commonwealth of Independent States, compatriots, and humanitarian cooperation, reported on a IV Regional Conference of Russian Compatriots of the Near Abroad Countries.

always been part of the Russian World. Ukraine's very name is to denote to its location at the edge of the Russian World (*'okraina bolshogo russkogo mira'*) (Satanovskii 2014, 443).

A particular understanding of Russia's national identity contributes to the portrayals of international relations. It is related to the way Russia constructs its international status and how it reads other states' perceptions of this status. Russian academic and policy discourse of the 1990s took Russia's great power status for granted, with only a few voices of dissent (Baev 1997, 185).[7] In political discourse, great-powerness was presented as an almost natural feature, a quality of Russia's character. Following the dissolution of the USSR, neither all democrats nor all nationalists accepted that some Soviet republics were no longer part of Russia, unwilling to come to terms with the break-up of empire. The loss of the international superpower status was experienced as a national humiliation (Light 1996, 36–7).

In addition to historical and geographical interpretations and the identity debate, what continues to have a bearing on the production of specific representations of the international is the heritage of Soviet International Relations scholarship. The emergence, or at least the significant appraisal, of the discipline of IR in Russia is usually located in the post-Stalinist period. In Soviet times policy practice was statutorily motivated by Marxist-Leninist ideology (Lynch 1987). Theory employed elements of Marxist doctrine or stood as an outright synonym to Marxist ideology. It was repeatedly expounded but with little precision and much of it was left vague. Importantly, theory and practice were considered interdependent. Practice could not exist without theory, due to the latter's purported 'organising, mobilising and transforming' function (Light 1988, 1, 4).[8] Soviet policy was deemed scientific because it was guided by Marxist-Leninist ideology based on objective laws of social development and revealing the objective truth (Light 1988, 8). Soviet theory enabled, so it was believed, Soviet decision-makers to anticipate the direction and the outcome of international affairs. Policy, in turn, was to have a feedback effect on theory (Light 1988, 316). The claim of a close relation between theory and practice was not, however, substantiated by any exposition of the connection between particular foreign policy action and relevant theoretical grounds for it.

It was not only in the Soviet times that disciplinary developments and the policy world impacted on IR knowledge claims. There have been important parallels between the official narrative of Russia's place in the world and the

---

[7] The 1990s discourse was also pervaded by the perception of defeat and humiliation, hence the objective for Russia to 'get off its knees' and regain the great power status became principal goals of Russian foreign policy under Vladimir Putin (Jonson 2004, 135–6).

[8] See also Zimmerman on how Marxism assumed the revolutionary unity of theory and practice (Zimmerman 1969).

trajectory of International Relations as a discipline in Russia. The Russian policymaking elite has been vocal about its exasperation at performing in the role of a student on the supposed trajectory towards a liberal democratic system (Putin 2007). Similar voices in Russian social sciences have been expressing disappointment with the process of domesticating Anglo-Saxon theoretical approaches (Fenenko 2016). Frustration with being outside of the English-language mainstream and the rejection of the role of pupil result in a greater push for the development of national interpretations and national methodologies. This process has its roots in the perceived bias in Western scholarship against Russia, the strong conviction of Russia's special circumstances requiring different approaches than those pursued in the West, and the observed non-engagement with Russian rhetoric on the part of the majority of Western scholarship.

Alexei Fenenko captures key grievances permeating Russian International Relations scholarship. Pointing to a dissociation of Anglo-American and Russian paradigms of thinking about international relations, he attributes it to the fact that the first camp largely shares the 'liberal faith', whereas Russians as well as Chinese do not share the liberal worldview (2016, 176). Fenenko explains that American IR is suffused with ideology, meaning that it relies on a list of axioms that one simply believes in rather than engages critically with. One such axiom is that the US is, by right, legitimate to act for the strengthening of liberal international order. Fenenko goes on to suggest that there are no grounds for engagement between an American professor and someone who does not consider liberal democracy to be a progressive political system, who would like to see the US defeated in a military conflict (2016, 174), and who considers the annexation of a territory a 'normal instrument' of international relations (2016, 175). This discussion is based on a superficial engagement with American IR but an important, if disturbing, voice looms behind it. Fenenko suggests that at least some of Russian IR scholars oppose the American worldview and the world map which is constructed as a result. Fenenko points to the great mismatch between Russian and American world maps as well as the disjuncture in how the future of world order is imagined in Russia and the US (2016, 178–9). His contribution, an example of growing unease with ideas circulating in academia outside Russia, is also a plea for renationalization of IR knowledge.

The need to produce *national* knowledge about international politics has recently grown stronger in Russia, where the ruling elite intends to show that value competition is taking place globally,[9] that the Western normative agenda is not universal, and that soft power can be effective *due to* it being

---

[9] Already the 2013 Russian Foreign Policy Concept stated that 'global competition for the first time... translates into the competition of different value orientations and models of development' (MFA RF 2013).

underpinned by conservative rather than liberal values. The Russian elite has been increasingly vocal about its dissatisfaction with the West's claim to authority in international politics (Bordachev 2014). In 2007 in Munich Putin declared he would not 'play the game' if the rules were established without Russia (Putin 2007). Russia, believing itself to occupy a 'unique place in the political scheme of the world, history and development of civilization', refused to be the 'object of civilizing influences on part the of other states' and required to be treated as an equal among equals (Deputy Foreign Minister Vladimir Chizhov, quoted in Allison 2006, 166). The drive for equality has been mixed with the feeling of superiority over the West and the perception of Russia's 'historic mission' as separate from the West (Clunan 2009, 111–13). Following the global economic crisis of 2008, key documents started describing international relations in terms of rivalry among power centres (MFA RF 2013, points 28, 29).

ROLES PERFORMED BY REPRESENTATIONS OF THE INTERNATIONAL

The implication of my argument is that the Western academia must stop thinking of the Russian view of the world as reflective of Russia's history, ideology, and culture, *while at the same time neglecting to reflect* on the historical, ideological, and cultural situatedness of Western thinking about IR, which finds one clear statement in Bull's idea of international society. Rather than ignoring or dismissing representations such as the Russian World as politically inspired, we need to take them seriously. By this I mean that in addition to paying greater attention to specific social and historical contexts from which diverging interpretations of world politics arise, it is vital to analyse their roles and impact, the way they shape the discipline of IR, and how they interact with the policymaking world. It is with these concerns in mind that I would like to offer suggestions concerning both international society and the Russian World.

The first is that both representations arguably contribute to, and facilitate building, national schools of IR. If not the 'international society' perspective on its own, then certainly the English School more broadly, tends to be linked with British IR. Some are even willing to bestow the name of a 'brand' on the English School for the role it has been playing in establishing the 'independence of British IR from the otherwise dominant American profession' (Brown 2009, 221; Brown 2011, 309).[10] A national demarcation of a discipline based

---

[10] On the contested theme of British IR, see also Dunne (1998a).

on a specific viewing of the world is problematic in several important ways. A *national* representation of the *international* may contribute to the construction of a relatively powerful discourse, one which will foreclose other avenues through which to interpret world politics. Thinkers imprisoned within their own perspective and insensitive to the situatedness and subjectivity of their own viewpoint are prone to disregard other perspectives from which to perceive—and construct—the world. A national school producing knowledge on international relations may exploit feelings of national pride and foster uncritical pretensions to objectivity. The development of national perspectives challenges IR as a field open for productive engagement and mutual comprehension by sharing concepts, questions, and concerns.

Secondly, posing as a neutral, abstract, and/or logical systematization, as pragmatic and functional, or as a description read out of practice, a representation provides a way for masking ideology, which unavoidably accompanies its production. Bull states at the outset of his book that his study was not value-free. However, he does not spell out how he deals with his value-laden premises. We only know that 'it is important in an academic inquiry into politics not to exclude them' (Bull 1977, xv). The employment, explicit or otherwise, of specific values transgresses the East–West split. If we are to recognize that choice, rather than objectivity, is driving the questions we ask and the elements that we emphasize when we provide answers, it will be necessary to engage with, rather than dismiss, the fact that knowledge production is embedded in value preferences. Such choices are motivated by value commitments (Suganami 2008, 334) and the idea of international society has enjoyed high currency due to the fact that it accommodates the socio-culturally underpinned estimation of harmony, order, and integration. Liberal values play an important role in the way the idea of international society has been constructed and has asserted itself in IR. Bull's liberal ideology impacted on the way he interpreted the world, which manifests itself in his definition of goals common to all societies: of limiting violence, the honouring of agreements, and the stability of possession (Bull 1977, 4–5). These 'goals of social life' are, to him, those of individual human beings, which illustrates most vividly his emphasis on individualism. Bull's liberalism is also present in the value he attaches to order as well as in his objection to world government. The latter he considered highly unlikely. However, had a 'universal monarchy', as Bull calls it, to be established, it would be based on the ascendancy of a single nation or race, and therefore most possibly tyrannical (Bull 1977, 254). Bull's endorsement of the values of 'life, truth, and property' as universal differs starkly from the values upon which the conception of the Russian World has been built. These are, above all, the respect for hierarchy, state-authority, and the superior value of the interests of the group over those of the individual.

Thirdly, a representation of international politics is a powerful identity-building and policy-legitimizing tool. In a recent intervention, Richard Ned

Lebow suggested that IR theories can be read as discourses, contributing to identity construction, even if this function remains their unacknowledged goal (2016). The interpretation of world politics in terms of an orderly society, put forward by Bull in *The Anarchical Society*, was in conformity with the interests of states-architects of the post-Second World War and post-decolonization international institutions. It expressed the dominant thinking shared by those living in a specific era and a particular location. The Russian World, in turn, allows for some conclusions to be drawn in the debate on Russia's identity. It reinforces Russia's self-image as a distinct civilization. In current-day Russia, a representation of the international has become an issue beyond scholarly concern. The very fact of being able to define what the international is and which values should underpin it is now approached as yet another credential of a great power. In addition, an academically sanctioned way of speaking about international politics may be used by the ruling elite for political gains, i.e. for domestic and international legitimization of specific policies and actions. In that respect, the idea of the Russian World has helped justify Russia's intervention in Ukraine, which, rather than an independent state, has been portrayed as part of a greater civilizational whole.

CONCLUSION

Several elements and processes spur the need for constructing idiosyncratic narratives of international relations. In this chapter I approached Hedley Bull's concept of international society as one such representation of the international realm. International society has been particularly influential as it came to be taken for granted by some as the legitimate representation of world politics. For Bull and for many other IR scholars, international society has worked as a framework through which to view and assess Russia. I pointed to several limitations in Bull's approach to Russia, primarily his tendency to dismiss Soviet views on international politics.

Indeed, I argued to the contrary that views and representations of the international constructed in Russia should be engaged with rather than disregarded as mere rhetoric. The study of Russian conceptions of international politics alerts us to the need to think reflexively about the situatedness of Bull's own approach and the specific values that it embodies and projects on to the world. It also sheds light on key concerns and grievances animating the knowledge production process in IR.

Apart from contemporary political differences between Russia and the West, several long-term trends have been affecting Russia's worldview and contributing to the construction of idiosyncratic narratives of international relations. These include: the interpretation of historical experience and geography; the conundrums of national identity debates; Russian political thought; and the heritage of the Soviet IR scholarship which impacts approaches to, and objectives of, studying international politics. IR analysis in Russia, driven by a specific intellectual and political culture, is far from uniform but the strand concerned with the Russian World presents Russia's role in, and the nature of, international politics in a light that diverges starkly from the idea of international society. This suggests a pressing need for qualifying the idea that the world as a whole now takes on the attribute of 'international society' associated with *The Anarchical Society*.

Some representations are powerful enough to inspire an entire school of thought. The drawback is that they become accepted as not only legitimate but self-evident. Contrary to Bull's own intentions, for whom international society has not been self-evident, the way the subsequent literature dealt with the concept made it into a neutral descriptor, which took on the aura of self-evidence. As a consequence, scholarly attention to other viewpoints has been muted. This chapter pointed to the roles different representations of the international play in facilitating the creation of national schools of IR, how they make it easier to present knowledge as sanitized of ideology, and how they work as a potential legitimizing tool for policymakers. Bull's *The Anarchical Society*—and particularly the opportunity to revisit it forty years after—is the best reminder of how tentative what we claim to be knowledge is.

17

The International Society of 'Civilized States'

Andrew Linklater

The relationship between culture, civilization, and international society has long been central to the English School perspective on world politics (Wight 1977, 21–45). Members of the School have shown that from the latter part of the eighteenth century, the constituent political units of European international society identified with a common civilization that was sharply contrasted with the 'savage' or 'barbarian' non-European world. They have discussed in detail how a society of sovereign states that was exclusively European was enlarged during the twentieth century to include 'social inferiors' in colonized and semi-colonized regions (Bull and Watson 1984). In various writings, Bull argued that the traditional cultural underpinnings of the modern society of states had been eroded in the course of its global expansion. He posed the important question of whether a new cosmopolitan culture is emerging that can unite different societies in the quest to maintain international order and promote global justice.

In *The Anarchical Society*, Bull extended Wight's reflections on culture, civilization, and international society by introducing a novel distinction between a 'diplomatic culture' and an 'international political culture' (the 'two cultures' as they will be described below). The former consisted of the 'common stock of ideas and values possessed by the official representatives of states', and the latter of the 'intellectual and moral culture that determines the attitudes towards the states system of the societies that compose it' (Bull 1977, 316–17). Bull argued that a powerful international political culture had underpinned the diplomatic culture of the nineteenth-century society of states. With the expansion of that society, the argument was, shared commitments to the international political culture were weakened. The diplomatic culture therefore lost much of its earlier foundation in the normative commitments that had united the constituent units of European international society. Bull maintained that it is entirely possible that a cosmopolitan culture will appear that strengthens diplomatic endeavours to preserve international order. But its contribution would be severely limited, he added, if it simply expressed dominant Western values and reminded non-Western peoples of the colonial era.

There has been too little discussion of the brief sections of *The Anarchical Society* that considered the relationship between the international political culture and the diplomatic culture.[1] This essay contains preliminary observations about how the analysis can be taken further. It does so by drawing on Norbert Elias's sociological exploration of the relationship between European state formation and elite convictions in the last quarter of the late eighteenth century that Europe was the supreme civilization that other societies should emulate (Elias 2012 [1939]). Central to that inquiry was the focus on the role that absolutist court societies played in the 'civilization' of manners that bound aristocratic elites together in 'supranational' court arrangements. In Bull's terms, ruling class conceptions of civilized manners were fundamental to the international political culture of the era. They were interwoven with specific images of legitimate statehood and presumed rights of colonial expansion that suffused the European diplomatic culture. In the nineteenth century, non-European governments in China, Japan, and the Ottoman Empire confronted the immense challenge of understanding and complying with European images of civilized existence in their quest for admission to the international society of states. They were engaged in attuning themselves to the European diplomatic culture and the international political culture with which it was inextricably interconnected.

This chapter argues that the globalization of core features of the European 'civilizing process' occurred as a result of the combined effect of 'top-down pressures' to conform to the 'two cultures' and 'bottom-up' efforts by non-European elites to shed feelings of inferiority by imitating the practices of the great power establishment. Bull argued that a gradual convergence of different value-systems that was especially evident in the late nineteenth century came to a halt with the 'cultural revolt against the West' in which post-colonial regimes struggled to emancipate themselves from Western cultural hegemony. But general support for the core institutions of international society and for the diplomatic culture survived 'Third World' initiatives to end colonial 'civilizing missions' that expressed the global dominance of the Western international political culture. The question posed by Bull was whether the

---

[1] In a useful summary of Bull's position, John Vincent emphasized Bull's distinction 'between a diplomatic culture uniting the official representatives of States, and an international political culture reaching out into the societies making up the States-system, a mass culture as opposed to an elite one on whose successful cosmopolitanization the future of international society might be said to depend' (1980, 254). Vincent's position on universal human rights recognized the importance of the two cultures for Bull's analysis of the current challenges faced by the first universal society of states.

centrifugal forces that had weakened the 'intellectual and moral culture that determines the attitudes towards the states-system' were increasingly checked by shared cosmopolitan orientations (1977, 316). As many discussions of culture and civilization have shown, the issue remains central to understanding contemporary world politics.

To explore those issues in more detail, this chapter summarizes Bull's perspective on the relationship between civilization and international society. It considers the dominance of the European 'standard of civilization' in the nineteenth century, the concomitant globalization of the European 'civilizing process', and core features of the 'cultural revolt' against the West. The chapter ends by sketching recent standpoints on world politics that have particular importance for understanding the evolving relationship between the international political culture and the diplomatic culture. The thesis is that Bull's analysis of the cultural dimensions of international society provides valuable resources for understanding the ever-changing balance of power between the elements of cultural convergence and countervailing forces of cultural divergence in the first universal society of states.

ORDER, CIVILIZATION, AND INTERNATIONAL SOCIETY

In the opening chapter of *The Anarchical Society*, Bull restated Wight's argument about a 'common feature' of the 'historical international societies', namely that each had been 'founded upon a common culture or civilisation', or on 'some of the elements of such a civilisation' that underpinned 'common interests' in addition to 'common rules and institutions' (Bull 1977, 16). Every one of those societies of states had been shaped by shared cultural phenomena such as 'a common language, a common epistemology and understanding of the universe, a common religion, a common ethical code, a common aesthetic or artistic tradition' (ibid.). Significant points of unity between 'civilized' states helped to 'validate or authenticate the rules of international society' and to strengthen diplomatic efforts to preserve order and stability (Bull 1977, 64). Moreover, as Wight had argued, a sense of 'cultural differentiation from what lay outside'—from the world consisting of 'barbarians'—had reinforced the sense of belonging to an exclusive society of states. A deeply-held conviction was that the 'code of conduct' that governed relations between 'civilized' states 'did not apply...in their dealings' with 'lesser societies' (Bull 1977, 33–4). Restraints on force could be relaxed, it was presumed, in colonial struggles with 'savages' who did not themselves observe the 'civilized' laws of war.

Throughout the history of the modern society of states, members of the English School have observed, support for foreign policy restraints crumbled when 'civilized' states were embroiled in violent conflict but, in the main, they did not abandon commitments to the basic institutions of international society such as diplomacy and international law. Willingness to keep faith with the relevant practices was stronger when the diplomatic culture did not rest only on utilitarian calculations about overlapping interests but was reinforced by attachments to a deeper international political culture (Bull 1977, 316–17). To extend the argument, it is useful to examine more closely the relationship between international society and European conceptions of civilization that have been the subject of major sociological investigations (Elias 2012 [1939]). Of particular value in understanding the link are historical studies of the eighteenth-century diplomatic community which have shown that its 'aristocratic-courtly and cosmopolitan' ethos reflected the manners and rituals that were most highly developed in French absolutist court society (Scott 2007; Elias 2012 [1939]). The rules that were intrinsic to the 'diplomatic culture' were linked with the international political culture that bound the ruling aristocratic elites together in a 'supranational court society' (Elias 2010, 4–5).

The point can be illustrated by recalling Heeren's classic definition of a states system as a 'union of several contiguous states, resembling each other in their manners, religion, and degree of social improvement, and cemented together by reciprocity of interests' (Heeren 1834, vii–viii). The decision to include manners in the list of defining features is worth noting since their refinement was central to the whole European 'civilizing process' (Elias 2012 [1939]). That 'process of civilization' was fundamental to the 'aristocratic-courtly and cosmopolitan' culture that was noted earlier. It shaped the international political culture that embraced different court societies. As the following discussion shows, the 'civilized manners' of absolutist court societies were also central to the diplomatic community. One consequence was that non-European governments that hoped to become members of the society of states had to demonstrate their ability to comply with the 'civilized' standards of 'social superiors'. The investigation of the European 'civilizing process' therefore sheds important light on the globalization of specific social ideals in the age of empire when the diplomatic culture was connected with the international political culture in that distinctive way.

The eighteenth-century 'aristocratic-courtly' culture reveals how the society of states did not rest simply on utilitarian calculations about the value of inter-state order—on the 'reciprocity of interests'—but on a deeper substratum of elite affinities and shared values. The global order lost the unifying role of 'a common culture or civilization' with the 'expansion of international society' but, as noted above, support for European principles of international relations did not melt away (Bull 1977, 16–17). Foreshadowing recent studies of the interrelations between international society and world society (Buzan 2004; Clark 2007), Bull asked whether a 'cosmopolitan culture' of modernity could emerge that replicates the role that the older European solidarities played in supporting commitments to inter-state order. He observed that 'the future of international society is likely to be determined' by the extent to which a cosmopolitan culture appears that embraces 'both common ideas and common values, and [is] rooted in societies in general as well as in their elites'; such a development, he maintained, could 'provide the world international society of today with the kind of underpinning enjoyed by the geographically smaller and culturally more homogeneous international societies of the past' (1977, 317).

Exhibiting his characteristic scepticism, Bull added that there was little reason to believe that a cosmopolitan culture is 'likely to become dominant around the world, engulfing cultural particularisms'; moreover, one had to ask if it was 'desirable that such a development should take place' (1977, 317). The fear was that such a culture would be the property of affluent ruling elites that profited most from globalization and would seem alien to mass populations who were struck by its blanket indifference to their basic requirements. The evidence was that the fundamentals of a global culture—the 'intellectual culture of modernity'—revolved around some shared scientific and technological orientations but not on a deeper 'common moral culture or set of common values'; its principal features were biased towards Western interests and preferences, and its 'roots' were unsurprisingly 'shallow in many societies' (1977, 317).

Bull proceeded to argue, without developing the point, that weaving 'non-Western ideas' into the constitution of international society would go some way towards addressing the problem of legitimacy that stood in the way of a cosmopolitan culture of modernity given the 'cultural revolt against the West' (Bull and Watson 1984, 217–28). The key issues were addressed directly in Vincent's later study of human rights which discussed the feasibility of a global moral and political consensus on the urgent need to eradicate starvation. Especially notable given the argument of this chapter was Vincent's contention that international society could be strengthened by collective action to protect human rights that were, for many, the hallmarks of a civilized form of life (Vincent 1986, 138). Whether such transformations are possible has been a central issue in recent analyses of world politics especially since the publication of Huntington's influential polemic on the 'clash of civilizations' (1993). The 'religious revolt' against secular modernity—an extension of the earlier 'cultural revolt against the West' that Bull examined—suggests that cultural differences are widening after several centuries in which the globalization of European 'civilized' values took place. To understand the relationship between cultural convergence and divergence in contemporary world politics, it is useful to discuss the nineteenth-century European 'standard of civilization' which was used to assess the 'progress' of non-European peoples in complying with 'civilized manners' and 'civilized' conceptions of statehood.

THE GLOBAL DOMINANCE OF THE EUROPEAN 'STANDARD OF CIVILIZATION'

In their study of the expansion of international society, Bull and Watson (1984) maintained that each of the regional international systems that existed prior to the waves of European colonial expansion had its own 'standard of civilization'. Each had a clear conception of what distinguished 'civilized' peoples from 'barbarians'. Each possessed its distinctive account of how to conduct relations with 'inferiors', and each had its established position on the rituals that 'social subordinates' were expected to observe assiduously in the presence of 'superiors'.

A parallel investigation added that the 'confrontation' between peoples that took place as Europeans expanded into non-European regions was primarily 'a confrontation of civilizations' and 'standards of civilization' that 'regulated their international relations' (Gong 1984, 3). As Bull stated, the 'standard of civilisation' (1977, 34), which was a central element in European international legal thinking in the latter part of the nineteenth century, was used to defend Europe's presumed right to stand in judgement of other peoples, to colonize or in other ways control them, and to refashion their social and political institutions in accordance with 'civilized' self-images (Gong 1984). Especially significant was the conviction that the modern sovereign state was the crucible of 'civilized' existence.

On that premise, only European states could belong to the society of states which was, in the words of one late nineteenth-century legal treatise, a 'product of the special civilization of modern Europe' that could not easily be 'understood...by countries differently civilized' (Hall 1880, 34). The international lawyer, Oppenheim, advanced a similar claim when he argued that international law is 'the body of rules which civilised states' regard as 'legally binding' in their relations with each other (1955, 117). To be admitted into international society, a state had to demonstrate that it was sufficiently 'civilized' to be trusted to observe its defining legal conventions. States such as Imperial China were placed in the middle rank of a presumed hierarchy of peoples that consisted, in the words of the international lawyer, James Lorimer (1883, vol. 1, 101) of 'civilized', 'barbaric' and 'savage' humanity. It was located in the 'barbaric' zone because of the inability to grant European traders and travellers the level of protection to which they were accustomed in 'civilized' societies. Imperial China was forced by 'unequal treaties' to abandon its traditional hegemonic conception of world order in which there was no notion of the sovereign equality of states. The principle of 'extraterritoriality' dictated that disputes involving Europeans would be subject not to any local jurisdiction but to legal principles that were overseen by the relevant European consular office.

As for 'savages' who did not inhabit state-organized societies, international lawyers presumed that they had no right to sovereign recognition because they lacked exclusive occupation of a particular territorial area. Contributing to colonial legal discourse, Westlake argued that 'the occupation by uncivilised tribes of a tract, of which according to our habits a small part ought to have sufficed for them, was not felt to interpose a serious obstacle to the right of the first civilised occupant' (1914, 139). Restating the thesis that 'the rules of the international society [exist] only for the purpose of regulating the mutual conduct of its members', he maintained that international law took 'no account' of 'uncivilised natives' whose treatment was best left to the 'conscience of the state to which the sovereignty is awarded' (1914, 138; 145).

The interwoven development of European state formation, the emergence of international society, and overseas expansion shaped civilized self-images that found distinctive expression in colonial discourses. The general direction of social and political change was captured by the idea of the European 'civilizing process'—the process in which Europeans came to regard themselves as more advanced than other peoples. Understanding that pattern of development sheds light on the emergence of the nineteenth-century 'standard of civilization' which embodied the European sense of cultural superiority and the presumed right to launch 'civilizing missions' or 'civilizing offensives' (Linklater 2016). It is useful to recall the observation that the

> evolution of the European system of interstate relations and the expansion of Europe across the globe were simultaneous processes... which influenced and affected each other. Both began at the end of the fifteenth century, and both were concluded by the end of the Second World War, by which time European dominance was clearly at an end and the global international system, while still evolving, was being shaped less by Europeans than by others.
>
> (Bull and Watson 1984, 6–7)

The upshot was that the European 'standard of civilization' which reflected global asymmetries of power in the nineteenth century fell into disrepute as power relations became more even. Understanding the 'civilizing process' of which the standard was part—and conceptions of 'civilized' manners in particular—reveals how the interaction between European state formation, imperialism, and the construction of international society shaped the interdependencies between the international political and diplomatic cultures.

'CIVILIZED MANNERS'

Bull's standpoint on the society of states has been criticized for failing to recognize that the European political order was cemented by agreements on 'domestic values of a social and cultural nature', and on 'common assumptions' about religion and ideology, and not just on shared beliefs about the utility of 'procedural rules of coexistence' (Neumann and Welsh 1991). The preferred interpretation here is that Bull appreciated that all 'historical international societies' have been connected with 'a common culture or civilisation', and he specifically highlighted the importance of understanding how the diplomatic culture and the international political culture were inter-related in recent centuries. In a direct parallel with Heeren's definition of a states-system, Bull emphasized the part that 'common *values*—such as a common religion or a common moral code' played in reinforcing 'the sense of common interests' (1977, 316, italics in original). What he did not explore was the relationship between European conceptions of civilization and the 'two cultures'. Contemporary scholars can trace the interconnections between those phenomena in detail by drawing on the sociological literature on the 'civilizing process'. Of special importance is the analysis of the development of social standards with respect to 'civilized' manners which were one of the main links between the 'courtly-aristocratic' international political culture and the elite diplomatic culture of the eighteenth century. They were central to European conceptions of their incontestable superiority over other peoples and pivotal to subsequent political dynamics as non-European ruling elites attempted to imitate the great power establishment.

The sociological analysis of the process by which European came to see themselves as uniquely civilized used numerous extracts from 'manners books', especially in the period between the thirteenth and eighteenth centuries, to reveal how people became increasingly concerned with observing new standards of propriety (Elias 2012 [1939], 142ff.). Changing table manners and everyday orientations to basic bodily functions such as nose-blowing and spitting reflected shifting expectations about the social restraints that 'refined' individuals should observe in routine encounters. The relevant behaviour codes appeared within European court societies. Notions of 'polished' behaviour at the court of Louis XIV became standard-setting for other elite groups in Europe. Subsequently, the relevant norms spread downwards to the lower strata in the main European societies and outwards to non-European elites as a result of colonial expansion. Feelings of social inferiority coupled with a strong desire to imitate 'upper class' conduct and to win the acceptance of the global establishment were pronounced amongst members of the lower ranks within Europe and amongst many non-European governing elites.

The whole European 'civilizing process' was inextricably connected with colonialism. The idea of civilization which became prominent in elite discourse in the final part of the eighteenth century conveyed the supreme 'self-confidence of colonising peoples' and their 'continuously expansionist tendency' (Elias 2012 [1939], 15ff.). It summarized 'everything in which Western society of the last two or three centuries believes itself superior to earlier societies or "more primitive" contemporary ones' (ibid.). By employing the concept, Western society highlighted 'its special character' and what it was most proud of: 'the level of *its* technology, the nature of *its* manners, the development of *its* scientific knowledge or view of the world, and much more' (ibid., italics in original). European societies emphasized the growing intolerance of violence within their respective 'civilized' borders and displayed their repugnance towards the 'cruelties' of 'barbaric' societies. Confidence in their civilized existence was an essential part of the 'group charisma' of a great power colonial establishment that used acts of stigmatization to persuade other societies of their 'group disgrace' and to encourage them to modify their systems of government in order to demonstrate progress towards 'civilization' (Mennell 1998, 138).

Such distinctions between the 'advanced' and 'backward' peoples were not confined to perceptions of relations between the imperial overlords and colonized subjects; they were also important features of developments within the European society of states, and specifically of dominant Western European attitudes to Eastern European ruling elites. There are many illustrations of how the gradual 'civilization of manners' within 'supranational court society' was linked with the development of the diplomatic culture. As discussed elsewhere, Polish royal instructions in 1601 to diplomats who were about to be dispatched to higher status Western European capitals stressed the imperative of complying with court etiquette (Linklater 2016). Social acceptance in the most powerful courts depended on conformity with behaviour codes governing basic bodily functions such as spitting (Bogucka 1991). Parallel developments occurred in Tsarist Russia about a century later when Peter the Great ordered the compilation of extracts from the standard-setting, Western European manners books (the volume, entitled *The Honourable Mirror of Youth,* was published in 1717) to ensure that diplomats who visited 'Western court society' behaved in 'polished' ways that symbolized their distinction from 'peasants' (Wortman 2006, 54). Those examples reveal how 'civilized' manners were integral to 'supranational court society' and the aristocratic diplomatic culture. The relevant social standards revealed that the international political and diplomatic cultures were interdependent parts of one long 'civilizing process'. The sociological examination of that trajectory of development shows how they were bound together by conceptions of civilized behaviour that 'outsiders' became anxious to emulate. The latter understood that complying with those standards was not merely about decorum; it was about winning the respect of the European political establishment and strengthening the case for eventual admission into the 'civilized' society of states.

Similar dynamics can be found in attempts by South-East and East Asian ruling elites to live in accordance with 'refined' European behaviour. The efforts by the Siamese government to learn from the courts at St Petersburg, London, and Berlin in the late nineteenth century, and from the Japanese court which had paved the way in adapting to the European 'civilizing process', exemplified the broader trend in which outsiders attuned themselves to the manners and institutions of the global imperial establishment. One requirement, which was to dress in a 'civilized manner', was illustrated by the decision of the Japanese Iwakura mission that visited the United States in 1871 to replace kimonos with Western suits (Gong 1984, 20, 179). The Siamese King, Chulalongkorn, ordered members of the mission that visited colonial authorities in South-East Asia in 1871–2 to dress 'à l'européen' (Gong 1984, 201–37; Winichakul 2000). Similar changes occurred in the Turkish Republic under Kemal Ataturk when wearing traditional Ottoman-Muslim head gear for men (the fez) was made illegal and replaced by Western-style hats which were regarded as symbols of 'civilization' and 'modernization' (Cagaptay 2006, 11–40).

Those developments may seem trivial when compared to the great affairs of state. But as Elias (2012 [1939], 123ff.) contended, behaviour patterns that seem insignificant—such as changing orientations to 'natural' functions in court societies—provide insights into the larger totality of social and political relations. They shed light on the means by which a 'civilized' establishment asserted its superiority over 'less civilized' outsiders (see Elias and Scotson 2012 for a discussion of established–outsider relations). Non-European state initiatives to modernize governing institutions accompanied the project of 'civilizing' manners as 'outsiders' sought to internalize the standards of the global colonial establishment. Those strategies contributed to the globalization of core elements of the European international political and diplomatic cultures.

There is no shortage of examples of internally driven transformations of non-European state structures that had precisely that effect. To demonstrate that it was a 'civilized monarchy', Siam in 1873 promoted the separation of public institutions from the royal household (see Gong 1984, 220) and, in so doing, it reflected the European political development which is usefully captured by the contrast between Louis XIV's alleged declaration that 'l'état c'est moi' and Frederick II's statement that 'the king is the first servant of the state'. Parallel movements which took place in the foundational years of the Turkish Republic included government decisions to abolish the caliphate, the shari'a courts and the religious schools (*madrassa*), and to adopt the Swiss civil and Italian penal codes. Those 'top-down' initiatives were designed to incorporate all citizens in the 'imagined community' of the nation which many non-European observers quickly realized was one of the principal foundations of the uniquely destructive capabilities of the states that threatened to overwhelm them (Cagaptay 2006, 11–40). They were important examples of 'Western-style civilizing offensives' (see Sutton and Vertigans 2005, 138) through which the European international political culture spread to other regions.

To return to Bull's exploratory comments on the 'two cultures'—the effects of the 'civilization' of manners were apparent in those domains which were also linked by European images of civilized state structures and refined diplomatic conduct. Government reforms in Japan, China, and the Ottoman Empire were responses to the ways in which European notions of civilization were embedded in the international political and diplomatic cultures. Only by reconstructing public institutions and by adapting to the dominant diplomatic culture could non-European ruling elites demonstrate that they were making the social and political progress that was demanded by the 'civilized' global establishment.

THE GLOBALIZATION OF THE 'CIVILIZING PROCESS'

'Learning how to be a modern, civilized state' and how to accumulate the 'symbolic power' that enhanced the prospects of gaining entry into international society required a detailed understanding of Western international law. Highlighting 'numerous Chinese blunders in diplomatic transactions', the American missionary, W.A.P. Martin, translated Wheaton's *Elements of International Law* into Chinese in 1864; the work was introduced into Japan the following year (Gong 1984, 151ff.). One other development was crucial— embarking on 'mimetic' imperial projects with the explicit objective of contributing to the larger European 'civilizing mission'. Recognizing that the 'civilized' great powers believed that they should spread 'civilization' to less 'advanced' peoples, the Japanese government proceeded to initiate its own 'civilizing offensive' in societies such as Taiwan in the latter part of the nineteenth century (Eskildsen 2002). One of the objectives of government policy would be repeated in Japan's participation in the West's suppression of the 1899–1901 Boxer Rebellion in China, namely to promote its recognition as a 'civilized' power that was entitled to join the society of states as an equal member. That goal was significantly advanced in 1905 by Japan's military defeat of Russia which had pursued a similar colonial strategy in the nineteenth century (Buranelli 2014; Neumann and Welsh 1991). European reactions did not always endorse Russia's 'progressive' self-image however. The dominant tendency was to look down on Russia as a 'less civilised civiliser'—as a 'semi-Asiatic' autocratic society (Buranelli 2014). Japan was deemed to be the more advanced of the two powers in the early twentieth century although that was not sufficient to secure its full admission into the exclusive club of 'civilized' sovereign states. Japan joined international society in 1899/1900 but Western governments continued to display their sense of superiority by rebuffing the Japanese proposal to enshrine the principle of racial equality in the Covenant of the League of Nations (Shimazu 1998).

Nevertheless, the European 'standard of civilization' encouraged mimetic imperialism that had the effect of globalizing the European 'civilizing process'. Also important was the role that societies such as Japan played as a model for other non-Western states, including the Ottoman Empire (Worringer 2004). The upshot was that the rapid convergence of Western 'civilized' societies and non-Western elite perspectives seemed to be well under way in the late nineteenth and early twentieth centuries (Elias 2012 [1939], 426). Contrary trends were evident in quests to borrow core features of Western scientific and technological developments while blocking what were regarded as harmful cultural practices (Worringer 2004). The anti-colonial sentiments of that period were part of a longer process of resistance to European imperialism that was often ignored or poorly understood by the ruling strata and by populations at large in colonizing societies. Most believed that struggles against imperial rule would be short-lived and that the globalization of 'civilized' values was unstoppable. Confidence reigned that the global hegemony of the 'two cultures' was guaranteed to survive.

THE 'CULTURAL REVOLT AGAINST THE WEST'

Western certainty about the future of the international order was expressed in Article 22 of the League of Nations Covenant which declared that the governance of peoples who were 'not yet able to stand by themselves' had to observe the principle that the 'well-being and development of the (colonial) peoples form a sacred trust of civilisation' (cited in Bain 2003, 101). At that time, imperialism was a source of group pride. Central to 'civilized' self-images was the conviction that European rule was the indispensable instrument of 'progress' and 'civilization' with respect to the internal political organization and diplomatic behaviour of 'backward' societies.

A revolutionary cocktail of Third World nationalism, the ascendancy of competing super-powers with their explicit anti-colonial rhetoric, and the military and political decline of the European great powers led to the unanticipated 'expansion of international society'. The nineteenth-century 'standard of civilization' fell into disrepute along the way. The international lawyer, Hersch Lauterpacht argued that 'modern international law knows of no distinction, for the purposes of recognition, between civilised and uncivilised States or between States within and outside the international community of civilised States' (1947, 31). As Bull observed, where the idea of the 'law common to all civilised states' survived at all—as in the Statute of the International Court of Justice—it was a source of 'embarrassment' (1977, 39). The 'shrinking of the globe', he added, had produced new 'tensions' between societies that identified with 'different cultures or civilisations' (1977, 273). The 'cultural revolt against the West' and the uncoupling of the diplomatic culture from an international political culture were amongst the main consequences.

The 'cultural revolt' is an example of a recurrent feature of human history, namely 'integration conflicts' in which social groups struggle against their enforced incorporation within longer webs of economic and political interconnectedness that radiate outwards from centres of power governed by elites that do not disguise their contempt for them (Elias 2008, 136–7). The sociological challenge is to explain how the balance of power between the dynamics of cultural convergence and divergence shifts over time. Given the global power asymmetries, the gradual absorption of non-European societies into European structures of civility and civilization was the dominant trend for about five centuries. The overall direction of change was checked by the upsurge of political demands for the equal respect of non-Western ways of life. Comprehending the relations between those forces was a central aim of Bull's investigation of the 'revolt against the West', of his reflections on the survival of a diplomatic culture that had been shorn of its earlier normative underpinnings, and of his observations about the prospects for a 'cosmopolitan culture' of modernity that might come to have the integrating role that the European international political culture had until recently.

Several new lines of investigation into the main patterns of cultural convergence and divergence in world politics have appeared over approximately the late twentieth century though none has engaged directly or in detail with Bull's deliberations on the international political and diplomatic cultures. There is no space here to do more than provide an outline of four distinctive standpoints, to reflect on their relationship with the analysis of the 'two cultures', and to underline the continuing importance of Bull's reflections for future inquiries into cultural dynamics in the contemporary society of states.

Exponents of the *first* perspective have defended a 'cultural convergence thesis' which states that there has been significant movement in recent times from a world of 'multiple civilisations to a single global civilisation' suffused with Western liberal-democratic, capitalist values. Any assumption that the modern period has witnessed the voluntary 'coming together of a universal civilization' is emphatically rejected; what has emerged instead is 'the application of a standard of civilization based on Western values' that has contributed to globalizing a liberal-democratic image of international society (Mozaffari 2001). To connect that analysis with Bulls' writings, top-down initiatives have sought to ensure global 'progress' through interconnected shifts in the international political and diplomatic cultures. The details have been discussed in investigations of strategies to promote a contemporary variant on the European 'standard of civilization'—they include measures to increase support for universal human rights and democratic government, to secure submission to the dictates of global 'market civilization' and, with respect to war-torn societies, to launch state-building projects that echo the classical European conviction that stable territorial concentrations of power are the key to civilized interaction. For reasons that were discussed earlier, the dominant political actors are generally reluctant to invoke the idea of civilization to defend those initiatives. Nevertheless, traces of the colonial past survive in dichotomies between the 'developed' global establishment and 'developing' societies that are presumed to require external guidance and support in order to escape their predicaments. As noted above, that reality led Bull to argue that what there is in the way of a cosmopolitan culture in the contemporary era—a culture with shallow 'roots' in societies that were admitted into international society in the post-Second World War era—could be strengthened by importing non-Western ideas.

There are major differences between that perspective and the *second* orientation which replaced predictions of the ascendancy of universal, liberal-democratic civilization with a powerful polemic about the coming 'clash of civilizations' (Huntington 1993, 1996). The contention was that 'civilizational consciousness' and associated political tensions had increased as a result of rising levels of human interconnectedness combined with the ascent of new centres of military and political power that are not subservient to the West (Huntington 1993). The core argument mirrors late nineteenth-century Western reflections on lengthening webs of global interdependence which feared that 'civilizing missions' to pacify non-Western peoples might be overwhelmed by the imperative of containing 'barbarian' peoples (Hobson 2012, 106–30; 257–84). Contemporary renditions maintain that 'civilization' is increasingly under siege from 'barbarism' and, more specifically, that 'liberal *pacific civilization*' is faced with threats emanating from the 'zone of *autocratic barbarism*' and a realm of 'anarchic savagery' comprising failed states that provide safe havens for anti-Western terrorist organizations (Hobson 2012, 260, italics in original). Those reflections on cultural divergence stated that predictions of an international political culture that is anchored in Western liberal-democratic values had been falsified by an upsurge of divisive 'civilisational consciousness'. The implication was that new pressures on the diplomatic culture had increased because of emergent difficulties in maintaining shared commitments to the non-violent resolution of major political disputes.

In response to the question of whether Western and non-Western civilizations can agree on 'elements of commonality' that can support amicable coexistence, Huntington (1993; 1996, 57) argued that peoples are at least able to agree—even in the context of growing civilizational rivalries—that murder is evil. In common with exponents of the first standpoint, some analysts have extended such claims by contending that the liberal universal human rights culture gives 'progressive' expression to the principle that 'international legitimacy and full membership in international society must rest in part on standards of just, humane or civilised behaviour' (Donnelly 1998, 21). The contention is that the 'fatal tainting' of colonial images of civilization has been superseded by the shift from an 'exclusive or particularistic' to an 'inclusive and universal' understanding of civilization (Donnelly 1998, 11ff.).

The proponents of *a third* perspective take a less optimistic view by arguing that liberal standpoints do not resonate with many social strata outside the West. They have highlighted the diplomatic challenge of reaching an agreement about common values that seem just from different cultural positions and are therefore able to command the consent of peoples elsewhere. Vincent's defence of the fundamental human right to be free from the tyranny of starvation remains the most important statement within English School inquiry of the need for a consensual approach to universal entitlements (Vincent 1986). The argument was that a global consensus on such basic rights would strengthen international society as well as satisfy aspirations for justice. Transposed into Bull's terminology, the contention was that an elite diplomatic culture that supports cosmopolitan values could develop alongside an international political culture in which different peoples are freely united in a 'civilized' quest to protect human rights. The implicit supposition was that the discourse of universal rights could play an equivalent role to 'civilized' manners and notions of civilized statehood in previous centuries in supporting a diplomatic culture that is reinforced by social ideals that link not just elites but different peoples together in a genuinely cosmopolitan political culture (see also n. 1).

Cautious optimism about the prospects for a global value-consensus on human rights was checked in the aftermath of 9/11 by a *fourth* perspective that focused on how liberal-conservative forces in the United States harnessed the language of civilization in defence of 'preventive warfare' and 'regime change'. Analysts discussed several statements by President George W. Bush that condemned 'acts of barbarism' that had been committed by the 'enemies of civilization' in order to construct a 'standard of sovereign responsibility' that permitted 'injured states' to override the sovereignty of governments that were believed to harbour terrorist organizations (Reinold 2013, 99ff.). Recent inquiries have shed light on how efforts to unite social groups by appealing to shared 'civilized' values did as much to divide as to unite the members of international society and populations more generally. There was robust political resistance to the Administration's efforts to use the discourse of civilization to connect an international political culture that was centred on liberal values to a 'civilized' diplomatic culture that lifted traditional restraints on violence in struggles with 'barbarians'. What has been described as 'coercive solidarism' (Hurrell 2014) has been criticized not only for fostering divisions between the major powers but also for contributing to cycles of 'reciprocal stigmatization' in which opposing Western and Islamic political forces developed self-fulfilling, demonic images of each other that entrenched commitments to violence (Sutton and Vertigans 2005, 151ff.). For such reasons, sharp divisions arose over the use of a new 'standard of civilization' to construct an image of how a diplomatic culture (consisting of 'the stock of ideas and values' shared 'by the official representatives of states') could be supported by a revitalized international political culture (an 'intellectual and moral culture' of liberal-democratic values that all 'civilized' societies were assumed to share).

With the partial exception of Vincent, none of the exponents of the four perspectives engaged with Bull's analysis of the 'two cultures' and with the interrelated discussion of 'civilization' and international society. They have not recognized the importance of one of the main arguments of *The Anarchical Society* which is that international society is the arena where the dynamics of cultural convergence and divergence unfold in distinctive and often dangerous ways. Bull's references to the changing relationship between the international political culture and the diplomatic culture in a society of states that has come to include all state-organized human groups provide a useful framework for analysing the ever-shifting balance of power between those central dimensions of world politics. His observations can be extended by drawing on the process-sociological investigation of how Europeans acquired their unique civilized self-images. The inquiry contributes to understanding the interdependencies between the 'two cultures' in the past and in the contemporary era. As Bull argued, the diplomatic culture that developed in Europe is no longer anchored in a single international political culture or civilization. Their recent separation led Bull to ask whether a cosmopolitan culture is emerging that can provide international society with the reinforcement of core values and beliefs that are freely shared by different peoples who identify with a world society. Outlining the key issues was one the main achievements of *The Anarchical Society* and one of its enduring legacies.

CONCLUSION

Bull's distinction between an international political culture and a specialist diplomatic culture, and his comments on the possibility of a cosmopolitan culture of modernity, advanced earlier English School analyses of the relationship between civilisation and international society. His argument was that harmony between the two cultures existed in Europe in the period in which international society consisted of self-defining civilized states that asserted the right to impose a specific 'standard of civilization' on non-Western societies. His analysis of the decline of the old international political culture and the survival of the diplomatic culture can be extended by foregrounding the rise of European civilized self-images and their impact on non-European societies from the earlier period of emulation to the recent era of political contestation and rejection. The latter had the effect of delinking the diplomatic culture from an international political culture of 'civilized' values.

The question posed by Bull in *The Anarchical Society* was whether a cosmopolitan culture may be evolving that has a similar role to the international political culture of old in cementing commitments to the practices and principles of international society. For many liberals, the human rights culture is the prime candidate to play that role. Bull doubted that any single moral code could bind the two cultures together in the way they had been linked when international society consisted of so-called civilized states. He did so in recognition of the scale of the political challenge to expand the range of shared values in the post-European society of states where the traditional problem of how to maintain order has been compounded by wholly unprecedented demands for global justice.[2]

---

[2] I am indebted to Hidemi Suganami for his searching and incisive comments on two earlier drafts of this essay, and to Adam Humphreys for his advice on the penultimate version.

Conclusion

18

Bull's Political Vision

Adam Humphreys

Both Bull and his principal work, *The Anarchical Society* (1977), are best known for developing the concept of international society and for establishing it as the centrepiece of the so-called English School of International Relations (IR) (Wight 1987, 222; Dunne 1998b; Alderson and Hurrell 2000; Buzan 2004, 1, 35; Williams and Little 2006, 1).[1] Bull's work is also of wider disciplinary significance. His defence of a 'classical' approach in IR theory (Bull 1966a) was, for example, a key staging post in the still ongoing debate about the nature and merits of a scientific approach to the study of world politics (see Jackson 2011). It is, however, the concept of international society that has proved the most enduring of Bull's legacies, as demonstrated both in key debates within the English School, such as those over humanitarian intervention (Wheeler 2000) and the prospects for greater solidarity in world politics (Hurrell 2007), and in how other theorists, especially constructivists, have drawn on the English School (Finnemore 1996; Wendt 1999).

Forty years after its publication, reading *The Anarchical Society* as a treatise on international society can make it seem somewhat dated (Alderson and Hurrell 2000, 54; Williams and Little 2006, 2). As the contributors to this volume make clear, many of Bull's central insights do remain relevant, notably his appreciation of the obstacles to cooperation presented by competing interests and values, of the importance of informal norms and understandings, and of the capacity of the great powers both to sustain and to undermine world order. This is most obvious in relation to security questions (Ayson; Ruzicka; Toros and Dionigi; Carr; see Chs. 7–10).[2] Yet Bull's insistence on the relative unimportance, as compared to the dynamics of the states system, of the kinds of transnational interactions highlighted, even in his own time, by

---

[1] The concept of international society did not, however, originate with Bull (see Linklater and Suganami 2006).

[2] Throughout this essay, I refer to other contributions to this volume by author and chapter number.

Keohane and Nye (1972) cannot be sustained today (Pauly; Falkner; see Chs. 11 and 12). Reading Bull's text narrowly as a study of international society also makes it hard to relate it constructively to dimensions of world politics that have since become significant in IR, such as gender (True, Ch. 14) and empire, the legacy of which, Pasha argues (Ch. 6), Bull's account of the demands for 'Third World' justice captures only inadequately.

In asking how persuasive *The Anarchical Society* remains today, one difficulty is, as Suganami (Ch. 2) points out, that the book does not do quite what it sets out to. The subtitle indicates that it will be a study of *order in world politics* but Bull in fact focuses more narrowly on *international order*, as provided by the modern, global, *international* society, treating *world order* and the *world society* that might support it as a distinctly secondary concern (Buzan 2004). This may go some way to explaining why the book is remembered chiefly for its treatment of international society. A key contribution of this volume, however, is to make clear that there is more to *The Anarchical Society* than international society, narrowly construed. Whereas Bull is often understood subsequently to have expanded his vision, most notably in the 1983 Hagey Lectures (Bull 2000c), it would be more accurate to observe that the potential for an expanded vision of world politics is present within the conceptual framework Bull develops in *The Anarchical Society*, but that he chose, in that book, to restrict his focus. He judged, at the time he was writing, that a study of order in world politics should *focus* on international society. This was, however, a provisional judgement: it was very much for 'the present time', a kind of phraseology he uses repeatedly. Forty years on, we are not compelled to endorse such judgements and nor should we presume that Bull would reproduce them today.

Bull described his argument as 'an implicit defence of the states system, and more particularly of that element in it that has been called international society' (1977, 307). This is reflected in the organization of the text. Part I presents the concept of international society and argues for its significance, Part II shows how the master institutions of international society produce order, and Part III makes the case for the continuing merits of international society as the basis of world order. Yet it is important to recognize, as not all readers have (see Alderson and Hurrell 2000, 7), that *The Anarchical Society* is concerned, above all, with the prospective decline of international society. This concern explains why, in Part III, Bull explores potential alternatives to international society as the basis for world order. Although he stressed the significance of international society for world order, he also recognized that it is only a contingent part of a broader world political arena. Bull's conceptual framework is, in this sense, more flexible than is often appreciated. The contributions to this volume may be collectively understood as exploring that flexibility forty years on, noting where Bull's judgements seemed prescient, but also recognizing where we now need to push his framework in different directions, and acknowledging, of course, that this flexibility has its limits. The key insight of this volume is that Bull's framework is richer than is suggested by his focus on international society and that much of this richness can be productively developed today, even if Bull himself did not maximize that potential.

With that in mind, this concluding essay proceeds as follows. First, it outlines the flexibility of Bull's conceptual framework, paying particular attention to his oft-neglected concept of the 'world political system'. Second, it lays out the range of contingent judgements that Bull reached when writing *The Anarchical Society* and indicates which of these judgements the contributors to this volume have endorsed or deemed in need of updating. Third, it highlights some of the limits the contributors have identified to this project of reading Bull more flexibly. Finally, it offers some suggestions about future inquiry.

THE FLEXIBILITY OF BULL'S CONCEPTUAL FRAMEWORK

Writing in and on the English School has long recognized that there is more to Bull and to *The Anarchical Society* than international society. In fact, Bull is often interpreted as offering a conceptual trichotomy which, corresponding to Wight's distinction between realist, rationalist, and revolutionary traditions of thought, is composed of international system, international society, and world society (Buzan 2001, 474–6; Linklater and Suganami 2006, 52). Of these, Bull elaborated world society the least. Indeed, Buzan describes it as 'the Cinderella concept of English school theory, receiving relatively little attention and almost no conceptual development' (2004, 11). This is a notable deficiency given that Bull purports to be writing a study of world order (not just international order) and that the development of a world society offers one obvious alternative to international society as the basis for world order. However, this volume shows that reading *The Anarchical Society* through the lens of this trichotomy obscures a small but important part of the sophistication and flexibility of Bull's conceptual framework. For Bull is careful to situate the states system, and its element of international society, in relation to a broader world political system of which the states system is only a part.

As is well known, Bull identifies modern international society, which is global in scope, as responsible for providing the degree of 'international order' ('order among states') currently enjoyed in world politics and as contributing thereby to 'world order' (order 'among mankind as a whole') (1977, 21–2). However, he identifies international society as only one 'element' of the states system: it coexists with 'the element of war and struggle for power among states' and 'the element of transnational solidarity and conflict' (1977, 41). Moreover, he expresses concern that the modern, global, international society 'enjoys only a precarious foothold' within contemporary world politics: it, and the order it underpins, has been undermined by 'ideological divisions... the revolt of non-European peoples and states against Western dominance, and the expansion of the states system beyond its originally European or Western confines' (1977, 257–8).

Bull acknowledges that '[o]rder in world politics may one day take the form of the maintenance of elementary goals of social life in a single world society or great society of mankind', but he rejects the idea that such a society 'is already a going concern' (1977, 23). If we view Bull (and the English School more broadly) as operating with the trichotomy outlined above, this implies that although we can speculate about possible future forms of order within world society, there is, at present, nowhere else to look for order in world politics than in international society: world order consists of the international order provided by international society plus domestic order within states (Suganami, Ch. 2). If so, then this would limit the capacity of Bull's framework to illuminate today's increasingly globalised world. For as Buzan points out, if we follow Bull in conceiving of world society as being concerned with 'shared identity at the individual level' then this 'begs the question of where the organised but non-state components of global civil society', such as transnational firms and NGOs, should be located (2001, 477). As Suganami (Ch. 2) notes, the answer lies in what Bull (1977, 276) terms the 'wider world political system' constituted by 'the world-wide network of interaction that embraces not only states but also other political actors, both "above" the state and "below" it'.

Bull explicitly recognized that the 'study of world politics should be concerned with the global political process as a whole, and this cannot be understood simply in terms of interstate politics'; he identified business enterprises, trade unions, political parties, professional associations, churches, and international organizations as part of a 'transnational nexus' (1977, 277). He insisted, however, that 'the existence of a political system involving other actors as well as states' was not 'a new or recent development. The states system has always been part of a wider system of interaction' (1977, 278). Indeed, he noted that the growth of a genuinely 'global political system' in the nineteenth century 'was not simply the work of states; private individuals and groups played their part as explorers, traders, migrants, missionaries and mercenaries, and the expansion of the states system was part of a wider spread of social and economic exchange' (1977, 20–1). This led him to downplay the significance of this broader world political system in relation to world order: he doubted that, at the time he was writing, transnational relations played 'a more important role, relatively to the relationship of states, than in earlier phases of the wider political system in which they both figure' (1977, 278). He focused, instead, on the 'political structure' to which relations within the world political system have given rise, viz. 'a global system and society of states' (1977, 21). In considering the utility of Bull's conceptual framework forty years on, however, this concept must be given a more central role.

One reason is that the transnational dimension of world politics is much more significant than it was in Bull's day. In this volume Pauly (Ch. 11) shows how the management of systemic risk in a global economy characterized by the rapid deepening of cross-border economic integration increasingly involves regulatory frameworks which, though created by states, also draw in private, market actors (see also Büthe and Mattli 2013). Similarly, Falkner (Ch. 12) argues that the global climate regime is becoming 'transnationalized' as sub-national political authorities, businesses, and NGOs take the initiative in setting climate norms, developing low-carbon strategies, and establishing governance mechanisms. In terms of Bull's conceptual framework, such developments are, as Pauly notes, best characterized as taking place not in international society, or even in world society, but in the 'world political system'. Indeed, Falkner's contention that such developments are not easily accommodated within either international society or world society points toward the need to resuscitate this aspect of Bull's framework. This is not to say that transnational relations are now more important than inter-state relations: Carr (Ch. 10) points out, for example, that, despite the privileged role of US-based private transnational organizations, the states system continues to be the key mechanism for governing cyberspace. Armed with the concept of the world political system, however, we are better able to consider questions about the relative influence of competing sources of governance.

Second, Bull defines (an embryonic) 'world society' as being 'characterised by a sense of the common interests and values of all mankind—as distinct from a world political system characterised merely by global interdependence and global awareness' (1977, 289). The world political system therefore accommodates, within Bull's conceptual scheme, those transnational developments which fall short of expressing any common values espoused by mankind as a whole. It is a consistent theme of *The Anarchical Society* that, on the one hand, world order will be best served by the preservation of international society but that, on the other hand, international society is precarious and can best be strengthened by extending the consensus which underpins it, a consensus which Bull presumes will be cosmopolitan (1977, 88, 316). In the last forty years, however, we have seen numerous developments within what Bull terms the 'world political system' which do not involve the development of a cosmopolitan consensus and which, therefore, cannot be situated within world society as Bull imagines it. For example, True (Ch. 14) argues that the fight against patriarchy has been transnational, but it does not (yet) command a consensus. The same is true of the battle for indigenous rights (Keal, Ch. 13). Non-state groups such as the so-called Islamic State (Toros and Dionigi, Ch. 9) symbolize the lack of a cosmopolitan consensus in contemporary world politics, yet also occupy a transnational space from which they are able to both mimic and contest the norms of international society.

Developing Bull's ideas about the emerging 'world political system... of which the system of states is only part' therefore adds a new dimension of flexibility to his framework (1977, 21). It is widely recognized that Bull's understanding of international society and its place within the states system allows us to employ his framework to ask a wide range of questions about, for example:

- the geographical scope of both the states system and the element of society within it;
- the degree to which the elements of war and struggle, regulated intercourse, and transnational solidarity are present and/or dominant within the states system;
- the degree to which rules of coexistence within international society are accompanied by rules of cooperation;
- how effectively the institutions of international society operate to produce order;
- the degree to which international society is underpinned by a common culture;
- the norms which prevail in international society and whose interests they serve.

This flexibility in Bull's framework is reflected not only in the historical and normative inquiry for which the English School is well known but also, for example, in more recent empirical inquiry into regional international societies (Stivachtis 2015).

Focusing additionally on the world political system and how it relates to international society on the one hand and to a prospective future world society on the other makes accessible a further range of questions which can be asked from within Bull's framework, including questions about:

- the relative importance of states and the states system, including its element of society, as compared to other actors within the world political system;
- the emergence of new actors, rules and understandings within the world political system;
- the extent to which developments in the world political system work for, or undermine, international and also domestic order;
- the extent to which developments in the world political system advance or undermine the prospects for the development of a world society, whether cosmopolitan or not.

This additional flexibility does not rule out a more traditional focus on international society, but it does open up the possibility of extending Bull's approach, not only, for example, by exploring the role of non-state actors in global governance, but also by exploring dimensions of world order, such as patriarchy, which do not fit neatly within a narrowly construed international society or a strictly cosmopolitan world society.[3]

Recognizing this flexibility in Bull's framework also highlights the fact that his claims about order in world politics are, for the most part, contingent judgements. It is often noted that Bull combines multiple modes of inquiry: he is known for his critical exposition of the key concepts necessary for studying world order, for historical inquiry into the forms that world order has taken, and for his normative judgements about the relative value of order and justice and about how world order can best be provided. He also famously advocated an 'approach to theorizing...that is characterised above all by explicit reliance upon the exercise of judgement' (Bull 1966a, 361). Yet it is not often recognized how provisional Bull's judgements are. His assessment of the functions performed by the institutions of international society in relation to order are not abstract, but concrete: he assesses what role they play at 'present' (1977, 101, 127, 162, 184, 200). Similarly, his judgements about the prospects for international society being superseded as a source of world order concern what is likely between the time he was writing 'and the end of the century' (1977, 257), that is, by the year 2000. His central argument that 'such prospects as there may be for order in world politics' lie in attempts to arrest the decline of international society (1977, 319) reflect these provisional judgements. It is often noted that this style of theorizing contrasts strongly with the deductive reasoning and hypothesis testing which is associated, however inaccurately (Humphreys 2012), with another famous text from the same period, Waltz's *Theory of International Politics* (1979), and which continues to dominate mainstream IR theory, especially in the US. Yet in appraising *The Anarchical Society*, it is equally important to note that, Bull's judgements being provisional, it is quite proper now to revise them.[4]

---

[3] There has, of course, been no shortage of work that has used English School ideas as a springboard from which to launch very different kinds of enquiries (Keene 2009, 104), of which Linklater (1998) is one outstanding example. In exploring the flexibility of Bull's framework, this volume, by contrast, and in Bullian fashion, pursues a middle ground between focusing, narrowly, as *The Anarchical Society* does, on international society, and radically reshaping Bull's approach.

[4] In the Introduction to *The Anarchical Society* Bull asks how order is 'maintained within the *present* system of sovereign states' and whether that system '*still*' provides 'a viable path to world order' (my italics) (1977, xi).

BULL'S JUDGEMENTS

As previously noted, Bull recognized that there is much more to world politics than international society. Several years before *The Anarchical Society* was published he observed that

> there is now a global political system of which the 'international system' or states-system is only part (even if it is the most important part), and that many of the issues that have arisen within this global political system... cannot be satisfactorily dealt with in a framework that confines our attention to the relations of sovereign states. To deal with them properly we need to consider, alongside states, not only organisations of states global and regional, but international non-governmental organisations, transnational and subnational groups, individual human beings, and *in posse* if not *in esse*... [the] *magna communitas humani generis*. (1972a, 255)

One question that arises, therefore, is why, in *The Anarchical Society*, Bull focused so centrally on international society. One of his judgements, clearly, was that such a focus was required, at the time he was writing, given the project in which he understood himself to be engaged. But this judgement is open to revision today, as are Bull's empirical and evaluative judgements, which are considered subsequently.

Judgements about Intellectual Priorities

There are two notable features of Bull's decision to focus on international society as a source of world order, despite his awareness that it forms only part of a broader world political system. First, Bull was operating in a disciplinary environment in which, he believed, the case for world politics being a *social* realm still needed to be made. It is often maintained, he notes, that

> the existence of international society is disproved by the fact of anarchy... A persistent theme in the modern discussion of international relations has been that, as a consequence of this anarchy, states do not form together any kind of society; and that if they were to do so it could only be by subordinating themselves to a common authority. (1977, 46)

He therefore considered it important to show that 'the modern international system is also an international society' the existence of which is not 'disproved by the fact of international anarchy' (1977, 51). Second, as previously noted, Bull believed that such world order as was provided by international society was 'precarious and imperfect' (1977, 52).[5] In other words, he focused on

---

[5] As Bain (Ch. 4) points out, this may be, in part, because of Bull's very understanding of order as constructed and contingent.

international society because of its significance (as he judged) for world order at the time he was writing and because of the threats to it (as he judged) resulting from its expansion and consequent lack of a common culture, from the Cold War, and from the revolt against the West.

We need not now endorse either of these judgements and nor is there any strong reason for believing that Bull would reproduce them today. It is important to note, however, that Bull's decision to focus on international society does not imply an abstract judgement that it offers the best *possible* basis for world order. As captured by his criticisms of Richard Falk's more radical urgings (Falk, Ch. 3), Bull's defence of international society stems in part from his belief that 'the best could all too often be the enemy of the good' (Alderson and Hurrell 2000, 61). This indicates that Bull is not unreflexively statist or conservative. Bull's position is certainly not statist qua ontology: if, as Jackson and Nexon (2013) argue, IR theories are best understood as advancing ontologies, then Bull's is quite rich. And while Bull is in some respects a conservative thinker, Edkins and Zehfuss's complaint (2005, 461) that by concentrating on order Bull defines away politics is not wholly fair: just as Edkins and Zehfuss's analysis is motivated by their sense of what is 'important in the present circumstances' (2006, 454), so Bull's judgement about the urgency of particular questions represents a political and ethical stance.

That said, despite the continuing utility of many of Bull's insights into the make-up and functioning of international society, his narrow focus is neither warranted by the state of IR today nor adequate for comprehending world order in its entirety. Kaczmarska (Ch. 16) shows, through her exploration of Russian ideas about world politics, that we cannot assume that Bull's conception of world politics as an international society is shared throughout the world. Pasha (Ch. 6) suggests that Bull's focus on the capacity of international society to provide order makes it impossible for him to recognize the true nature of the injustice felt by the victims of colonialism and the extent to which this undermines world order. Bull's narrow focus also causes him to neglect domestic order (Suganami, Ch. 2). Had he addressed it more directly, as a constituent part of world order, he might have recognized that issues such as patriarchy and indigenous rights (True; Keal; see Chs. 13 and 14) are not only questions of justice, but also questions of order.

The contributions to this volume indicate, therefore, that we now need to look beyond international society in a way which Bull did not do in *The Anarchical Society*, but which his conceptual framework very much facilitates. For Linklater (Ch. 17), although Bull was right to highlight the significance of cultural convergence and divergence for international society and hence for world order, his analysis did not go deep enough. For both Pauly and Falkner (Chs. 11 and 12), it is necessary to focus on the transnational dimension of world politics much more centrally than Bull did. For Keal, True, Reus-Smit, and Pasha (Chs. 5, 6, 13, and 14), Bull's dividing line between order and justice can no longer (if it ever could) be sustained.

Empirical Judgements

The idea that world politics is a social realm now being familiar, many of Bull's empirical judgements seem quite banal, for example that, at the time he was writing, there were sufficient common rules and institutions to diagnose the existence of an international society. For the most part, the contributors to this volume do not contest these judgements, either as judgements about the world Bull inhabited or even as they apply to the present day. Ayson (Ch. 7) and Ruzicka (Ch. 8) argue that Bull's emphasis on the importance of restraint and informal understandings in great power relations remain highly relevant. They also endorse Bull's concern (1977, 117, 200-1) about the dangers that the US becoming a preponderant power would pose to world order. Carr (Ch. 10) argues that even though the attribution problem makes the application of international law in cyberspace problematic, states have resorted to informal rules and norms in a fashion consistent with Bull's observations about the operation of international society. Bull's observation that the US and Soviet Union each often recognized a need to limit the other's power, but failed to recognize why their own actions might be interpreted as threatening (1977, 110), also speaks directly to the apparent failure of the EU and NATO, in our own time, to recognize that Russia might legitimately regard their wooing of Ukraine as threatening (Patomäki, Ch. 15; Mearsheimer 2014).

However, if Bull's judgements about international society remain insightful today, the contributors to this volume find his judgements about the broader world political system less convincing. As Pauly, Falkner, and Patomäki (Chs. 11, 12, and 15) all point out, Bull's claim that there is nothing new about transnational forces (1977, 277-9) cannot be sustained today and was questionable even forty years ago. Moreover, even if Bull was right that international society was then the only political structure worthy of note within the world political system, the subsequent growth of transnational regimes, most notably in the world economy but also, for example, in relation to climate change, suggests that such a claim would require greater scrutiny today. Indeed, Patomäki (Ch. 15) notes that recent regulatory changes may be construed as first steps towards the development of world government. The discussions in this volume of human rights (Reus-Smit, Ch. 5) and indigenous rights (Keal, Ch. 13) also bring into question the contemporary plausibility of Bull's contention that the great society of mankind is nothing but an idea, while Pasha's discussion (Ch. 6) of the colonial underpinnings of international society suggests that Bull misunderstood the nature of the justice claims of former colonial countries. More generally, Reus-Smit, Pasha, Falkner, Keal, and True (Chs. 5, 6, 12, 13, and 14) all provide reason to doubt that Bull's judgement that 'ideas of cosmopolitan or world justice play very little part' in world politics (1977, 85) remains true today. The collective message, in short, is that Bull's empirical judgements about his principal focus, international society, were often quite perspicacious, but that many of his judgements about the broader world political system must today be revisited.

Evaluative Judgements

Bull's evaluative judgements largely concern the prospects for world order in the future and hence involve consideration not only of international society but also of the world political system and the relationship between them. Falk acknowledges in his essay (Ch. 3) that Bull's judgement about the likely enduring primacy of the states system proved more accurate than Falk's own belief that radical change could be achieved imminently. Yet Bull's inadequate theorization of the dynamics of change (see Patomäki, Ch. 15; Reus-Smit, Ch. 5) limited his capacity to predict the future. In some respects international society has in fact proved more durable than Bull imagined. He argued that 'the states system can remain viable only if the element in it of international society is preserved and strengthened', which depends 'on maintaining and extending the consensus about common interests and values that provides the foundation of its common rules and institutions, at a time when consensus has shrunk' (1977, 315). Contrary to Bull's expectations, however, international society has survived even though there has not, at a global level, been a significant growth in consensus, let alone an extension of the 'cosmopolitan culture' that, he believed, this required (1977, 316). As Linklater (Ch. 17) observes, Bull's appreciation that the norms of international society can become divorced from attitudes towards it in domestic societies is a crucial insight. Yet Bull failed to recognize how the civilizing process associated with the expansion of international society might sustain those norms even in the absence of an underlying cosmopolitan culture. More generally, Bull's lack of appreciation of the complex interplay between the domestic and the international may explain why he failed to recognize the potential impact on international society of changing ideas about empire, gender, and human rights (Pasha, Ch. 6; True, Ch. 14; Reus-Smit, Ch. 5).

In respect of the broader world political system, what Bull seems to have missed is the possibility that there could be such a radical extension of transnational governance without threatening the endurance of the states system and the element of international society within it. This suggests, in turn, that Bull was wrong to suppose that the prospects for change lay chiefly in international society. As Falkner (Ch. 12) points out, Bull surmised that, in the short run, 'effective action' to tackle ecological challenges would depend 'primarily on the action of states' (1977, 294). Bull was not wholly wrong, but he failed to recognize that transnational regimes might develop to the degree that it no longer makes sense to single out the state and the states system as the sole, or even the most important, object of study.

There is some disagreement among the contributors to this volume about whether, as Bull judged, international society remains the best bet for world order. Ayson (Ch. 7), Carr (Ch. 10), and Toros and Dionigi (Ch. 9) all implicitly endorse the contribution of contemporary international society to world order. However, Falkner (Ch. 12) argues that sustained action on climate change requires a transition to more solidarist forms of governance that cannot be achieved from within a pluralist international society. Pasha (Ch. 6) argues that Bull's international society cannot adequately accommodate the justice demands of former colonial states insofar as its rules and institutions are continuous with those of the European international society that imposed colonial rule in the first place. Keal (Ch. 13) and True (Ch. 14) agree with Pasha that it is no longer plausible (if it ever was) to claim that an international society structured around the prioritization of order over justice is the only global political structure capable of providing world order. Claims to indigenous sovereignty also bring into question Bull's presumption that an emergent world society would be cosmopolitan: Keal points out that the idea of indigenous sovereignty involves a kind of group right that is not straightforwardly compatible with Bull's individualist understanding of world justice. What these essays reveal is that contemporary world politics involves dimensions of normative contestation that Bull did not imagine. He not only misunderstood the nature of the justice claims being advanced against Western states, but also failed to anticipate that a major power such as Russia might reject international society as an organizing idea for world politics (Kaczmarska, Ch. 16).

Reflecting on Bull's judgements in this fashion offers an insight into the limitations of his political vision. In respect of the workings of international society his thinking showed great dexterity. He often identified surprising ways in which developments that appeared, on the surface, to undermine world order might, in roundabout fashion, support it. For example, he argues that even when states fail to comply with a rule, to the extent that they feel compelled to offer an explanation for their non-compliance that may, in the long run, strengthen the rule (1977, 45, 137–8). This kind of normative enmeshment has proved to be a key driver of the global human rights regime (Foot 2000). By contrast, however, Bull had a relatively restricted vision of the range of alternative possibilities for world order and justice. Revealingly, although he recognized that there may be alternatives to the modern states system which do 'not conform to any previous pattern of universal political organisation', he refused to 'speculate as to what these non-historical alternatives might be' (1977, 256). The only alternatives he would consider were those for which he found evidence in the history of previous, non-global international systems. This may explain why he was reluctant to develop the concept of the wider world political system any further than was strictly required to accommodate the transnational forces observable in the 1970s.

THE LIMITS OF BULL'S PROJECT

To the extent that the contributors to this volume question Bull's judgements, it is important to recognize that they are judgements which Bull could, and perhaps would, have revised forty years on. His conceptual framework is, moreover, sufficiently flexible to allow for many of his judgements to be revised quite considerably, especially once we broaden our focus to encompass the world political system. However, the contributors to this volume also identify limits to the flexibility of Bull's framework. These limits arise in three main respects: its capacity to illuminate difference, its adequacy as a basis for causal inquiry, and the normative agenda it implicitly imposes.

Reus-Smit (Ch. 5) describes Bull as a 'master of taxonomy': the distinguishing feature of Bull's theorizing, Reus-Smit argues, is his 'drive to classify and categorize, to carve up a phenomenon or issue into elements or dimensions, and then compare, contrast, and relate them'. One weakness of a taxonomic approach, however, is its inability to accommodate the in-between. As previously noted, transnational forces have often been thought to sit uncomfortably between Bull's concepts of international and world society, a problem which can be somewhat rectified by rehabilitating his concept of a world political system. Yet even with this additional dimension of flexibility, some aspects of contemporary world politics are difficult to situate within Bull's framework. For example, competing conceptions of world politics, such as the idea of the 'Russian world' (Kaczmarska, Ch. 16), appear to be part of international society while simultaneously undermining its status as a 'constitutional principle of international order' (Bull 1977, 68). This suggests that, like all taxonomies, Bull's framework may be better suited to the study of some kinds of phenomena than others. It is, in this respect, an obvious limitation of *The Anarchical Society* that there are some dimensions of world politics which it does not make visible, including not only patriarchy and coloniality (True, Ch. 14; Pasha, Ch. 6) but also, for example, race (Anievas et al. 2015).

Reus-Smit (Ch. 5) argues, however, that Bull's taxonomic approach causes problems even in relation to the dimensions of world politics that Bull explicitly discusses, such as human rights. Bull is led by his taxonomy, Reus-Smit observes, to classify human rights as an issue of individual justice rather than of international justice, from which he infers that human rights claims are potentially subversive of international order. What Bull therefore fails to see is that human rights are power mediators: arguments about the rights of individuals are also arguments about the limits of state authority. In Bull's terms, Reus-Smit suggests, human rights are therefore about both individual and international justice, exposing the inflexibility of a taxonomic architecture in which they are required to be one or the other. Pasha (Ch. 6) argues, similarly, that Bull's dichotomy between order and justice prevents him from recognizing the true depth of what he later (1984b; 2000c) termed the 'revolt against the West'. Because he classified Third World demands as being about justice, rather than order, because he believed that justice could not be secured without order, and because he believed that such world order as was currently available was provided by international society, Bull argued that international society would have to accommodate

> the demands of Asian, African and Latin American countries and peoples for just change in respect of the elimination of colonialism and white supremacist governments, the redistribution of wealth and resources, and the ending of the relationship of dependence of subordination in which most of them stand to the rich countries. (1977, 300)

What Bull therefore failed to recognize, Pasha argues, is that these demands were also, and fundamentally, about order. Because Bull classified them as questions of justice, he failed to see that no order in which the institutions complicit in colonialism were preserved could be satisfactory.

Bull's lack of vision in this regard is connected to the second major limitation of his approach: his failure adequately to theorize change. As noted in Suganami's introduction (Ch. 1), Bull is often thought of as an interpretive rather than a causal thinker. Indeed, my focus on the flexibility of his conceptual framework underlines the primarily interpretive thrust of *The Anarchical Society*. Bull does, nonetheless, claim that the rules and institutions of international society contribute causally to international order (1977, 74). As Patomäki (Ch. 15) points out, however, this claim is underdeveloped: Bull does not specify the range of causal powers, mechanisms, or processes that a systematic causal approach would have to consider. Reus-Smit (Ch. 5) links this failure directly to Bull's taxonomic approach—such an approach, he argues, is oriented toward static rather than dynamic analysis: toward classifying phenomena as being one thing or the other, rather than toward developing a generative account of their emergence, evolution, and impact. Patomäki argues that Bull's failure to anticipate the extent to which developments in the global economy would impact upon international security reflects his failure to develop this kind of generative theorizing.

The final major limitation in Bull's approach identified in this volume is his inadequate account of the normative basis of his own theorizing. Bain (Ch. 4) argues that whereas Bull describes his approach as Grotian, in fact his account of order is Hobbesian: Bull understands order as constructed and contingent, rather than as reflecting any natural ordering of things. The cause of this confusion lies in Bull's use of Augustine's definition of order, which was itself part of a medieval dispute about the nature of God and the extent of his power (1977, 3-4). One implication of Bain's argument is that international society, as Bull understands it, has not outgrown its European and Christian roots to the extent that Bull suggests. The problem this creates is twofold. First, whereas Bull represents the goals of life, truth, and property as 'elementary, primary, or universal goals of social life' (1977, 5), he was presenting a normative vision which is more substantively shaped by Christian ideas of freedom, autonomy, and moral responsibility than he admits, a vision which is then somewhat concealed by his subsequent distinction between order and justice. Second, as previously noted, the conceptual framework he goes on to develop fails to illuminate key dimensions of normative contestation in world politics today, such as the legacy of colonialism and the unravelling of patriarchy (Pasha, Ch. 6; True, Ch. 14).

FUTURE DIRECTIONS

Bain's suggestion (Ch. 4) that we can improve our understanding of Bull by recognizing what his analysis owes to debates in medieval theology brings us to the directions for further inquiry suggested by this volume. Some of these are familiar. For example, while many contributions indicate the need to resuscitate Bull's conception of the world political system, the further development of Bull's conceptual vocabulary forms a key part of Buzan's agenda for 'reconvening the English School' (2001, 479). Similarly, while Reus-Smit, True, and Linklater (Chs. 5, 14, and 17) all point to the need to revise Bull's narrative of the emergence of international society so as better to incorporate, respectively, the role of contestation over human rights, of patriarchal structures within domestic societies, and of Western ideas about civilized manners, this form of inquiry, too, is a well-established part of the English School's research agenda. This volume has, though, identified three newer avenues of inquiry which those interested in developing Bull's approach in *The Anarchical Society* and in relating it to contemporary world politics might also pursue.

The first of these is to develop a more substantive theorization of dynamic processes. Its lack of causal inquiry has long been noted as a weakness of the English School (see Finnemore 2001, 510), but there is an outstanding question about what form such inquiry should take. Keene articulates one possibility, arguing that although international society is often construed as an ideal type, Bull's inquiry into international order fails to 'fulfil the *causal* aspirations of the Weberian project' (2009, 116). This is not, however, the kind of causal inquiry that is prized by most mainstream IR theorists. The contributions to this volume identify three alternative possibilities. Patomäki's discussion (Ch. 15) implies that in order to develop a more satisfactory causal analysis of the dynamics of world order it is necessary to engage in a more systematic specification of underlying causal powers, mechanisms, and processes. Reus-Smit (Ch. 5) indicates how we might develop a generative theory of international social change by focusing on how rights regimes have, by distributing legitimate social powers, empowered some actors and disempowered others, thereby creating powerful incentives for change. Linklater (Ch. 17), meanwhile, illustrates the potential of a more sociological inquiry into the complex relationship between cultural ideas, norms, and practices at the domestic and international levels.

A second possible direction for further inquiry consists in identifying more clearly the situatedness of Bull's approach, that is, the extent to which it draws on assumptions of which Bull himself may not have been fully aware. Bain's (Ch. 4) contention that Bull's account of international order is shaped by a dispute in medieval theology is significant in this regard because, as Bain points out, Bull was so hostile to religion. This suggests that Bull himself was not aware of the roots of the concepts and arguments on which he drew, from which we might infer that he was equally unaware of the normative slant they brought to his framework. Kaczmarska (Ch. 16) emphasizes the importance of viewing Bull's conceptual framework as offering a representation of the world, a representation that is no less situated than alternative conceptual framings, such as the 'Russian world', which liberal, Western scholars may more readily regard as ideologically loaded. Insofar as our focus is on the value of the interpretive framework Bull provides, these contributions remind us that, as Weber observed, all knowledge of social life is 'knowledge from a *specific point of view*' (2004, 381).

The final direction of further inquiry suggested by this volume is to revisit Bull's ideas about what a just world order might potentially consist in. As previously noted, Bull offers a provisional defence of international society, despite the injustices associated with it. Yet he also surmises that '[w]orld justice may be ultimately reconcilable with world order' in a 'world or cosmopolitan society that provides for both' (1977, 88). However, he has little to say about the content of a just world order beyond his supposition that it will be underpinned by a 'cosmopolitan society' or 'cosmopolitan community' (1977, 26, 68, 152, 275), a supposition which appears to be rooted in his belief that the modern international society is itself underpinned by a cosmopolitan culture (1977, 316–17). This lack of interest in the form which an alternative to the states system might take is, once again, illustrative of Bull's restricted political vision. The contributions to this volume open up some tantalizing possibilities. Pasha (Ch. 6) demonstrates how closely the cosmopolitan culture which Bull prized is implicated in the historical injustice of colonialism. Keal's (Ch. 13) analysis of claims to indigenous sovereignty indicates the need for a just world order to accommodate group rights. True's (Ch. 14) inquiry into the unravelling of patriarchy indicates the backlash that the spread of Western values can create. Falkner (Ch. 12), meanwhile, raises the question of how a transition to a more solidarist basis for human affairs might be possible.

These possible future directions of inquiry all relate, broadly, to Bull's political vision. If *The Anarchical Society* remains relevant today partly because it is so much more than a treatise on international society, then we must also accept that, in looking beyond international society, Bull's vision is limited. In developing that vision, however, we would do well to retain something of Bull's commitment to justice, his appreciation of the value of order, his sensitivity to the difficult trade-offs that are the stuff of politics, and his caution about pressing our knowledge claims too far and too fast.

Consolidated Bibliography

Aalto, Pami. 2007. 'Russia's Quest for International Society and the Prospects for Regional-level International Societies'. *International Relations* 21(4): 459–78.
Achkasov, V.A. and V.A. Gutorov (eds.). 2008. *Politologiya*. Moscow: Vysshee obrazovaniye.
al-Baghdadi, Abu-Bakr. 2014. 'ISIS Abu Bakr al-Baghdadi first Friday sermon as so-called "Caliph"'. https://english.alarabiya.net/en/webtv/reports/2014/07/07/ISIS-Abu-Bakr-al-Baghdidi-first-Friday-sermon-as-so-called-Caliph-.html, accessed 23 August 2016.
al-Muhajirah, Umm Sumayyah. 2014. 'Slave-girls or prostitutes'. *Dabiq* 9: 44–9.
al-ʿUbaydi, Muhammad et al. 2014. 'The Group That Calls Itself a State: Understanding the Evolution and Challenges of the Islamic State'. West Point: The combating Terrorism Center at West Point: 105.
Albert, Mathias. 2016. *A Theory of World Politics*. Cambridge: Cambridge University Press.
Albert, Mathias, Barry Buzan, and Michael Zürn (eds.). 2013. *Bringing Sociology to International Relations: World Politics as Differentiation Theory*. Cambridge: Cambridge University Press.
Albert, Mathias, Gorm Harste, Knud Jørgensen, and Heikki Patomäki. 2012. 'Introduction: World State Futures'. *Cooperation and Conflict* 47(2): 145–56.
Alderson, Kai, and Andrew Hurrell. 2000. *Hedley Bull on International Society*. Basingstoke: Macmillan Press.
Alfred, Taiaiake. 1999. *Peace, Power, Righteousness: An Indigenous Manifesto*. Ontario: Oxford University Press.
Alfred, Taiaiake. 2005. 'Sovereignty'. In *Sovereignty Matters: Locations of Contestation and Possibility in Indigenous Struggles for Self-Determination*, ed. Joanne Baker, 33–50. Lincoln and London: University of Nebraska Press.
Alkhshali, Hamdi and Dana Ford. 2014. 'ISIS announces new currency'. <http://edition.cnn.com/2014/11/13/world/meast/isis-currency/>, accessed 23 August 2014.
Allan, Pierre and Kjell Goldmann (eds.). 1992. *The End of the Cold War: Evaluating Theories of International Relations*. Dordrecht: Martinus Nijhoff.
Allen-Ebrahimian, Bethany. 2014. 'Putin Hits on China's First Lady'. *Foreign Policy* (November): 10.
Allison, Graham. 2010. 'Nuclear Disorder: Surveying Atomic Threats'. *Foreign Affairs* 89(1): 74–85.
Allison, Roy. 2006. '"Russia in Europe" or "Russia and Europe"'. In *Putin's Russia and the Enlarged Europe*, ed. Roy Allison, Margot Light, and Stephen White, 160–80. London, Oxford: Royal Institute of International Affairs Blackwell Pub.
Anghie, Antony. [2004] 2007. *Imperialism, Sovereignty and the Making of International Law*. Cambridge: Cambridge University Press.
Anievas, Alexander, Nivi Manchanda, and Robbie Shilliam. 2015. *Race and Racism in International Relations: Confronting the Global Colour Line*. Abingdon: Routledge.

Anonymous. 2014a. 'This is the Promise of Allah'. < https://ia902505.us.archive.org/28/items/poa_25984/EN.pdf >, accessed 30 September, 2015.

Anonymous. 2014b. 'The Words of the Enemy: The American crusader Gary Berntsen'. *Dabiq* 8: 57.

Anonymous. 2014c. 'The Islamic State in the Words of the Enemy'. *Dabiq* 1: 32–3.

Anonymous. 2014d. 'Erasing the Legacy of a Ruined Nation'. *Dabiq* 8: 22–4.

Anonymous. 2014e. 'Introduction'. *Dabiq* 1: 4–5.

Anonymous. 2014f. 'The Birth of Two Wilayat'. *Dabiq* 3: 18–20.

Anonymous. 2014g. 'A Window into the Islamic State'. *Dabiq* 4: 27–9.

Anonymous. 2014h. 'From Hijra to Khilafah'. *Dabiq* 1: 34–41.

Anonymous. 2015. 'Why Islamic State's Gold Coins Won't Replace the Global Banking System'. *The Economist* (3 September). <http://www.economist.com/blogs/economist-explains/2015/09/economist-explains-1>, accessed 23 August 2016.

Aquanno, Scott M. 2015. 'Crisis, Continuity and Learning: The institutional origins of sub-prime management at the Federal Reserve'. *Competition & Change* 19(1): 3–18.

Arat, Zehra F. Kabasakal. 2015. 'Feminisms, Women's Rights and the United Nations: Would Achieving Gender Equality Empower Women?' *American Political Science Review* 109(4): 674–89.

Armstrong, J.D. 1993. *Revolution and World Order: The Revolutionary State in International Society*. Oxford, New York: Clarendon Press; Oxford University Press.

Aseev, Y.A., I.A. Kants, and I.I. Kravchenko. 2014. *Russkii Mir: Analiz sostoyaniya, problemy*. Stavropol: Argus.

Augustine. 1982. *Eighty-Three Different Questions*, trans. David Mosher. Washington, DC: Catholic University of American Press.

Augustine. 1998. *The City of God Against the Pagans*, ed. and trans. R.W. Dyson. Cambridge: Cambridge University Press.

Avant, Deborah D. 2016. 'Pragmatic Networks and Transnational Governance of Private Military and Security Services'. *International Studies Quarterly* 60(2): 330–42.

Averre, Derek. 2008. 'Russian Foreign Policy and the Global Political Environment'. *Problems of Post-Communism* 55(5): 28–39.

Ayer, Alfred J. 1971 [1936]. *Language, Truth and Logic*. Harmondsworth: Penguin.

Ayson, Robert. 2012. *Hedley Bull and the Accommodation of Power*. Basingstoke: Palgrave Macmilllan.

Ayson, Robert. 2015. *Asia's Security*. London: Palgrave Macmillan.

Baev, Pavel. 1997. 'Russia's Departure from Empire: Self-assertiveness and a New Retreat'. In *Geopolitics in Post-wall Europe: Security, territory and identity*, ed. P. Baev, V.I. Einagel, and O. Tunander, 174–95. Oslo, London: PRIO, Sage.

Bain, William. 2003. *Between Anarchy and Society: Trusteeship and the Obligations of Power*. Oxford: Oxford University Press.

Bain, William. 2015. 'Thomas Hobbes as a Theorist of Anarchy: A Theological Interpretation'. *History of European Ideas* 41(1): 13–28.

BBC. 2015. 'Palestinian Flag Raised at United Nations Headquarters'. *BBC News Online*. 30 September. <http://www.bbc.co.uk/news/world-middle-east-34398174>, accessed 30 September 2015.

Beck, Ulrich. 1992. *Risk Society: Towards a New Modernity*. London: Sage.

Beitz, Charles. 1979. *Political Theory and International Relations*. Princeton: Princeton University Press.
Beitz, Charles. 2011. *The Idea of Human Rights*. Oxford: Oxford University Press.
Behrendt, Larissa. 2003. *Achieving Social Justice*. Sydney: Federation Press.
Benton, Ted. 1977. *Philosophical Foundations of the Three Sociologies*. London: Routledge and Kegan Paul.
Berger, Mark T. 1994. 'The End of the Third World?' *Third World Quarterly* 15(2): 257–75.
Berlin, Isaiah. 1953. *The Hedgehog and the Fox: An Essay on Tolstoy's View of History*. London: Weidenfeld & Nicolson.
Bernstein, Richard J. 1976. *The Restructuring of Social and Political Theory*. Oxford: Blackwell.
Bhaskar, Roy. 1975. *A Realist Theory of Science*. Brighton: Harvester Press.
Bhaskar, Roy. 1993. *Dialectic. The Pulse of Freedom*. London: Verso.
Biermann, Frank, Philipp H. Pattberg, Harro v. Asselt, and Fariborz Zelli. 2009. 'The Fragmentation of Global Governance Architectures: A Framework for Analysis'. *Global Environmental Politics* 9(4): 14–40.
Black, Julia. 2008. 'Constructing and Contesting Legitimacy and Accountability in Polycentric Regulatory Regime'. *Regulation & Governance* 2: 137–64.
Bogucka, Maria. 1991. 'Gesture, Ritual and Social Order in Sixteenth- to Eighteenth-Century Poland'. In *A Cultural History of Gesture*, ed. J. Bremmer and H. Roodenburg, 190–209. Cambridge: Polity.
Boothby, William H. 2016. Interview with author, July 14, 2016.
Boothby, William H., Wolff Heintschel von Heinegg, James Bret Michael, Michael N. Schmitt, and Thomas C. Wingfield. 2012. 'When is a cyberattack a use of force or an armed attack?'. *Computer*, 45(8): 0082–4.
Bordachev, Timofei. 2014. 'Sila, moral, "spravedlivost"'. *Rossiya v Globalnoi Politike* 13(2). http://www.globalaffairs.ru/number/Sila-moral-spravedlivost-16584.
Borko, Yuri. 1997. 'Possible Scenarios for Geopolitical Shifts in Russian-European Relations'. In *Geopolitics in Post-wall Europe: Security, Territory and Identity*, ed. P. Baev, V. I. Einagel, and O. Tunander, 196–213. Oslo, London: PRIO, Sage.
Bouchet, Nicolas. 2016. 'Russia's "Militarization" of Colour Revolutions. Since Ukraine's EuroMaidan, Russia Sees Mass Anti-Regime Protests at Home and Abroad as a Military Threat'. *CSS Policy Perspectives* 4(2), (January). http://www.css.ethz.ch/content/dam/ethz/special-interest/gess/cis/center-for-securities-studies/pdfs/PP4-2.pdf (8 July 2016).
Bourdieu, Pierre. 2004. *Science of Science and Reflexivity*. Chicago: University of Chicago Press.
Brennan, Frank. 1995. *One Land One Nation: Mabo - Towards 2001*. St Lucia: University of Queensland Press.
Brenton, Anthony. 1994. *The Greening of Machiavelli. The Evolution of International Environmental Politics*. London: Earthscan/RIIA.
Brenton, Anthony. 2013. '"Great Powers" in Climate Politics'. *Climate Policy* 13(5): 541–6.
Bridge, Carl and Kent Fedorowich. 2003. 'Mapping the British World'. *The Journal of Imperial and Commonwealth History* 31(2): 1–15.

Brodie, Bernard, Frederick Sherwood Dunn, Arnold Wolfers, Percy Ellwood Corbett, and William Thornton Rickert Fox. 1946. *The Absolute Weapon: Atomic Power and World Order*. New York: Harcourt & Brace.

Brooks, Stephen G. and William C. Wohlforth. 2016. 'The Once and Future Superpower', *Foreign Affairs* 95(3) (May/June): 11.

Brown, Chris. 2009. 'The Development of International Relations Theory in the United Kingdom: Traditions, Contemporary Perspectives and Trajectories'. *International Studies* 46(1–2): 221–37.

Brown, Chris. 2011. 'The Development of International Relations Theory in the UK: Traditions, Contemporary Perspectives, and Trajectories'. *International Relations of the Asia-Pacific* 11(2): 309–30.

Browning, Christopher. 2008. 'Reassessing Putin's Project: Reflections on IR theory and the West'. *Problems of Post-Communism* 55(5): 3–13.

Brummer, Chris. 2012. *Soft Law and the Global Financial System*. Cambridge: Cambridge University Press.

Brunkhorst, Hauke. 2012. 'The Co-Evolution of Cosmopolitan and National Statehood – Preliminary Theoretical Considerations on the Historical Evolution of Constitutionalism'. *Cooperation and Conflict* 47(2): 176–99.

Brunner, Emil. 1948. *Christianity and Civilisation*, vol 1. London: Nisbet & Co.

Brzezinski, Zbigniew. 1970. *Between Two Ages: America's Role in the Technetronic Era*. New York: Viking Books.

Bukovansky, Mlada, Ian Clark, Robyn Eckersley, Richard Price, Christian Reus-Smit. and Nicholas J. Wheeler. 2012. *Special Responsibilities: Global Problems and American Power*. Cambridge: Cambridge University Press.

Bulkeley, Harriet, Liliana Andonova, Michele M. Betsill, Daniel Compagnon, Thomas Hale, Matthew J. Hoffmann, Peter Newell, Matthew Paterson, Charles Roger, and Stacy D. VanDeveer. 2014. *Transnational Climate Change Governance*. Cambridge: Cambridge University Press.

Bull, Hedley. 1958. 'World Opinion and International Organization'. *International Relations* 1(9) (April): 428–39.

Bull, Hedley. 1959a. 'Disarmament and the International System'. *The Australian Journal of Politics and History* 5(1) (May): 41–50.

Bull, Hedley. 1959b. 'The Arms Race and the Banning of Nuclear Tests'. *Political Quarterly* 30(4): 344–56. Reprinted in *Hedley Bull on Arms Control*, selected and introduced by Robert O'Neill and David N. Schwartz, 235–48 (1987). Basingstoke: Macmillan.

Bull, Hedley. 1961. *The Control of the Arms Race: Disarmament and Arms Control in the Nuclear Age*. London: Weidenfeld & Nicolson.

Bull, Hedley. 1965a. 'Disarmament and Arms Control'. *The British Survey* 190 (January): 1–10.

Bull, Hedley. 1965b. 'Introduction to the Second Edition'. *The Control of the Arms Race*, 2nd edn. New York: Praeger.

Bull, Hedley. 1966a. 'International Theory: The Case for a Classical Approach'. *World Politics* 18(3): 361–77.

Bull, Hedley. 1966b. 'Society and Anarchy in International Relations'. In *Diplomatic Investigations: Essays in the Theory of International Politics*, ed. Herbert Butterfield and Martin Wight, 35–50. London: George Allen & Unwin.

Bull, Hedley. 1966c. 'The Grotian Conception of International Society'. In *Diplomatic Investigations: Essays in the Theory of International Politics*, ed. Herbert Butterfield and Martin Wight, 51–73. London: Allen & Unwin.

Bull, Hedley. 1967. 'Western Policy and Nuclear Proliferation in Asia'. *World Review*. 6(3) (October): 1–15.

Bull, Hedley. 1968. 'The Political and Strategic Background to Australia's Defence'. In *The Economics of Defence*, ed. R.H. Scott, Economic Papers 29 (November) Economics Society of Australia and New Zealand, NSW & Victorian Branches: 1–16.

Bull, Hedley. 1969. 'International Theory: The Case for a Classical Approach'. In *Contending Approaches to International Politics*, ed. Klaus Knorr and James N. Rosenau, 20–38. Princeton: Princeton University Press.

Bull, Hedley. 1971a. 'Order vs. Justice in International Society'. *Political Studies* 19(3) (September): 269–83.

Bull, Hedley. 1971b. 'Civil Violence and International Order'. In *Civil Violence and the International System*, part 2: *Violence and International Society*. Adelphi Paper 83 (December): 27–36. London: IISS.

Bull, Hedley. 1971c. 'The New Balance of Power in Asia and the Pacific'. *Foreign Affairs* 49(4) (July): 669–81.

Bull, Hedley. 1971d. 'Europe and the Wider World'. *The Round Table* 244 (October): 455–63.

Bull, Hedley. 1972a. 'International Relations as an Academic Pursuit'. *Australian Outlook* 26(3): 251–65.

Bull, Hedley. 1972b. 'The Theory of International Politics 1919-1969'. In *The Aberystwyth Papers: International Politics, 1919-1969*, ed. Brian Porter, 30–55. London: Oxford University Press for the University College of Wales.

Bull, Hedley. 1975. 'Rethinking Non-Proliferation'. *International Affairs* 51(2): 175–89.

Bull, Hedley. 1976. 'The West and the Third World'. *Dyason House Papers* 2(5) (June): 1–5.

Bull, Hedley. 1977. *The Anarchical Society. A Study of Order in World Politics*. London: Macmillan.

Bull, Hedley. 1979a. 'Human Rights and World Politics'. In *Moral Claims in World Affairs*, ed. Ralph Pettman, 79–91. London: Croom Helm.

Bull, Hedley. 1979b. 'The Third World and International Society.' *The Year Book of World Affairs* 33: 15–31.

Bull, Hedley. 1979c. 'Natural Law and International Relations'. *British Journal of International Studies* 5(2): 171–81.

Bull, Hedley. 1979d. 'The Universality of Human Rights'. *Millennium: Journal of International Studies* 8(2): 155–9.

Bull, Hedley. 1980. 'The Great Irresponsibles? The United States, the Soviet Union and World Order'. *International Journal* 35(3): 437–47.

Bull, Hedley. 1984a. 'The Emergence of a Universal International Society'. In *The Expansion of International Society*, ed. Hedley Bull and Adam Watson. Oxford: Clarendon Press.

Bull, Hedley. 1984b. 'The Revolt against the West'. In *The Expansion of International Society*, ed. Hedley Bull and Adam Watson, 217–28. Oxford: Clarendon Press.

Bull, Hedley. 1991 [1976]. 'Martin Wight and the Theory of International Relations'. In *International Theory: The Three Traditions*, by Martin Wight, ed. Gabriele Wight and Brian Porter, ix–xxiii. Leicester: Leicester University Press for The Royal Institute of International Affairs.

Bull, Hedley. 1995. *The Anarchical Society: A Study of Order in World Politics*, 2nd edn. Houndmills: Macmillan.

Bull, Hedley. 2000a. 'The Grotian Conception of International Society (1966)'. In *Hedley Bull on International Society*, ed. Kai Alderson and Andrew Hurrell, 95–118. Basingstoke: Macmillan.

Bull, Hedley. 2000b. 'Natural Law and International Relations (1979)'. In *Hedley Bull on International Society*, ed. Kai Alderson and Andrew Hurrell, 157–69. Basingstoke: Macmillan.

Bull, Hedley. 2000c. 'Justice in International Relations: The 1983 Hagey Lectures (1984)'. In *Hedley Bull on International Society*, ed. Kai Alderson and Andrew Hurrell, 206–27. Basingstoke: Macmillan.

Bull, Hedley. 2000d. 'International Relations as an Academic Pursuit (1972)'. In *Hedley Bull on International Society*, ed. Kai Alderson and Andrew Hurrell, 246–64. Basingstoke: Macmillan.

Bull, Hedley. 2002. *The Anarchical Society: A Study of Order in World Politics*, 3rd edn. Houndmills: Palgrave.

Bull, Hedley. 2012. *The Anarchical Society: A Study of Order in World Politics*, 4th edn. New York: Columbia University Press.

Bull, Hedley and Adam Watson (eds). 1984. *The Expansion of International Society*. Oxford: Clarendon Press.

Bunzel, Cole. 2015. 'From Paper State to Caliphate: The Ideology of the Islamic State'. *Analysis Paper*, Centre for Middle East Policy at Brookings 19: 48.

Buranelli, Filippo C. 2014. 'Knocking on Heaven's Door: Russia, Central Asia and the Mediated Expansion of International Society'. *Millennium* 42(3): 817–36.

Busby, Joshua W. 2008. 'Who Cares about the Weather? Climate change and US national security'. *Security Studies* 17(3): 468–504.

Büthe, Tim and Walter Mattli. 2013. *The New Global Rulers: The Privatization of Regulation in the World Economy*. Princeton: Princeton University Press.

Butterfield, Herbert and Martin Wight (eds.). 1966. *Diplomatic Investigations: Essays in the Theory of International Politics*. London: Allen & Unwin.

Buzan, Barry. 2001. 'The English School: An Underexploited Resource in IR'. *Review of International Studies* 27(3): 471–88.

Buzan, Barry. 2004. *From International to World Society?: English School Theory and the Social Structure of Globalisation*. Cambridge: Cambridge University Press.

Buzan, Barry. 2005. 'International Political Economy and Globalization'. In *International Society and its Critics*, ed. Alex J. Bellamy, 115–33. Oxford: Oxford University Press.

Buzan, Barry. 2014. 'The "Standard of Civilization" as an English School Concept'. *Millennium: Journal of International Studies* 42(3): 576–94.

Buzan, Barry and George Lawson. 2015. *The Global Transformation*. Cambridge: Cambridge University Press.

Cagaptay, Soner. 2006. *Islam, Secularism, and Nationalism in Modern Turkey: Who is a Turk?* Abingdon: Routledge.

Callahan, William A. 2004. 'Nationalising International Society: Race, Class and the English School'. *Global Society* 18(4): 305–22.

Caporaso, James A. 1996. 'The European Union and Forms of State: Westphalian, Regulatory or Post-Modern?' *Journal of Common Market Studies* 34(1): 29–52.

Carr, Edward H. 1939. *The Twenty Years' Crisis 1919–1939*. London: Macmillan.

Carr, Edward H. 1946. *The Twenty Years Crisis 1919–39. An Introduction to the Study of International Relations*. London: Macmillan & Co.

Carr, Madeline. 2016a. *US Power and the Internet in International Relations: The Irony of the Information Age*. Basingstoke: Palgrave Macmillan.

Carr, Madeline. 2016b. 'Public–private Partnerships in National Cyber-security Strategies'. *International Affairs* 92(1): 43–62.

Carter, Jimmy. 2014. 'Patriarchy and Violence against Women and Girls'. *The Lancet* 385, 9977: 40–1.

Chakste, Mintauts. 1949. 'Soviet Concepts of the State, International Law and Sovereignty'. *The American Journal of International Law* 43(1): 21–36.

Chebankova, Elena. 2016. 'Contemporary Russian Conservatism'. *Post-Soviet Affairs* 32(1): 28–54.

Checkel, Jeffrey T. 2005. 'International Institutions and Socialization in Europe: Introduction and Framework'. *International Organization* 59(4): 801–26.

Choucri, Nazli. 2012. *Cyberpolitics in International Relations*. Cambridge: The MIT Press.

Cimoli, Mario and Gabriel Porcile. 2011. 'Global Growth and International Cooperation: A Structuralist Perspective'. *Cambridge Journal of Economics* 35(2): 383–400.

Clark, David and Susan Landau. 2011. 'Untangling Attribution'. *Harvard National Security Journal* (2): 323–52.

Clark, Ian. 2007. *International Legitimacy and World Society*. Oxford: Oxford University Press.

Clark, Ian. 2011. *Hegemony in International Society*. Oxford: Oxford University Press.

Clark, Ian. 2013. *The Vulnerable in International Society*. Oxford: Oxford University Press.

Clayton, Mark. 2010. 'Stuxnet: Ahmadinejad admits cyberweapon hit Iran nuclear program'. *The Christian Science Monitor* (November 30). http://www.csmonitor.com/USA/2010/1130/Stuxnet-Ahmadinejad-admits-cyberweapon-hit-Iran-nuclear-program.

Clunan, Ann L. 2009. *The Social Construction of Russia's Resurgence: Aspirations, Identity, and Security Interests*. Baltimore: Johns Hopkins University Press.

Confortini, Catia. 2012. *Intelligent Compassion: Feminist Critical Methodology in the Women's International League for Peace and Freedom*. New York: Oxford University Press.

Cordesman, Anthony H. 2014. 'Russia and the "Color Revolution". A Russian Military View of a World Destabilized by the US and the West'. *CSIS Center for Strategic and International Studies* 28 (May). https://www.csis.org/analysis/russia-and-%E2%80%9Ccolor-revolution%E2%80%9D (6 July 2016).

Cox, Robert W. with Timothy J. Sinclair. 1996. *Approaches to World Order*. Cambridge: Cambridge University Press.

Craig, Campbell. 2003. *Glimmer of a New Leviathan: Total War in the Realism of Niebuhr, Morgenthau, and Waltz*. New York: Columbia University Press.

Craig, Campbell and Jan Ruzicka. 2013. 'The Nonproliferation Complex'. *Ethics and International Affairs* 27(3): 329–248.
Craig, Campbell and Jan Ruzicka. Forthcoming. *Unipolarity and the Politics of Nuclear Nonproliferation*. Ithaca: Cornell University Press.
Crawford, Neta C. 1994. 'A security regime among democracies: cooperation among Iroquois nations'. *International Organization* 48(3) (Summer): 345–85.
Credit Suisse Research Institute. 2012. *Gender Diversity and the Impact on Corporate Performance 2005–2011*. Zurich: Credit Suisse.
Dangerfield, George. 1966 [1935]. *The Strange Death of Liberal England*. London: MacGibbon & Kee.
Davies, Sara and Jacqui True. 2017. 'Norm entrepreneurship in foreign policy: William Hague and the prevention of sexual violence in conflict'. *Foreign Policy Analysis*.
Derrida, Jacques. 1994. *Specters of Marx: The State of the Debt, the Work of Mourning, and the New International*, trans. Peggy Kamuf; with introd. by Bernd Magnus and Stephen Cullenberg. New York: Routledge.
Delcour, Laure and Wolczuk, Kataryna. 2015. 'Spoiler or Facilitator of Democratization? Russia's Role in Georgia and Ukraine'. *Democratization* 22(3): 459–78.
Demchak, Chris. 2011. *Wars of Disruption and Resilience: Cybered Conflict, Power, and National Security*. Athens: University of Georgia Press.
Department of Justice. 2014. 'U.S. Charges Five Chinese Military Hackers for Cyber Espionage Against U.S. Corporations and a Labor Organization for Commercial Advantage'. US Department of Justice press release (19 May). https://www.justice.gov/opa/pr/us-charges-five-chinese-military-hackers-cyber-espionage-against-us-corporations-and-labor.
Deudney, Daniel. 2007. *Bounding Power: Republican Security Theory from the Polis to the Global Village*. Princeton, NJ: Princeton University Press.
Deutsch, Karl W. 1954. 'Cracks in the Monolith: Possibilities and Patterns of Disintegration in Totalitarian Systems'. In *Totalitarianism. Proceedings of a Conference Held at the American Academy of Arts and Sciences March 1953*, ed. C.J. Friedrich, 308–33. Cambridge, MA: Harvard University Press.
Deutsch, Karl W. 1957. *Political Community and the North Atlantic Area. International Organization in the Light of Historical Experience*. Princeton, NJ: Princeton University Press.
Dodson, Mick. 1998. 'Linking International Standards with Contemporary Concerns of Aboriginal and Torres Strait Islander Peoples'. In *Indigenous Peoples, the United Nations and Human Rights*, ed. Sarah Pritchard, 18–29. Annandale NSW: The Federation Press.
Donnelly, Jack. 1998. 'Human Rights: A New Standard of Civilization?' *International Affairs* 74(1): 1–23.
Drezner, Dan. 2014. *The System Worked: How the World Stopped Another Great Depression*. Oxford: Oxford University Press.
Du Bois, W.E.B. 1925. *The New Negro, An Interpretation*. New York: Albert and Charles Boni.
Duncan, Peter J.S. 2013. 'Russia, the West and the 2007–2008 Electoral Cycle: Did the Kremlin Really Fear a "Coloured Revolution"?' *Europe-Asia Studies* 65(1): 1–25.

Dunne, Tim. 1995. 'The Social Construction of International Society'. *European Journal of International Relations* 1(3): 367–89.
Dunne, Tim. 1998a. 'A British School of International Relations'. In *The British Study of Politics in the Twentieth Century*, ed. B. Barry, A. Brown, and J. Hayward, 395–424. Oxford: Oxford University Press.
Dunne, Tim. 1998b. *Inventing International Society: A History of the English School*. Basingstoke: Palgrave Macmillan.
Dunne, Tim and Christian Reus-Smit (eds). 2017. *The Globalization of International Society*. Oxford: Oxford University Press.
Eckersley, Robyn. 2007. 'Ambushed: The Kyoto Protocol, the Bush Administrations Climate Policy and the Erosion of Legitimacy'. *International Politics* 44(2–3): 306–24.
Edkins, Jenny and Maja Zehfuss. 2005. 'Generalising the International'. *Review of International Studies* 31(3): 451–71.
Efremenko, Dmitri. 2014. 'Za Flazhki'. *Rossiya v Globalnoi Politike* 13(3): http://www.globalaffairs.ru/number/Za-flazhki-16764.
Elias, Norbert. 2008. 'Towards a Theory of Communities'. In *Essays II: On Civilizing Processes, State Formation and National Identity*. Dublin: University College Dublin Press.
Elias, Norbert. 2010. 'The Fate of German Baroque Poetry: Between the Traditions of Court and Social Class'. In *Mozart and Other Essays on Courtly Art*. Dublin: University College Dublin Press.
Elias, Norbert. 2012 [1939]. *On the Process of Civilization: Sociogenetic and Psychogenetic Investigations*. Dublin: University College Dublin Press.
Elias, Norbert and John Scotson. 2012. *The Established and the Outsiders*. Dublin: University College Dublin Press.
Ellsberg, Mary, Diana J. Arango, Michael Morton, Floriza Gennari, Sveinung Kiplesund, Manuel Contreras, and Charlotte Watts. 2015. 'Prevention of Violence against Women and Girls: What Does the Evidence Say?' *The Lancet* 385, 9977: 1555–66.
Engels, Friedrich. 1884 [2010]. *The Origins of the Family, State and Private Property*. London: Penguin Classics.
Eriksson, Johan and Giampiero Giacomello. 2006. 'The Information Revolution, Security and International Relations: (IR)relevant Theory?' *International Political Science Review* 27(3): 221–44.
Erskine, Toni and Madeline Carr. 2016. 'Beyond "Quasi-Norms": The Challenges and Potential of Engaging with Norms in Cyberspace'. In *International Cyber Norms: Legal, Policy and Industry Perspectives*, ed. Anna-Maria Osula and Henry Rõigas, 87–109. Tallinn: NATO CCD COE Publications.
Eskildsen, Robert. 2002. 'Of Civilisation and Savages: The Mimetic Imperialism of Japan's 1874 Expedition to Taiwan'. *American Historical Review* 107(2): 388–418.
Fabian, Johannes. 1983. *Time and the Other: How Anthropology Makes Its Object*. New York: Columbia University Press.
Falk, Richard. 1975. *A Study of Future Worlds*. New York: Free Press.
Falk, Richard. 1999. *Predatory Globalization: A Critique*. Cambridge, UK: Polity.
Falk, Richard. 2000. 'A "New Medievalism"?' In *Contending Images of World Politics*, ed. Greg Fry and Jacinta O'Hagan, 106–16. Basingstoke: Macmillan.

Falk, Richard. 2002. *The Great Terror War*. Northampton, MA: Olive Branch Press.

Falk, Richard. 2012a. 'Global Climate Change, Human Security and the Future of Democracy'. In *Global Crises and the Crisis of Global Leadership* ed. Stephen Gill. Cambridge: Cambridge University Press.

Falk, Richard. 2012b. 'The Second Cycle of Ecological Urgency: An Environmental Justice Perspective' and 'Towards a Necessary Utopianism: Democratic Global Governance'. In *The Writings of Richard Falk: Towards Humane Global Governance*, 173-91, 430-47. New Delhi, India: Orient Blackswan.

Falk, Richard. 2015. 'Henry Kissinger: Hero of Our Time'. *Millennium* 44(1): 155-64.

Falk, Richard. 2016. 'Climate Change, Policy Knowledge, and the Temporal Imagination'. In *Reimagining Climate Change*, ed. Paul Wapner and Hilal Elver, 49-68. Milton Park, UK: Routledge.

Falk, Richard and David Krieger. 2012. *The Path to Zero: Dialogues on Nuclear Dangers*. Boulder, CO: Paradigm.

Falk, Richard A. 1971. *This Endangered Planet: Prospects and Proposals for Human Survival*. New York: Random House.

Falkner, Robert. 2003. 'Private Environmental Governance and International Relations: Exploring the Links'. *Global Environmental Politics* 3(2): 72-87.

Falkner, Robert. 2012. 'Global Environmentalism and the Greening of International Society'. *International Affairs* 88(3): 503-22.

Falkner, Robert. 2016a. 'A Minilateral Solution for Global Climate Change? On Bargaining Efficiency, Club Benefits and International Legitimacy'. *Perspectives on Politics* 14(1): 87-101.

Falkner, Robert. 2016b. 'The Paris Agreement and the New Logic of International Climate Policy'. *International Affairs* 92(5): 1107-25.

Falkner, Robert, Hannes Stephan, and John Vogler. 2010. 'International Climate Policy after Copenhagen: Towards a "Building Blocks" Approach'. *Global Policy* 1(3): 252-62.

Farrell, Henry and Abraham Newman. 2014. 'Domestic Institutions Beyond the Nation State: Charting the New Interdependence Approach'. *World Politics* 66(2): 331-63.

Farwell, James and Rafal Rohozinski. 2011. 'Stuxnet and the Future of Cyberwar'. *Survival: Global Politics and Strategy* 53(1): 23-40.

Faure, Michael G. and Ton Hartlief. 2003. *Insurance and Expanding Systemic Risks*. Paris: OECD.

Feaver, Peter D. 1995. 'Optimists, Pessimists, and Theories of Nuclear Proliferation Management'. *Security Studies* 4(4): 754-72.

Fenenko, Alexei. 2016. 'Pochemu v Amerike ne lubiyat publikovat' rossiiskikh avtorov'. *Mezhdunarodnyye protsessy* 14(1): 172-80.

Finnemore, Martha. 1996. *National Interests in International Society*. Ithaca: Cornell University Press.

Finnemore, Martha. 2001. 'Exporting the English School'. *Review of International Studies* 27(3): 509-13.

Fishman, Brian. 2007. 'Fourth Generation Governance: Sheikh Tamimi Defends the Islamic State of Iraq'. West Point: Combating Terrorism Center at West Point.

Fomenko, Aleksandr V. 2009. *Russkii Mir i Geopoliticheskiye Strannosti. Istoriya kak faktor politiki*. Moscow: Izdatelstvo RGTEU.

Foot, Rosemary. 2000. *Rights Beyond Borders: The Global Community and the Struggle over Human Rights in China*. Oxford: Oxford University Press.

Fraser, Nancy. 1997. *Justice Interruptus: Critical Reflections on the Post-Socialist Condition*. New York: Routledge.

Fraser, Nancy. 2005. 'Reframing Justice in a Globalized World'. *The New Left Review* 36 (November–December): 69–88.

Frieden, Jeffry A. 2006. *Global Capitalism: Its Rise and Fall in the Twentieth Century*. New York: W.W. Norton.

Friedrichs, Jörg. 2001. 'The Meaning of New Mediaevalism'. *European Journal of International Relations* 7(4): 475–502.

Fritel, Jérôme. 2014. 'D.A.E.C.H, naissance d'un Etat terroriste'. <http://info.arte.tv/fr/daech-naissance-dun-etat-terroriste> Accessed 23 August 2016.

Fukuyama, Francis. 1998. 'Women and the Evolution of World Politics'. *Foreign Affairs* 77(5): 24–40.

Gallagher, Kevin P. 2015. *Ruling Capital: Emerging Markets and the Reregulation of Cross-Border Finance*. Ithaca, NY: Cornell University Press.

Gartzke, Erik. 2013. 'The Myth of Cyberwar: Bringing War in Cyberspace Back Down to Earth'. *International Security* 38(2): 41–73.

Gavin, Francis J. 2012. 'Politics, History and the Ivory Tower-Policy Gap in the Nuclear Proliferation Debate'. *Journal of Strategic Studies* 35(4): 573–600.

Gemenne, François, Jon Barnett, W. Neil Adger, and Geoffrey D. Dabelko. 2014. 'Climate and Security: Evidence, Emerging Risks, and a New Agenda'. *Climatic Change* 123(1): 1–9.

Germain, Randall, ed. 2016. *Susan Strange and the Future of Global Political Economy: Power, Control and Transformation*. Abingdon, UK: Routledge.

German Advisory Council on Global Change. 2008. *Climate Change as a Security Risk*. London: Earthscan.

Gill, Stephen. 1998. 'New Constitutionalism, Democratisation and Global Political Economy'. *Pacifica Review: Peace, Security & Global Change* 10(1): 23–38.

Gill, Stephen. 2008. *Power and Resistance in the New World Order*, 2nd edn. New York: Palgrave Macmillan.

Gill, Stephen and David Law. 1989. 'Global Hegemony and the Structural Power of Capital'. *International Studies Quarterly* 33(4): 475–99.

Gong, Gerrit. 1984. *The 'Standard of Civilization' in International Society*. Oxford: Clarendon Press.

Goodhart, Charles. 2011. *The Basel Committee on Banking Supervision*. Cambridge: Cambridge University Press.

Goodhart, Charles and Dirk Schoenmaker. 2006. 'Burden Sharing in a Banking Crisis in Europe'. *Sveriges Riksbank Economic Review* 2: 34–57.

Gramsci, Antonio. 1971. *Selections from the Prison Notebooks of Antonio Gramsci*, ed. and trans. Quintin Hoare and Geoffrey Nowell-Smith. New York: International Publishers.

Grande, Edgar and Louis Pauly. 2005. *Complex Sovereignty: Reconstituting Political Authority in the Twenty First Century*. Toronto: University of Toronto Press.

'Greenland reaps benefits of global warming'. *The Independent* 31 March 2013, at: http://www.independent.co.uk/environment/climate-change/greenland-reaps-benefits-of-global-warming-8555241.html.

Grotius, Hugo. 1988. *Meletius Or Letter on the Points of Agreement Between Christians*, translated by Guillaume H.M. Posthumus Meyjes. Leiden: E.J. Brill.

Grotius, Hugo. 2001. *De Imperio Summarum Potestatum Circa Sacra*, vol. 1, ed. and trans. Harm-Jan Van Dam. Leiden: Brill.

Grotius, Hugo. 2004. *The Free Sea*, ed. David Armitage. Indianapolis: Liberty Fund.

Grotius, Hugo. 2005. *The Rights of War and Peace*, vol. 1, ed. Richard Tuck. Indianapolis: Liberty Fund.

Grotius, Hugo. 2006. *Commentary on the Law of Prize and Booty*, ed. Martine Julia van Ittersum. Indianapolis: Liberty Fund, 2006.

Grotius, Hugo. 2012. *The Truth of the Christian Religion*, ed. Maria Rosa Antognazza. Indianapolis: Liberty Fund.

Grynkewich, Alexus. 2008. 'Welfare as Warfare: How Violent Non-State Groups Use Social Services to Attack the State'. *Studies in Conflict & Terrorism* 31(4): 350–70.

Gunning, Jeroen. 2008. *Hamas in Politics: Democracy, Religion, Violence*. New York: Columbia University Press.

Guseinov, A.A., A.A. Kara-Murza, and A.F. Yakovleva (eds.). 2011. *Russkii Mir kak Tsivilizatsionnoye Prostranstvo*. Moscow: RAN Institut Filosofii.

Hague, William. 2010. 'Speech: Britain's Foreign Policy in a Networked World', Foreign and Commonwealth Office, 1 July. https://www.gov.uk/government/speeches/britain-s-foreign-policy-in-a-networked-world-2.

Hale, Thomas and Charles Roger. 2014. 'Orchestration and Transnational Climate Governance'. *The Review of International Organizations* 9(1): 59–82.

Hall, Catherine. 2002. *Civilising Subjects: Metropole and Colony in the English Imagination, 1830–1867*. Oxford: Polity.

Hall, Ian. 2011. 'The Revolt against the West: Decolonisation and its Repercussions in British International Thought, 1945–75'. *The International History Review* 33(1): 43–64.

Hall, Rodney Bruce and Thomas J. Biersteker (eds.). 2002. *The Emergence of Private Authority in Global Governance*. Cambridge: Cambridge University Press.

Hall, William E. 1880. *International Law*. Oxford: Clarendon Press.

Harik, Judith P. 2004. *Hezbollah: The Changing Face of Terrorism*. London, New York: I.B. Tauris.

Harré, Rom and Paul Secord. 1972. *The Explanation of Social Behaviour*. Oxford: Blackwell.

Harris Rimmer, Susan. 2015. 'A Critique of Australia's G20 Presidency and the Brisbane Summit 2014'. *Global Summitry* 1(1): 41–63.

Hart, Herbert L.A. 1961. *The Concept of Law*. Oxford: Clarendon Press.

Hart, Herbert L.A. 2012. *The Concept of Law*. 3rd edn. Oxford: Oxford University Press.

Hashim, Ahmed S. 2014. 'The Islamic State: From al-Qaeda Affiliate to Caliphate'. *Middle East Policy* 21(4): 69–83.

Hayek, F.A. 1944. *The Road to Serfdom*. Chicago: University of Chicago Press.

Healey, Jason. 2011. 'Beyond Attribution: Seeking National Responsibility for Cyber Attacks'. *Issue Brief*. The Atlantic Council.

Heeren, Arnold H.L. 1834. *A Manual of the History of the Political System and its Colonies, volume one*. London: D.A. Talboys.

Held, David and Anthony McGrew. 1998. 'The End of the Old Order? Globalization and the Prospects for World Order'. *Review of International Studies* 24: 219–43.

Held, David and Heikki Patomäki. 2006. 'Problems of Global Democracy: A Dialogue'. *Theory, Culture & Society* 23(5): 115–33.

Helleiner, Eric. 2014. *The Status Quo Crisis*. Oxford: Oxford University Press.

Hitchens, Christopher. 2001. *The Trial of Henry Kissinger*. New York: Twelve.

Hjerpe, Mattias and Björn-Ola Linnér. 2010. 'Functions of COP Side-Events in Climate-Change Governance'. *Climate Policy* 10(2): 167–80.

Hobbes, Thomas. 1840. 'Of Liberty and Necessity'. In *The English Works of Thomas Hobbes*, vol. 4, ed. William Molesworth. London: John Bohn.

Hobbes, Thomas. 1996 [1651]. *Leviathan*, rev. student edn., ed. Richard Tuck. Cambridge: Cambridge University Press.

Hobbes, Thomas. 2012. *Leviathan*, vol. 2, ed. Noel Malcolm. Oxford: Oxford University Press.

Hobson, John. 2012. *The Eurocentric Conception of World Politics: Western International Theory, 1760–2010*. Cambridge: Cambridge University Press.

Hoffman, Stanley. 1986. 'Hedley Bull and his Contributions to International Relations'. *International Affairs* 62(2): 179–95.

Hoffmann, Matthew J. 2011. *Climate Governance at the Crossroads: Experimenting with a Global Response after Kyoto*. New York: Oxford University Press.

Hoffmann, Matthew J. 2013. 'Global Climate Change'. In *The Handbook of Global Climate and Environment Policy*, ed. Robert Falkner, 3–18. Cheltenham: John Wiley & Sons Ltd.

Hoffmann, Stanley. 1990. 'International Society'. In *Order and Violence: Hedley Bull and International Relations*, ed. J.D.B. Miller and R.J. Vincent. Oxford: Clarendon Press.

Hoffmann, Stanley. 1995. 'Foreword to the Second Edition: Revisiting *The Anarchical Society*'. In Hedley Bull, *The Anarchical Society: A Study of Order in World Politics*, 2nd edn., vii–xii. Houndmills: Macmillan.

Hollis, Martin and Steve Smith. 1990. *Explaining and Understanding International Relations*. Oxford: Clarendon Press.

Honneth, Axel. 1995. *The Struggle for Recognition: The Moral Grammar of Social Conflicts*. Cambridge MA: The MIT Press.

Hopgood, Stephen. 2013. *The End Times of Human Rights*. Ithaca: Cornell University Press.

Horovitz, Liviu. 2015. 'Beyond Pessimism: Why the Treaty on the Non-Proliferation of Nuclear Weapons Will Not Collapse'. *Journal of Strategic Studies* 38(1–2): 126–58.

Hozic, Aida and Jacqui True (eds). 2016. *Scandalous Economics: The Politics of Gender and Financial Crises*. New York: Oxford University Press.

Huang, Reyko. 2015. 'The Islamic State as an Ordinary Insurgency'. In *Islam and International Order*. POMEPS Studies 15: 13–15.

Hume, David. 1985 [1739/1740]. *A Treatise of Human Nature*. Ed. and Introd. Ernest C. Mossner. London: Penguin Books.

Humphreys, Adam R. C. 2012. 'Another Waltz? Methodological Rhetoric and Practice in *Theory of International Politics*'. *International Relations* 26(4): 389–408.

Hunnicutt, Gwen. 2009. 'Varieties of Patriarchy and Violence against Women'. *Violence against Women* (15)5: 553–73.

Hunt, Krista. 2002. 'The Strategic Co-optation of Women's Rights: Discourse in the "War on Terrorism"'. *International Feminist Journal of Politics* (4)1: 116–21.

Huntington, Samuel P. 1993. 'The Clash of Civilizations?'. *Foreign Affairs* 72(3): 22–49.

Huntington, Samuel P. 1996. *The Clash of Civilizations and the Future of World Politics*. New York: Simon and Schuster.

Hurrell, Andrew. 2002. 'Foreword to the Third Edition: The Anarchical Society 25 Years On'. In Hedley Bull, *The Anarchical Society: A Study of Order in World Politics*, 3rd edn., vii–xxiii. Houndmills: Palgrave.

Hurrell, Andrew. 2007. *On Global Order: Power, Values, and the Constitution of International Society*. Oxford: Oxford University Press.

Hurrell, Andrew. 2012. 'Foreword to the Fourth Edition'. In Hedley Bull, *The Anarchical Society: A Study of Order in World Politics*, 2nd edn., vii–xxvii. Houndmills: Macmillan.

Hurrell, Andrew. 2014. 'Order and Justice'. In *Guide to the English School in International Studies*, ed. Cornelia Navari and David M. Green. Chichester, West Sussex: Wiley Blackwell.

Hurrell, Andrew and Benedict Kingsbury. 1992. 'The International Politics of the Environment: An Introduction'. In *The International Politics of the Environment*, ed. Andrew Hurrell and Benedict Kingsbury, 1–47. Oxford: Clarendon Press.

Hurrell, Andrew and Sandeep Sengupta. 2012. 'Emerging Powers, North-South Relations and Global Climate Politics'. *International Affairs* 88(3): 463–84.

Ikenberry, G. John. 2011. *Liberal Leviathan: The Origins, Crisis, and Transformation of the American World Order*. Princeton, NJ: Princeton University Press.

IMF 2014. *Global Financial Stability Report*. (April): 104. Washington, DC: International Monetary Fund.

Irons, Catherine J. 1992. 'Indigenous Peoples and Self–Determination: Challenging State Sovereignty'. *Case Western Reserve Journal of International Law* 24(2) (Spring): 235–76.

Ivanov, Igor. 2012. 'Anatomia Evropeiskikh Tsennostei'. *Sovremennaya Evropa* 2.

Ivanova, Maria. 2015. 'Paris Climate Summit: Why More Women Need Seats at the Table'. *The Conversation* (5 November).

Ivison, Duncan. 2015. '"Indigenous people" are a Polity: On Sovereignty and Constitutional Recognition'. *The Conversation* 6 July. http://theconversation.com/indigenous-people-are-a-polity-on-sovereignty-and-constitutional-recognition-44287.

Jackson, Patrick Thaddeus. 2011. *The Conduct of Inquiry in International Relations: Philosophy of Science and its Implications for the Study of World Politics*. London: Routledge.

Jackson, Patrick Thaddeus and Daniel H. Nexon. 2013. 'International Theory in a Post-Paradigmatic Era: From Substantive Wagers to Scientific Ontologies'. *European Journal of International Relations* 19(3): 543–65.

Jackson, Robert H. 1990. *Quasi-States: Sovereignty, International Relations and the Third World*. Cambridge: Cambridge University Press.

Jackson, Robert. 2000. *The Global Covenant: Human Conduct in a World of States*. Oxford: Oxford University Press.

James, Harold. 2014. 'The Insuring Instinct'. In *The Value of Risk: Swiss Re and the History of Reinsurance*, ed. Harold James et al. Oxford: Oxford University Press.

Jameson, Frederic. 1999. 'Marx's Purloined Letter'. In *Ghostly Demarcations: A Symposium on Jacques Derrida's Specters of Marx*, ed. Michael Sprinker, 26–67. London and New York: Verso.

Jeffery, Renee. 2006. *Hugo Grotius in International Thought*. Basingstoke: Palgrave Macmillan.

Jessop, Bob. 2012. 'Obstacles to a World State in the Shadow of the World Market'. *Cooperation & Conflict* 47(2): 200–19.

Johnston, Alastair Iain. 2005. 'Conclusions and Extensions: Toward Mid-Range Theorizing and beyond Europe'. *International Organization* 59(4): 1013–44.

Jones, Roy E. 1981. 'The English School of International Relations: A Case for Closure'. *Review of International Studies* 7(1): 1–13.

Jonson, Lena. 2004. *Vladimir Putin and Central Asia: The shaping of Russian foreign policy*. London: I.B. Tauris.

Kaldor, Mary. 2003. 'The Idea of Global Civil Society'. *International Affairs* 79(3): 583–93.

Kaldor, Nicholas. 1972. 'The Irrelevance of Equilibrium Economics'. *Economic Journal* 82(328): 1237–55.

Kandiyoti, Deniz. 1989. 'Bargaining with Patriarchy'. *Gender and Society* (2)3: 274–90.

Kaplan, Morton. 1957. *System and Process in International Politics*. New York: Wiley.

Kaplan, Morton. 1966. 'The New Great Debate: Traditionalism vs. Science in International Relations'. *World Politics* 19(1): 1–20.

Kapstein, Ethan. 1998. *Governing the Global Economy: International Finance and the State*. Cambridge, MA: Harvard University Press.

Karaganov, Sergei. 2014. 'Rossiya-SShA: Dolgoye protivostoyaniye'. *Rossiya v Globalnoi Politike* 13(4). http://www.globalaffairs.ru/number/Rossiya-SShA-dolgoe-protivostoyanie-16923.

Keal, Paul. 2003. *European Conquest and the Rights of Indigenous Peoples: The Backwardness of International Society*. Cambridge: Cambridge University Press.

Keat, Russell and John Urry. 1975. *Social Theory as Science*. London: Routledge and Kegan Paul.

Keck, Margaret E. and Kathryn Sikkink. 1998. *Activists Beyond Borders*. Ithaca: Cornell University Press.

Keck, Margaret E. and Kathryn Sikkink. 1999. 'Transnational Advocacy Networks in International and Regional Politics'. *International Social Science Journal* 51(159): 89–101.

Keene, Edward. 2002. *Beyond the Anarchical Society: A Study of Order in World Politics*. Cambridge: Cambridge University Press.

Keene, Edward. 2009. 'International Society as an Ideal Type'. In *Theorising International Society: English School Methods*, ed. Cornelia Navari, 104–24. Basingstoke: Palgrave Macmillan.

Kello, Lucas. 2013. 'The Meaning of the Cyber Revolution: Perils to Theory and Statecraft'. *International Security* 38(2): 7–40.

Kelsen, Hans J. 1961 [1945]. *General Theory of Law and State*, trans. Anders Wedberg. New York: Russell & Russell.

Kelsen, Hans. 1967. *Pure Theory of Law*, trans. Max Knight. Berkeley. University of California Press.

Keohane, Robert O. (ed.). 1986. *Neorealism and its Critics*. New York: Columbia University Press.

Keohane, Robert O. and Joseph S. Nye, Jr. (eds). 1971. *Transnational Relations and World Politics*. Cambridge, MA: Harvard University Press.

Keohane, Robert O. and Joseph S. Nye, Jr. 1972. *Transnational Relations and World Politics*. Cambridge, MA: Harvard University Press.

Keohane, Robert O. and Joseph S. Nye. 1977. *Power and Interdependence*. Boston: Little, Brown.

Keohane, Robert O. and David G. Victor. 2011. 'The Regime Complex for Climate Change'. *Perspectives on Politics* 9(01): 7–23.

Kerry, John. 2015. In 'ISIS? ISIL? Kerry discusses what to call "Islamic State"'. *The Washington Post* (8 September). <http://wapo.st/XMsccE>. Accessed 23 August 2016.

Keynes, John Maynard. 1920. *The Economic Consequences of the Peace*. New York: Harcourt, Brace and Howe.

Kissinger, Henry. 2014. *World Order*. New York: Penguin.

Klußmann, Uwe, Matthias Schepp, and Klaus Wiegrefe. 2009. 'NATO's Eastward Expansion: Did the West Break Its Promise to Moscow?'. *Der Spiegel* 26 (November). http://www.spiegel.de/international/world/nato-s-eastward-expansion-did-the-west-break-its-promise-to-moscow-a-663315.html (1 July 2016).

Knake, Robert K. 2010. 'Untangling Attribution: Moving to Accountability in Cyberspace'. *Prepared Statement before the Subcommittee on Technology and Innovation, Committee on Science and Technology*. Hearing: Planning for the Future of Cyber Attack. Washington DC: Subcommittee on Technology and Innovation, Committee on Science and Technology.

Knorr, Klaus and James N. Rosenau (eds.). 1969. *Contending Approaches to International Politics*. Princeton: Princeton University Press.

Köhler, Gernot. 1999. 'What Is Global Keynesianism?', Working Paper, http://wsarch.ucr.edu/archive/papers/kohler/kohler2.htm (11 July 2016).

Kosachev, Konstantin. 2012. 'Ne Rybu, a Udochku'. *Rossiya v globalnoi politike* 11(4): http://www.globalaffairs.ru/number/Ne-rybu-a-udochku-15642.

Kroenig, Matthew. 2009. 'Beyond Optimism and Pessimism: The Differential Effects of Nuclear Proliferation'. *Managing the Atom Working Paper Series* 2009–14. Cambridge, MA: Harvard University.

Kurki, Milja. 2012. *Democratic Futures: Re-Visioning Democracy Promotion*. London & New York: Routledge.

Kymlicka, Will. 1989. *Liberalism, Community and Culture*. Oxford: Clarendon Press.

Kymlicka, Will. 2007. *Multicultural Odysseys: Navigating the New International Politics of Diversity*. Oxford: Oxford University Press.

Lake, David A. 2009. *Hierarchy in International Relations*. Ithaca: Cornell University Press.

Lauterpacht, Hersch. 1947. *Recognition in International Law*. Cambridge: Cambridge University Press.

Lebow, Richard Ned. 2003. *The Tragic Vision of Politics: Ethics, Interests, and Orders*. New York: Cambridge University Press.

Lebow, Richard Ned. 2016. 'IR Theory as Identity Discourses'. In *International Relations Theory Today*, ed. K. Booth and T. Erskine 53–68. Cambridge: Polity.

Legrand, Tim. 2014. 'Of Citadels and Sentinels: State Strategies for Combating Cyber-Terrorism'. In *Cyber-Terrorism*, ed. Tom Chen, Lee Jarvis, and Stuart Macdonald, 137–54. London: Springer.
Lessnoff, Michael. 1974. *The Structure of Social Science: A Philosophical Introduction*. London: George Allen and Unwin.
Lewis, Bernard. 2002. *What Went Wrong? The Clash between Islam and Modernity in the Middle East*. New York: Oxford University Press.
Light, Margot. 1988. *The Soviet Theory of International Relations*. Brighton: Wheatsheaf.
Light, Margot. 1996. 'Foreign Policy Thinking'. In *Internal Factors in Russian Foreign Policy*, ed. N. Malcolm, A. Pravda, R. Allison, and M. Light, 33–100. Oxford: Oxford University Press.
Lijphart, Arend. 1981. 'Karl W. Deutsch and the New Paradigm in International Relations'. In *From National Development to Global Community. Essays in Honour of Karl W. Deutsch*, ed. Richard L. Merritt and Bruce Russett, 233–51. Allen and Unwin: Boston, MA.
Lindley, M.F. 1969 [1926]. *The Acquisition and Government of Backward Territory in International Law: Being a Treatise on the Law and Practice Relating to Colonial Expansion*. New York: Negro Universities Press.
Lindsay, Jon. 2013. 'Stuxnet and the Limits of Cyber Warfare'. *Security Studies*, 22(3): 365–404.
Ling, Lily M. and Anna Agathangelou. 2004. 'Power, Borders, Security, Wealth: Lessons of violence and desire from September 11'. *International Studies Quarterly* (48)3: 517–38.
Linklater, Andrew. 1982. *Men and Citizens in the Theory of International Relations*. London: Macmillan/London School of Economics and Political Science.
Linklater, Andrew. 1990. *Beyond Realism and Marxism: Critical Theory and International Relations*. London: Macmillan.
Linklater, Andrew. 1998. *The Transformation of Political Community: Ethical Foundations of the Post-Westphalian Community*. Cambridge: Polity Press.
Linklater, Andrew. 2011. *The Problem of Harm in World Politics: Theoretical Investigations*. Cambridge. Cambridge University Press.
Linklater, Andrew. 2016. 'The "Standard of Civilization" in World Politics', *Human Figurations: Long-Term Perspectives on the Human Condition* 5(2). Available at http:hdl.handle.net/2027/spo.11217607.0005.205.
Linklater, Andrew and Hidemi Suganami. 2006. *The English School of International Relations: A Contemporary Reassessment*. Cambridge: Cambridge University Press.
Lister, Charles. 2014. 'Profiling the Islamic State'. *Brookings Doha Center Analysis Paper* 13: 57.
Little, Richard. 2000. 'The English School's Contribution to the Study of International Relations'. *European Journal of International Relations* 6(3): 395–422.
Lo, Bobo. 2014. *Russia's Eastern Direction – Distinguishing the Real from the Virtual*. Paris: Institut Français des Relations Internationales.
Locke, John. 1988. *Two Treatises of Government*. Cambridge: Cambridge University Press.
Lorimer, James. 1883. *The Institutes of the Law of Nations*. Edinburgh: William Blackwood and Sons.

Lynch, Allen. 1987. *The Soviet Study of International Relations*. Cambridge: Cambridge University Press.

Malcolm, Noel. 2002. 'Hobbes's Theory of International Relations'. In *Aspects of Hobbes*. Oxford: Clarendon Press.

Malia, Martin E. 1999. *Russia under Western Eyes: From the Bronze Horseman to the Lenin Mausoleum*. Cambridge, MA, and London: The Belnap Press of Harvard University Press.

Mandelbaum, Michael. 1977. 'Review of *The Anarchical Society: A Study of Order in World Politics*'. *Political Science Quarterly* 92(3): 574–5.

Mandelbaum, Michael. 2002. *The Ideas that Conquered the World: Peace Democracy, and Free Markets in the Twenty-first Century*. New York: Public Affairs.

Mandelbaum, Michael. 2005. *The Case for Goliath: How America Acts as the World's Government in the Twenty-first Century*. New York: Public Affairs.

Manjikian, Mary McAvoy. 2010. 'From Global Village to Virtual Battlespace: The Colonizing of the Internet and the Extension of Realpolitik'. *International Studies Quarterly*, 54(2): 381–401.

Manning, Charles A. W. 1962. *The Nature of International Society*. London: Macmillan.

Manning, Charles A. W. 1975. *The Nature of International Society*, reissue. London: Macmillan.

Markwell, Donald. 2006. *John Maynard Keynes and International Relations. Economic Paths to Peace*. Oxford: Oxford University Press.

Mazrui, Ali. 1967. *Towards a Pax Africana*. London: Weidenfeld and Nicolson.

McCarthy, Daniel. 2015. *Power, Information Technology and International Relations Theory: The Power and Politics of US Foreign Policy and the Internet*. Basingstoke: Palgrave.

McKeen-Edwards, Heather and Tony Porter. 2013. *Transnational Financial Associations and the Governance of Global Finance*. Abingdon, UK: Routledge.

McKinsey and Company. 2007. *Women Matter, Gender Diversity: A Corporate Performance Driver*. New York.

McLuhan, Marshall. 1962. *The Gutenberg Galaxy*. Toronto: University of Toronto Press.

Meadows, Donella H. and Dennis L. Meadows. 1972. *The Limits of Growth*. New York: New American Library.

Mearsheimer, John J. 2014. 'Why the Ukraine Crisis is the West's Fault: The Liberal Delusions that Provoked Putin'. *Foreign Affairs* 93(5): 77–89.

Mendelsohn, Barak. 2012. 'God vs. Westphalia: Radical Islamist Movements and the Battle for Organising the World'. *Review of International Studies* 38(3): 589–613.

Mendelsohn, Barak. 2015. 'The Jihadi Threat to International Order'. *The Washington Post* (15 May). <http://www.washingtonpost.com/blogs/monkey-cage/wp/2015/05/15/the-jihadi-threat-to-international-order/>, accessed 7 December, 2015.

Menkiszak, Marek. 2013. 'Greater Europe. Putin's Vision of European (Dis)integration'. *OSW Studies* 46. Warsaw: Centre for Eastern Studies.

Mennell, Stephen. 1998. *Norbert Elias: An Introduction*. Dublin: University College Dublin Press.

Midgley, E. Brian F. 1979. 'Natural Law and the "Anglo-Saxons": Some Reflections in Response to Hedley Bull'. *British Journal of International Studies* 5(3): 260–72.

Mies, Maria. 1986. *Patriarchy and Accumulation on a World Scale*. London: Zed Books.
Ministry of Foreign Affairs, Russian Federation. 2013. 'Concept of the Foreign Policy of the Russian Federation'. *Approved by President of the Russian Federation V. Putin on 12 February*. Ministry of Foreign Affairs. Moscow.
Morgenthau, Hans. 1961. *Politics among Nations. The Struggle for Power and Peace*. 3rd edn. New York: Alfred A. Knopf.
Morozova, Nina. 2009. 'Geopolitics, Eurasianism and Russian Foreign Policy under Putin'. *Geopolitics* 14(4): 667–86.
Moyn, Samuel. 2010. *The Last Utopia: Human Rights in History*. Cambridge MA: Harvard University Press.
Mozaffari, Mehdi. 2001. 'The Transformationalist Perspective and the Rise of a Global Standard of Civilization'. *International Relations of the Asia-Pacific* 1(2): 247–64.
Muhammad, Kh. Husein, F. Kodir, L. Marcoes-Natsir, and M. Wahid. 2007. *Dawrah Fiqh Concerning Women: Manual for a Course on Islam and Gender*. 2nd edn. West Java: Fahmina Institute.
Nagel, Thomas. 2005. 'The Problem of Global Justice'. *Philosophy and Public Affairs* 33(2) (March): 113–47.
NATO. 2014. *Wales Summit Declaration*, Issued by the Heads of State and Government participating in the meeting of the North Atlantic Council in Wales, 5 September 2014. http://www.nato.int/cps/en/natohq/official_texts_112964.htm.
Naumkin, Valeri V. 2014. 'Tsivilizatsii I Krizis Natsii-Gosudarstv'. *Rossiya v Globalnoi Politike* 13(1). http://www.globalaffairs.ru/number/Tcivilizatcii-i-krizis-natcii-gosudarstv-16393.
Neumann, Iver B. 2007. 'Russia's Quest for Recognition as a Great Power, 1489-2007'. *Institute of European Studies and International Relations Working Paper* (1).
Neumann, Iver. 2008. 'The Body of the Diplomat'. *European Journal of International Relations* (14)4: 671–95.
Neumann, Iver B. 2011. 'Entry into International Society Reconceptualised: The Case of Russia'. *Review of International Studies* 37(02): 463–84.
Neumann, Iver B. and Jennifer M. Welsh. 1991. 'The Other in European Self-Definition: An Addendum to the Literature on International Society'. *Review of International Studies* 17(4): 327–48.
Nexon, Daniel H. 2009. *The Struggle for Power in Early Modern Europe*. Princeton NJ: Princeton University Press.
Nicholas, S. 2003. '"Brushing up your Empire": Dominion and Colonial Propaganda on the BBC's Home Services, 1939–45'. *The Journal of Imperial and Commonwealth History* 31(2): 207–30.
Niezen, Ronald. 2003. *The Origins of Indigenism: Human Rights and the Politics of Identity*. Berkeley: University of California Press.
Northedge, F. S. 1976. *The International Political System*. London: Faber & Faber.
Nye, Joseph S. 2010. *Cyber Power*. Cambridge: Belfer Center for Science and International Affairs.
Nye, Joseph S. and Robert O. Keohane. 1971. 'Transnational Relations and World Politics: An Introduction'. *International Organization* 25(3): 329–49.
O'Brian, Robert, Anne Marie Goetz, Jan Aart Scholte, and Marc Williams (eds.). 2000. *Contesting Global Governance: Multilateral Economic Institutions and Global Social Movements*. Cambridge: Cambridge University Press.

O'Neill, Robert and David N. Schwartz. 1987. *Hedley Bull on Arms Control*. Basingstoke: Macmillan.

O'Reilly, Marie, Andrea Ó Súilleabháin, and Thania Paffenholz. 2015. *Reimagining Peacemaking: Women's Roles in Peace Processes*. Washington DC: International Peace Institute.

Oakeshott, Michael. 1975. 'Introduction to *Leviathan*'. In *Hobbes on Civil Association*. Indianapolis: Liberty Fund.

Oakley, Francis. 1979. *The Crucial Centuries: The Medieval Experience*. London: Terra Nova Editions.

Oakley, Francis. 1984. *Omnipotence, Covenant, and Order: An Excursion in the History of Ideas from Abelard to Leibniz*. Ithaca: Cornell University Press.

Oakley, Francis. 1999. 'Legitimation by Consent: The Question of the Medieval Roots'. In *Politics and Eternity: Studies in the History of Medieval and Early-Modern Political Thought*. Leiden: Brill.

Oakley, Francis. 2005. *Natural Law, Laws of Nature, Natural Rights: Continuity and Discontinuity in the History of Ideas*. New York: Continuum.

Obama, Barack. 2015a. 'Letter from the President—Authorization for the Use of United States Armed Forces in connection with the Islamic State of Iraq and the Levant', (11 February). Washington DC: The White House. https://www.whitehouse.gov/the-press-office/2015/02/11/letter-president-authorization-use-united-states-armed-forces-connection. Accessed 23 August 2016.

Obama, Barack. 2015b. 'Statement by the President on ISIL' (10 September). Washington DC: The White House. https://www.whitehouse.gov/the-press-office/2014/09/10/statement-president-isil-1. Accessed 23 August 2016.

Obama, Barack. 2015c. 'Executive Order—Imposing Additional Sanctions with Respect to North Korea' (2 January). Washington DC: The White House. https://www.whitehouse.gov/the-press-office/2015/01/02/executive-order-imposing-additional-sanctions-respect-north-korea.

Ockham, William of. 1990. '*Quodlibeta*, III, Q. xiii'. In *Philosophical Writings*, ed. and trans. Philotheus Boehner. Indianapolis: Hackett.

Ollivant, Douglas and Brian Fishman. 2014. 'State of Jihad: The Reality of the Islamic State in Iraq and Syria'. (21 May). Accessed at http://warontherocks.com/2014/05/state-of-jihad-the-reality-of-the-islamic-state-in-iraq-and-syria/.

Omarova, Z. M. 2011. 'Rossiya i "Russkii mir" Blizhnego Zarubezhya'. *Uchebnoye posobiye*. Moscow: Vostok-Zapad.

Ophuls, William. 1977. *Ecology and the Politics of Scarcity: Prologue to a Political Theory of the Steady State*. San Francisco: W. H. Freeman.

Oppenheim, Lassa. 1955. *International Law: A Treatise*, volume one, *Peace*, ed. H. Lauterpacht. London: Longmans, Green and Co.

Ostrovsky, E. and P. Shchedrovitskiy. 1997. 'Orel raspravliyayet kryliya'. *Ekspert*, 15 December.

Oushakine, S. 2015. 'We are good at keeping quiet—about many things...'. *Free4-Russia*, 23 June.

Paffenholz, Thania, Nick Ross, Steven Dixon, Anna-Lena Schluchter, and Jacqui True. 2016. *Making Women Count—Not Just Counting Women: Assessing Women's Inclusion and Influence on Peace Negotiations*. New York: Inclusive Peace and Transition Initiative and UN Women.

Pagden, Anthony. 1998. *Lords of All the World: Ideologies of Empire in Spain, Britain and France, 1492–830*. New Haven: Yale University Press.
Panetta, Fabio et al. 2009. 'An Assessment of Financial Sector Rescue Programmes'. *BIS Papers* 48. Bank for International Settlements.
Panetta, Leon. 2012. 'Remarks by Secretary Panetta on Cyber Security to the Business Executives for National Security'. (October 11). New York City. http://archive.defense.gov/transcripts/transcript.aspx?transcriptid=5136.
Pasha, Mustapha Kamal. 2013. 'The "Bandung Impulse" and International Relations'. In *Postcolonial Theory and International Relations: A Critical Introduction*, ed. Sanjay Seth, 144–65. Abington and New York: Routledge.
Pateman, Carole. 1988. *The Sexual Contract*. Stanford, CA: Stanford University Press.
Pateman, Carole. 1989. *The Disorder of Women: Democracy, Feminism and Political Theory*. Stanford: Stanford University Press.
Paterson, Matthew. 2005. 'Global Environmental Governance'. In *International Society and Its Critics*, ed. Alex J. Bellamy, 163–77. Oxford: Oxford University Press.
Patomäki, Heikki. 1992a. 'From Normative Utopias to Political Dialectics: Beyond a Deconstruction of the Brown-Hoffman Debate'. *Millennium: Journal of International Studies* 21(1): 53–75.
Patomäki, Heikki. 1992b. 'What Is It That Changed With the End of the Cold War? An Analysis of the Problem of Identifying and Explaining Change'. In *The End of the Cold War. Evaluating Theories of International Relations*, ed. Pierre Allan and Kjell Goldmann, 179–225. Dordrecht: Martinus Nijhoff.
Patomäki, Heikki. 2002. *After International Relations: Critical Realism and the (Re) Construction of World Politics*. London & New York: Routledge.
Patomäki, Heikki. 2003. 'Problems of Democratizing Global Governance: Time, Space and the Emancipatory Process'. *European Journal of International Relations* 9(3): 347–76.
Patomäki, Heikki. 2008. *The Political Economy of Global Security*. London & New York: Routledge.
Patomäki, Heikki. 2010. 'What Next? An Explanation of the 2008–9 Slump and Two Scenarios of the Shape of Things to Come'. *Globalizations* 7(1): 67–84.
Patomäki, Heikki. 2011. 'Towards Global Political Parties'. *Ethics & Global Politics* 4(2): 81–102.
Patomäki, Heikki. 2013. *The Great Eurozone Disaster. From Crisis to Global New Deal*. Zed Books: London.
Patomäki, Heikki. 2014. 'Piketty's Global Tax On Capital: A Useful Utopia or a Realistic Alternative to a Global Disaster?'. *real-world economics review* 69 (7 October): 51–7.
Patomäki, Heikki. 2016. 'Explaining the Emergence of Global Regulation of Private Security Service Providers'. *International Studies Quarterly Symposia*, will be available at http://www.isanet.org/Publications/ISQ.
Patomäki, Heikki and Colin Wight. 2000. 'After Post-Positivism? The Promises of Critical Realism'. *International Studies Quarterly* 44(2): 213–37.
Pauly, Louis. 2014. 'Governing Global Risks: The Evolution of Policy Capacity in the Financial Sector'. *Discussion Paper*, Global Governance Department, Wissenschaftszentrum für Sozialforschung, Berlin (May). (SP IV 2014-103; http://bibliothek.wzb.eu/pdf/2014/iv14-103.pdf.)

Pauly, Louis. 2014. 'The Political Economy of Global Financial Crises'. In *Global Political Economy*, ed. John Ravenhill, 198–222. 4th edn. Oxford: Oxford University Press.

Pavlova, Y. and T. Romanova. 2014. 'Ideinoye Sopernichestvo Ili «Tresh-Diskurs»'. *Rossiya v globalnoi politike* 13(3): http://www.globalaffairs.ru/number/Ideinoe-sopernichestvo-ili-tresh-diskurs-16767.

Pearson, Noel. 1993. 'Reconciliation: to Be or Not To Be – Separate Aboriginal Nationhood or Aboriginal Self-Determination and Self-Government Within the Australian Nation?', *Aboriginal Law Bulletin* 3(61) (April): 14–17.

Perlo-Freeman, Sam, Aude Fleurant, Pieter Wezeman, and Siemon Wezeman. 2016. 'Trends in World Military Expenditure, 2015'. *SIPRI Fact Sheet* (April). Stockholm: SIPRI, http://books.sipri.org/files/FS/SIPRIFS1604.pdf (9 July 2016).

Peterson, V. Spike (ed). 1992. *Gendered States: Revisioning International Relations*. Boulder, CO: Lynne Rienner Publishers.

Pierson, Paul. 2004. *Politics in Time. History, Institutions and Social Analysis*. Princeton, NJ: Princeton University Press.

Piketty, Thomas. 2014. *Capital in the Twenty-First Century*, trans. A. Goldhammer. Cambridge, MA: The Belknap Press (Harvard University Press).

Plato. 1961. 'Timaeus'. In *The Collected Dialogues of Plato*, ed. Edith Hamilton and Huntington Cairns, trans. Benjamin Jowett. Princeton: Princeton University Press.

Pogge, Thomas W. 1994. 'Cosmopolitanism and Sovereignty'. In *Political Restructuring in Europe: Ethical Perspectives*, ed. Chris Brown, 89–112. London: Routledge.

Polanyi, Karl. 1944. *The Great Transformation*. New York: Farrar & Rinehart.

Pritchard, Sarah (ed). 1998. *Indigenous Peoples, the United Nations and Human Rights*. Annandale: The Federation Press.

Putin, Vladimir. 2005. 'Annual Address to the Federal Assembly of the Russian Federation'. The Kremlin: Moscow.

Putin, Vladimir. 2007. 'Speech and the Following Discussion at the Munich Conference on Security Policy'. Munich. 10 February.

Putin, Vladimir. 2014. 'Obrashcheniye Prezidenta Rossiiskoi Federatsii', 18 March. Moscow.

Quijano, Anibal. 2000. 'Coloniality of Power, Eurocentrism and Latin America'. *Nepantla: Views from the South* 1(3): 533–80.

Quilliam Foundation. 2015. 'Women of Islamic State, an English Translation from Arabic' (January).

Rawls, John. 1971. *A Theory of Justice*. Cambridge. Cambridge University Press.

Reinold, Theresa. 2013. *Sovereignty and the Responsibility to Protect: The Power of Norms and the Norms of the Powerful*. Abingdon: Routledge.

Rengger, Nicholas. 2006. 'Seeing (Double) in the Darkness: The Moral Vision of The Anarchical Society'. *The Anarchical Society in a Globalized World*, ed. Richard Little and John Williams. Basingstoke: Palgrave Macmillan.

Reus-Smit, Christian. 2013a. *Individual Rights and the Making of the International System*. Cambridge: Cambridge University Press.

Reus-Smit, Christian. 2013b. 'The Liberal International Order Reconsidered'. In *After Liberalism*, ed. Rebekka Friedman, Kevork Oskanian, and Ramon Pachero-Pardo, 25–48. London: Palgrave.

Rid, Thomas. 2012. 'Think Again: Cyberwar'. *Foreign Policy*, 192 (March/April): 80–4.
Rid, Thomas. 2013. *Cyberwar Will Not Take Place*. London: Hurst & Company.
Rid, Thomas and Ben Buchanan. 2015. 'Attributing Cyber Attacks'. *The Journal of Strategic Studies*, 38(1–2): 4–37.
Rinaldo, R. 2011. 'Muslim Women, Moral Visions: Globalization and Gender Controversies in Indonesia'. *Qualitative Sociology* 34: 539–60.
Risse, Thomas, Stephen C. Ropp, and Kathryn Sikkink (eds). 1999. *The Power of Human Rights*. Cambridge: Cambridge University Press.
Risse, Thomas, Stephen C. Ropp, and Kathryn Sikkink (eds). 2013. *The Persistent Power of Human Rights*. Cambridge: Cambridge University Press.
Risse-Kappen, Thomas (ed). 1995. *Bringing Transnational Relations Back In: Non-State Actors, Domestic Structures and International Institutions*. Cambridge: Cambridge University Press.
Robinson, Mary. 2016. 'Gender Equality and Climate Change: The Vital Link for Success beyond Paris'. *The Elders* 7 (March).
Rosenau, James N. 1990. *Turbulence in World Politics*. Princeton: Princeton University Press.
Rosenberg, Justin. 2016. 'International Relations in the Prison of Political Science'. *International Relations* 30(2): 123–53.
Rubin, Lawrence. 2015. 'Why the Islamic State won't become a Normal State'. *The Washington Post* (9 July). <http://www.washingtonpost.com/blogs/monkey-cage/wp/2015/07/09/why-the-islamic-state-wont-become-a-normal-state/>, accessed 29 September 2015.
Ruggie, John. 1993. 'Territoriality and Beyond: Problematizing Modernity in International Relations'. *International Organization* 47(1): 139–74.
Ruthven, Malise. 2007. *Fundamentalism. A Very Short Introduction*. Oxford: Oxford University Press.
Ruzicka, Jan and Nicholas J. Wheeler. 2010. 'The Puzzle of Trusting Relationships in The Nuclear Non-Proliferation Treaty'. *International Affairs* 86(1): 69–85.
Sagan Scott D. and Kenneth N. Waltz. 1995. *The Spread of Nuclear Weapons: A Debate*. New York: W.W. Norton & Company.
Sakwa, Richard. 2011a. 'Russia and Europe: Whose Society?' *European Integration* 33(2): 197–214.
Sakwa, Richard. 2011b. 'Russia's Identity: Between the "Domestic" and the "International"'. *Europe–Asia Studies* 63(6): 957–75.
Satanovskii, Yevgeny. 2014. *Shla by ty... Zametki o Natsionalnoi Idee*. Moscow: Eksmo.
Scheffran, Jürgen and Antonella Battaglini. 2011. 'Climate and Conflicts: The Security Risks of Global Warming'. *Regional Environmental Change* 11(1): 27–39.
Schelling, Thomas C. 1960. *The Strategy of Conflict*. Cambridge MA: Harvard University Press.
Scheve, Kenneth and David Stasavage. 2016. *Taxing the Rich. A History of Fiscal Fairness in the United States and Europe*. Princeton, NJ and New York: Princeton University Press and Russell Sage Foundation.
Schimmelfennig, Frank. 2014. 'European Integration in the Euro Crisis: The Limits of Postfunctionalism'. *Journal of European Integration* 36(3): 321–37.

Schmitt, Michael N. 2013. *Tallinn Manual on the International Law Applicable to Cyber Warfare*. Cambridge: Cambridge University Press.
Scholte, Jan Aart. 2005. *Globalization: A Critical Introduction*. 2nd edn. Houndmills, Basingstoke: Palgrave Macmillan.
Scholte, Jan Aart (ed). 2011. *Building Global Democracy?: Civil Society and Accountable Global Governance*. Cambridge: Cambridge University Press.
Scott, Hamish. 2007. 'Diplomatic Culture in Old Regime Europe'. In *Cultures of Power in Europe During the Long Eighteenth Century*, ed. H. Scott and B. Sims. Cambridge: Cambridge University Press.
Sergounin, Alexander. 2000. 'Russian Post-Communist Foreign Policy Thinking at the Crossroads'. *Journal of International Relations and Development* 3(3): 216–55.
Shadian, Jessica. 2010. 'From States to Polities: Reconceptualizing Sovereignty through Inuit Governance'. *European Journal of International Relations* 16(3) (May): 485–510.
Shakleina, T. A. and A. A. Baikov. 2014. *Megatrendy. Osnovnyye Trayektorii Evolutsii Mirovogo Poriyadka v XXI veke*. Moscow: Aspekt Press.
Shaw, Karena. 2002. 'Indigeneity and the International'. *Millennium: Journal of International Studies* 31(1): 55–81.
Shaw, Martin. 2010. *Theory of the Global State*. Cambridge: Cambridge University Press.
Shepherd, Laura. 2006. 'Veiled References: Constructions of Gender in the Bush Administration Discourse on the Attacks post 9/11'. *International Feminist Journal of Politics* (8)1: 19–41.
Shimazu, Naoko. 1998. *Japan, Race and Equality: The Racial Equality Proposal of 1919*. London: Routledge.
Shue, Henry. 1996. *Basic Rights*, 2nd edn. Princeton NJ: Princeton University Press.
Simmons, Beth A. 2009. *Mobilizing for Human Rights*. Cambridge MA: Harvard University Press.
Singer, David. 2007. *Regulating Capital*. Ithaca, NY: Cornell University Press.
Sjoberg, Laura. 2012. 'Gender, Structure and War: What Waltz Couldn't See'. *International Theory* (4)1: 1–38.
Stanner, W. E. H. 2009. 'Continuity and Change among the Aborigines (1958)'. In *W.H.E. Stanner: The Dreaming and Other Essays*, ed. Robert Manne, 146–71. Melbourne: Black Inc, Agenda.
Stansfield, Gareth. 2014. 'Kurdistan Rising: To Acknowledge or Ignore the Unraveling of Iraq'. *Middle East Memo* 33: 1–16.
Stern, Nicholas. 2015. *Why Are We Waiting? The Logic, Urgency, and Promise of Tackling Climate Change*, Boston: The MIT Press.
Stevis, Dimitris. 2014. 'The Trajectory of International Environmental Politics'. In *Advances in International Environmental Politics*, ed. M. M. Betsill, K. Hochstetler, and D. Stevis, 13–44. Houndsmills: Palgrave Macmillan.
Stivachtis, Yannis A. 2015. 'Interrogating Regional International Societies, Questioning the Global International Society'. *Global Discourse* 5(3).
Suchman, Mark C. 1995. 'Managing Legitimacy: Strategic and Institutional Approaches'. *Academy of Management Review* 20(3): 572–610.

Suganami, Hidemi. 1983. 'The Structure of Institutionalism: An Anatomy of British Mainstream International Relations'. *International Relations* 7(5): 2362–81.
Suganami, Hidemi. 1989. *The Domestic Analogy and World Order Proposals*. Cambridge: Cambridge University Press.
Suganami, Hidemi. 2004. Review of '*The Emergence of Private Authority in Global Governance*. Rodney Bruce Hall and Thomas J. Biersteker (eds.) Cambridge. Cambridge University Press. 2002'. *International Relations of the Asia-Pacific*. 4(1): 197–9.
Suganami, Hidemi. 2007. 'Understanding Sovereignty through Kelsen/Schmitt'. *Review of International Studies* 33(3): 511–30.
Suganami, Hidemi. 2008. 'Narrative Explanation and International Relations: Back to Basics'. *Millennium-Journal of International Studies* 37(2): 327–56.
Sutton, Philip W. and Stephen Vertigans. 2005. *Resurgent Islam: A Sociological Approach*. Cambridge: Polity.
Tetlock, Philip. 2005. *Expert Political Judgement. How Good Is It? How Can We Know?* Princeton, NJ: Princeton University Press.
Thomas, Daniel C. 2001. *The Helsinki Effect*, Princeton NJ: Princeton University Press.
Tikk Ringas, Eneken (ed). 2015. *Evolution of the Cyber Domain: The Implications for National and Global Security*. London: International Institute for Strategic Studies.
Tilly, Charles. 1985. 'War Making and State Making as Organized Crime'. In *Bringing the State Back In*, ed. Peter Evans, Dietrich Rueschemeyer and Theda Skocpol, Cambridge: Cambridge University Press.
Timermanis, I. E. (ed). 2015. *Politologiya. Uchenbnik Dliya Bakalavrov*. Moscow: Yurait.
Tlostanova, M. 2014. 'Towards a Decolonization of Thinking and Knowledge: A Few Reflections from the World of Imperial Difference'. *Antville*. http://antville.org/static/m1/files/madina_tlostanova_decolonia_thinking.pdf.
Tooze, Roger and Christopher May (eds.). 2002. *Authority and Markets: Susan Strange's Writings on International Political Economy*. London: Palgrave Macmillan.
Torney, Diarmuid. 2015. *European Climate Leadership in Question: Policies Toward China and India*. Cambridge, MA: The MIT Press.
Tosa, Hiroyuki. 2009. 'Anarchical Governance: Neoliberal Governmentality in Resonance with the State of Exception'. *International Political Sociology* 3(4): 414–30.
Towns, Ann E. 2010. *Women and States: Norms and Hierarchies in International Society*. Cambridge: Cambridge University Press.
Trenin, Dmitri. 2006. *Integratsiya i identichnost': Rossiya kak 'novyi Zapad'*. Moscow: Evropa.
True, Jacqui. 2004. 'Feminism'. In *International Society and its Critics*, ed. Alex J. Bellamy, 151–62. Oxford: Oxford University Press.
True, Jacqui. 2012. *The Political Economy of Violence against Women*. New York: Oxford University Press.
Tsygankov, Andrei P. 2013. *Mezhdunarodnyye Otnosheniya: Traditsii Russkoi politicheskoi mysli*. Moscow: Alfa-M, Infra-M.
Tsygankov, P. A. (ed). 2008. *Mezhdunarodnyye Otnosheniya: Teorii, Konflikty, Dvizheniya, Organizatsii*. Moscow: Alfa-M: INFRA-M.

Tully, James. 1994. 'Aboriginal Property and Western Theory: Recovering a Middle Ground', *Social Philosophy and Policy* 11(2) (Summer): 153–80.

Turkmani, Rim. 2015. 'ISIL, JAN and the War Economy in Syria'. London: The London School of Economics and Political Science, Civil Society and Human Security Research Unit, 1–27.

Turner, Dale. 2001. 'Vision: Towards an Understanding of Aboriginal Sovereignty'. In *Canadian Political Philosophy: Contemporary Reflections*, ed. R. Beiner and W. Norman, 318–31. Ontario: Oxford University Press.

UN. 2012. 'General Assembly Votes Overwhelmingly to Accord Palestine "Non-Member Observer State" Status in United Nations'. *UN Press Release* (29 November). <http://www.un.org/press/en/2012/ga11317.doc.htm>, accessed 30 September 2015.

United Nations. 1992. *An Agenda for Peace. Preventive Diplomacy, Peacemaking and Peace-Keeping*. A/47/277—S/24111. 17 June 1992. New York: United Nations, https://www.un.org/ruleoflaw/files/A_47_277.pdf (8 July 2016).

United Nations. 2015. A/70/74 Report from the Group of Governmental Experts on Developments in the Field of Information and Telecommunications in the Context of International Security. 22 July 2015. https://www.un.org/disarmament/topics/informationsecurity/.

United Nations Women. 2011. *Progress of the World's Women: In Pursuit of Justice*. New York: UN.

Vasilenko, I. A. 2014. *Sovremennaya Rossiiskaya Politika. Uchebnik dlia magistrov*. Moscow: Yurait.

Vasquez, John. 1996. *The Power of Power Politics: From Classical Realism to Neotraditionalism*. Cambridge: Cambridge University Press.

Vattel, Emmerich de. 1916 [1758]. *The Law of Nations*, trans. C.G. Fenwick. Washington, DC: Carnegie Institute of Washington.

Victor, David G., M. Granger Morgan, Jay Apt, John Steinbruner, and Katharine Ricke. 2009. 'The Geoengineering Option: A Last Resort Against Global Warming?' *Foreign Affairs* 88(2): 64–76.

Vincent, R. John. 1974. *Nonintervention and International Order*. Princeton: Princeton University Press.

Vincent, R. John. 1980. 'The Factor of Culture in the Global International Order'. *The Year Book of World Affairs* 34: 252–64. London: Stevens and Son.

Vincent, R. John. 1986. *Human Rights and International Relations*. Cambridge: Cambridge University Press.

Vogler, John. 2016. *Climate Change in World Politics*. Basingstoke: Palgrave Macmillan.

Voller, Yaniv. 2014. *The Kurdish Liberation Movement in Iraq: From Insurgency to Statehood*. London: Routledge.

Walker, William. 2012. *A Perpetual Menace: Nuclear Weapons and International Order*. London: Routledge.

Wallstrom, Margot. 2016. 'State of the Government Policy in Parliamentary Debate on Foreign Affairs' (24 February). http://www.government.se/speeches/2016/02/statement-of-government-policy-in-the-parliamentary-debate-on-foreign-affairs-2016/.

Walt, Stephen. 2015. 'What Should We Do if the Islamic State Wins? Live with it'. *Foreignpolicy.com* (10 June). <http://foreignpolicy.com/2015/06/10/what-should-we-do-if-isis-islamic-state-wins-containment/>, accessed 30 September 2015.

Waltz, Kenneth N. 1959. *Man, the State and War: A Theoretical Analysis*. New York: Columbia University Press.
Waltz, Kenneth N. 1979. *Theory of International Politics*. New York: McGraw-Hill.
Waltz, Kenneth N. 1981. *The Spread of Nuclear Weapons: More May Be Better*. Adelphi Paper 171. London: International Institute for Strategic Studies.
Ward, Barbara. 1966. *Spaceship Earth*. New York: Columbia University Press.
Watson, Adam. 1984. 'Russia and the European States System'. In *The Expansion of International Society*, ed. Hedley Bull and Adam Watson, 61–74. Oxford: Clarendon.
Weber, Max. 2004. 'The "Objectivity" of Knowledge in Social Science and Social Policy'. In *The Essential Weber: A Reader*, ed. Sam Whimster, 359–404. London: Routledge.
Wendt, Alexander. 1999. *Social Theory of International Politics*. Cambridge: Cambridge University Press.
Wendt, Alexander. 2003. 'Why a World State Is Inevitable'. *European Journal of International Relations* 9(4) (December): 491–542.
Westlake, John. 1914. *The Collected Papers of John Westlake on Public International Law*, ed. L. Oppenheim. Cambridge: Cambridge University Press.
Wheeler, David A. and Gregory N. Larsen. 2003. 'Techniques for Cyber Attack Attribution'. *Institute for Defense Analyses*, IDA Paper P-3792.
Wheeler, Nicholas and Timothy Dunne. 1996. 'Hedley Bull's Pluralism of the Intellect and Solidarism of the Will'. *International Affairs*. 72(1): 91–107.
Wheeler, Nicholas J. 1992. 'Pluralist or Solidarist Conceptions of International Society: Bull and Vincent on Humanitarian Intervention'. *Millennium: Journal of International Studies* 21(3): 467–8.
Wheeler, Nicholas J. 2000. *Saving Strangers: Humanitarian Intervention in International Society*. Oxford: Oxford University Press.
White, Hugh. 2012. *The China Choice: Why American Should Share Power*. Collingwood Victoria: Black.
White, Stephen and Ian McAllister. 2014. 'Did Russia (Nearly) Have a Facebook Revolution in 2011? Social Media's Challenge to Authoritarianism'. *Politics* 34(1): 72–84.
Wight, Martin. 1956. 'The Power Struggle in the United Nations.' *Proceedings of the Institute of World Affairs*, 33rd session: 247–59. Los Angeles: USC.
Wight, Martin. 1960. 'Why Is There No International Theory?' *International Relations* 2(1): 35–48.
Wight, Martin. 1966a. 'Why Is There No International Theory?' In *Diplomatic Investigations: Essays in the Theory of International Politics*, ed. Herbert Butterfield and Martin Wight, 17–34. London: Allen & Unwin.
Wight, Martin. 1966b. 'Western Values in International Relations'. In *Diplomatic Investigations: Essays in the Theory of International Politics*, ed. Herbert Butterfield and Martin Wight, 89–131. London: Allen & Unwin.
Wight, Martin. 1968. 'Western Values in International Relations'. In *Diplomatic Investigations: Essays in the Theory of International Politics*, ed. Herbert Butterfield and Martin Wight. Cambridge, MA: Harvard University Press.
Wight, Martin. 1977. *Systems of States*. Leicester: Leicester University Press.

Wight, Martin. 1987. 'An Anatomy of International Thought'. *Review of International Studies* 13(3): 221–7.

Wight, Martin. 1991. *International Theory: The Three Tradition*, ed. Gabriele Wight and Brian Porter. New York: Holmes & Meier.

Williams, John and Richard Little. 2006. 'Introduction', in *The Anarchical Society in a Globalized World*, ed. Richard Little and John Williams, 1–9. Basingstoke: Palgrave Macmillan.

Williams, Michael C. 2005. *The Realist Tradition and the Limits of International Relations*. Cambridge: Cambridge University Press.

Winch, Peter. 1958. *The Idea of Social Science and its Relation to Philosophy*. London: Routledge.

Winichakul, Thongchai. 2000. 'The Quest for "Siwilai"?: A Geographical Discourse of Civilizational Thinking in Late 19th and Early 20th C. Siam'. *Journal of Asian Studies* 59(3): 528–49.

Wolin, Sheldon. 2010. *Democracy Incorporated: Managed Democracy and the Specter of Inverted Totalitarianism*. Princeton, NJ: Princeton University Press.

Worringer, Renée. 2004. '"Sick Man of Europe" or "Japan of the Near East"?: Constructing Ottoman Modernity in the Hamidian and Young Turk Eras'. *International Journal of Middle East Studies* 36(2): 207–30.

Wortman, Richard S. 2006. *Scenarios of Power: Myth and Ceremony in Russian Monarchy from Peter the Great to the Abdication of Nicholas II*. Princeton: Princeton University Press.

Zagladin, Nikita V. 2004. 'Natsionalno-tsivilizationnaya Identichnost Rossii: Istoriya i sovremennost'. In *Poisk natsionalno-tsivilizatsionnoi identichnosti i kontsept 'osobogo puti' v rossiiskom massovom soznanii v kontekste modernizatsii*, ed. V. V. Lapkin and V. I. Pantin, 15–23. Moscow, IMEMO RAN.

Zhade, Zuriyet A. 2014. 'Rossiiskaya Tsivilizatsionnaya Identichnost v Meniyayushchimsiya Mire'. *Vlast'* (4).

Zimmerman, William. 1969. *Soviet Perspectives on International Relations*. Princeton: Princeton University Press.

Zoellick, Robert B. 1997. 'Economics and Security in the Changing Asia-Pacific'. *Survival* 39(4) (Winter): 29–51.

Zürn, Michael and Jeffrey T. Checkel. 2005. 'Getting Socialized to Build Bridges: Constructivism and Rationalism, Europe and the Nation-State'. *International Organization* 59(4): 1045–79.

Index

Aboriginal 221, 224, 225
Abu 'Umar al-Baghdadi 150
Afghanistan 53, 118–19, 243, 247
Al Qaeda 118, 120, 121, 149, 150, 151
al-Baghdadi, Abu Bakr 151, 155–6
al-Thamimi, Utham 156
al-Zarqawi, Abu Musab 150
Alexander, Samuel 7
Alfred, Taiaiake 225–6
Allison, Graham 15, 129
anarchy 5, 10, 45, 50, 68, 97, 140, 163–4, 235, 237, 312
Anderson, John 6–7, 70
anti-religious 61, 70
Aristotle 95
armed intervention 118–19
arms control 115, 125, 133, 142
Asia
  Bull and 112
  Central 257, 279
  East 257, 294
  Southeast 294–5
  and violence 123–6
attribution in cyberspace 16, 163, 166–7, 176, 178
Augustine of Hippo 61–4, 67, 70, 318
austerity 264
Australia 115–16, 118, 241
Ayson, Robert 14, 46, 130, 314, 316

Bain, William 13, 19, 20, 318, 319, 320
balance of power 28, 77, 79, 111, 114, 117, 133–4, 143, 182, 298
Balkans 263
Bandung Conference 101, 104, 107
Bank for International Settlements 188, 191
Basel Committee on Banking Supervision 188, 191
Basel Process 189, 192, 194, 196
Basel I 188
Basel II 189–90
Basel III 192
Behrendt, Larissa 225
Bolshevik Revolution 29
Bosnia 120
Brazil 132
Brenton, Tony 208
Bretton Woods 180, 188, 190
Britain *see* United Kingdom

British Committee on the Theory of International Politics 278
British orthodoxy 19–20
Brunner, Emil 62
Bush, George W. 300
Buzan, Barry 9, 59, 181, 182, 183, 197, 205, 214, 307, 308, 319

Caliphate, caliphate 15, 146, 149, 151, 153, 154–5, 247
Carr, Edward Hallett 3, 65
Carr, Madeline 3, 5, 15–16, 316
Carter, President 76
causation, causality 10, 11, 18, 29, 39, 258–9, 261, 319–20
China 14, 48, 53, 116, 117, 118, 238, 241
  armed intervention 118, 119
  as 'barbaric' 291
  and cyber security 172, 177
  and European civilization 296
  and terrorism 121
China/US relations 123–6
Christendom 25, 28, 146, 222
Christian theological doctrine 13
Christianity 72
'civilizing process' 19, 93, 100, 287–8, 289, 290, 295, 297
clash of civilizations 18, 48, 93, 290, 299
Clausewitz 138, 163
  Clausewitzian 114
climate change 4, 15, 16, 39, 199, 203–204
climate regime 17
Cockburn, Patrick 159
Cold War 4, 14, 47–8, 101, 106, 112, 113, 217
  and nuclear deterrence 107, 114, 134, 142
  post- 18, 52, 53, 116–17, 118, 254–5, 257, 259, 261
collective security 257
colonialism, coloniality 13–14, 30, 44, 50, 55, 94, 100–6, 108, 293, 313, 318–20
common culture 71, 286, 288
conceptual vocabulary
  Bull's 17, 25–6, 34, 319
Congress for Peace 1915 245
consensus, shrinking 29–30, 103, 315
Control of the Arms Race (Bull) 112, 137, 140
Copenhagen Accord 208, 211

cosmopolitan culture 17, 20, 30, 39, 61, 71–3, 182, 219, 227, 286, 289–90, 298–9, 301–2, 315, 320
  and gender 242
  and indigenous peoples 227, 230–1
  and Third World 104
cosmopolitanism 97, 103, 107, 108, 226–7, 231, 268
  and world society 289–90, 301, 309, 310–11, 316
Covenants on Civil and Political Rights and Economic, Social and Cultural Rights 90
Cox, Robert 12, 42, 43, 49
Creation 62–4, 67, 72
Crimea 14, 127, 265
crisis prevention 187–9, 192, 195–6
cultural convergence and divergence 298–9, 301
cultural revolt 298
cyberspace 16, 164, 172–7
  deterrence 167
  and international law 163, 168, 172–7
  security 162–3, 167

D'aesh 159
Dabiq 154, 157, 159
Declaration of the Rights of Man and of the Citizen 86
Declaration on the Rights of Indigenous Peoples 220
decolonial perspective, decolonial reading 92, 97, 100, 101, 107
decolonization 47, 82, 84, 86, 88, 89–90, 93–5, 97, 99, 100–3, 106, 220, 240
Denmark 222
depoliticization 99
Derrida, Jacques 106
Deutsch, Karl 254, 259–60
differentiation and hierarchy 93–4
Dionigi, Filippo 15, 316
diplomatic culture 19, 245, 286–8, 289, 292, 293–6, 297, 298–9, 300–1
diplomatic mechanism 28
disarmament 113
Dodson, Mick 220
domestic analogy 6
domestic order 27, 35–6, 308, 310, 313
Dunne, Tim 8, 9, 45
Duterte, Rodrigo 125

Eastern Europe 263, 294
ecological *see* environmental
economic and social justice 23, 29, 32, 33, 38, 71, 248, 249, 260
economic factors 264–7
economic forces 16

economic inequality 266–7
economic integration 117, 181
Elias, Norbert 19, 287, 295
Empire, empire(s) 27, 71, 81, 82, 86, 88–90, 94, 98, 101, 104, 106–8, 218, 274, 278, 280, 287, 289, 296–7, 306, 315
Emergency management 187, 191–2, 194–6
English School 4, 9, 13, 15, 16, 18–20, 31, 45, 60, 70, 74, 156, 182–3, 305
  and climate change 198, 199
  and coloniality 100, 102, 106
  and common culture 286
  and globalization 181
  and human rights 75, 300
  on Russia 274
environmental issues 16–17, 43, 200, 203
environmental management 23, 29, 33, 37, 38
ethical concerns
  Bull's 50–1
  see also normative
EU *see* European Union
Europe, financial governance 194
European Central Bank 194
European civilization 293–6
European system of central banks 194
European Union 185, 208, 255, 262, 263, 264–5, 314
Eurozone 192, 194
Expansion of International Society (Bull and Watson) 82, 83–4, 95, 273

Falk, Richard 6, 12, 25, 200, 212, 313, 315
Falkner, Robert 12, 15, 16–17, 309, 313, 314, 315, 316, 321
Federal Reserve 191–2, 194
feminism, feminist 18, 234–6, 243, 246, 248, 249–50
financial crisis, financial crises 15, 188, 194, 264
financial crisis management 191–3, 194
Financial Stability Forum (later Board) 188, 191, 192, 196
First World War 30, 47, 88, 90, 156, 188, 200, 245, 254
Fishman, Brian 151, 159
Floating exchange rates 179
France 104, 114, 118, 122, 143,
Frederick II 295

G20 188, 191, 241
Gaddafi 119
gender equality 240–1
gender justice 18
Genesis 62–3
Georgia 118, 119, 263

Germany 90, 132, 190, 255
global civil society 42, 145, 256, 308
global economy 179, 196
global finance 179, 181, 193–4, 197
global financial governance 184–97
global risks 186, 196
global warming *see* climate change
globalization 17, 51, 52, 183, 220, 240, 255–6, 268
    and 'civilizing process' 287–8, 289, 290, 295, 297
    and gender 243
    and great powers 182
    and indigenous peoples 228, 232
Gold standard 179
Goodwin, Geoffrey 3
Gorbachev 259
Gramsci, Antonio 42, 196
great power peace 123
great powers 28, 30, 32, 34, 77, 117–18, 305
    and cyberspace 176–7
    and global economic governance 180, 190
    and global environmental management 202, 207–10, 211, 214
    in international society 97, 104, 271
    and management of violence 113–16, 120, 132
    and nuclear order 133, 142–4
great society of all mankind, great society of mankind 26, 27, 33, 180, 216, 218, 232–3, 239, 268, 308, 314
Greenland 204, 222
Grotius, Hugo 59, 60, 66–7, 69, 70, 72, 73–4
    Grotian 13, 20, 24, 26, 42, 43, 46, 54, 65, 224, 234, 240, 241, 253, 268, 272, 318
Guatemala 53

Hagey Lectures (Bull) 3, 76, 78, 219, 228, 306
Hague, William 245
Hart, Herbert L. A. 6, 27, 31, 33
Hayden, Michael 173
Hayek, F. A. 184
Heeren, Arnold H. L. 289, 293
Hegelian 33
Helsinki Effect (Thomas) 76
hermeneutics 8
hierarchy 239
historic injustice 218
historical erasure 100, 101, 107, 108
historical narratives 278–9
Hizb ut-Tahrir 149
Hobbes, Thomas 13, 45, 59, 61, 65–8, 70, 71–4, 139
    Hobbesian 15, 20, 24, 26, 65–8, 73, 97, 135, 140, 221, 234, 240, 254, 258, 318
Horn of Africa 118

human rights 13, 17, 75–6, 317–18
    and change 84–6
    consensual not objective 72
    and cosmopolitan values 300
    and gender 242–3, 247
    and indigenous peoples 220–1, 229
    as political principles 80–1
    as power mediators 81
    and sovereignty 87–8
    as subversive 78–80
    universality 80, 85
Hume, David 27, 31
Humphreys, Adam 11, 12, 20
Huntington, Samuel 48, 290, 299
Hurrell, Andrew 143, 183

identity 219, 224, 225
identity politics 44
India 124, 132
indigenism 220
indigenous peoples 14, 17, 85, 216–33
information and communication technologies 165
Institute for Strategic Studies 113
Institute of International Finance 189
institutions 10, 28–9, 43, 77–9, 272
    Europeanized 100
    of international society 7, 33–4, 78, 240, 248, 268, 311
    and IS 146–7, 160
    and nuclear proliferation 142
    and violence 111–12
insurance 185, 187–8, 191–2, 194–6
International Association of Deposit Insurers 188
International Association of Insurance Supervisors 188
international change, theory of 83–4
International Court of Justice 172
International Criminal Court 43
international environmental governance 205, 207, 215
international law 28, 34
    and climate politics 211
    and cyberspace 163, 168, 172–7
International Monetary Fund (IMF) 51, 188, 194
international order 10, 27–8, 34–6, 217–18
    and attribution in cyberspace 163–4
    and colonialism 93–4, 100–1
    and gender relations 240, 250
    and nuclear proliferation 129–30, 137–8
    and patriarchy 235–9, 249–50
    and sovereignty 217, 223–4
    and theology 69–74
    and world order 27, 35–6, 38, 76–7, 231

International Organization of Securities Commissions 188
international political and diplomatic cultures 287, 292, 293, 301–2
international political culture 19
international society 24–6, 28, 29, 30, 31, 32, 36, 37, 38, 39
　and civilization 293
　and cyberspace 165
　and decolonization 100–1
　and economy 268
　and environmentalism 200–1, 204, 206
　and European 'civilizing process' 100, 289
　goals of 27–8
　Grotian conception of 60
　and human rights 79–80, 90–1
　and IS 146, 152–3, 158
　and non-state actors 148–50, 160
　and nuclear proliferation 130, 138–41
　and order 65, 70–1, 171
　and patriarchy 238, 249
　and regulation of violence 112, 113–15, 126–7
　and representation 282–5
　and Russia 271, 274–5
　and standard of civilization 291–2
　and states system 310
　and unravelling patriarchy 244–5, 247–8
　and world order 306, 312
　see also international system; world political system; world society
international system 7, 9, 10, 11, 12, 23, 25, 26, 28, 65, 75, 77, 94, 95, 111, 114, 132, 139, 149, 201, 312
　see also international society; world political system; world society
Internet 5, 15, 16, 162, 169
Interpretivism 8
Inuit 222
Inuit Circumpolar Conference (ICC) 222
Inuit Declaration on Arctic Sovereignty 222
IR in Russia 275, 278, 280–1, 284–5
Iran 53, 122, 170–1
Iraq 53, 122, 143, 243
　and Al Qaeda 150
　and IS 152, 153
IS *see* Islamic State
ISI (Islamic State in Iraq) 150–1
ISIS (Islamic State of Iraq and Sham) 151
Islam 44, 156, 244
Islamic State 15, 122–3, 127, 146, 150–61
　as caliphate 15, 122, 149, 151, 153, 155–8, 247
　early evolution 150–2
　and gender 246–7
　and international society 160–1
　state building 152–5, 158–9

Islamist movements 149, 150
Israel 171
Ivanov, Igor 172, 175

Japan 117, 124, 125, 238, 240
　and European civilization 294–5, 296
Joseph, king of Spain 89
just war 257
justice 13, 31–2, 34–6, 50, 209, 214
　and coloniality 92, 93–4
　deferral of 99
　and global financial order 180, 184
　and indigenous peoples 216, 227–8
　international and human 13, 77–8, 81–2, 227, 317–18
　and nuclear weapons 136–7
　Third World demands 96
　See also economic and social justice; order and justice

Kaczmarska, Katarzyna 18, 19, 313, 320
Kant 59
Kantian 20, 24, 26, 46, 234, 240, 241
Kaplan, Morton 135, 260
Keal, Paul 13, 17, 313, 314, 316, 320
Kelsen, Hans 33
Kennan, George 41, 50
Keohane, Robert 18, 25, 182, 306
Keynesian 265
Kissinger, Henry 12, 41, 48–9, 50–1
Korean War 123
Kothari, Rajni 42
Krasner 50
Kurdish activists 147
Kymlicka, Will 223, 228, 229–30
Kyoto Protocol 208, 211

Lavrov, Sergei 263
League of Nations Covenant 296, 297
Leviathan (Hobbes) 73, 74
liberal institutionalism 8
liberalism 96, 218–19
Libya 14, 53, 118, 119, 143
life, truth, and property 13, 27, 28, 29, 31, 35, 36
Linklater, Andrew 8–9, 18, 19, 33, 223, 226, 313, 319, 320
Locke, John 80, 224
Logical Positivism 6
Lorimer, James 291
Louis XIV 295

Mandelbaum, Michael 20, 59
Manning, C. A. W. 6, 24, 272
Mao Zedong 116
marriage 236–7, 242
Martin, W. A. P. 296

Martinez Cobo, Jose 219
Marx, Karl 42, 242
masculinity 234, 249
Mazrui, Ali 105
medieval theology 60
Middle East 53, 121, 257
Midgley, E. B. F. 6, 61, 73
modernity 17, 72, 101, 290, 298, 301
Montreal Protocol 44
Morgenthau, Hans 12, 41, 50
mutual nuclear deterrence 134

Napoleon 89, 115
NATO 118, 119, 169, 257, 262, 314
natural law 6, 28, 61, 69, 72–3
  minimum content of 27
neo-Malthusian 201
New Mediaevalism 25, 222–3, 255–6
Nigeria 122
Nixon, President 116
Noel-Baker, Philip 113
Non-aligned Movement 53
non-governmental 37, 186, 217, 312
non-state actors 11, 17, 20, 25, 26, 37, 38, 44, 145–6, 147–8, 152, 181, 311
  and cyber security 162, 166, 167, 174
  and environment 207, 212, 213
  and financial governance 189, 197
  and gender 239, 240, 242
  and indigenous peoples 222
  Islamist 149, 150, 246
  and statebuilding 155, 160
  and violence 14, 15, 112, 121–2, 127–8, 158, 255
Non-Western countries and peoples 50, 51–2, 53, 71, 84, 88, 247, 287, 297, 299
non-Western elements 17–18, 30, 39, 102, 104, 107, 219, 230–1, 298
  and gender 234, 242, 244, 246, 248
normative
  advocacy 31, 33
  authority 46
  theory 11, 31, 33, 254
  see also ethical concerns
North Korea 125, 143
nuclear deterrence 15, 47–8
Nuclear Non-Proliferation Treaty 114, 130, 133, 137, 143–4
nuclear proliferation 14–15, 132–8
  restraint 129–30, 142–4
  and states system 138–41
nuclear war 30
Nye, Joseph 25, 182, 306

Obama, Barack, President 118–19, 159, 209
Ockham *see* William of Ockham

Ollivant, Douglas 159
Omnipotence 64, 66–7, 72
Oppenheim, Lassa 291
order 31–2, 34–6, 39, 60
  Augustine 61–2
  Grotius 66–7, 69
  Hobbes 66, 67–8
  Plato 62–3
  and theology 61–5
  William of Ockham 64–5
  see also domestic order, international order, world order
order and justice 31–2, 34–5, 78, 83, 318
  decolonial perspective 92
  and financial crisis 195
  and indigenous peoples 232–3
  order prioritized over justice 95–6, 98–9
  and violence 115
  and women's rights 248

Pakistan 118
Palestine 148
Palestine Liberation Organization 147
Panetta, Leon 169
para-state 15, 153, 154, 155, 157, 160
Paris Agreement on Climate Change 2015 43, 44, 208, 211
Pasha, Mustapha Kamal 13–14, 19, 44, 306, 314, 316, 318, 320
Patomäki, Heikki 10, 18, 19, 38, 314, 318, 320
patriarchy 17–18, 234–5
  and international society 237–8, 249
  and violence 243
Pauly, Louis 15, 16, 309, 313, 314
peace and security 23, 29, 33, 38
Permanent Court of Arbitration 126
Permanent Court of International Justice 172
Peter the Great 294
Philippines 125, 126
Philo of Alexandria 63
Plato 62–3
pluralism, pluralist 16, 45–6, 48, 50, 52, 93, 97, 103, 106, 115, 183, 198, 211–14, 263, 316
  cultural 216
  pluralism/solidarism dichotomy 75, 78, 100, 196, 210, 316
  of the English School methodology 20
  and environmentalism 198, 200, 201, 202–210
  international system 94–5, 259
  and Russia 274
  and Third World 103, 106, 115
Polanyi, Karl 184
political economy 18, 101, 262, 267
positivism, positivist 8, 33, 260

post-colonial states 93–4
Putin, Vladimir 236, 279, 282

quantitative international politics 6

racial hierarchy 101, 103–4
Rationalism, Rationalist (Wight) 7–9, 10, 11, 13, 20, 60, 66, 272
　See also Realism, Realist; Revolutionism, Revolutionist
Realism, Realist (Wight) 7–8, 20, 60, 66, 275, 307
　See also Rationalism, Rationalist; Revolutionism, Revolutionist
realism, political 12, 50, 54, 87, 96, 97, 209, 258, 262
　classical realism 42, 45, 107, 262
　neorealism, structural realism 8, 106–107, 234
redistributive justice 13, 94, 96
reflexivity 19
religion 61, 70, 72
representation 282–5
Reus-Smit, Christian 13, 19, 183, 243, 313, 314, 317–18, 319, 320
revolt against the West 19, 40, 297
Revolutionism, Revolutionist (Wight) 7–8, 20, 275
　See also Realism, Realist; Revolutionism, Revolutionist
risk assessment 187–90, 194–6
risk management 185–6, 187–90, 194
Rousseau, Jean Jacques 253
rules
　informal rules 14, 125, 127, 314
　and institutions 10, 24, 26, 28, 29, 78, 94, 181, 248, 255, 258, 272, 288, 314, 315, 316, 318
Russia 18, 117, 118, 257, 265, 314
　and cyber security 172, 177
　and European civilization 296
　and IS 122–3
　and military intervention 118, 127, 262–3, 264
　and nuclear proliferation 133
　and terrorism 121, 122
　in world politics 270
　see also Soviet Union
Russian World 18, 276–7, 280, 284
Ruzicka, Jan 14–15, 314

Saleh, Mudher Mohammad 153
Sanger, David 171
Satanovskii, Yevgenii 279
Saudi Arabia 53
Scarborough Shoal 125

Schelling, Thomas 117
self-determination 90, 96, 98, 147
September 2001 attacks 14, 48, 120, 121, 122, 145, 300
Serbia 118, 263
Siam 294–5
situatedness 18, 20, 282–3, 320
social change 83–4, 86
social life 26–8, 31, 35, 36, 60, 71, 76–8, 80, 95, 203, 218, 235, 283, 308, 319, 320
socialization 100, 148–50, 158
solidarism, solidarist 17, 52, 98, 106, 183, 196, 202, 316, 321
　coercive 300
　English School 100
　and environmentalism 201–2, 210–13, 214, 215
　and global order 183
　pluralism/solidarism dichotomy 75, 78, 100, 196, 210, 316
　and Third World 103, 106
Somalia 118, 120
South China Sea 125
sovereign state 24, 27, 28, 33, 37
sovereignty 88
　and indigenous peoples 216, 220–5, 232
　and IS 156–7
　and patriarchy 235
　and Third World 98, 103, 105
Soviet Union 53, 149, 158
　breakup 255, 279, 280
　see also Russia
Soviet Union/US relations 113–14, 116, 120, 134, 136
Spain 89
spectrality 92, 99–100, 102, 106
standard of civilization 19
state of nature 15, 65–6, 68, 258
　and nuclear proliferation 74, 135, 139–40
state-building 152–3
states system *see* international system
Strange, Susan 182–3
Stuxnet 170–1, 173
Suganami, Hidemi 232, 306, 307, 318
Syria 14, 117, 119, 122, 257
　and ISIS 151, 152

Taiwan 119, 125, 296
Taliban 120
taxonomy 75, 81, 317
terrorism 44, 120–2, 169, 255
Thatcher, Margaret 51
theology 13, 70, 72
　see also order
theoretical perspective 9

Index

Theory of International Politics (Waltz) 311
Third World 13, 53, 92, 102, 297
   and justice 93-4, 96-7, 100, 104, 107, 318
   and sovereignty 98, 103, 105
   and violence 115-16, 119
This Endangered Planet (Falk) 42-3, 200
Tibet 119
Timaeus (Plato) 62, 63
Toros, Harmonie 15, 316
transnational feminist networks 18
transnational organizations 82, 145, 165, 181, 255
transnational relations 182, 308-9
Trenin, Dmitri 274
Trilateral Commission 53
True, Jacqui 17-18, 313, 315, 316, 319, 321
Trump, Donald, President 119, 123, 210
Turkey 241
Turner, Dale 225
Twenty Years' Crisis (Carr) 3, 65

Ukraine 14, 18, 118, 119, 127, 262-5, 279, 314
Umma 149, 247
Uncertainty 182, 196
UNGGE 175-6, 178
United Kingdom 118, 255
United Nations 44, 46, 53, 90, 148, 229, 257, 271
   United Nations Charter 173
   United Nations Declaration on Human Rights 227
   United Nations Framework Convention on Climate Change (UNFCCC) 199, 204, 206-7, 208, 209, 211, 213, 214
   United Nations General Assembly 147
   United Nations Security Council 51, 119
   United Nations Security Council Resolution 1540 121
United States 52, 53
   armed intervention 118-19, 127, 257
   and Asia 116
   and climate politics 209
   and cyber security 172, 177
   dominance 117-18, 314
   economic imbalance 190
   financial intervention 191-2
   and IS 123
   nuclear proliferation 133, 142
   and terrorism 120-1
United States/China relations 123-6
United States/Russia relations 113-14, 116-17, 120, 134, 136
Universal Declaration on Human Rights 90
universal international society 30
US Federal Reserve 191-2

Vattel, Emmerich de 7
Vietnam 53, 125
Vincent, R. John 5, 75, 80, 290, 300, 301
violence 14, 255
   against women 242-3, 245, 247
   and cyberspace 168-72
   and decolonization 100
   and gender 17, 235
   regulation 111-12, 115, 127
voluntarism 72

Wallström, Margot 246
Waltz, Kenneth N. 4, 8, 9, 15, 129, 311
war 28, 67, 69, 111, 114, 136, 138, 257
war on terror 48, 120
Watson, Adam 44, 46, 82, 83-4, 95
West Germany 132
West Java 244
Western culture 13, 17
Western Europe and Russia 274
Western powers in Middle East 152-3
Western scholarship 281
Western-centric conception 15, 146
Westphalian community 53
Westphalian system 49, 101, 149, 224
   and sovereignty 156
White, Hugh 124
Wight, Martin 6, 7-8, 20, 24, 65-6, 70, 104-5, 272, 275, 286, 288, 307
   See also Rationalism, Rationalist; Realism, Realist; Revolutionism, Revolutionist
will and artifice 70, 74
William of Ockham 64-5, 70, 71
Wilson, Woodrow, President 245
women 14
   and diplomatic culture 245
   exclusion 238
   inclusion 250
   as leaders 240-1, 246
   and peace 242, 245
women's empowerment 246
Women's International League for Peace and Freedom 245
Working Group on Indigenous populations (WGIP) 219, 220
World Bank 51, 188
World Climate Conference 198, 199
World Economic Forum 53
world government 11, 24-5, 140
world international society 18, 30, 39
world order 13, 20, 27, 29, 30, 35-6, 38, 39, 42-5, 47, 48, 49-51, 52, 54, 77, 200, 216, 217-19, 226-7, 231, 256, 268, 281, 306, 309, 311, 320-1
   and coloniality 94, 102

world order (*cont.*)
  globalized 46
  and indigenous peoples 216, 221, 231–2
  and international order 13, 27, 35–6, 75, 76–7, 81, 90, 218, 231, 307, 308
  and nuclear proliferation 140–1
  and patriarchy 235, 249
  and sovereign states 76, 291
  and Westphalian principles 49–51, 53
world political system 11, 12, 20, 23, 34, 36–9, 146, 180–2, 231, 270–1, 307–310, 312, 314–15, 317, 319
  as distinct from world society 20, 25–6
  central to Bull's conception of world politics 26, 310
  see also international society; international system; world society
world politics 34, 36, 37, 38, 39

world society 20, 26–7, 59, 71, 182–3, 202, 218, 239, 247, 289, 301, 307–8, 309, 310
  and climate change 211, 213, 214–15
  and cosmopolitanism 289–90, 301, 309, 310–11, 316
  and human rights 82, 90
  and indigenous peoples 228, 230, 231
  and international society 13, 75, 77–8, 82, 146, 250, 301, 306, 317
  and patriarchy 18, 234, 244, 248
  see also international society; international system; world political system
world state 256, 258–9

Xinjiang 119

Yanukovych, Viktor 264–5
Yemen 14, 53, 128
Yugoslavia 255